The Essesntial Herb Gardening Handbook

How Any Home Cook Can Grow Flavors from Around the World

Daniel I Stein

RMC Publishers

Contents

Introduction 5

1. Planning your Herb Garden 13
2. What Type of Herb Garden is Right for Me 23
3. Twenty Popular Herbs to Grow 41
4. How to Sow, Propagate and Divide Herbs 83
5. Soil Improvement and Companion Planting 91
6. History and Basic Techniques 99
7. What Could Go Wrong? (and how to fix it) 127
8. Cooking with Herbs 155

Conclusion 165
Glossary 167

Introduction

Flowers are fantastic. They look lovely, smell nice, and I can definitely see the appeal. But once you have grown your flowers, and they are sitting there in a nice vase or pot, you're kind of at the end, aren't you?

At least for me, there's only so much looking and appreciating and rose-smelling I can do before those flowers start blending into the scenery; I start forgetting to water them, and then one day, there just happens to be a dead brown mess on the windowsill.

Herbs, on the other hand, are a different story. You're not planting a decoration; you're planting food, or more accurately, planting flavors. At the end of this journey, you'll have dozens of recipes, meals, and experiences to enjoy, and of course, most herbs produce flowers too. You also won't have to give up your entire yard or balcony; just a few pots, or planters, or a windowsill is all you need.

Introduction

The promise at the end of herb gardening is just that little bit of extra motivation to keep things exciting, and to see your garden through the seasons.

In your dream herb garden, does the sun pour in a sunny window, with the light shining on a row of green tips with aromatic scents? Do sweet-smelling herbs thrive in pots on your windowsill all winter long?

Do you reach over while you're cooking and cut a sprig of rosemary. Or pinch a few leaves of cilantro on the spur-of-the-moment? Or do you have a cabinet full of fresh and dried herbs that you have grown yourself?

No matter what your dream herb garden looks like, this book will help you devise a plan for your herb garden, guide you through choosing your herbs, and teach you how to use these unique plants in your cooking.

Think of this book as having two friendly neighbors.

The first is a gardener who knows exactly when to add fertilizer for the beans to grow well, which seeds are the best for the local soil, or where to put sunflowers to catch as much light as possible.

The second is a chef who knows exactly what spices to pair together, always has the perfect twist to brighten up an old family recipe, and understands how to use fresh ingredients to the most impressive effect. This book will guide you through selecting and planting a set of herbs to suit your taste so that you will always have the flavors you need on hand to enhance your culinary masterpieces.

Let's start with the first questions new gardeners often ask.

Introduction

Don't worry about getting all of the answers now. These first questions are just to get you thinking and to get your creative juices flowing. After that, we're going to go through everything step-by-step, and by the time you finish this book, you'll know everything you need to create your perfect herb garden.

1. How much space do I need to grow herbs?

The short answer is you can make any space suitable to grow herbs.

First, look at the space where you're thinking of planting your herb garden. If it is a windowsill, is the sun direct? What time of the day does it get sun? What size of pots or containers could fit here? If it's a balcony, is it sunny or shaded? Is there room to build a planter? Is there a shelf or a table to put pots on? Is there concrete on the surface or a grass lawn, a garden shed, or just a pile of junk? Take a few pictures and give yourself a day or two to imagine the space filled with herbs of your choice. Next, look at Chapter 1 for more help designing and planning your herb garden. In Chapter 2, you can read about herb gardens that have worked around the world for many gardeners. See if any of these gardens appeal to you, then check if you have a suitable climate, soil, and sunlight and try one!

2. How important is the climate for my plants?

Next, think of herbs growing in your chosen space and the environmental conditions you will provide. For example, there may be frost in certain areas overnight or in winter. Or maybe it is desert-like in summer so that plants may need lots of water? What is your annual rainfall? Will herbs get water-logged if it rains every day? Most plants enjoy bright sunshine and warm weather, but you will be surprised at how many herbs also thrive in part sun, part shade when the hottest after-noon sun is glaring down! Mint is one of these. It seems to gasp in hot sunshine, so this is a plant to give some welcome shade so that you can enjoy peppermint tea or mint in roasted dishes.

3. How much light and how much room will my plants need?

If your proposed herb garden is going to be in pots, will you construct a special area for your herbs? Is there a large tree in your garden that may compete with your little herbs for light and soil? Are there any high walls that shelter the area from the wind? Some herbs like shelter, and some are pretty used to windy coastal shorelines. If you have walls, will they throw a lot of shade? Check if something shades parts of your patio, the backyard, or the balcony where you will place your plants. Annual herbs grow happily in pots and you can re-seed them each spring, but perennial herbs (which can stay outdoors in winter, too) need enough soil and space to thrive. All of these factors will determine where you should place your pots, planters, or herb garden.

To get started, snap a photo of your future herb gardening space in the early morning, at midday, and again in the late afternoon. Start noticing where the sun arrives first thing in the morning and at what time the light disappears. In spring and summer, this will be where you put a chair with a coffee to welcome in the day. You are gaining knowledge about what time the sun rises, and at what time the shade hits certain areas of your garden. The pictures will enable you to draw in plants over the areas to visualize what type of plant will grow best where.

To keep track of your progress, at this stage, I usually tell people to take these pictures and to start making your gardening journal, so take down some notes.

- What areas get full sun all day, partial sun for a few hours, or no sun at all?

- Are there nearby buildings or trees that shade or shelter certain spots from the wind or rain?
- What is the temperature like, does the spot get frost in the morning, is it covered from the rain, or is it indoors and next to a drafty window or a warm space heater?

I thoroughly recommend recording your notes and ideas, including any herb gardens you visit and would like to copy. If you add photos, this becomes a treasured memento of your gardening journey. When you look back at the empty place when you started, you will notice a considerable change in your herb garden over a season. These photos are your reminder of success (and maybe failures) so that you can learn and improve. Now you have an idea of what is possible in your space, let's look at another critical question.

4. What kind of soil do herbs need to thrive?

The next important factor for plants is the soil in which they grow. In a pot, you can control this completely, and if these are annual herbs like basil, parsley, or cilantro, then you can change the soil in pots whenever you need to. However, if these plants will live there for a longer period like sage, rosemary, or thyme, you need to consider what conditions these plants have in their native Mediterranean landscapes. Some grow in dry, impoverished soils, so don't worry if your garden soil isn't all that fertile. It may be precisely what your herb needs. You can always add fertilizer and other nutrients to boost your soil's fertility at a later date. Read Chapter 4 for more information about soil, composting, and improving your soil.

5. Which herbs grow well together?

We will look at combinations of herbs that grow well together. Companion planting is the term for growing plants side by side that will benefit each other, or if one is being used as a sacrificial offering to pests so that your precious herbs do not get targeted. For example, nasturtiums are often grown next to other plants simply because aphids love them! Aphids will ignore every other plant if nasturtiums are close by. The cheerful blooms of nasturtiums can be eaten in salads, and their delicate little leaves are also edible, but if they distract pests away from your chosen herb, even better. See Chapters 3 and 4 for detailed information about companion planting and the needs of 20 of the most popular garden herbs.

6. What kind of herb garden should I grow? What kind of herbs are best for the foods I like to cook and eat?

Maybe you envisage an Italian garden, planning meals with basil in pesto, accompanied by tomatoes, marjoram, and cilantro? Mediterranean perennial herbs can be grown well together, such as sage, rosemary, thyme, and lavender. Many combinations of herbs can grow well together, and only you can decide which combinations will suit your space, climate, and taste. The time you have available is another factor in planning your garden. Are you going to be watering before work or before taking children to school and mulching plants to improve fertility, or do you fancy a low-maintenance herb garden that looks after itself? Are you keen to encourage beneficial wildlife into your garden by growing flowers to attract bees and butterflies? In this book, we will examine various options so that you can make an informed choice. Chapter 5 explains the uses of herbs in cooking. Chapter 6 will delve into the history of herbs grown for aromatic or medicinal use, the medieval cottage garden, and some more unusual herbs and recipes to try.

7. How do you use herbs properly?

This book will help you as a complete beginner and guide you as you learn more about the needs of individual herbs and how you can use them. Nothing is set in stone. If your herbs are in pots and you are not keen on one herb, you can just try a different combination the following year. If your herb garden is in a planter, you can remove plants for indoor winter use or decide which herbs may prefer another space after one season. If you've planted annual herbs, you can dry their leaves for winter use, make herb oils for yourself and your friends, and you can leave the perennial herbs in situ until the next active growing season. Some herbs are super easy to propagate or plant from seed. Save the seeds, dry the herbs and then give these as gifts to other gardeners.

It is helpful to find another keen gardener or join a gardening club, and this is a great way to get advice, swap plants, and maybe participate in a community project working with groups that need keen gardeners. Chapter 6 will guide you through some unusual herbs you can try once you have gained confidence with your first herbs. Chapter 4 will provide valuable propagation methods, how to remove your delicate plants indoors for winter, and how to save seeds and dry herb leaves for use in colder seasons.

In addition, Chapter 7 offers ways to deal with common problems and pests which affect herbs. For example, why are my basil leaves turning yellow? Or what's eating my cilantro? You can try organic cures and ancient tricks that will attract the right pollinator bees but keep the aphids and pests at bay. In midsummer, you can enjoy fresh basil chopped into tomatoes and salads. When the fall arrives, you can admire the dried herbs you've hung in a shady patch in your house, relax in sweet-smelling homemade lavender oil in your bathtub or nip out to a rosemary bush and pick a few leaves to add to soup or casseroles. Enjoy!

Chapter 1
Planning your Herb Garden

IF THIS IS YOUR FIRST ATTEMPT AT GARDENING, THEN LET'S assume that herb plants are a bit like humans. Like us, they need food, warmth, water, and shelter, and different plants have different preferences. Like humans, some plants crave the hot sun, while others prefer to bask in the shade during the afternoon heat. Some prefer rich, deep soil, while others can survive in the impoverished, dusty ground.

Food for your herb plants is the soil they grow in and any extra fertilizers you provide.

Warmth is usually provided by the sun but can also come from a greenhouse or a more sheltered spot indoors or an area with stones, which attracts heat and loses it slowly as the sun sets; these all make a cozy place for plants.

Water is essential for germinating most seeds, and without enough moisture, your herbs will die. On the other hand, too much water and their roots get waterlogged, so you need to understand how much water is correct for the herbs you choose. It is usually best to plant herbs with similar needs together.

Shelter is the last on the list, and remember that you will see smaller plants using shrubs as protection in the wild. You may be familiar with the way bluebells choose to grow in woodlands in the late spring, protected by the cover of the larger trees above but also making full use of the available light before the summer leaf cover fully shades them.

Choosing your Herbs

Are you familiar with all the herbs you can grow? Do you want to try particular ones? Chapter 3 of this book gives you a list of 20 popular herbs with detailed instructions on their ideal planting conditions. You can go straight there now or read on for some factors to consider first.

For example, an herb like basil needs deep, rich soil and lots of water because, in the countryside where they grow wild, that's what they are used to. If you choose basil and want to try other herbs like rosemary, thyme, and French tarragon (the Mediterranean herbs), be aware that these herbs would probably be better off in a different pot. Mediterranean herbs often start their lives on the edge of sunny, arid cliffs close to the sea, where the soil tends to be sandy and not so rich. These herbs have long, deep roots so that they cannot be uprooted easily by windy breezes but also so they can dig deep to find any water that is deep underground. So if you want basil and one of these Mediterranean herbs, you may want to place them either in separate pots or in a different section of your herb garden.

Let's go over some things to consider when deciding where to plant our herbs.

Where should they be planted?

Planning your garden means deciding if your herbs will all grow in pots or if you want to design a particular part of the garden in soil for your herbs. You may already know not to plant sage close to other herbs, and there are groups of herbs that do well together. If you grow tomatoes in pots, you can also pop a basil plant in there. Cilantro, marjoram, and chives are a good match for tomatoes too, as they all like a bit of shade in the afternoon, and the larger tomato plant will provide that.

Pots

Pots are a trick most experienced gardeners know. You can start seeding all your herbs indoors in pots early in spring and then put them outside when all danger of frost has gone. The pots can enjoy the long, balmy days in the summer sunshine, and then you can bring some of them back indoors when the fall arrives. This way, you can have basil all year round in your kitchen, as well as parsley and chives. Some herbs like tarragon, lovage, and mint will die back naturally in colder temperatures, but if you want some of these during the winter, you can dry their leaves.

So are you planning to grow your herbs in pots indoors, outdoors, or both?

If your herbs are going to grow on a sunny windowsill or a balcony, make sure they get lots of direct sunlight and plenty of fresh air. However, it might infrequently rain in summer in their natural environment, so my advice is not to overwater them. Rainwater often does the job for you. As a general rule, indoor herbs tend to get overwatered.

Your herbs will provide you with gorgeous aromatic smells as you walk past, which will also brighten your mood in a work area. Humanity has used herbs like this for centuries. Think of lavender bath oil and rose-scented soap, and most people will instantly relax, which is precisely what these scents do for the human body.

The soil in pots is usually sufficient for only one growing season. After that, you may need to add a top mulch or a layer of compost, leaf mulch, or ash to the pots to keep plants going. All of these settle quickly with watering, but a problem with soil in pots is that soil gets compacted over time and that the tap water used is full of chlorine which can start to build up in the soil. As an alternative, you could save any available rainwater from roof collection into a water barrel. Try to ensure that water barrels are covered though because this is the perfect breeding ground for mosquitoes in temperate climates.

Be careful with annual herbs in pots that try to flower too soon. Usually, this happens because all the goodness in the pot has been used up. The plant's instinct is to turn to seed as soon as soil nutrients are depleted, there is a lack of available water, or the temperatures drop.

Re-pot any herbs immediately when you can see roots coming out the end of the pot. It's also a good idea to add more soil to pots when you take them indoors for winter so that they have enough energy to get through the colder season. Many perennial herbs go dormant in winter when the weather turns chillier, but they are alive and will spring back into life when the warmer air of spring comes around.

Planters or beds

If you plan to build a herb garden either as a raised bed or in the soil, then choose an area that gets a lot of sunshine as most herbs thrive in bright sunshine. Basil, parsley, chives, sage, rosemary, and thyme all love direct sunlight, and they will reward you with abundant foliage for your efforts. Indoors, as long as they get some sunshine every day, your herbs will be fine, but you will probably not be rewarded by the enormous bunches of fresh foliage they can produce outdoors. Some exceptions to this rule do exist – for example; mint prefers some shade. However, note that mint is an herb that needs to be contained because it spreads like crazy and can take over your whole herb garden.

Raised beds are fantastic for people who cannot kneel or whose backs need some tender care. A raised bed for herbs is perfect for a community garden or shared space because it allows a wide range of people to enjoy it. A raised bed is the ideal solution if herb gardeners need some support, such as a walker or a wheelchair. The deep soil makes it very fertile, the height makes it accessible, and you can plant rows of herbs so that everybody can pick some tasty leaves. Making a raised bed from bricks allows you to place all the tools you need and seeds or pots on the edge of the bed, as well as that welcome cup of tea all gardeners seem to enjoy while they admire the results of their hard work.

Making a new bed in soil

If you can, place a cover over the area in the months prior to planting to warm it up and kill off any weeds. Prepare your ground well by digging out any weeds and their roots so that you are starting with fresh, weed-free soil. Bindweed and dandelion roots left in the soil tend to spread like crazy, so if you see long, thick white roots resembling string, this is Bindweed or Morning Glory, which has fantastic tubular white flowers. Lovely as these are, they spread by underground roots, so take out every piece you see and dispose of them. Do not put these segments of root in your compost bin. Each little segment is viable as a plant due to the root suckers you will notice; it is a complete triumph of nature's ability to propagate new plants. Shame it's not a herb! However, these roots will happily absorb all the rich goodness of your compost heap, so get rid of them another way.

One option is to dump the whole lot (roots, leaves, flowers) into a bucket of water and let them rot for 4-5 days. Strain the resulting mixture into a watering can or bottle as a fertilizer for tomatoes or some of your hungry herbs later. Dig deep to remove any long roots of dandelions, or you will see these in your herb garden for many years to come. However, although classed as a weed, dandelion does provide beneficial color and nectar for bees in spring. Dandelion leaf tea is drunk all over Europe. You can even use these dandelion leaves to make homemade fertilizer for your other plants – see Chapter 2 for details of nutrients these "weeds" can provide.

The final question is, has this area been dug before?

If you have lived here for years, you will know the answer, but if you just moved in, it is an excellent idea to discover if this area was used to grow anything in the past. Pests love soil that has been undisturbed, and a multitude of lurking slugs and snails may be licking their lips at the idea of the tasty herb supper you are about to plant. However, another consideration comes from what farmers call crop rotation. You may remember this from history or geography or botany lessons. The basic idea is that to grow healthy plants; you should not grow the same crop in the same soil year after year. See more about this in Chapter 3. For now, let's assume this is year 1 in your herb planning for your garden or pots.

It is essential in designing your herb bed to think about each herb and how much space it will need. Next, a word about how long your plants will stay in the ground and how experienced gardeners describe this.

How long will they last?

What exactly are annual, biennial, and perennial herbs?

Parsley, basil, cilantro, and marjoram all grow well together. These are all annual herbs; this means you plant them, they grow, and they live only for one growing season. These herbs die back naturally at the start of the cold weather in the fall or winter, and the seeds they make may fall to the ground and start to grow as new plants when the soil gets warmer the following year.

Some herbs are biennial; this means they grow well from seed in their first year, then flower in the second year and die back after this. Typical flowers that do this are foxgloves and Sweet William. Biennial herbs are more unusual – chervil is one example; it grows well in the first year, but it usually dies back after flowering in the second year. However, chervil will seed itself in the second year if you leave the plant in the same place, and there will always be plants if you allow it to self-seed. It is a vibrant herb for salads, providing an unusual aniseed taste. It is used (like Sweet Cicely) in cooking to balance bitter plants like rhubarb and cuts down on the amounts of added sugar you use. It likes semi-shade, so that it can be planted under a raspberry or blackcurrant bush.

Perennial herbs start pretty small but gradually grow larger and spread, often turning woody as they do. In hot climates, this is a method of propagation. Many of the pieces of branches knocked off by animals or wind will sprout roots where they land, making an entirely new plant. They are usually frost-tolerant, and you can plant them from seeds, cuttings, or small plants. They grow over many years and will last in your garden for five years, and often a lot longer.

Lavender is like this. You have probably seen large, overgrown plants with thick stems and felt maybe it was time to prune these branches at times. Sage and rosemary do the same and can spread into substantial shrubs, which may cause a space problem if they overhang some of the annuals in your herb garden. Sage is a perennial herb that is also notorious among experienced gardeners because it tends to kill off anything that grows too close to it. Its delicious smell is fabulous in cooking but lethal for some other plants. Strawberries are an exception, and borage flowers love being next to sage. Thyme does not grow as tall as sage and rosemary, but it does have beautiful flowers! Bees also love rosemary, sage, and thyme, and they snack on their attractive flowers as they pass. Sage and rosemary spread a lot, but the thyme bush is small and compact, and it allows you to pick fresh thyme whenever you need it. This plant survives snow in England, so unless your weather is extreme, your thyme plant should be fine. All of these perennial herbs come back year after year, flowering in early summer and attracting bees and beneficial insects to your herb garden.

Big perennial shrubs prefer a bit of space to grow – see soil, expected spread, and watering needs in detail for each herb in Chapter 5.

How much water do they need?

Think about watering them too. If you plan to use a watering can, make sure your water supply isn't too far away. If the herbs are indoors in less accessible spots or outdoors, you may not notice a herb drooping, so check them every few days. You probably will be picking them frequently in summer, or you could enlist the help of a younger gardener to take on the task for pocket money.

By now, have you gotten a clearer picture of your gardening space?

- Will your herbs grow indoors in small pots, or do you plan to grow these herbs outdoors in larger pots or beds? Will you create a raised bed?
- Is there enough sunlight? Shelter? And will you be able to water them easily?
- Have you chosen a selection of seeds yet? If not, you can move on to the herb details in Chapter 3 for help.

This is not a recipe book, but I can certainly point you towards some of the delightful tastes herbs provide in kitchens around the world (Chapter 8) and encourage you to try at least one unusual one. Chapter 2 describes the herbs that people use and grow worldwide from Canada to Latin America, from Asia and Africa to Europe.

Chapter 2
What Type of Herb Garden is Right for Me

THIS CHAPTER WILL FIRST EXAMINE 10 OF THE MOST POPULAR herbs for any herb garden or windowsill for the absolute beginner. These are 10 excellent choices that are popular, easy to grow, and are very versatile in the kitchen. After looking at these 10 herbs, you can then read about different styles of herb gardens around the world.

After seeing the other types of herb gardens, you may decide to add some exotic herbs to your list and adapt some less common flavors into your cooking.

Remember, while these herbs go well together in these cuisines, that doesn't necessarily mean that they will grow well together in a pot.

The beginner's (Italian) herb garden

Useful for anyone, and benefits almost any cooking style.

1. **Basil**. This staple herb from Italy offers fresh green leaves to eat raw or chopped into tomato salads. It is also the main ingredient for pesto sauce. It is usually grown as an annual herb, and most supermarkets sell pots of basil for cooks to use. You can use the leaves and flowers in your recipes.
2. **Bay leaves** are often picked from a shrub in your backyard and then dried for use by hanging them on some string in a cool area that does not get bright direct sunshine. Once dried, bay leaves can be added to soups, sauces, and casseroles, where the flavor of the leaves adds a subtle herb taste.
3. **Chives** add an onion-like flavor to many dishes. They can be eaten raw or chopped into dishes and cooked slightly. Garlic chives are somewhat thicker and have a stronger taste.
4. **Cilantro** is easy to grow but quick to go to seed. In cooking, you can use both leaves and flowers as well as the seeds. Indian cuisine uses ground coriander (the seeds) as an ingredient for several dishes.
5. **Garlic** is very easy to grow and is a tiny miracle for younger gardeners who plant one clove and dig up an entire bulb. Garlic is traditionally associated with French cuisine, but it is used worldwide and comes with a range of health benefits. See more about this in Chapter 6.
6. **Marjoram** is a Mediterranean herb and spreads like crazy in a herb garden. It is a favorite for bees to visit, so if you want to feed the wildlife or get some flowers pollinated, this is one to include. It adds a subtle taste to

many Mediterranean dishes and is widely used in recipes.

7. **Parsley** is famous for being an ingredient of parsley sauce, a white sauce used to flavor fish, and it comes in 2 types; flat-leaved and moss curled. This herb is very difficult to germinate from seed, requiring heat and moisture, so if you want an easy start to your herb garden, buy some pots to start you off.
8. **Thyme** is a perennial herb, that is, one that grows for many years. Its native habitat is on dry cliffs, where it provides bees with welcome nectar and provides any visitor to the garden a delicious scent as they walk by. It likes soil that is not too rich, loves the sun, and does not need much watering. An easy starter herb!
9. **Rosemary** is another perennial herb, and once planted, it will spread quite wide, so allow it plenty of space in your herb garden.
10. **Sage** is used fresh and dried and adds a delicious rich flavor to stews and winter casseroles.

Almost every single herb in the Beginner garden plan is used in Italian cooking, from bay leaves to basil, marjoram, chives, rocket, various salad leaves, and tomatoes. Home of pizza and pasta, Italy is also the inventor of pesto sauce, which is available around the world and in many variations. In Italy, the details of the family pesto recipe may be a closely-held secret. See Chapter 6 for using these Italian herbs to make pesto, some information about canning tomatoes and other produce with herb flavoring, etc. Olives are not herbs, but they are very Italian, and olive oil (organic if possible) can be used for herb oils and in Italian dishes. We do not include growing pine nuts for use in pesto, but if you have the space and climate, this is a challenge for your future herb garden once this one is established.

Essential herbs to include in your Italian herb garden:

Basil, garlic, chives, thyme, marjoram, sage, rosemary, pine nuts, bay leaves, peppers, chili peppers, and of course, tomatoes! See how to grow all of these herbs in detail in Chapter 3.

If you're unsure what kind of garden you want, these 10 herbs would be an excellent start. But if you have a favorite type of cuisine, take a look and see if any of these themed herb gardens would work for you.

(If the herbs have already been described, I will not include them in detail below.)

The French herb garden

Next, let's move on to the herbs found in parts of France, which is colder in the north with a warmer, temperate climate near the Mediterranean sea in the south, where the soil may be more sandy for your herbs. If you look for pre-mixed herb packages in stores, two French mixes are almost always included. The *Fines Herbes* and the *Herbes de Provence* collections are a reference for French cooks, and their fame has spread to other countries that enjoy French cooking.

France is famous worldwide for its champagne grapes, distinctive cuisine, olives, cheese, and patisserie pastry shops. It is also home to the renowned herb liqueur, the pea-green colored Chartreuse. Carthusian monks are reputed to have followed a recipe for "the elixir of long life" using 130 herbs and plants to make a medicinal alcoholic tonic in the monastery since 1737. You can read more about herbs used in history and how they control or aid recovery from various ailments in Chapter 6. For now, let's look at herbs necessary for inclusion in any French herb garden.

Essential herbs to include in your French herb garden:

1. **French Tarragon** is frequently used in many French recipes, but it is not a common herb in many countries due to the difficulty of sourcing the plant. It is very different from Russian Tarragon, which you can grow from seed but does not have the same flavor despite the name, whereas the delicate flavor of French Tarragon can only be added to your garden by getting a plant. The reason for this is that this herb rarely flowers, and even if it does, the seeds may not grow the same as the mother plant. The propagation of this herb commonly happens by cutting a stem, popping it in water, and then saving this indoors over winter. You can pot on tarragon when the roots show in water, and it can be planted outdoors again the following summer. Root divisions are also possible in early spring, but you need an actual plant to start with. This herb is fond of warm conditions, so if frost is expected in your garden, ensure that you keep it indoors in cold seasons after the fall arrives. If you have French Tarragon, make a few cuttings in any case, as it is temperamental. Having a few backup plants in pots is an excellent way to have a supply of this delicate flavor for culinary use. Do not plant it outside until all danger of frost has passed.
2. **Rosemary**, **thyme**, and **sage** are essential components of French herb gardens, so make sure you include these perennial herbs. Once planted, they will happily remain in your garden for several years. See detailed instructions for growing them in Chapter 3.
3. **Fennel** is a herb that should definitely grace any French herb garden. It is one of the ingredients of the infamous absinthe drink, which was drunk in vast quantities by many famous artists during the Belle Époque. At that time, the herb-infused drink was a treatment for epilepsy, kidney stones, and a multitude of others.

Vincent van Gogh, Pablo Picasso, and Henri Toulouse-Lautrec were said to enjoy the taste of the green mixture. However, modern doctors might disagree with the effect of including wormwood as an ingredient because nowadays, it is known to induce hallucinations! So although wormwood is NOT recommended, fennel is a valuable herb. The leaves can be eaten, and its seeds frequently flavor staple dishes in any French café. One word of advice with growing fennel. If grown very close to dill, the two herbs cross breed and create combinations of herbs with unpredictable tastes, so avoid placing these two herbs close to one another.

4. **Chives** add an onion flavor to salads, and they are commonly an addition to many white sauces for poultry and meat. They are also utilized in cold herb kinds of butter used to flavor fish dishes. Finally, chives are also one of the essential four herbs used in so many dishes in France called "Fine Herbs".
5. **Chervil** is included in Herbes de Provence as well as being an ingredient in salads and used as a natural sweetener of rhubarb and sour fruits.
6. **Herbs de Provence** is a mix of herbs used dried in recipes to add flavor to meat, poultry, fish, and vegetables which originates in the Provence area of France, where these herbs grow in abundance. Essential herbs included are fennel, marjoram, parsley, rosemary, tarragon, and thyme. You can also add basil, bay leaves, savory, chervil, sage, oregano, mint, and even the flowers of lavender.

The Spanish herb garden

In Spanish cooking, the main ingredients besides the herbs include olive oil, various kinds of vinegar, and dressings. Like other Mediterranean countries, Spain produces olives and olive oil, peppers, and some unusual herbs. For example, Spanish chorizo sausage has many herbs hardly known outside the country, yet the sausage is extremely popular. Secret recipes kept by the Spanish! This is the home of the paella; the classic seafood rice cooked to perfection with saffron. Although strictly not a herb, ñora is a round, ball-shaped pepper which is the secret ingredient only a Spanish cook knows! It is prepared by being first dried in direct sunlight and then ground into a seasoning. Its distinctive flavor is not well known outside Spain and is certainly worth tasting if you visit. Spain's traditional chorizo sausage owes much of its characteristic flavor to this herb, and ñora is added to patatas bravas, the spicy potatoes offered in tapas bars, and sometimes the whole plant is served as a vegetable after being cooked with garlic. Gazpacho is the refreshing cold summer soup first made to use up a glut of tomatoes, and today it is one of the most famous Spanish dishes on a hot summer's day, and it is flavored with garlic and pepper. Read on to see the herbs and spices included in traditional Spanish cooking.

1. **Saffron** is a traditional herb prepared from a particular type of crocus flower and collected painstakingly by Spanish farmers every year. These petals cause the rice to be tinted yellow shades through to maroon color in paella, the national seafood dish, and soups and sauces. Saffron is grown in La Mancha in Spain, and this spice is comparable to the price of gold when it is produced.
2. **Bay leaf** is grown as a small shrub and can even grow to tree size in the right conditions. The leaves are picked and dried, then hung until needed in the kitchen. You can dry them and store them in a herb jar in your kitchen.
3. **Garlic** is an essential Spanish ingredient for almost

every dish. It grows in bulbs, and one or two of these is enough to season a dish to perfection. Super easy to grow, this herb will survive frost, snow, and any conditions your local climate will throw at it.

4. **Ñora** is grown in Valencia on the west coast of Spain and is also known as **pimentón**. Columbus supposedly brought the first one back from Latin America, and he donated it to monks in the Yuste monastery. From this monastery garden, it traveled to La Nora in Murcia in the south of Spain. Typically dried and used as a powder, this is an essential dried plant seasoning for many Spanish dishes such as chorizo and is the secret ingredient that not many people know about!
5. **Oregano** is a small herb with tasty leaves which can be eaten fresh off the bush, but its delicate flavor escapes easily into a cooked dish. This herb is used in France, Italy, and Portugal as well as Spain and Greece.
6. **Chili pepper** is used sparingly in most Spanish dishes, and when it is too hot, the Spanish will complain saying it is picante. Chopped, it is added to dishes and cooked in stews.
7. **Nutmeg** (*Myristica fragrans*) and **cinnamon** (*Cinnamomum verum*), are used widely in Spanish cooking but are usually imported from India, Indonesia, and the West Indies. Both arrived with the return of the conquistadors to Spain after their long journeys trying to explore the New World. There is a rich tradition of use of these two in Spanish kitchens. The seeds of nutmeg are used in cooking, and you need to grate the nut to release the flavor in cooking. Cinnamon is edible tree bark from a variety of the Laurel family grown in Indonesia and Malaysia. These are not actually herbs, and unless you live in a hot climate you are unlikely to

be able to grow these, but they are essential tastes in Spanish cuisine.

Herbs from Greece, Turkey, and Lebanon

This is another Mediterranean herb garden similar to those used in Spain. However, the Greeks experimented by adding herbs and resin to wines which transformed into the retsina we recognize and relish on streetside tavernas on visits to Greece. Mastic is a cream-colored resin that grows near the Aegean sea on some Greek islands, which adds the famous taste to retsina, the national wine. The flavor of this drink is unique and, strangely enough, often disappoints if taken home and drunk outside of the Greek air and atmosphere.

1. **Dill** is a favorite herb here, and other herbs include **oregano**, **parsley**, and **marjory**.
2. **Nutmeg**, like in Spain, is also a common ingredient.
3. **Bay leaves** are frequently used in Greek cooking, and **oregano** and chopped mint add taste to many regional dishes. Remember that tasty bay leaves must be dried before you use them.
4. Greek seasoning you find in the supermarket is a mix of oregano, **garlic**, and onion powder mixed with dill and bay leaves, and sometimes mint.
5. **Mint** is often added to cooling dishes like tzatziki, which is a yogurt accompaniment to meat. Mint also features in delicious sweet desserts.
6. The seeds of **thyme** and **fennel** are used a lot, and olive oil is the main ingredient in many dishes.
7. **Cloves** are imported and used with many dishes, and parsley is occasionally used, particularly as a herb garnish.

8. **Cilantro** has been used in Greece for centuries, adding its sweet taste to various dishes.
9. Alongside mastic, which grows in the Aegean, pine honey is another exotic taste found in Greek cooking, and thyme-flavored honey is also popular. Honey is often added to Greek breakfast selections to flavor natural yogurt.
10. Citrus trees are abundant in Greece, and lemon often features as a garnish and a flavor.
11. Eggplant is vital in dishes like Moussaka, which offers layers of cheese and eggplant with meat and herbs. Zucchini flowers are a specialty, usually filled with generous helpings of rice, herbs, and spices.
12. Vine leaves are also cooked in these countries, and "Dolmades" in Greece is a lift straight from Turkish, where "dolma" means to fill. The taste of these leaves combined with herbs and spices makes them a very popular dish all over this region. Greek people often say that spring has arrived when they see fresh vine leaves being sold in markets, but they are not just available in the growing season either; the leaves are added to vinegar and dried to be used in every season. Dill, parsley, and lemon are the herbs and fruit grown in the region which are commonly added to dolmades.
13. Cheese is more often than not made from sheep's milk, where the land is not especially fertile for cattle. Feta cheese is a specialty in Greece and Turkey and is so well-known worldwide it hardly needs an introduction. Often served in feta cheese appetizers, with herbs to accompany it, including dill, parsley, and oregano, the cheese is usually mixed with a generous serving of olive oil. However, it is not the only available cheese, and if you visit, you will find a combination of cheeses you probably would only see in a New York deli! Ladotyn

cheese contains added olive oil, Graviera cheese with added thyme gives it a unique taste, and there is also a spreadable cheese called Katiki Domokou. Epiros cheese offers a salty, minty taste, so there are many herb-flavored cheese delights to try. A common use of herbs worldwide is to season meat dishes, and particularly in the north of Greece, the sweeter tasting, imported spices like cinnamon and cloves are added with local herbs.

14. **Parsley** is a typical garnish, and **tarragon** also features in this region's dishes, adding something extra to meat and chicken dishes and stews.

The Mexican herb garden

The Spanish conquistadors were amazed at the difference in the produce available in Mexico compared to their native country on their arrival. They saw many strange fruits and vegetables used in the Mexican dishes that are so familiar nowadays. For example, the avocado was a pear they had never seen, and cocoa was revered as a sacred drink the Spanish had never even imagined. Thanks to Mexican knowledge of the cacao plant, the world now enjoys hot chocolate. In Spain, it is enjoyed with a snack called churros.

Who has not heard of chile con carne? This super-hot mincemeat fried with red hot chili peppers is served in Mexican restaurants as the typical dish of this country. There are other famous dishes, such as guacamole, made of avocado, which calms down the hotter dishes common in Mexican cuisine, such as pozole rojo, the red stew that also utilizes the deep red chili peppers. This soup is usually accompanied by garnishes such as chopped radishes, cabbage, scallions, cilantro, and finally, the essential carbohydrate in Mexico: corn tortillas.

Herbs native to Mexico include **coriander**, **allspice**, **cloves**, **thyme**, **Mexican oregano**, **Mexican cinnamon**, and **cumin**. Other plants used are **Aloe Vera**, **Galangal root**, **Epazote**, and **chili pepper**, some of which were used as food but also as medicine.

Mexican oregano is not the same as the common oregano that is widely used in Europe and the Americas. This oregano has a slightly different flavor, and you should use less of it than you usually use because the taste is more intense.

Mint is widely used in dressings and drinks and often balances some of the heat in other dishes.

Herb gardens in India and Asia

The warmer climates found in both India and Asia offer a wider variety to choose from for your herb garden. Unusual herbs like **cinnamon** and **cloves** can grow in Indonesia, and **ginger** grows widely all over this part of the world. There are many ground and powdered flavors a visitor will recognize on the shelves of a supermarket here and others that we would find hard to recognize. In some areas of this region, **powdered mango**, **nutmeg**, and **lemongrass** grow.

Mystica fragrans is the tree that is the source for both **mace** and nutmeg. Nutmeg is the inner seed that is grated into cooking, and it grows inside another external layer (or aril) which is then ground into the herb we call mace. According to local knowledge, both of these herbs are said to aid digestion. Other medicinal uses in Asia for these two will be explored in Chapter 5.

Cinnamon comes from the Cinnamomum zeylanicum tree, and both trees grow in many parts of India, mainly in Kerala. These trees can also grow in the Tamil Nadu and Karnataka regions.

Cloves are flower buds of a tree in Indonesia, and they are exported widely because of their unique flavor. Clove trees need a lot of space as they can grow up to 40 feet. However, they are beautiful trees if you have the climate and lots of time! They will fruit for many years, some as long as 80 years.

You can grow almost anything here, and herbs can last all year round, providing you care for them. **Basil**, **cilantro**, **chives**, and **garlic** are all widely used to flavor many recipes as all of these herbs enjoy the hot weather and the direct sunlight that is on offer.

The Chinese herb garden

There are ingredients found in Chinese cooking which are not widely used in the West. Traditionally some of these are known as spices, not herbs, but as the origin is from plants that provide flavor to food, I will discuss one of these which the herb grower might not consider in other countries.

Ginger is not strictly a herb, but its roots are used to flavor food worldwide, and it grows well in Asia, where it is a common ingredient in cooking and present in the herb garden. It is slightly more challenging to grow than some leafy herbs, the plant has striking spiky dark green foliage, but it is the root we consume for culinary purposes. Even as a decorative plant, ginger is worth adding to your windowsill. If you're lucky, you may be able to eat a small section and then re-plant some of the remaining roots to grow again. Ginger also grows well in areas like conservatories, where it can have a deeper pot and will grow to a better height. The foliage is stunning, and you can eat your elegant plant roots from time to time, always allowing for enough root to allow the plant to survive.

African Herbs

The vast continent of Africa includes many types of climate, from the desert in Egypt to more verdant lands all along the Nile basin to sunny climates at the end of the continent in South Africa. So should we class cloves as a spice or a herb? Typical African herbs are **harissa**, **zanzibar**, **berbere**, **cloves**, **peri-peri** mix, and **grains of paradise**, which is counted as a spice, but as it comes from the grains of plants, I have included it as a herb. Some of these names are well known to Europeans, who travel to Morocco more frequently, and harissa is widely used in cooking and available to buy in markets. **Coconut** is not strictly classed as a herb either, rather a dried fruit. However, it is used in cooking, and its milk is a common ingredient in cuisine as far apart as from Africa to Brazil.

Herbs from Australia and New Zealand

Many of us associate Australia with tea tree oil. Other trees such as Eucalyptus were imported into the UK and Europe, where the gorgeous aroma added a wonderful scent as walkers passed by, and the elegance of the grown tree is a wonder! The leaves were used as herb oils in steam rooms and sauna buildings, where the infusion was reputed to help clear the air passageways and contribute to a calmer body in medicine. The legacy of the Aboriginal use of herbs before the arrival of colonizers to Australia included the use of plants such as native mint, which has approximately 90 species growing well in the wild. Ginger is also native to Australia and other parts of Asia, with hot temperatures ideal for cultivation. Often called Aniseed Myrtle, Myrtle is not the same as that grown in Europe, which is poisonous. There is a variety of Lemon Myrtle (Backhousia citriodora) classed as a rainforest tree native to Queensland.

In reality, an Australian Aboriginal herb garden would comprise all the land they covered on foot in their travels around the continent. Local knowledge of the siting of useful plants would have been recorded in the minds of adults who passed down both the location and the plant's use to the next generation. Although some knowledge has undoubtedly been lost, significant efforts have been made in conserving that knowledge for everyday use. When picking herbs like these in the wild, you must have an expert who can verify that the herbs you choose are safe for human consumption and their use and that picking them is legally permitted as some plants are protected by law. Buy seeds or plants from a reputable grower to grow in your own herb garden. Some to try:

1. **Native Ginger** (*Alpinia caerulea*). You will need warm conditions for this to grow well, but some European gardeners place them in warm greenhouses or indoors, where they are reported to thrive. The root is the part we know as ginger, and it is also dried for use in cooking.
2. **Bush Mint**. It is estimated that approximately 90 species of mint are native to Australia. Some types have gorgeous flowers, like those seen on traditional mint found in Europe, the US, and Canada. They make attractive hedge plants, and you can pick the leaves to use in tea and cooking.
3. **Lemon Myrtle** (*Backhousia citriodora*). This is more a tree than a herb, but if you live in Australia or a climate similar to Queensland, this tree is perfect! Traditionally it was used to cure headaches and also to cook with fish.
4. **Australian Ginger** (*Alpinia caerulea*).You can eat all parts of this native ginger plant, so this is an excellent addition to your herb garden if you can locate a root to start with. They can be divided as with other ginger, and a small piece of root is usually enough to begin with.

> The tastiest edible parts are the new young shoots, similar to the bamboo shoots that grow in many parts of the world. Keep this plant moist – remember its native habitat is the rainforest and keep those conditions.

Now you have a good overview of herbs from all over the globe. In Chapter 3, there are detailed instructions on how to plant your herbs from seed, stem cuttings, or root pieces, what soil they need, and the optimum conditions to get you started.

If you are enjoying '*The Essential Herb Gardening Handbook*' please don't be shy about saying so! My goal is to help as many people as possible appreciate the environment around us, so feel free to share this book with your friends and family (and please leave a review at your preferred retailer).

Chapter 3

Twenty Popular Herbs to Grow

1. Basil
2. Bay Leaf
3. Celery
4. Chives
5. Cilantro
6. Dill
7. Fennel
8. Garlic
9. Lavender
10. Lemon Balm
11. Marjoram
12. Mint
13. Oregano
14. Parsley
15. Rosemary
16. Sage
17. Savory (Summer)
18. Savory (Winter)
19. Tarragon
20. Thyme

Basil

This herb needs little introduction to herb lovers! Used all over the world in salads and cooking, its fame is often as the main ingredient in pesto sauce, that Italian favorite.

When to plant: Indoors in pots in late spring, plant outdoors in summer. Germination can be slow. Cover the pot with a plastic bag to keep it warm and then remove the bag when seeds sprout. For a winter crop, plant seeds again in August and take pots indoors for winter.

Best soil: Rich soil with plenty of humus, compost, and manure.

Best light: Full sun indoors; direct sunlight if outside.

Watering: Frequently; every day in hot water or if it flowers or goes to seed.

Plant next to: Tomatoes, chives, cilantro, marjoram, or in a greenhouse with these.

Harvesting: Pick leaves throughout the summer; plant new seeds in August for winter use indoors.

Cooking: Salads, Pesto, on pizzas, in pasta dishes, etc.

Problems: White flowers appear and the whole plant looks leggy. Trim off the flowers (you can eat them), water the plant more regularly, and give a top dressing of mulch. If you repot the whole plant you will give it a new life and more vigorous growth.

Bay Leaf

Bay is an evergreen shrub from the Laurel family and its leaves are dried for use in cooking. It likes shelter and grows tall, so a deep pot is required, or plant it in the ground if you can.

When to plant: Best to plant in a deep hole in autumn or spring outdoors.

Best soil: Rich soil with some lime content.

Best light: Full sun indoors; direct sunlight if outside.

Watering: Frequently once first planted. Then check weekly in summer.

Plant next to: It will grow tall but it smells fabulous next to other herbs. Rosemary and thyme are good companions.

Harvesting: Pick leaves when needed and hang them to dry. Use dried leaves in cooking.

Cooking: Dried leaves are used to add flavor to stews, soup, and cooked dishes and usually removed before serving.

Problems: This will grow into a tree if space permits. To stop it growing too tall, prune regularly and dry the leaves for culinary use.

Celery

Celery stems need to be fully covered to give them that yellowy-white color, so dig a deep trench and cover up the stems as they appear. When you pick a plant, make sure you cover up the stems of the plant next to it.

When to plant: Plant seeds in March/April indoors in pots and then plant outdoors in May/June, when there is no risk of frost. Prepare a trench outdoors then after your plant them in the ground, you can cover up the stems with earth as they appear.

Best soil: Celery grows for a long time in one place so needs lots of energy from the soil; make it as rich as you can. Manure the soil before planting and fertilize regularly during the growing summer season.

Best light: Bright sunshine for 40 weeks is needed for trench celery to mature so make sure the row is not shaded by summer crops.

Watering: Lots! Celery enjoys frequent watering and fertilizer. A very thirsty plant.

Plant next to: Give these plants lots of space and light and don't plant anything too close.

Harvesting: From October onwards. Pick stems from one plant, then cover up the next plant so that stems remain white.

Cooking: Use freshly cut in salads, raw for dipping into hummus instead of crackers, or as an addition to juices. Celery adds flavor to stocks and soups and we also use celery salt for seasoning.

Problems: Stems turn green when exposed to light. Cover them up well. These plants do not like frost or cold and if not watered and fertilized, your crop will be a disappointment. They take a long time to mature , this is not a plant for an impatient gardener.

Chives

Chives can be chopped into salads and sauces to add an onion flavor and garlic chives add a stronger, tangier taste. They are perennial – they will return each year once seeded.

When to plant: Tiny, little black chive seeds take ages to germinate so help them along with a sunny windowsill indoors and some central heating in the fall or spring. Then re-pot outdoors when the summer arrives.

Best soil: Rich soil or compost.

Best light: Full sun indoors; direct sunlight if outside.

Watering: Not usually necessary if planted in soil outdoors unless it is really hot and dry. Indoors, weekly should be enough but check the pot in warm weather.

Plant next to: You can plant them anywhere there is strong sunshine next to tomatoes, cilantro, and marjoram or in a flower bed. They have gorgeous purple flowers later in the summer.

Harvesting: Pick whenever you need them from late spring right through to the fall.

Cooking: A favorite in French cooking, chives are used in potato salads, omelets, and any recipe that needs an extra dash of fresh onion greenery.

Problems: Very few problems are reported with chives. Once established just add a top dressing of compost and water occasionally in warm weather.

Cilantro

In the UK, coriander is the name of the whole herb, whereas, in the US, cilantro is the name given to the little rounded seeds used in cooking.

When to plant: The seeds can be sown continuously indoors for a regular supply of fresh, tasty leaves. If grown outside, plant when there is no risk of frost (from May onwards normally). You can plant seed indoors then transplant it into the soil once the weather is warmer.

Best soil: Rich soil; add manure or homemade compost, with plenty of humus if available.

Best light: Full sun indoors; direct sunlight if outside.

Watering: If in the ground, water when the soil is dry at least once a week. When really dry, cilantro tries to go to seed so if you want seeds to save for your kitchen, that's perfect. Just make sure you keep planting new crops for leaves if you do this.

Plant next to: Tomatoes, chives, salads, marjoram.

Harvesting: Pick leaves regularly as needed. If you are growing for seeds, allow them to flower then let the plant die off and pick the seeds when they turn brown. When completely dry, store them in a glass jar for when you need them.

Cooking: A favorite ingredient in Mexican cooking, Italian dishes, and salads all over the world. Its fresh taste brings many dishes to life!

Problems: Often goes to seed but if that's why you are growing it, you won't mind! Keep planting new seeds to ensure you have a good supply of green cilantro leaves. Check if the leaves look wilted if cilantro is in pots, may need watering every day if hot.

Dill

Dill offers an attractive, feathery look for any flower bed with voluminous yellow flowers late in the summer, which turn to edible seeds. Dill leaves are long and very thin and look fabulous in fish dishes and cream sauces, adding a distinct flavor to cooking.

When to plant: Plant seeds in spring where you want them to grow. Dill does not take kindly to being re-planted and re-potted so or a little later when the soil is warm outside. Water them well.

Best soil: Dill requires well-drained soil and it grows up to 2 feet (60 cm) tall.

Best light: Full sun indoors; direct sunlight if outside.

Watering: Frequently, every day in hot weather or if the plant tries to go to seed.

Plant next to: Other flowering annual plants make good companions but not **fennel**. Fennel and Dill can cross-pollinate and the resulting plant will have an unpredictable taste. This plant can grow very tall and looks good at the back of a flower bed too, with other low flowering annuals placed in front.

Harvesting: Leaves can be harvested as required. The yellow flowers turn to seed heads. When they dry out and turn brown, you know when they are ready to pick. To collect, turn the seed head upside down into a paper bag and cut the stem so all the seeds fall into the bag.

Cooking: It is used in French cooking in sauces and fish dishes, particularly salmon. The dried herb leaves keep their flavor too, and you can hang them to dry in your kitchen. The seeds were traditionally used to make vinegar for pickling and they add a distinctive taste to cheese sauces.

Problems: Dill is usually happy to self-seed which may be a problem if you don't want too many plants. Pick the seed heads before they fall to avoid this. Some gardeners are not expecting the height to be so tall for an herb so seed it at the back of your flower bed, not the front.

Fennel

Fennel has an unmistakable smell – people seem to love it or hate it! Once established in a garden, it is there forever. It grows really tall and seeds hang on to the leaves all winter, enabling wind fertilization

When to plant: Plant the seeds in any patch where you want the herb, and more often than not, a plant will grow. Think carefully about its location. It will spread by seed dispersal and it grows taller than some adults in perfect conditions. Plant in April outside or slightly earlier indoors.

Best soil: Although it likes rich soil, fennel will grow anywhere! Fennel plants prefer well-drained soil.

Best light: Full sun indoors; direct sunlight if outside. Its height will shade smaller herbs so be careful where you plant it.

Watering:. Fennel loves frequent watering. However, it is native to windy, seaside cliffs so it can survive in conditions with infrequent rainfall. If fennel is in a pot, then water it weekly and avoid having the soil always moist.

Plant next to: Putting fennel at the back of a herb garden is perfect. You can plant fennel with other Mediterranean herbs like tarragon, thyme, rosemary, and even with tomatoes, chives, and cilantro, but not next to dill.

Harvesting: Pick leaves whenever you need them and eat as you walk, or add them to flavor soups and stews. You can dry fennel leaves too. Pick the seeds like dill, by placing a bag over the whole seed head and then catching the seeds as they fall.

Cooking: Try using fennel with oily fish, to use its distinctive taste. It is great steeped in a soup and removed before serving, along with a sprig of bay leaf and some thyme. The seed heads are excellent added as topping to homemade bread, bringing a taste of summer to the winter.

Problems: Fennel is a survivor and will spread like crazy so to avoid this, plant it at the back of a flower bed, cut the seed heads and save them for the kitchen and then use its stalks to support beans or peas..

Garlic

While you might not think of it as a herb, garlic is used all over the world and its health benefits, long-known to traditional knowledge have been confirmed by science..

When to plant: Garlic needs cold weather so plant in the fall, allow the winter to sharpen its taste, and gather the bulbs the following summer. Separate into individual cloves and plant each separately. Make sure the pointed end is up, as this will become the stalk. Sometimes you see a small root at the flatter end.

Best soil: Garlic needs good drainage and rich soil. Add manure if available, compost, and plenty of humus, such as leaf mold.

Best light: Best grown outside in pots or in a row in your garden. Bright summer sunshine is excellent.

Watering: Usually not necessary in winter except when first planted to establish the cloves in the ground. The rain normally does the work for you outside. Water weekly from spring onwards, especially if it is warm and sunny.

Plant next to: Some gardeners think planting peas and garlic together is a good idea as the peas fix nitrogen into the soil. Peas grow well in winter when the garlic is young and the soil will be enriched by the peas. However, peas can starve the garlic of nutrients at a time when they are establishing their first growth.

Harvesting: Garlic will tell you when it is ready to pick. The leaves turn brown and seem to die, allow a week or so for them to die off completely, then dig the garlic out. Store the bulbs by hanging them in a dry place.

Cooking: Used to make garlic bread, added to stews, soups, roasted, crushed into various Indian dishes, Chinese recipes, and all over the world.

Problems: Garlic has several diseases including root rot caused by extremely wet weather. There's nothing you can do apart from keeping an eye on the leaves. Plant them in rich soil with excellent drainage. The leaves also turn brown and appear dead when they are almost ready to harvest but this is just nature's way of telling you it is harvest time.

Lavender

This plant is used as a relaxant, lavender soap is used worldwide, and is added to clothes drawers and placed under pillows. Its delicious scent is a favorite with bees, so planting a few lavender plants will keep them very happy.

When to plant: Cuttings can be taken at any time, but best in spring or fall. More difficult to grow from seed, but if you do sow in early spring in pots. Give each plant space to expand because lavender will send shoots out in every direction. Most plants last at least 5 years but you will need to prune them regularly.

Best soil: Good drainage is essential. Lavender grows well on poor soil in native sites but if you give it some compost and enrich the soil with plenty of humus, your plants will thrive.

Best light: Loves full, direct sunlight outside.

Watering: Lavender does not need much water in the average garden. Once established, lavender does not need much unless it is an exceptionally hot, dry summer. Check the soil during those periods and water when it feels dry to the touch.

Plant next to: Plant it with other herbs in sunny spots and ensure that the taller lavender is at the back. In large pots, combine with nasturtiums, which add complementary colors to the silvery lavender leaves. The smell of lavender can confuse some garden flies, so try planting it next to anything attracting pests..

Harvesting: Cut your flowers in bloom in summer, which can be used to infuse oils with their scent You will need to replace the flowers in the oil every week by adding new ones until the scent remains firmly embedded. Compost the flowers after use.

Cooking: Lavender leaves can be used to flavor meat dishes or as a strong taste in soups. It can be added to cake mixtures and batters too. The flowers are edible but you may need to balance their strong taste with citrus fruit like lime or lemon..

Problems: Lavender is usually trouble-free until it ages, after about 5 years. Stems can become long and woody and it is best to prune these to keep the plant in good shape. You can prune when you pick flowers, in the fall and the spring.

Lemon Balm

Also known as Bee Balm, this herb has a long history adding a citrus scent to various dishes, as well as making herbal teas. Fresh leaves can be added to salads to add a citrus taste in the summer sunshine.

When to plant: Plant seeds in spring but it is widely available in garden centers for those who want to plant direct!

Best soil: This herb grows well in most environments and rich soil is not essential. Plant it direct into a pot or your flower bed and give it some homemade compost or fresh soil. It does not need to be fertilized if the soil is reasonably fertile.

Best light: Lemon Balm is often grown in shade or semi-shade. Like mint, it is not a lover of really direct sunlight if outside. So a spot with some afternoon shade is ideal and the plant will thrive.

Watering: You don't need to water this plant too much outdoors. If it starts to flower, this is a sign that the plant may think winter is coming so you can cut the flowers off and extend its season a bit longer. Water when the soil around it seems very dry.

Plant next to: Lemon Balm spreads a lot so make sure neighbors are far away. Give it space but small herbs like parsley will grow well with it. Tomatoes, chives, cilantro, and marjoram are also good choices..

Harvesting: Leaves can be harvested when you need them in spring, summer, and fall. In winter it is fairly dormant so taking leaves then is hard on the herb. Cut leaves only when it's growing and allow it to rest for the winter.

Cooking: The leaves add a zing to cooked fruit and cakes and it is also added to stuffing mixtures mixed with breadcrumbs, where the flavor is infused in the poultry or meat is cooked with. Herbal tea made with lemon balm leaves and mint is a favorite tisane in many central European countries.

Problems: This herb does not stay in one place and its roots need to be divided after about 3 years, into independent plants. Some advice for a herb gardener with little space: plant this herb in a pot where you can restrict its growth.

Marjoram

Marjoram is occasionally mistaken for oregano. There are many varieties of this herb to try from annual plants which last only one growing season to bigger bush types like Pot Marjoram, which can survive for a few years

When to plant: Plant marjoram starters into the desired position in your garden in late spring. Sow seeds in March, then transplant outdoors when there is no danger of frost.

Best soil: Marjoram will tolerate soil that is not the richest; it is used to growing in the wild on dusty roadsides and cottage gardens. So give it some fresh compost but it will grow happily in many spots in the average garden without any problems.

Best light: Full sun outside is necessary for about 4 hours per day but marjoram tolerates some shade. It dries out very easily so some shade is perfect for this herb.

Watering: If in a pot, marjoram dries out very easily so water it at least weekly and check it during hot weather. Marjoram does fine with a regular splash, so you might have a look at it most days. If it needs water, it tends to flower, then go to seed.

Plant next to: Some herbs that prefer the same conditions are Lemon Balm, thyme, or mint. Its green leaves make an excellent background color for bright annual flowers like pansies and carnations, take advantage of the color and shape of its pretty leaves to add some artistic touches to the garden.

Harvesting: You can pick marjoram leaves as you need them in the growing season. Leaves can be picked and dried for winter use and you can also plant seeds late in the summer for a ready supply indoors throughout the winter.

Cooking: Marjoram is used to add its unique flavor to poultry or meat prior to cooking. Cooks spread a little oil on the meat and then crush the herb firmly into the skin so that the flavor will cook through. Add it to savory baking and the subtle taste will infuse the dish. Complements other herbs like thyme.

Problems: Frost is not a friend of your perennial marjoram so if you get cold winters either cover the plant well during a cold spot or better still, take it indoors. Annual marjoram will die back naturally at the end of the season.

Mint

Peppermint, spearmint, and many other varieties of mint can be grown. Mint is adored by bees and pollinators and there will be a hum around these plants when they are in bloom. Their flowers are attractive and the leaves are used to make teas.

When to plant: Either in spring or autumn, place a root in a container that restricts it from spreading. Mint is often described as invasive, so keep it in check in a pot. Cover with a generous layer of new topsoil each year and change the soil completely every 3 years.

Best soil: Mint uses up the goodness in soil quickly so if it starts to look unhealthy, add some compost to cheer it up! Good drainage is essential for mint too.

Best light: Mint enjoys the sun early morning and late afternoon but it prefers shade when the sun is at its hottest so make sure you provide it with some respite during the hottest parts of the summer.

Watering: As it lives in the shade during the hottest part of the day, most mint plants do well if watered by rainfall or once a week with a watering can.

Plant next to: Lemon Balm likes the same conditions but be careful with putting mint into the ground because it spreads so easily. If it is in a pot, then its fragrance is really pleasant in a seating area on a patio or its flower spikes look well next to other colorful annual flowers like nasturtiums or cosmos.

Harvesting: Pick leaves when you need them and you can also dry mint leaves for winter usage when the plant has died back. Mint dies back completely in winter so pick leaves before this happens.

Cooking: Mint sauce is a well-known recipe with lamb, and mint is also excellent in cool, refreshing summer drinks and mint ice cream is divine. Alcoholic drinks which contain mint include the cocktail favorite Crème de menthe and Mexican mojitos often come garnished with a mint leaf.

Problems: Mint is often the problem! It tends to take over entire gardens if permitted so keep it contained. It does have a Mint beetle which likes to lay its eggs on any mint but the plant usually survives. If you spot them, they are a very attractive metallic color and you can remove them or use a mixture of soap and water.

Oregano

This herb is frequently called wild marjoram and is often confused with sweet marjoram, which is very closely related to it. Common oregano is a member of the mint family and is used in Mediterranean cooking.

When to plant: Common oregano can be grown indoors in compost from March to May, and then transplanted out after the last frost. Heat is useful for germination so make sure your pot is in a warm place such if you don't have a heated mat to propagate seeds.

Best soil: Use compost for seeds, but oregano does not need very rich soil after germination. In the wild, it grows on Mediterranean clifftops where the soil is very sandy, so oregano will tolerate a wide variety of conditions as long as it is well-drained and not too wet! It prefers slightly acidic soil so adding some tea leaves or coffee grounds will help to create this over time.

Best light: This herb is used to the sunny slopes of cliff tops in southern Europe so give it a sunny position and a place where it remains warm. Full sun with some shelter is ideal..

Watering: Oregano prefers the soil to be dry, so it only needs a watering if the soil feels dry. If in a pot, oregano will need watering occasionally but do not allow the roots to be in wet, moist soil for too long.

Plant next to: Oregano's very delicate spikes of purple flowers look fabulous in any flower bed but you can also place oregano close to other herbs such as cilantro, parsley, or mint. It is perennial and will last many years in the same spot so allow it some space to expand too. It can grow up to 31 inches (80 cm).

Harvesting: Pick leaves as required in the growing period from spring through to the fall. You can add the leaves to olive oil, where the taste infuses the oil, depending on the cultivar you have chosen. Fresh leaves taste much stronger than the dried herb..

Cooking: The taste of your oregano will depend on the cultivar grown. The taste ranges from sweet in Europe, to bitter in some hybrids, to a spicier taste in Greece and Turkey, and a quite strong flavor in Latin America. Often eaten raw as a topping, but traditionally included in roasted dishes in Italian cooking.

Problems: Sometimes oregano just exhausts the soil it is in and needs to be moved. However, it is often best to completely change the site or start with a new plant. Experienced gardeners try to grow it from seed produced and have success.

Parsley

This herb comes as a garnish on salads, fish, and many dishes. Parsley sauce is chopped parsley added to a white sauce, which is used widely in the UK. Comes in both flat leaved parsley and moss curled varieties.

When to plant: Notoriously difficult to germinate, your parsley seeds need excellent care in order to grow. Germination will not take place in cold, wet soil so I advise using a warm dark place such as a heated gardening propagator or even your airing cupboard.

Best soil: Only the best for parsley! It likes rich soil with any extras such as leaf mold or homemade compost will ensure a long supply of green, tasty foliage.

Best light: Full sun indoors once the seeds germinate and then place plants in direct sunlight when you transplant them outside. If placed in the shade, it will not be as happy as in full sun. You can plant seeds late in the summer to take indoors for winter use.

Watering: Water frequently - every day in hot weather. The leaves wilt in really hot weather..

Plant next to: Parsley will mix happily with plants that like the same conditions. Tomatoes or cucumbers will give it a little shade when the sun is at its hottest, and it accompanies chives, cilantro, oregano, and marjoram well too.

Harvesting: Pick as needed for fresh use, dried parsley is not ideal. Some cooks swear by dipping a few sprigs of parsley into boiling water for 1-2 minutes, then placing it to dry in the oven for a few minutes. As soon as it cools, place it in a spice jar to use in winter (or a late summer sowing to take some fresh parsley indoors for the winter).

Cooking: Eat fresh in summer salads, use as a garnish on fish, as a topping for scrambled eggs, and in white for potatoes. Parsley is one of the herbs in the French *Fines Herbes* and is often added as a last-minute topping on soups and stews.

Problems: The main difficulty is germination but once established, parsley is usually trouble-free. Slugs and snails are partial to the young leaves so keep your eyes peeled. You also need to pick regularly to stop it from going to seed. If flowers appear, cut them off to stop the plant from going to seed.

Rosemary

Rosemary for remembrance, because the scent of this herb will remain even in a dried sprig months later. Rosemary needs plenty of space, as this perennial herb will expand its branches and delight you with sky blue flowers in spring.

When to plant: You can sow seeds in April or May but they take quite a while to germinate. It might be better to buy a small plant and position it in a warm spot where it will thrive. Rosemary can tolerate a cold winter but it likes a sheltered spot. Frost may kill off the tips of an established plant but new shoots will emerge when the weather warms up.

Best soil: Rosemary grows wild on French and Italian coastlines. To imitate this, plant it in sandy, well-drained soil which does not retain excess moisture. A handful of compost won't go amiss every spring and fall but Rosemary grows happily in fairly poor soil.

Best light: Full sun is best. Provide heat and some shelter from winter weather by planting it next to a south-facing wall or near other shrubs which will protect it from winter frost.

Watering: As a cliff plant, Rosemary does not need to be watered once it is established. Allow rainfall to do that job for you! For the newly planted Rosemary plant, water it well and then keep an eye on it for a few months, giving it only the occasional watering.

Plant next to: Rosemary needs space to reach its full height and spread as an herb; however, it also needs shelter from very cold weather so planting it close to rose bushes and other garden shrubs often helps. Frost will kill off the growing tips but it shouldn't damage the roots so don't worry too much.

Harvesting: Pick the fresh leaves or a whole sprig to add flavor to stews, casseroles, and cooked dishes. Pick sprigs to dry indoors and hang them in clothes cupboards, or areas where you need a fresh smell, and then use the dried leaves as required throughout the winter.

Cooking: Rosemary leaves leave a scent on your hands long after cutting so use sparingly; the flavor is very strong. Usually, cooks add a sprig of Rosemary and remove it before serving. Rosemary accompanies lamb, pork, and veal in Mediterranean recipes and it adds depth to vegetarian meals.

Problems: Winter frost or snow appears to kill off the growing tips of Rosemary but it usually survives. If you are worried, then cover the plant with a cloth or bubble wrap for the cold period.

Sage

Sage looks elegant at all times of the year. The leaves have an unusual texture and the herb comes in various shades and colors from dark olive-green to gray, an attractive addition to any garden.

When to plant: Try not to plant sage into cold ground; spring is ideal once the last frosts have passed. Choose a sunny site and make sure you do not have other plants very close. Apart from strawberries and borage, sage emits a chemical signal to other plants which deters their growth.

Best soil: If planting into the ground, add compost and plenty of humus, which will decompose slowly and add essential nutrients. Sage will grow for many years so start the ground well. Do not expect sage to stay small – it can reach as high as 3 feet (91.5 cm) tall and expands in all directions.

Best light: Full sun is essential for sage to reach its growth potential. It will dominate after 2 years so do not plant delicate plants next to it.

Watering: Sage enjoys natural rainfall, don't bother watering sage unless you have just planted it. Water it weekly in its first few months but after that, let the rain do the work. Check the soil and make sure it is dry before watering.

Plant next to: Choose robust geraniums or annuals until a new sage plant reaches its full height. After that, surround it with strawberries and borage, maybe chives or parsley but not too close. Sage tends to kill off other plants that grow too close.

Harvesting: A little sage goes a long way. Pick leaves fresh before the plant has flowered, which is usually June or July.

Cooking: Sage is well known for the flavor it adds to stuffing for poultry and meat on festive occasions and modern bread makers have made it popular as a flavor too. It is a very strong herb and may overwhelm other herbs. Some cheesemakers use a little sage too and other uses (sparingly) are in soups, stews, and slow-cooked dishes where the herb can release its goodness slowly.

Problems: Sage can overwhelm other plants close to it. So if you have a favorite plant, think twice before adding a sage plant close by. As it grows, it gets woody and you will need to prune it hard every July after it flowers.

Savory (Summer)

Savory comes as a winter and summer herb, and summer savory tastes like a mixture of thyme, sage, and rosemary.

When to plant: Like its winter relative, this herb is best planted in Spring (April) and can be treated as an annual, so plant new seeds each year. Cover seeds with a thin layer of compost and watch it climb to over 1 foot (30 cm) tall

Best soil: The soil needs to have good drainage and to be light, not a clay type. Ensure you add some compost and if your soil is very thick, maybe add some sand and gravel to thin it a little.

Best light: Full sun is best in a new position each year.

Watering: As this herb likes good drainage you do not need to water very frequently. When it's very dry weather, feel the soil and if it's really parched give it a good soaking. When it flowers, it likes some water too so when you spot the buds, get your watering can out.

Plant next to: This is an annual herb so you can happily plant it next to any herb that likes similar soil and watering. If space is tight, then parsley, chives, cilantro, and marjoram are all good companions although some of these prefer the soil a bit richer.

Harvesting: You need to pick leaves before the plant flowers when the herb is about 1 foot (30 cm) high. After you've enjoyed the flowers, cut the whole plant back and then it should produce a second crop of leaves. Pick these until your winter savory appears!

Cooking: Savory can be used like thyme or rosemary in most dishes. It adds depth to the flavor and the silvery gray leaves emit a gorgeous scent when cut in the kitchen. Add them to egg dishes, they can go in salads and they are an extra taste to experiment with when cooking summer dishes.

Problems: When seeds are first planted, keep an eye out for slugs and snails which will gobble them up. You can grow them in a pot and transplant them, but these seeds are not fond of disturbance.

Savory (Winter)

Savory comes as a winter and summer herb, and winter savory offers the cook an herb they can pick when very little is in season.

When to plant: Winter savory is an evergreen plant, which provides leaves in the depth of winter like sage and thyme. For this reason alone, it is worth giving it a try! Plant it in your soil in April and make sure you trim it back in spring. It then goes quite dormant until the weather cools down and summer savory takes over

Best soil: Light soil with good drainage will suit winter savory very well. It is a low, ground-hugging herb that enjoys full sun when few other plants are there to compete. It grows in spikes, with leaves shooting out to each side which you can pick for salads, omelets, and winter poached eggs..

Best light: Full sun outdoors. Try to make sure bigger shrubs do not shade it or the foliage will be thin.

Watering: Frequently every day in hot water or it goes to seed.

Plant next to: Winter savory has fresh, new leaves from early fall and many other plants are dying back at this time so the usual plants to accompany this herb are winter flowering bulbs such as snowdrops, grape hyacinths, and later on, daffodils. The problem with these is that they tend to spread through an area and they may overwhelm your winter savory. My advice is to either give this herb its own, deep pot and have a label on it to remind you or you that you place a mulch on top of it to mark its position and then plant around it in the summer.

Harvesting: Pick leaves frequently for fresh use in the winter and spring months. Then ensure that you cut the herb back in late spring to allow it to rest before it appears again the following winter.

Cooking: Savory is traditionally used to season broad bean and lentil soup. Broad beans are ready to pick in late March, early April so herbs may still be growing fresh leaves. You can also use winter savory for fresh green garnishes to egg dishes and to accompany any green salads.

Problems: You may think your winter savory has completely died when the hot, midsummer sun is shining in your garden but it is just taking a rest! Otherwise, its leaves are munched by slugs and snails but it is usually not bothered by pests in the cold season.

Tarragon

There is no taste quite like tarragon! This herb is delicate with a hint of licorice. Two types of tarragon are available; French and Russian.

When to plant: You cannot plant French tarragon from seed. Normally it spreads through its rhizome root system and the seeds rarely grow into new viable plants. Buy a starter plant instead, but it will not tolerate frost and is quite difficult to grow. The Russian variety can be planted in spring indoors and then planted outdoors when the ground is warm. It is tolerant of frost once established, and is much less picky in general.

Best soil: French tarragon likes rich soil which drains well. Russian tarragon will grow happily in semi-shade in less fertile soil, which its choosier French cousin will not.

Best light: French tarragon loves being indoors in full sun. It needs to be indoors the minute the fall arrives because a frost will kill it immediately. Outdoors, give French tarragon a sunny position and it will grow the whole summer season. Russian tarragon enjoys bright sunlight if outside, but as long as it has 4 hours per day, this herb will continue to thrive..

Watering: In pots, both of these herbs need frequent watering but neither likes roots that sit in wet soil.

Plant next to: French tarragon does not take up a lot of space. Annual flowers and herbs like parsley are excellent but do not crowd it by planting it next to rosemary or other taller plants. You will need to dig it up carefully to take it indoors for winter so if you keep it in a pot, you can do this easily.

Russian tarragon needs less fertile soil, and foxgloves love the shade and similar conditions so this could be a good choice.

Harvesting: For drying, French tarragon is the better to use because the Russian variety tends to lose scent as it dries. Both herbs are rich in vitamin A and C so eat them fresh when you can.

Cooking: Tarragon is added to seafood, salads, sauces, flavored butter to melt onto poultry, as well as in sweet rice dishes and desserts. Both varieties work well with vanilla pods and sometimes you will find this served in French ice cream or sweet sauces. Tarragon vinegar is a favorite for salads and either herb can be used.

Russian tarragon stalks can be cooked fresh when they are young, similar to bamboo shoots and asparagus. It is a more vigorous plant so you can pick more leaves and add them to salads, giving them an unusual twist

Thyme

Thyme is a perennial evergreen herb, with dainty little pink flowers, which tends to creep along dry areas in impoverished soils. Plant it somewhere to enjoy the scent of the leaves and the herb's pretty blooms. You can pick its leaves all year round.

When to plant: You can plant the seed in late spring when the ground has warmed up, but most growers buy a plant instead. Thyme grows quite leggy with straggling branches over time. Plant it deep and make sure the soil has good drainage as thyme hates wet feet! Divide plants every 3 years and replant them separately.

Best soil: Thyme will thrive in poor soil; this herb is a great survivor. Give it a thin layer of compost (around the stem) in the spring, to encourage it to grow big and strong. Leaf mold will add humus and it seems to appreciate it. In the summer, make a mulch with grass cuttings which decompose slowly and reduce loss of moisture.

Best light: Full sun indoors or outdoors. Thyme thrives with lots of sunshine.

.

Watering: Infrequently. Most thyme plants survive very hot temperatures with little rainfall in their native Mediterranean environments so it is not necessary to water your thyme plant much. In a particularly dry period, check its soil and water if it feels really parched..

Plant next to: Any Mediterranean herb (chives, rosemary, cilantro, parsley). Thyme will not grow much higher than 1 foot (about 30 cm) so place it at the front of plants that grow taller. This makes it easier to pick leaves too.

.

Harvesting: Pick thyme leaves fresh throughout the year as you need them. This herb survives the winter and you can keep cutting to add flavor to cooking A great herb for climates where little else can be picked fresh.

.**Cooking:** Thyme often accompanies parsley in bread, and is often added to fish because it is a subtle taste that does not overwhelm delicate flavors. It adds flavor to soups like squash and pumpkin and can be added to pastry as a topping. Some cooks add it to desserts like lemon and thyme cake because the taste is accentuated by sugar and slow cooking releases the flavor.

Problems: Thyme gets very leggy if left unpruned. Most thyme plants use up the nutrients for the soil they are in after about 3 years so it is a good idea to divide the roots and re-plant them.

Chapter 4
How to Sow, Propagate and Divide Herbs

To have a steady supply of fresh herbs is very easy in summer and many herbs only last for just one season. However, some herbs can have a much longer life if divided or cut to make new plants. This chapter examines best practices for sowing herbs from seed and how to propagate new herbs so that you can have a steady supply year-round.

All seeds require soil, water, and heat to germinate. Use sterilized soil to start seeds off so you know there are no diseases, pests, or weeds present. Seeds take different times to begin life – see the soil requirements for each herb in Chapter 3.

Here are the ideal conditions for germinating seeds:

Temperature. Herbs, like most plants, have a minimum and optimum temperature to ensure they germinate. In the wild, this is so that the plant seed will not try to start growing until the temperature feels like spring or until the perfect growing conditions for the seed to be viable exist. This is approximately 18 or 19 degrees Celsius for most herbs (64 to 68 degrees Fahrenheit) but can be a slightly higher 20 to 23 Celsius (68 to 73 degrees

Fahrenheit) for tomatoes, chili peppers, and cucumbers, which may accompany your herbs. Buying a heated propagation mat will be very useful in a climate with cold winters.

Water the pot when you plant the seed and then wait a bit. The goal here is to keep the soil just moist. Once the seeds are established, follow the watering guidelines for each herb in Chapter 3. An optional trick is to leave your seeds in a bowl of warm water until you can see them start to sprout and then transfer them to the soil.

Light is another factor. Celery, for example, needs light to germinate, so you should just place the seeds on top of the compost and water them in. As soon as any of your herb seeds show some green growth, they will need light to photosynthesize. For early sowings in spring, you may need some help from artificial light to help your herb seedlings to thrive because light levels tend to be very low before the beginning of spring.

Choosing your Seeds

Not all seeds are the same, so choose your seeds carefully. Some seeds are called F1, which means they have been altered to make them resistant to disease or produce more fruit. These can be useful for plants that tend to become diseased (cabbage family, potatoes, etc.) or if you want to grow more productive crops (squash). However, the taste is another issue and for me, buying organic seed usually guarantees that my crops get the best possible start.

Starting your Seeds

A good trick for seeds that are difficult to get going (like parsley) is to give them a few hours in water to soften them up. You can place several seeds in a pot of compost, water them, then cover them up with a thin layer of soil. Then cover the whole seed pot with a transparent plastic bag to trap moisture. Use any plastic you have handy from shopping bags or food wrap; this will conserve moisture, retain heat better, and can be removed as soon as your seedlings show. Next, supply some heat! An airing cupboard is superb for this but only for one or two pots at a time! Some gardeners prefer to use a heated propagation mat, which supplies heat for many pots simultaneously and can keep seedlings at a steady temperature. Until seeds have germinated, they don't need light in general apart from celery and some salads.

Check each day for new seedlings, and if the soil feels dry, water the pot every 2 to 3 days. As soon as the seedlings appear, remove the plastic cover and move them into the light in a protected environment. For example, a sunny windowsill indoors in spring is perfect but be careful with drafts when the nighttime temperature falls. As the days get warmer, place the seedlings outdoors to harden them off; this is a time outside in the sunshine to help them get used to being outdoors, but take them back in at night away from pests and from dangerous drops in temperature.

Thinning out

This is the process of separating the seedlings and keeping only the strongest ones. It is not such a big issue with herbs, but when growing basil, cilantro, and salad crops, I grow plenty of herb seeds and then space them into the final growing spot. I usually plant them all because this allows for some spoilage by slugs and snails but usually ensures that many plants will survive.

It is essential to check how tall and wide your final herb will reach. For example, if you grow a tomato next to your basil, chives, and cilantro, you need to remember that some tomato varieties can reach over 2 feet tall and spread to at least 2 feet wide. A tiny tomato in a pot gives you no indication of the maximum height it can reach, so check the seed packet, stake the tomato before you add the plant to the soil, and allow it some space away from its herb neighbors. Your basil will be completely shaded unless you think about this before you dig in the companion tomato, and you already know that basil likes the sun. With herbs that will grow much bushier like sage, allow the herb enough space to grow into its final size.

Potting on

When your herb seedlings start to look cramped, their roots begin to show at the base of the pot, and the sunny weather has arrived, it is time to pot your herbs on. This means either giving them a bigger pot or planting them directly into the soil in the ground or a planter bed. First, check the soil needs for your particular herb in Chapter 3. Some herbs do not need rich soil, and some prefer it. When sowing seeds directly into the soil, make sure you dig a hole big enough for the root ball of your herb (only slightly larger than the root ball size), that the soil is crumbly, and that you water them in well.

Propagation: making more plants

Why should you do it?

1. Cost – you can make new, free plants. If your neighbors have a plant you like, just ask them for a cutting!
2. Some herbs do not grow from seed (e.g., French tarragon). Making new plants will make welcome gifts for family and friends.
3. All herbs eventually get old, so this allows you to replace your favorites with new vigorous ones just like their parent.

4. Hormone rooting powder or gel makes it a straightforward process. However, commercial ones are very reliable, and there are some natural alternatives in the Tips below.

The main ways to propagate your herbs

Take stem cuttings

Cut a small part of a healthy secondary stem approximately 3-6 inches (8-15 cm) long off of the plant. Make your cut close to the main stem if possible. Ensure there are no flower buds on the stem piece you remove because the herb will try to flower, not root. Next, remove the leaves at the end of the stem. Now you can either root the stem in water or plant it directly into the soil.

Place the stem(s) in a jar of water and allow it to sit in a shady area for a few weeks. Roots should start to grow, and as soon as you see a robust root system, you can pot this new plant in the soil. Dip the end of the stem into hormone rooting powder to help the process along (see natural alternatives below). Make a hole for the cutting in a pot of sterilized compost and ease the soil around the new root. Water it generously to assist the plant in stabilizing.

Woody stems from herbs like rosemary and sage will take longer to root, so be patient. Rooting is easier with some help from either a commercial hormone rooting powder or a natural one. Water it well every 3 to 4 days and place it in a sunny location. Check the soil daily and watch for any new leaves forming. If they start growing, your plant is ready to go.

This works for: bay, basil, lavender, oregano, sage, rosemary, tarragon, thyme.

TIPS: A natural hormone rooting powder is the gel from Aloe

Vera if you have a plant. Other alternatives used by gardeners worldwide include cinnamon, turmeric, honey, willow tea, comfrey tea, and even cow dung! Run the cut end of the stem over the gel and then place the stem directly in the soil.

Take root cuttings

This is also known as plant division. Many herbs become very overgrown over time, and my advice is to pick herb leaves frequently as a natural pruning process. After all, you grew them for a reason, don't forget to use them! Herbs like mint quickly outgrow any pot they live in, and every three years or so, you need to divide the roots and re-pot to keep the plant healthy. Dig up the whole herb carefully, and then use a spade or knife to cut sections of the herb off with stem, leaves, and roots intact. If you grow this division in soil, it will usually make a brand new plant.

This works for chives, mint, oregano, Lemon Balm, thyme, winter savory.

TIPS: Check the herb at the end of the season and decide if it needs division. Are there very woody branches? Does it hang over the edge of the pot? If so, you can prune it back vigorously or divide the roots

OTHER PLANTS REPRODUCE BY GROWING SMALL PLANTLETS (Spider plant and Aloe vera), or they self-seed by throwing ripe seeds into the soil in areas at a distance from the mother herb.

This is true for dill, fennel, parsley, and Russian tarragon.

TIPS: If your herb is becoming invasive, make sure to remove seed heads just after flowering.

Chapter 5
Soil Improvement and Companion Planting

THIS CHAPTER WILL EXAMINE WAYS TO IMPROVE YOUR SOIL USING composting and other free methods of recycling waste to create richer soil for all your plants and wildlife in general. Companion planting means using Mother Nature to pair plants up that help each other in some way. Finally, we will look at what can go wrong with your herbs in Chapter 7 and include crop rotation.

Your herbs may be the only crop you want to grow. However, it is worth knowing how to improve your soil if you plan on growing herbs for more than one season. Soil is food for your herbs, and the microscopic creatures that inhabit our soil can create their own thriving ecosystem, even in a pot on your windowsill. So let's look at some easy ways to ensure that your soil is healthy and some ways to improve it so that it can support your herbs (and plants) for years to come.

Ways to improve your soil for your herbs

If you buy a bag of compost in the garden center, it will undoubtedly have enough nutrients to feed your herbs for one growing season. However, if you dig into your soil outdoors, you should expect to see some wildlife! If you find earthworms, they are aerating the soil as they tunnel through it, and you will often see centipedes scurrying back under cover. Worms deposit their waste, which adds to soil fertility, and there may be other creatures alive in a handful of soil, this is a living substance.

Soil gets quickly depleted if one type of plant keeps extracting all the goodness so, in order to continue to grow healthy plants and herbs, you need to add a top layer to pots or herbs in the ground. For herbs, a soil pH of about 6.8 is usually recommended, and soil should be crumbly like the texture of bread crumbs. However, individual herbs may have preferences, so check Chapter 3 when you are planting for detailed information.

To test what type of soil you have in the ground, dig a hole at least 1 foot (approximately 30 cm) deep and then pour a whole watering can of water into it. Watch how the water drains away. If it's straight through, you probably have sandy soil. If the water still has not drained away 24 hours later, you may have clay soil. The ideal soil is loam – see more below.

Sandy soil is found near the ocean, and it is not as full of nutrients as other soils, mainly because these drain away every time it rains. It can be dug relatively easily has excellent drainage, but conversely, this means goodness is leached out of the soil. To counteract this, add some sawdust, well-rotted manure, and compost to enrich it for hungry vegetables. Sandy soil is perfect for some herbs because it is the norm in their native environments, so check the details of your particular herb in Chapter 3.

Loam soil (the best soil!) has a texture like crumbs; you can dig it easily when it is dry, it drains well, and usually has high fertility. It retains moisture well but not to the extent that rainfall gathers in puddles on the top of the soil when it rains. If that happens, you probably have clay soil.

Clay soil sticks together like modeling clay. Imagine this around a plant's roots. It may cause the ground to get waterlogged, so if your soil has a lot of clay, it is good to add other ingredients to help make it looser. For example, some sand can be added, and some homemade compost is another good idea. Both of these will add other nutrients and allow for better drainage.

Before you plant any herbs, check for the exact conditions they like in Chapter 3. Then use the ways below to improve fertility generally for soil which grows crops year after year.

HERE ARE EIGHT EASY WAYS YOU CAN IMPROVE YOUR SOIL YEAR on year.

1. Use well-rotted manure: Manure adds richness and nutrients to any garden, and if you cannot find a local farmer or stable to supply it, buy a bag from a supplier or garden center. If you have any friends who have chickens, a bucket full of soil from wherever they run is equally good to increase the quality of your soil. Dig it in well, and it needs to be well-rotted. Manure is really useful to feed hungry crops like tomatoes, and if you are planting basil right next door, both crops will benefit from a bucket full of manure. Plant cilantro, chives, and lettuce in the same bed next to the tomatoes; all of these plants will guzzle up the manure to make sumptuous tomatoes and lots of fantastic herb foliage and green leaves to add to salads.

2. Compost your waste: This recycling of green waste brings many nutrients into the soil and stops it from going to a landfill. I cannot recommend this enough. Even a small worm composter is helpful if you only have a small space. If you have soil and a backyard, buy a big plastic composting bin with a top lid to place material in easily and a door below to extract the finished product. Start with a layer of twigs or cardboard on the soil. Then empty your tea bags, coffee grounds, potato peelings, apple cores, orange peels, and anything that has ever grown in there. Composting is a method of reducing your environmental waste by decomposing it into planting material in as little as six months. It can take longer, but there are guides to the best methods available, and your local authority is a good start.

For simple composting, you need to alternate layers with green waste like vegetable peelings, then add a second layer of paper or wood waste from garden twigs, leaves, etc. Paper waste like newspapers, envelopes, and household bills can also be added but tear them into tiny pieces to aid in decomposition. Grass lawn cuttings, twigs chopped finely, any skin or peels from fruit or vegetables, and the dust from the vacuum bag waste is fine in there. Crush eggshells and these will add keratin and calcium.

DO NOT ADD cooked meat, fish or dairy products, or pet litter trays for fear of attracting rodents or risk of cross-infection. Instead, you can make a DIY composting area by using pallets or old wooden planks and then using an old carpet or cardboard to cover up the whole area.

3. **Mulches**: Gardeners often speak about adding a layer of mulch to the top of a plant pot or flower bed. This is simply spreading a layer of material on the topsoil such as composted wood chips, freshly cut lawn mowings, straw, hay, comfrey leaves, leaf mold (see below), or green manure material (such as ryegrass and corn salad).

You can do the same with your pots. Just add a layer on the top and water it in. The idea is often to block weeds with this layer and retain moisture in very hot weather. Wood chips should be used with care, as some gardeners complain that they deplete the soil underneath. However, they are great for use on walkways or paths between your herb garden pots or growing beds.

4. Seaweed: This is a method used by Irish farmers for centuries, and if you live close to the sea, this is a free resource. You can buy seaweed liquid feed in any garden center! Simply gather some seaweed and spread it on the top of the soil at the end of the growing season in winter or early in spring. This will give it time to decompose, and it not only adds goodness to the soil but also helps as a technique for water retention. Make sure you keep it away from the stems of the plants you want to grow though – keep it at the edges of the border. A layer of seaweed keeps the soil moist at ground level. If you find it difficult to weed, this layer reduces weeding because other plants find it difficult to survive with a blanket of salty, decomposing seaweed. It is a tried and tested method to deter slugs and other pests. In addition, it enriches the soil and can give lethargic plants a boost. Finally, it helps lighten dense soil, and it's free! Some gardeners are not so keen on the smell of seaweed, but if, like me, you love the ocean smells, just try it.

5. Ash: Do you burn logs in winter to keep warm, and maybe you have access to ash from bonfires during the year? Ash is the remains of wood, and it is high in nutrients which can raise fertility. Just add a layer to the topsoil. When you add it to either pots or soil, make sure you mix it in equal parts with compost because otherwise, it can change the pH of the soil very quickly, and the life forms within the soil may not be entirely happy with a layer of ash thrown all over them. Using compost and ash together provides the nutrients you can water in so that the combined goodness soaks into the soil below.

6. Leaf mold: If you ever have to sweep up garden leaves, this will make that job more manageable. Make some holes in a big plastic bag and then add the leaves and simply leave them until the spring. The holes will allow air to circulate, and the leaves will decompose naturally. Come springtime, have a look and there will be a crumbly, dry leaf textured mixture that adds extra humus to the soil. You will probably find that creatures have found this safe, warm place (like earthworms and caterpillars) so when you empty the bag, remove these to a safer place. Add it to seed mixes with compost, and you can also dig it into any planter box with herbs in it.

7. Green manures: are seeds that are sown either in winter or spring when land lies fallow for a season or two. Sowing these crops fixes nitrogen into the soil and makes it available for the next crop you plant – your herbs. Sow the seeds in the pot the winter before you plant herbs and let the green manure crop grow freely until the spring. Then turn the whole plant upside down in the pot, which will become nutrients for your hungry herbs. Examples of green manures are clover, phacelia, Hungarian ryegrass. If you ask more experienced gardeners or your local seed supplier, they may know others more suitable for your local climate and soil.

8. Crop rotation: Over the centuries, gardeners have noticed that soil cannot support the same crop in the same soil every year. In agricultural terms, this is known as monoculture, and it makes crops more liable to infestation by pests and disease. To counteract this, crop rotation is a system that rotates the crop in the same area every 3-4 years.

Companion planting for herbs

On the next page, we will look at various herbs which grow well (or poorly) with other plants. Some gardeners use herbicides, pesticides, and barrier methods to remove pests and most herbs have aromatic scents, which are helpful. You may be able to avoid a lot of the damage caused by pests merely by planting a good neighbor, so let's walk ourselves through this!

Herb	Possible Companion	Reason
Basil	Asparagus, tomatoes, and parsley	Asparagus root fly and aphids hate the smell of basil.
Celery	Lettuce and salad crops	Short growing season – no competition and they have similar soil is required. Not parsnips, turnips, or carrots
Chives	Carrots, parsley, marjoram, tarragon	They repel aphids and the smell of chives is hated by carrot root flies and other pests
Dill	Coriander	Beneficial insects, and dill is taller and shades it. Attracts insects away from coriander.
Fennel	Broad beans	Ladybugs love fennel flowers and will eat blackfly on broad beans. Not dill or cilantro, cross breeds with dill and crowds out cilantro.
Garlic	Asparagus	The strong smell keeps pests away, so can be helpful near any vegetables.
Lemon Balm	Mint – but keep it in a pot	Similar growing conditions. Both attract beneficial insects.
Marjoram	See chives	Nasturtiums work well with this herb too and attract aphids away from it.
Mint	Shade-loving plants like Lemon Balm	Attracts beneficial insects, but will crowd out most other plants.
Oregano	Other Mediterranean herbs	Similar soil and watering (keep soil dry).
Parsley	See basil	Grows well in rich soil, more foliage if well-watered.
Rosemary	Bay leaf	Deters pests. Great pollinator flowers and strong scent.
Summer savory	Onions	Next to onions, they say it makes onions sweeter. Attracts pollinators.
Winter savory	Lavender or thyme	
Sage	Strawberries and borage, or cabbages and carrots	Its strong smell deters pests from visiting berries, cabbages, and carrots. Also deters growth in some plants, so give it some
Tarragon	Dill and lavender	They attract pollinators. Remember to take indoors in winter.
Thyme	Mediterranean herbs – rosemary	Same soil needs and both attract pollinators

Chapter 6
History and Basic Techniques

This chapter will examine how herbs were used in times gone by, and provide some basic techniques for using herbs. For example, cottage gardens were used to provide herbs to contemporary doctors in the Middle Ages, and herbs have been used worldwide to soothe colds, improve appetite, cure headaches, and reduce fever. In addition, monastery gardens often produced fine wines and spirits for monarchs, and some of these were infused with herbs. Read on for a whistle-stop tour of herbs in history and how you can use that knowledge today to make your own herb oils, in cooking, and to replace various household products.

Herbs in history

When you think of a time without refrigeration or freezing, herbs were used dried, preserved in oil, and as a way to cover up the smell of food that may have passed its sell-by date. Midwives and mothers widely recognized that certain herbs provided relief from pain, fever, and other symptoms. Physicians often had a patch in the cottage garden for herbs believed to have medicinal benefits, even if these cannot be proven today. At a time when no pharmaceutical drugs were available, herbs were used as substitutes for medicine. Digitalis, for example, extracted from foxglove flowers, is still utilized for heart conditions. While this book does not recommend the exclusive use of herbs, chat to your doctor about using them alongside your medicine. For each herb, I have added ways it was used in the past and ways you can use it now. Have fun!

Drying herb leaves for winter use, making herb oil, and making teas from fresh leaves are simple ways to benefit from your homegrown herbs. In the days before freezers, kitchens would dry lots of herbs for use in colder weather when the fresh herb was unavailable; this makes for delightful smells in the area where you hang them to dry. Children love helping with this activity, and if you give them a long piece of string, they can help by tying individual herbs together as they become ready for picking. Alcohol and oil-infused herbs preserved the scent and the goodness well, and you can find several recommendations below for the best herbs to do this. Herb oils have a long history in usage and are referred to in ancient Egyptian texts and medical writings from India, Babylon, the Middle East, and China. Every culture prized certain herbs for specific characteristics, and a trip to your local aromatherapist can enlighten you on their usage today.

Read on for a discussion of each herb below, along with a basic recipe or technique. Make sure you experiment and get creative with these basics, and develop your own herb creations!

Basil

is an essential ingredient of Italian cooking in salads, pizzas, and sauces. Pesto sauce is a firm favorite in many households. Here is a recipe to make your own.

You will need:

- a cup or a good handful of fresh basil leaves
- 2-3 tablespoons of pine nuts
- at least half a cup of olive oil
- 2-3 cloves of garlic
- half a cup of grated Parmesan cheese
- freshly ground black pepper, and
- a pinch of sea salt

Method:

To make a smooth sauce, you need to liquefy the basil leaves in a food processor or blender. Next, remove the skins of the garlic and chop the garlic into smaller pieces. Then mix all the ingredients except the olive oil in a bowl. You can add these ingredients to the bowl of a food processor to arrive at a smooth paste. Next, add small amounts of the olive oil, and continue stirring this in. It will gradually become absorbed, and you can keep adding the oil until you get to whatever consistency you prefer. This will store in the fridge for a week, and then you can make another fresh batch.

Bay leaf

is grown as a shrub or tree, and besides its use in cooking, it can also be added to bottles of herb oil to add its unique flavor over time. Bay leaves must be dried before you use them. So prune several branches of your bay and then hang them in a shady spot for several weeks – 2-4 is ideal. This will infuse the air where you store them, and I thoroughly recommend allowing them to hang for the whole winter and just picking them when you need them!

Remember that botulism is sometimes a problem for herbs that you add to oil, so check all your herb leaves carefully for pests and remove them first. Do not use damaged leaves. Some gardeners recommend using a citric acid wash for herbs before adding them to oil. Once added, you need to seal the bottle, so use screw top lids or a cork but make sure it remains closed. When in use, just sniff the bottle. Anything that smells good is usually an indication that everything is perfect for use.

You will need:

A bottle of olive oil; I recommend virgin olive oil or whatever oil is produced closest to you for a more sustainable version. Check the provenance of your closest suppliers and purchase locally if possible. If you have a decorative empty wine bottle, this is a great way to use it!

Method:

Ensure the bottle is completely clean by sterilizing it or washing it well in a bowl of boiling water, then dry it in an oven at low heat. Next, fill half of the bottle with oil and add one or two bay leaves on a twig stem. You can include other herbs such as a sprig of thyme, some tarragon, and rosemary, which also grow on twigs but make sure there are not too many flavors, or they will compete! Then fill the bottle up to the top and seal it.

Make sure it looks aesthetically pleasing and allow the bottle to sit in a shady place, without direct sunlight for 2-3 weeks, by which time the oil will be infused with flavor.

This makes a fabulous salad dressing oil, and it looks terrific sitting on the dinner table too. How about making a perfect, homemade gift? Make a fresh bottle about a month before the festive season, add a red ribbon bow, and it is ideal for Christmas presents.

CELERY

has water-filled celery stems which are fantastic if added to homemade juices, adding an unexpected zing to the flavor. It is a fresh taste all on its own, and you can combine it with apples for a sweeter taste.

Celery seed can be saved as it arrives and then used as a seasoning like salt) or made into tea. Celery seed tea is said to be useful for the elimination of toxins from the body but just once a day. Check with your medical professional if in doubt. Parsley tea is also recommended for this, but please seek medical advice, and if you are taking medication, check with your physician first.

Chives

are not as good dried as they are fresh, but you can grow spring onions all year round for a similar flavor. I love chive butter when these delicious greens are in season.

You will need:

- 200g of butter
- a handful of chives
- some salt and pepper, and
- a handful of parsley is also recommended.

You can increase quantities if you have more guests.

Method:

Allow the butter to soften slightly at room temperature for half an hour before use. Then, place it in a bowl. Chop your chives finely to release that gorgeous, oniony flavor, and then mix them into the butter. You can simmer in a pan at a low temperature on the stove for a few minutes to help the chive flavor absorb into the butter.

Use melted onto fish dishes and also on baked potatoes. Very fattening but delicious!

Cilantro

is known as coriander in the UK, but in the US and Canada, cilantro is the leaf and coriander is the seed. Cilantro leaf is now a favorite for infusion in gins and is widely available commercially. Cilantro's sweet taste adds an unusual flavor to desserts like rice puddings if you can add it at low heat, allowing the herb to infuse. However, coriander seed is essential for making your own curry mixture so let's get started!

You will need:

- 1 tablespoon each of coriander
- fenugreek and cumin seeds
- a small piece of grated ginger
- a teaspoon of turmeric
- some chili to suit your taste.

You also need a mortar and pestle (or a bowl to crush seeds).

Method:

Using the mortar and pestle, crush the seeds into powder, enjoying the whiff of fresh herbs as you do this. Add the ginger, salt, turmeric and mix all the ingredients together. Be careful adding the chili; not everybody loves spicy, but add a teaspoon to the mixture for moderate heat. If you love hot spicy paste, add as much as you like, and I suggest some cool yogurt dressing to accompany the dish.

Use it immediately, although you can store the mixture for up to four weeks.

Dill

is traditionally used in gripe water, a medicine that has relieved teething problems in young children for hundreds of years. Its effect is to soothe the gums and aid sleep. Dill has a gentle flavor and delicate, feathery leaves. However, I advise that dill be used on its own, as more potent herbs will overwhelm its flavor.

Dill is often used with eggs, and I love dill on pancakes with honey. Fresh or dried, it adds a unique taste sensation, and I don't add sugar because the honey provides enough sweetness. These no-sugar dill and honey pancakes are an example of the versatility of dill when combined with sweet flavors.

You will need:

- one cup of plain flour
- one cup of milk
- 30 grams of butter
- one egg
- some oil to fry the pancakes
- honey, and
- a teaspoon of dill leaves

Method:

Soften the butter for 15-20 minutes before use. While you're waiting, break the egg into a cup, whisk it, and add to a bowl. Mix the softened butter with the egg, and then add the milk and flour. Cream in the dill leaves; they add a feathery texture to the mix, and they infuse your pancake with its scent. Put some oil in a frying pan and allow it to heat up for a minute, then pour a cup of the mixture into the pan and let it cook gently until the edges turn a slightly golden brown. Flip the pancake! This is always fun with young children. At this stage, I like to add the honey into the center so that it heats up, but you can add this later if you prefer. If you want soggy pancakes, remove them quicker than if you like crispy ones; for these, keep cooking until the edges turn brown. Finally, roll the pancake and put it on a plate. If you are the cook, you will find it difficult to resist, so make sure you do a taste test. That dill will not shout at you, but it certainly is noticeable. Enjoy.

FENNEL

has a robust aniseed flavor evident in the leaves and the seeds. Fennel is an ingredient in Absinthe, the famous drink of the Belle Époque in France, consumed by artists such as Picasso, Van Gogh, and Toulouse-Lautrec. In those days, it was the recommended drink for treating epilepsy. However, nowadays it is not recommended for this use!

Fennel survives the winter outside, and its seeds are used to flavor bread and add a licorice flavor for culinary use in savory egg and cheese tarts. If you have fennel in your garden, you can enjoy fresh leaves all winter long. This herb provides fresh greens when few are available, and the seed heads can be collected as you need them.

Garlic

is famous for having medicinal benefits, and many doctors recommend taking garlic capsules. I have friends who eat a clove of fresh garlic daily, but the smell on your breath can be a bit off-putting for work colleagues, so maybe do this on weekends. Traditionally garlic is reputed to reduce cholesterol and blood pressure. You can make garlic-infused oil, and it is wonderful but be careful with how long you keep it as it tends to go rancid quickly once opened. Instead, store it in the refrigerator and discard it after about 4-5 days, especially if it smells bad.

Garlic soup is a French recipe that tourists can enjoy on holiday or which you can recreate in your kitchen. The strong taste is reduced by cooking, and the flavor is unbeatable on a cold winter's evening.

You will need:

- 5 bulbs of garlic (which you will separate into individual cloves)
- a liter of water (or slightly more if you have a lot of guests)
- 2-3 slices of bread made into bread crumbs
- a sprig of thyme, and
- some grated cheese and black pepper as a topping

Method:

Add the cloves and a bay leaf to a liter of water – no need to take off the skins; they will slip off after 30 mins in boiling water. Then remove the pot from the boil, take off the skins and discard them. Mash the garlic at this stage, or use a food processor if you like. Next, add herbs like thyme and other Mediterranean herbs. Tarragon is terrific in this if you have some fresh leaves to pick. Finally, add salt and pepper and bread crumbs and allow the soup to simmer on warm heat. (You can pour your friends a herb cocktail in this interval). Before serving remove the bay leaf, add parsley and grated cheddar as a topping, and there you go. Garlic soup! I like to serve it with homemade garlic bread if you have the time and patience.

Lavender

is used all over the work as an aid for relaxing. Added to soaps, bath oils, and many herbal bubble baths, this herb is famous for helping you sleep. A sprig of lavender in a clothing drawer allows the scent to permeate the fabric over time. It is a beautiful addition to a funeral bouquet, as the smell spreads through the ceremony, soothing all present. Here is an easy way to make lavender oil.

You will need:

A recycled clean glass container, 12 sprigs of freshly cut lavender, some base oil – olive is fine for this, but you can shop in your local health food store. Almond oil is also extraordinarily sweet-smelling, and the lavender will add an extra scent.

Method:

Sterilize the glass container by washing in the dishwasher or placing it in a bowl of hot water and drying it off in the oven for a few minutes. Then half fill the jar with your chosen oil. Cut the flowers from the stems and add them to the oil, then top up the jar with oil to the top. Allow to sit in a shady place for 4-5 days, then remove the flowers and add new ones. You will need to change the flowers at least three times for the scent to remain. Then close up your jar and store it in a dark cupboard or your bathroom. Add 8-12 drops at bath time for a relaxing soak after a hard day's work or energetic sports.

Lemon Balm

Tea made from its leaves is said to settle a sick stomach, especially nerves before an exam, a driving test, or whatever makes you nervous! Collect fresh leaves if available; if not, use dried leaves you saved during the summer. Lemon Balm tea used to be a remedy for feverish colds in the UK, and its lemon scent adds a delicious reminder of summer in a basket full of dried herbs in a bathroom or hallway.

For many ideas here, you need to dry some herb leaves. To do this, dry leaves, pick several stems with a lot of foliage and use the stem to hang them to dry in a shady area until you need them.

You can tie the stems with string and then hang them upside down to dry. Above a fridge is a good location, as the area is usually cozy. The herb leaves begin to turn a brown color which tells you the goodness within them is being retained. When you need some leaves, just pick them from a stem. The scent will fill the whole area but be careful not to place bay and lavender too close to more delicate tastes. These powerful scents will dominate some subtler flavors like French Tarragon.

Marjoram

is famed for its fantastic taste in French and Italian cooking, this herb has also been used for years to soothe aching joints and conditions related to inflammation. Like lavender, marjoram oil can be soothing on painful joints. Make oil in the same way as lavender oil, and then use a few drops in bathwater or on a compress to help soothe aching joints and muscles after a long day in your garden. Marjoram and oregano can be used interchangeably in recipes – if no fresh leaves are available, make sure you dry some in summer so that you can add them to winter dishes.

Mint

can be used in tea to ease morning sickness in some women and is even better if combined with ginger. In fact, for nausea of any type, if you smell a drop of mint or ginger oil onto a tissue, it usually helps. In addition, mint is a traditional aid to ease flatulence in some cultures. Perhaps this is why the fresh leaves are often offered after a meal has finished, accompanied by fennel seeds, and with chocolates, mint provides after-dinner relief. Of course, another reason may be the fresh taste its leaves bring in the mouth, as most of us are used to the taste of mint in toothpaste.

Peppermint tea is recognized as a drink to cool people down in hot weather, and many discover drinking too much causes them to feel cold, so don't drink too many cups even if it is very hot! Mint tea can be made in advance and left in a jug in the fridge for when you need a cooling drink on a hot day. Finally, mint is a common herb that you find in every cocktail bar, and its green leaves often adorn the edge of a glass. Crème de menthe is a popular alcoholic French drink that is now drunk worldwide.

To make peppermint tea at home, make sure you dry some of the leaves before the plant dies off for the winter. See how to do this in Lemon Balm above. You can pick as many as possible, then hang them to dry in a shady corner. Then add a few fresh or dried leaves to some boiling water whenever you need a refreshing drink and sit down for a few moments of peace.

Oregano

like marjoram, is useful for adding flavor to soups and winter stews. You can dry the leaves when it is growing well in summer for use in winter. Oregano is excellent added to stuffing mixtures for festive occasions and is often combined with thyme or sage.

Parsley

can be used like celery seed, and the fresh leaves of parsley tea reputedly help remove toxins from the system. Chop a teaspoon of fresh parsley and cover with boiling water to make a pleasant tea. However, dried parsley never gives me the same satisfaction as the fresh herb, so I recommend a late sowing of parsley in August so that you can pick the fresh herb indoors for winter use.

Rosemary

for remembrance, the old saying goes. Although delicious in taste, rosemary oil is not recommended for anybody in the first months of pregnancy or for people with high blood pressure. This is because some herb oils affect the uterine muscles, and rosemary is one of these. However, its scent offers users an uplifting aroma, as any gardener knows as they pass by the herb in the outdoors.

The smell can outdo other herbs in cooking, so use it sparingly. However, it is delicious if added to a sprig of herbs such as thyme and sage and used to make vegetable stock for soups and stews.

Rosemary alcohol tincture is often recommended as an aid to improve circulation. Chat to your doctor first and if they agree, rub it into affected areas such as legs that are tired or have varicose veins. Traditionally, rosemary is an antiseptic oil, and its strong flavor can be recognized in the world-famous Benedectine liqueur.

Sage

is a strong-smelling herb, best grown apart from many plants, although it grows well with strawberries and even borage. The medical profession has been testing the quality of sage oil for many digestive conditions, and the common belief is that sage oil helps reduce excessive perspiration. The leaves are high in vitamins A and C and also contain a high amount of vitamin K.

Its extremely strong flavor is used in conjunction with other Mediterranean herbs like oregano, garlic, dill, parsley, marjoram, and thyme to make a herb-based stock. Stock adds body to many cooked soups and stews, and you can make it when the herbs are ready, then freeze it for use later on in the year. If you have old yogurt or cream pots, these are fabulous to store stock. Make sure you label it!

You will need:

A handful of herb leaves, including 3-4 sage leaves, a sprig of thyme, a bay leaf, a sprig of rosemary, and then any others you have available – marjoram, parsley, etc. An onion, chopped, three cloves of garlic, some water to boil the herbs, and salt and pepper to taste.

Method:

Chop the garlic and onion and fry this in a bit of vegetable oil to start. Fine chop all the herbs as this will release the flavor. Add these to the garlic and onion mixture and add a liter of water (top up as required). For non-vegetarians, if you have any leftover chicken bones, these can be added to make a rich taste to this stock but make sure you do not add this to dishes if you have vegetarian or vegan guests. Allow the mixture to bubble away. If you use bones, allow to cook for at least 30 mins, but for herb stock, about 20-30 minutes if perfect. Then let the mixture cool, pour into pots, and freeze until you need it. Add this to any stew or soup where the flavor of herbs adds depth to your cooking.

Winter Savory

offers leaves to the cook when there are very few growing, so this one is so worth including in the garden. Also, perhaps because it was so important historically, the leaves and stems were used to make teas and tonics, which were believed to help indigestion and nausea. Nowadays, some herbalists recommend its use as a natural remedy for winter coughs and colds that are hard to shift but take the advice of a professional or your chemist on this.

Summer Savory

adds a unique flavor to summer salads. Still, it also has a history of usage as an anti-inflammatory and antimicrobial herb derived from oil-soaked in the leaves. You can make your own oil in the same way suggested for lavender above and try this in the same way – to apply to sore muscles. Some herbalists recommend this for internal use, so please discuss this with your doctor. The Romans reputedly believed that this herb was an aphrodisiac. However, I can only sing the praises for the fantastic, fresh taste the leaves offer to many dishes and leave you to decide if the claims have any truth in them!

Tarragon

is an ingredient in many French dishes, but here I must recommend the qualities of the fresh herb. One hint from midwives was that eating tarragon used to bring on menstruation, and it is also said to aid digestion.

This is one of my absolute favorites and is not very well-known due to its inability to grow from seed. However, it is so worth getting a plant, and from here on in, you can propagate it, look after it, and spread this herb joy among friends and family.

No other herb tastes like tarragon. Just a tiny amount of it in soups, egg dishes, and cooked tarts make it an essential herb in my garden.

In France, it makes Bearnaise sauce and tarragon vinegar. For me, this is the perfect topping for scrambled eggs, as it releases its fresh, slightly licorice flavor through every mouthful. Here is how to make the perfect tarragon scrambled eggs.

You will need:

- a small teaspoon of butter
- 2 eggs beaten in a cup of milk
- some fresh tarragon leaves (dried leaves will have to do if no fresh ones are available), and
- black pepper to taste

Method:

Heat and melt a tiny amount of butter in a pan, and then add the eggs and milk mixture, stirring continuously. Chop the tarragon into small pieces and add this to the mixture.

The eggs will thicken naturally; add more milk if it is too thick. Serve immediately on hot toast with black pepper.

Thyme

thrives in low fertility soil, almost a herb of neglect. You can pick thyme all winter long, so there is no need to dry leaves. The cheerful pink flowers are a magnet for bees, and I use this herb in dishes that need slow cooking because its taste infuses the dish that way.

There are many studies involving the compounds contained in thyme-infused oil. Thymol, linalool, and camphor are some of the elements. In European monasteries, it was believed that thyme was an anti-bacterial oil that could effectively preserve food, and treat stomach pains from eating spoiled food. Nowadays, there are also studies investigating thyme oil to promote healthy hair growth.

Whatever the case for the medical benefits of this gorgeous herb, I think it adds a unique, exceptional taste to squash soup.

You will need:

- 1 squash, cut into pieces with skin intact and seeds removed
- 2 cloves of garlic, chopped
- an onion
- some vegetable stock
- several sprigs of thyme and a bay leaf
- salt and pepper to taste, and
- natural yogurt to serve on top with a garnish of either parsley or whatever fresh herb is available.

Method:

Partially cook the squash in the oven for about 25 minutes until it is soft. While it is cooking, start frying the garlic and onion in a pan. Remove the cooked squash from the oven and add them to the pan with a liter of water, a bay leaf, and the sprigs of thyme. A pinch of salt and pepper added here will add to the flavor. Then allow the soup to cook slowly on low heat. When the squash is cooked through (after 20-30 minutes), add the vegetable stock and simmer on low heat for another 5 minutes. Then serve in bowls, with natural yogurt and cheese with a fresh herb topping like parsley.

On a final note, there are many examples of herbs used in alcoholic drinks, such as the famous Chartreuse green liqueur and, more recently, herbs infused in gin, adding a rich dimension to the taste. In medicine, many studies are trying to prove the abilities that humanity has attributed to various herbs. Hopefully, this chapter has inspired you to learn more about what herbs contain and how they can be used in your daily life. In the next chapter, we will examine what could go wrong when growing herbs and how to fix these problems.

Chapter 7
What Could Go Wrong? (and how to fix it)

IN THIS CHAPTER, WE EXAMINE SOME OF THE TYPICAL PROBLEMS that occur with herb plants and suggest ways to fix them.

1. **Roots:** root rot, eelworm, vine weevil.
2. **Leaves:** yellowing leaves, brown spots, leaf curl, wilting leaves, leaf rust, and leaf mold (botrytis).
3. **Stem:** Brown stem, stem rot, damping-off fungi, scale insects, mealybugs.
4. **Growth:** slow growth, excessive leaf foliage.
5. **Flowers:** lack of flowers, feeding flowers, flowers go to seed.
6. **Pests:** aphids, caterpillars, earwigs, greenfly, slugs, snails, whitefly, red spider mite, scale insects.

Some problems with herbs may be due to a lack of nutrients in the soil. Composting, mulching, leaf mold, and crop rotation can help with any nutrient-related issues; see more below.

1. Problems with roots

Root rot refers to healthy roots becoming pot-bound or water-logged, leading to brown, diseased roots. Healthy roots should be white or cream colored. *Oregano* and *thyme* are both prone to root rot if conditions are damp and drainage is poor.

If roots start to lose their natural shape growing straight downwards, as they would in the ground, it is called being **pot-bound**. Often pot-bound roots make a plant unstable, and it keeps falling over. Being pot-bound means the roots start to curl around the end of the pot. This does not make for good drainage, so it is best to re-pot this herb.

To examine the roots of the herb in a pot, soak the pot in a bucket of water for at least 15 minutes to loosen up the roots and then turn the pot upside down. Place your hand around the stem so that it falls gently into your palm, and then lay the plant out on a cloth or recycled paper to take a look. Root rot is often preceded by the roots becoming bound by the edges of a pot that is too small. Support the plant in your hand while you tease out the roots and try to aim them vertically downwards. This will help the roots grow naturally as soon as they are planted.

Now is the time to remove any brown or black roots using cleaned cutting shears or a pruner. Clean the blade before each cut to avoid spreading diseases.

How do I know if my herb is pot-bound?

- You can see tiny roots at the end of the pot when you look at it.
- The whole plant guzzles water – and dries out again really quickly.
- The whole plant looks unhealthy, there is not a lot of

new growth at the tips, and overall, leaf growth is extremely slow.

How do I fix it?

Pot-bound roots are curled in the shape of the pot, so you need to tease these out carefully. Soaking the plant in water for an hour will aid this process. Try to ease roots into a vertical direction, and shape them into how you imagine the roots of a tree grow underground – expanding sideways and downwards. If you find any brown or black roots, your herb has root rot.

How do I fix root rot?

To treat root rot, use a sterile cutting knife or pruning shears and cut all the diseased roots off. Wipe down the blade before each cut so that you do not spread disease. If the remaining roots look a healthy white or cream color, allow them to dry for a few hours and then re-pot them into a bigger pot with fresh compost. Do not overwater this plant again, and keep an eye for new leaves to ensure it makes a full recovery.

If your herb is in soil, dig around the roots gently with a stick or trowel and examine the roots. If you see black or brown, you need to dig out the herb immediately. Feel the soil around the roots. Is it very moist? You know what the problem is here! Over-watering. Remember, many herbs survive well on rainfall alone, so stop watering for several days, and then check the soil for dryness before you water again.

Root rot is a serious condition, and your herb plant will not survive if you continue as usual. Check again how often your herb needs to be watered, and then favor not watering if you are in doubt. French Tarragon is prone to root rot in very heavy soils, so make sure the soil you provide has some sand, gravel, and humus to avoid it.

Other problems with roots are usually caused by eelworm or vine weevils. See pests below for how to treat these.

2. Problems with leaves

- **Yellowing leaves** are often a sign that your herb has been getting too much water. Has somebody been looking after your herb while you went on holiday? Excessive overwatering can result in yellow leaves. Another culprit could be aphids eating the leaves. See more on pests below. If the herb is also showing roots at the end of the pot, it usually means the whole herb needs to be repotted and given more nutrition via the soil. Yellow leaves on herbs planted in the ground can also indicate that the herb is coming to the end of its natural life if it is an annual plant. Basil leaves often start to look paler from late August onwards.

How do I fix it?

Hard water can be the culprit too, so if your tap water is hard, run it through a filter or use saved rainwater.

Yellow coloring between the veins can indicate a shortage of trace elements like nitrogen in your soil. See more on this in Number 7 below.

Brown spots on leaves are often the result of under-watering, and pests cause leaves to look mottled and unhealthy. Another possible is too much sun, but this is unlikely for most herbs that crave a lot of sunshine. *Mint* and *Lemon balm* leaves may turn brown in too much sunshine, but the problem is likely one of the above.

If under-watering is the problem, water the plant well and see if it recovers. If so, continue to water more regularly and pick leaves too. Pick the brown leaves off, and regular picking will encourage healthy growth. Pests may be aphids and greenflies – see how to deal with these below.

Consult the guide to the best conditions again. For example, if the herb likes shade, make sure it is in the shade at the hottest part of the day.

- **Leaf curl** tends to happen when there is a sudden drop in temperature or a lack of manganese in the soil.

How do I fix it?

If your plant is indoors, is it in a draft? Has the weather changed recently? If the herb is outdoors, check the location. For example, maybe you moved the herb to a larger pot, which exposed the herb to drafts or blocked the sunlight it was used to. Move the herb to a more sheltered location out of drafts and then leave it for a few weeks to recover. If the fall is approaching, maybe it is time for the plant to move indoors.

If it lacks manganese, then try feeding using a fertilizer mix in your watering can. If it helps and the plant improves, feed the herb monthly.

- **Wilting leaves** can show that your plant is not being watered enough; this is easy to spot with parsley, basil, and cilantro when the whole plant seems to collapse.

How do I fix it?

First, water the plants generously and see if it recovers. After this, water more regularly!

- **Leaf rust** is exceptionally unusual on herbs. It presents as small round patches of brown rings on the underside of the herb's leaves. It usually indicates not enough sunshine combined with excessive watering.

How do I fix it?

If you can, move the herb to a sunnier spot, remove the affected leaves and limit your zeal for watering this herb.

- **Leaf mold**, or **botyritis**, commonly affects cucumber plants, so if your herbs are in close proximity, there may be a danger of them coming into contact with affected leaves. This is a gray, soft, fluffy mold that attacks large cucumber leaves but spreads easily to other parts and plants nearby. Basil is very susceptible to this.

How do I fix it?

The affected leaves should be removed immediately with gloves and destroyed. Do not add these to compost bins! Try to improve the airflow to get rid of leaf mold; it spreads in damp conditions too, so avoid overwatering plants for a spell.

- **Holes in leaves** can be a result of flea beetles, earwigs, and caterpillars, so see the section on pests below.

3. Stem problems

- A **brown color** that appears on a normally green stem is sometimes caused by overwatering the plant and leaving moisture on its leaves. It sometimes occurs in the middle of the stem, and the gardener feels as if the plant is dying. The cause may be too much watering and where you water.

How do I fix it?

Try to aim for the soil around the stem when you water and not the leaves or the actual stem. Leaving drops of water on the leaves or stems higher up is not ideal for most herbs, which usually prefer some sunshine and drier conditions.

- Sometimes a **brown stem** can indicate a lack of calcium, often spotted on the tomato plants growing beside basil, cilantro, parsley, and chives.

How do I fix it?

In this case, you can save eggshells and crush them once they have dried. Place them at the base of the stem of the affected plants. The eggshells will slowly release calcium (via the keratin in eggshells), which will help the tomatoes recover gradually. Some gardeners also use crushed eggshells, with spiky edges to persuade slugs and snail visitors not to nibble the surrounding plants.

- **Damage from pests** is another possibility. Pests like leather jackets like stems and roots. They are gray creatures, about an inch long, and they thrive in light soils and very moist soil.

How do I fix it?

Keep the soil dry for a while and remove them if you see them. They are an unusual and challenging pest because you rarely see them, as they live underground.

4. Problems with growth

- Why is my **herb growing so slowly**?

First, check the predicted height of your herb. Some herbs do not grow very tall, and summer savory and tarragon are often weeded out by inexperienced gardeners because they "look like a weed". The following reason may be insufficient sunshine or a lack of trace elements in the soil. It may be that another plant is shading your herb for a lot of the active, sunny hours in the day? Next, check the season. If it is September or October, it is possible that the herb has reached the end of its life cycle or that it is going into a dormant phase for the winter. If it is still mid-summer, there may be a pest lurking.

How do I fix it?

Usually, I recommend turning the pot upside down, holding it carefully in your hand, and checking the roots. If the roots are pot-bound, you need to tease the roots out gently by soaking them in water. Then, replace the pot with a bigger one and give it fresh soil. This should provide your herb with excellent conditions to start growing bigger.

Try moving the herb into more direct sunshine (not shade-loving herbs, though, like mint or Lemon balm). If the plant recovers, leave it in the new location. See more about soil and nutrients in Number 7 below.

A final solution could be a massive aphid infestation. First, check for a sticky residue on the leaves or brown patches on the undersides. If this is the case, then wipe the leaves with some dish soap in water applied with a soft cloth.

- What herbs **survive the winter**?

To survive, some herbs need to be taken indoors as soon as the temperature plunges. Tarragon and lovage are two of these.

Some herbs are annuals and only last one growing season, such as basil, coriander, and parsley.

Frost hardy herbs.

However, some herbs are fine outdoors even in winter, and you can continue picking leaves throughout the winter season. These include Bay leaf, sage, mint, rosemary, and thyme, which will all be fine outdoors.

5. Problems with flowers

Flowers are a part of the herb's life cycle. Starting with a seed that germinates in soil, the plant produces green foliage with aromatic tastes and smells, and then it flowers to be pollinated, and then it goes to seed. Some herbs have flowers that pollinators adore, such as sage, rosemary, thyme, and lavender. Bees will flock to your garden, as will butterflies, to enjoy their nectar. Flowers are a sign that the herb has finished its growing cycle and has decided to finish its life cycle.

- **Going to seed**: Basil and cilantro are notorious for this! Both have attractive flowers, but to extend the plant's life cycle for foliage, remove the flowers and add them to salads or as a garnish on soups. Chives usually go to seed at the end of a season. They offer a dash of circular purple flowers to any flower bed they are in, and usually, they will return the following year. Just enjoy the color!

How do I fix it?

Often, the reason is the herb's natural life-cycle but is increased by a lack of water or a lack of nutrients in the soil. If you want to keep picking leaves from your herbs, then cut the flowers and re-pot the herb. Give it a thorough watering, and this gives the herb a new lease of life.

To prevent this, cut the seed heads as they develop or cut the flowers for display inside because the scent of the foliage will add a delicious fragrance to your flower arrangements.

If you want to collect the seed, coriander is collected from cilantro herbs for culinary use, so do not remove the flowers and allow the herb to seed. Collect them in a paper envelope to dry them out well, then store them in the kitchen in a spice jar.

French tarragon rarely flowers, so do not be disappointed. Its Russian cousin does flower profusely, and if you let it go to seed, it will happily spread through a shady area of your garden and even become invasive.

- If **no flowers** develop at all, you may have an aphid problem. These devour the tips of herbs, including aromatic flower buds and flowers.

How do I fix this?

Dish soap and water is an easy method - see how to remove them below. Some gardeners use neem oil and water, and others recommend citrus oil.

6. What pests target herbs?

- **Aphids** love a variety of plants and can be spotted by the sticky residue they deposit on plant leaves. Herbs they target include almost all of them apart from herbs with a strong scent like chives, garlic tarragon, and lavender. Also known as greenflies, these pests attack growing tips, and flowers are their favorite. Every experienced gardener has a tale about greenfly, or blackfly, or even orange fly raiding the leaves and flowers of their favorite rose, geranium, and any flowering tip they find.

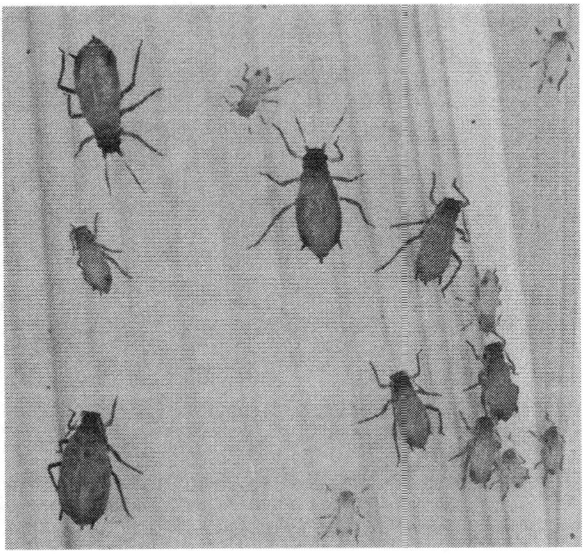

How do I fix it?

The pest depletes the strength of the whole plant, so physically remove them using a tablespoon of dish soap added to a watering can full of water, then apply to the affected area with a soft sponge or cloth.

- **Scale insects** love the long, thin leaves of tarragon, but they also enjoy Bay leaf and many other indoor house plants, so check the undersides of leaves for brown shades that are difficult to remove. Be careful when bringing herbs back in for winter. Check for scale insects before they come in, or they will spread like wildfire among your favorite house plants.

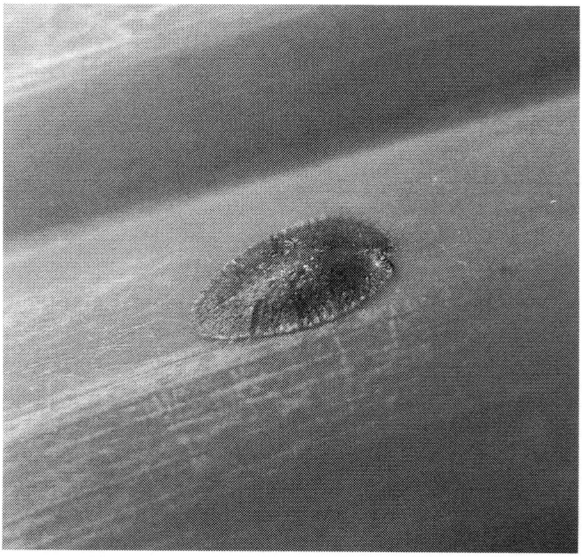

How do I fix it?

These insects stick to the back of the leaves, and they have to be removed one by one in a long, painful process. If you miss even one, you will be back to this again in 6 months! On tarragon, they are not difficult to locate. Often I just cut the leaf off and dispose of the whole leaf and any insects.

- **Red spider mite** prefers dry, warm conditions, and herbs in a greenhouse often fit this bill, so remove the bugs with a mixture of 1 tablespoon of dish soap in a liter of water. Add this to a spray bottle and aim it directly at the red spots on the leaves.

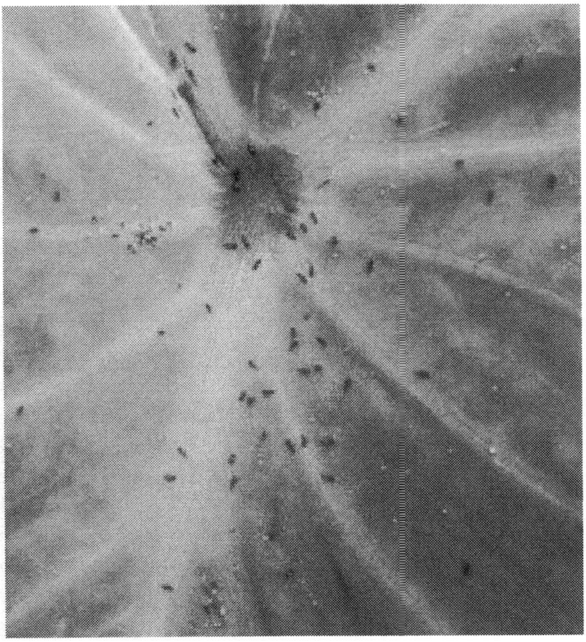

How do I fix it?

Spray the pests, then wipe the leaves down with a damp sponge or cloth. This bug hates to be damp, so it should leave. To keep it away long-term, water the herb more frequently for a while and spray the leaves if affected. Then wipe them down with a cloth. Aerate the whole area, too, because red spider mites like dry, warm conditions, and if you keep it damp and drafty, they can be encouraged to abandon the plant.

- **Leafhoppers** and **leaf-miners**. If you see trails, or tunnels, on basil leaves, you may have leafhoppers nearby. These pests also enjoy munching oregano and parsley, and these herbs often grow close to each other.

How do I fix it?

Plant lots of extra herbs. These bugs are challenging to eliminate, but if you have extra herbs, they can munch on some, and you still have lots of foliage to pick.

- **Slugs** and **snails** eat any tiny seedlings, and they prefer fresh green leaves from new growth.

How do I fix it?

These two pests are the scourge of gardeners, and there are millions of ideas from beer traps to eggshells, but some possible ideas include

1. Cut bramble pieces and surround your herb plants with these. Physical spikes often send these slimy pests searching for more accessible food supplies. The sharp edges of eggshell pieces can also deter them.
2. Use leaves as decoy bait! Comfrey or nasturtium leaves are a favorite of these slugs, but if they are super hungry, you may still find them on the herbs in the morning.
3. Physically remove them. Get handy with a flashlight late at night and go slime detective hunting. If you find

some, relocate them to your compost bin where they can decompose plants that need it.

A final note: If you develop a fool-proof method to keep slugs and snails away, you are destined to become a millionaire and to be loved by every gardener in the world.

- **Eelworm** and **vine weevils** attack the roots of plants. In addition, many herb leaves exude an aromatic fragrance that keeps airborne pests at bay, but the roots of any plant are vulnerable to these two.

How do I fix it?

This is extremely difficult as you need to access the roots. If the herb is in a pot, upend it carefully to sneak a look at the roots. Are there bulbous swellings in the roots? This is definitely eelworm. There is no saving this herb, and the important thing is to dispose of the plant safely.

Vine weevils devour the whole root system, causing the herb to collapse, which is also impossible to save. The best idea is to buy sterilized compost in the future. A cold spell will kill these pests, but if your herbs are in the soil, it may be worth transferring them to pots for one season, using fresh compost, and then covering the infected area.

If you also grow vines, plant your herbs some distance away from them to avoid this problem.

- **Caterpillars**, **earwigs**, and **flea beetles** eat small or large holes in leaves. Butterfly lovers may be delighted to see wildlife in their garden.

How do I fix it?

You can don some gloves and move caterpillars to other plants if you prefer to allow them to continue their life cycle. I recommend this, by the way. Most butterfly and moth species are in trouble, and allowing a few of them to munch on your plants will also bring some spectacular pollinators to admire on your flowers later on.

Earwigs are challenging to catch, but if you and a partner work together, they can be teased into collecting jars and placed back in compost bins.

Flea beetles do not like soap and water mixtures sprayed on the leaves, and they can also be lured onto sticky traps. So if you use this method, remember to wash edible herbs before use.

7. Lack of nutrients. Improve the soil for your herbs.

In Chapter 5 we looked at different ways to improve the soil, so please refer back to that for information about composting, mulching, and using leaf mold. Companion planting for herbs discussed in Chapter 4 will be helpful to decide which herbs to plant together. Finally, this section will examine the benefits of crop rotation in a growing plan for a garden over a four-year period and how this can boost your soil and ultimately help your herbs thrive.

First, let's see which nutrients are needed in the soil where your herbs will grow. If you have ever bought a bag of plant fertilizer, you will see these letters in brackets in the ingredients on the packaging, sometimes labeled as NPK feeds. See what these letters mean below!

- Nitrogen (N) is the leaf maker of your herb. It is used for plants to photosynthesize, that is, to make food from sunshine using their leaves. If there isn't enough nitrogen available, the leaves may be yellow and the overall growth of your herb may be less than you would like.
- Phosphorus (P) is what gives the roots their healthy glow.
- Potassium (K) is needed for flowers and helps the herb utilize nitrogen. This is the element that keeps the stem healthy, which then strengthens the whole plant. Leaves are often mottled with strange patterns if potassium is missing from the soil.
- Calcium (Ca). Without this nutrient in the soil, the whole plant can die because it adjusts the acidity, enabling nutrient absorption.
- Magnesium (Mg) is one nutrient that helps the initial

germination of the seed and helps the herb produce chlorophyll. Without this, leaves can fall off the plant.

There are other parts of fertile soil called trace elements or minerals. These are often called minor elements because the main growth elements are the ones above. However, without these in the soil, your herbs will not thrive.

- Iron (Fe) is used to make chlorophyll, the food a plant uses to grow. Without it, leaves are pale or yellow. Think of a human who needs an iron tonic, and you get the idea!
- Manganese (Mn) is essential to avoid curling leaves, which are often pale in color. Fe and Mn are used to form chlorophyll.
- Boron (B) (or the lack of it) is the culprit when you notice brown centers in a vegetable and also causes patches on leaves and fruit. If there is a supply of boron in the soil, other nutrients are absorbed efficiently.
- Molybdenum (Mo) is present in the soil that has added lime, and it ensures that nitrogen is available for the herb to use. The growing tips will look malformed without this trace element, so it is an essential part of your soil.
- Copper (Cu) is essential, especially for the young plant, and it gives a boost to the whole herb when it is present. Leaves may wilt without it.
- Zinc (Zn) is a big helper in plant nutrition. Chlorophyll, several proteins, and carbohydrates are not formed well without zinc. Many commercial fertilizers contain high levels of phosphorous, which then makes it more difficult for the herb to use zinc. So try to add compost to the soil, which aids zinc availability.

What is crop rotation?

Crop rotation is a method devised by farmers who noticed that growing the same plant in the same ground year after year resulted in poorer yields, depletion of the soil, and often allowed diseases and pests to take hold in the soil. The basic idea is that some plants take a lot of energy from the soil and deplete certain nutrients. Instead of continuing to add manure or compost to replace those, the next set of plants can add those things to the soil instead. For example, beans and peas can add nitrogen back into the soil, which the cabbage family loves. So if you plant cabbages after a season of peas, the cabbage will benefit from the peas planted before it.

Even if you plan to grow herbs in pots, use this same idea for not growing the same herb in the same pot if it is an annual. Change the crop so that the soil gets a different herb, and you can keep topping up the fertility of your pots by adding mulches, compost, leaf mold, and wood ash.

This is a 4-year plan. For example, if you plant potatoes in year 1, they will not be planted again in the same ground until year 5. The herbs you choose can work with many of the crops listed below, but this is a guide to vegetable and fruit growing which will help you decide which herbs can be planted alongside your vegetables. Please refer back to companion planting for each individual herb in Chapter 4.

Crop Rotation and where to fit your herbs

Year 1

Fertilizer

Manure in spring. Compost mixed into manure will improve soil texture too. Plant feeds are required in summer.

Plants

Potatoes and 'hungry' plants like eggplant, radishes, tomatoes, squashes, pumpkins, zucchini, and cucumber

Herbs

Basil, parsley, chives, cilantro, and oregano. Bay leaf is an option, but it may be too big to be a permanent companion.

Notes

Potatoes "clear" the ground. The others are very hungry, annual plants. Feed them weekly when flowering and fruiting in summer.

Watering

All the vegetable plants need a lot of regular watering. Include special feeds such as nettle, comfrey, dandelion leaves to help them grow better. Use herbs that enjoy these conditions.

Year 2

Fertilizer

Manure in spring. Add general compost too. Fertilize with plant feeds every 2-3 weeks.

Plants

Legumes, or a mix of peas, beans, and onions.

Herbs

Garlic, chives, and summer savory. If you plant broad beans, consider adding fennel to attract blackflies.

Notes

Nitrogen fixers that will feed the Brassicas which follow. These can all be planted separately.

Watering

All need regular watering. Can be enriched with comfrey or nettle leaves and feed.

Year 3

Fertilizer

Lime is needed (or slightly acid soil) for Brassicas to grow well. Do not manure. Apply general compost—mulch with leaf mold.

Plants

Brassicas – Cabbage family (Brussels sprouts, cauliflower, broccoli, cabbage)

Herbs

Nasturtiums. Aphids will go directly to the leaves and flowers, not your vegetables: chives, savory, cilantro, and oregano. Marigolds and mint reputedly deter cabbage root fly.

Notes

Do not manure - plant with leaf mold and comfrey leaves in the bed, which decompose during the season. They love nitrogen from peas and beans.

Watering

Make sure the soil is firm around young plants. Then, they can be moved from a nursery bed to a permanent bed in autumn.

Year 4

Fertilizer

Do not manure. Spread general compost. Remove stones.

Plants

Roots (carrots, bets, turnips, parsnips).

Herbs

Chives (to distract pests), parsley, marjoram.

Notes

Do not manure - it will cause the roots to split. Remove large stones, or roots will grow around them!

Watering

Water well to improve germination. May need protective netting.

Perennial Crops

Fertilizer

All benefit from manure. Fruit and asparagus love ash (from fires) as fertilizer – spread in winter to boost growth

Plants

Strawberries, raspberries, fruit bushes, asparagus.

Herbs

Sage, basil, mint, lemon balm.

Notes

Move the fruit every 3-4 years or when fruiting stops. Asparagus can stay in the same place for up to 25 years.

Watering

Water these plants only in spring and summer.

General guidelines for healthy herbs.

- Try to give herbs the optimum conditions – direct sunlight or semi-shade as appropriate, suitable soil and not crowd them altogether. Allow some air to circulate between them for best results.
- Try to pick them regularly. Otherwise, several herbs tend to "bolt", which means if it is basil or cilantro, they flower then go to seed about a month after germination. If you pick them often, you will notice any pests, brown leaves, or drooping branches, and you can take action. Prune any branches that look too heavy or spoil the overall shape.
- Weed between them and remove dead leaves to help stop the pests from arriving. Slugs and snails often move in to munch on decaying leaves, and other pests will do the same. Weed out any unintended plants and pick your herbs.
- Know how much water they need, and then make sure the ones that need water get watered regularly. This stops them from going to seed early. Feel the soil before you water. Without disturbing the roots, dig with your finger and see if the soil an inch down seems dry too. If so, water! Herbs like this include basil, chives, cilantro, and garlic.
- If you know a herb does not need much water, then place it further away from the tap, and you are less likely to have a full watering can when you get there. Herbs like this include mint, lemon balm, lavender, sage, rosemary, and thyme. These usually survive on sparse rainfall in Mediterranean climates and go for a long time without water. So you really only need to water these if they are visibly wilting in a heatwave.

- Include sweet scents like lavender, lemon balm, rosemary, and thyme. You will enjoy walking past these herbs, and the bees and butterflies will visit your garden a lot more.
- Finally, decoy flowers and leaves like nasturtiums and comfrey are a natural way to keep pests off your precious plants. Both of these have flowers that bees love too, so they are a colorful addition to a herb garden.

Chapter 8
Cooking with Herbs

WHILE COOKING IS MORE ART THAN SCIENCE, YOU CAN STILL follow some basic rules and techniques. Start with the basics here, and as you learn how these flavors work and interact with each other, you can branch out and get more creative.

First, identify the type of cuisine you are cooking. If you aren't sure what region or style your recipe is from, don't worry; just compare the flavors in the recipe for the main dish against the flavor summary table further on in this chapter. If you still aren't sure what to do, check the individual herb cheat sheets and pick something with a flavor type you think would complement the dish. There are no wrong answers, only experiments!

Once you know the general flavor profile, you can pick a few herbs to add. If you are a beginner, I would recommend adding only one herb (or two at most), so you can get a feel for how they influence the taste. After all, if you add all of your herbs to everything, it will all start to taste the same.

Finally, check the Cheat Sheets for each herb to see what types of dishes they usually work best in (soup, poultry, seafood, etc.), how to add them (dry or fresh, before or after cooking), and the type of flavor they will add (floral, spicy, citrus, etc.). There can be a substantial difference in flavor (and amounts used in recipes) between fresh and dry herbs. While most herbs can be used fresh, I have highlighted the herbs that can just as easily be used dry when cooked. A general rule of thumb is that herbs with more woody stems and stiffer leaves work better dried compared to softer, more delicate herbs, which tend to lose all of their flavors when dried out or overcooked.

Nothing in this section will be correct all of the time, and cooking is full of exceptions, but these can be seen as general rules of thumb to follow as you're learning.

One rule that doesn't have an exception is always to remember and remove herb stems or inedible leaves (like bay leaves or raw sage) before serving. These can be very unpleasant to bite into.

What flavor profile are you working with?

Depending on what type of herb garden you planted, you might have most or all of the flavors needed to create cuisines from around the world. Generally, the flavors of herbs in these categories go well with each other.

However, you will almost certainly have to supplement with spices and other additions. Here is a quick summary of the flavors you would need to re-create some popular cooking styles.

Herbs	**Italian**	**French**	**Spanish**	**Mediter-ranean**	**Mexican**	**Indian/ Asian**	**African**
Basil	X					X	
Bay Leaf	X		X	X			
Chives	X	X				X	
Cilantro				X	X	X	
Dill				X			
Fennel		X		X			
Garlic	X		X		X	X	
Marjoram	X	X					
Mint				X	X	X	
Oregano			X	X	X		
Parsley		X		X			
Rosemary	X	X					
Sage	X	X					
Summer Savory		X					
Tarragon		X		X			
Thyme	X	X		X	X		
Winter Savory		X					
Supplementary Flavors							
Allspice					X	X	
Berbere							X
Chervil		X					
Chili pepper			X				
Cinnamon					X	X	
Cloves				X	X	X	X
Coconut						X	X
Cumin					X	X	
Ginger						X	
Grains of Paradise							X
Harissa							X
Lemon grass						X	
Mastic				X			
Nutmeg			X	X		X	
Olives			X	X			
Paprika			X		X		X
Per-peri							X
Pimentón			X				
Saffron			X				
Sesame						X	
Turmeric						X	
Vanilla					X		
Zanzibar							X

Herb Cooking Cheat Sheets

Basil

How to use: Fresh or raw

Types of dishes: soups, salads, seafood, meat, poultry, vegetables, eggs, cheeses

When to add: after cooking is complete or just before serving

Flavor description: strong and sharp, can be slightly peppery and sweet

Bay Leaf

How to use: Fresh or dried (fresh Bay leaves are very potent but do not last long)

Types of dishes: soups, seafood, meat, poultry, vegetables

When to add: before cooking, then removed before serving

Flavor description: very subtle minty-peppery flavor that is used more as an enhancement to proteins and sauces rather than a distinct flavor of it's own

CELERY

How to use: fresh or raw

Types of dishes: soups, salads, meat, poultry

When to add: before or after cooking (cooking removes the bitter flavor)

Flavor description: Adds a salty or onion-like flavor that can be spicy and slightly bitter

CHIVES

How to use: fresh or raw

Types of dishes: soups, salads, poultry, vegetables, eggs, cheeses

When to add: just before serving, typically as a garnish

Flavor description: very mild and slightly sweet onion flavor

CILANTRO

How to use: fresh

Types of dishes: soups, salads, seafood, meat, desserts

When to add: after cooking is complete or just before serving

Flavor description: bright citrus flavor

Note: some people get an unpleasant soap-like taste from cilantro, unfortunately this is genetic and there is nothing to remedy it, these people will just have to avoid cilantro

Dill

How to use: fresh

Types of dishes: soup, salad, seafood, poultry, vegetables, eggs, cheeses

When to add: near the end or after cooking

Flavor description: grassy and sweet with mild hint of licorice

Note: flavor changes quite a bit (for the worse) after flowering

Fennel

How to use: fresh

Types of dishes: soups, salad, seafood, meat

When to add: before or after cooking

Flavor description: sharper and stronger licorice flavor than dill, that becomes much milder and sweeter after being cooked

Garlic

How to use: fresh or roasted

Types of dishes: put in everything but dessert, if a dish is missing something, it probably needs garlic

When to add: before cooking

Flavor description: Earthy, warm, and savory, becomes sweeter after cooking or roasting

Lavender

How to use: fresh

Types of dishes: soups, salads, desserts

When to add: before cooking

Flavor description: sweet and floral

Lemon Balm

How to use: fresh

Types of dishes: salads, desserts, teas (can use as a substitute for mint)

When to add: before or after cooking

Flavor description: bright and citrus

Marjoram

How to use: fresh or dried

Types of dishes: soups, salads, meat, poultry, vegetables, eggs, cheeses (can use as a substitute for oregano or thyme)

When to add: before or after cooking

Flavor description: woody and floral, milder than oregano and sweeter than thyme

Mint

How to use: fresh

Types of dishes: salads, meat, eggs, cheeses, desserts

When to add: before (dried) or after cooking, or just before serving (fresh)

Flavor description: sharp and sweet, producing a cooling effect on the tongue, there are countless varieties, each with their own subtle differences

Oregano

How to use: fresh or dried

Types of dishes: soups, salads, seafood, meat, poultry, vegetables, eggs, cheeses

When to add: before cooking, heat removes the bitterness

Flavor description: aromatic, earthy, and slightly bitter

Parsley

How to use: fresh, but it does not keep well once cut

Types of dishes: soups, salads, seafood, poultry

When to add: after cooking or just before serving

Flavor description: very mild and clean, peppery flavor that is just bitter enough to balance out sweet dishes

Rosemary

How to use: fresh or dried

Types of dishes: seafood, meat, poultry, vegetables, cheeses

When to add: before cooking

Flavor description: strong pine tree or evergreen-like woody flavor

Sage

How to use: fresh or dried

Types of dishes: soups, meat

When to add: near the end of cooking, often removed before serving

Flavor description: savory and pine

Savory

How to use: fresh or dried

Types of dishes: soups, meat, vegetables

When to add: before cooking

Flavor description: sweet, spicy and peppery

Tarragon

How to use: fresh

Types of dishes: salads, seafood, poultry, vegetables, eggs, cheeses

When to add: near the end of cooking (becomes bitter with heat)

Flavor description: sweet and bitter with hints of vanilla and licorice

Thyme

How to use: fresh or dried

Types of dishes: soups, salads, meat, poultry, vegetables

When to add: before or after cooking

Flavor description: sweet and savory, like a milder version of oregano

Conclusion

Congratulations, you have all the tools you need to plan, grow, harvest, and use your own herbs.

Remember to share your successes, learn from your mistakes, and enjoy every moment!

A Special Gift Just for You

Use my **'Outdoor Space Planner'** to:

- Get inspired, and choose what elements you *like*, *want*, or *need* to have in your new outdoor space
- Identify any special requirements or restrictions that might be roadblocks to improving your backyard or balcony
- Create an easy to follow budget so you don't run out of money, space, or time
- Draw out your personalized design and plan a schedule for everything to get delivered, built, and installed.

Go to https://www.subscribepage.com/danielistein to get it now!

Glossary

Acidic: This usually refers to the type of soil. Some plants prefer acidic soil to grow. See PH below.

Alkaline: This usually refers to the type of soil. See PH below.

Annual: This is a plant which you sow, it grows and then dies back in one year.

Biennial: This is a plant that is sown and grows well in year 1 but flowers in year 2. It has a 2-year cycle and usually tried to go to seed in year 2.

Compost: This can be purchased or made by you as a free homemade resource, often called "Black Gold" by experienced gardeners. See how to make your own by recycling any household vegetable and fruit waste, combining it with paper waste and thicker twigs from your garden pruning to make an excellent plant fertilizer for your garden, herbs, and fruit trees. See Chapter 5.

Crop rotation: A growing system that is used to ensure that soil does not get depleted by growing the same crop in the same location every year. This helps to produce healthy soil and reduce pests. See Chapter 7.

Drying herbs: how to do this. See Lemon Balm in Chapter 6.

Green manure: also called a cover crop, is withered or dying plant material that is added as a soil amendment. Any green plant material that hasn't decomposed is green manure.

Harden off: This is when your new seedlings are placed outdoors during the day to get them used to being outdoors and then taken back indoors overnight. They are getting used to being outdoors.

Leaf mold: This is a process to use any leftover, dropped leaves in the fall. It is a free resource that provided bulk for soil and can be used in potting plants on.

NPK feeds: These plant foods are sold in gardening stores and they provide 3 critical nutrients for plants.

- N is for nitrogen which makes healthy leaves.
- P is for phosphorus which makes healthy roots.
- K is for potassium or potash which is essential for flowers, keeps the stem healthy, and allows your herb to use nitrogen.

PH of soil: The PH of soil measures the contents on a scale. Soil types vary, depending on the underlying stone formation, usage of the soil in the past, etc.

- Soil with a PH from 6.5 to 7.5 is *neutral.*
- Soil with a PH of less than 6.5 is *acidic*. Any soil less than 5.5 is strongly acidic.
- Soil with a PH of more than 7.5 is *alkaline*.

The soil you choose will depend on the needs of your particular herbs. You can buy composts made for ericaceous plants, which like acid soil and a normal grow bag will be quite fertile with a balance of nutrients. Check what soil your herbs enjoys before planting and check the PH with a testing kit if you are not sure.

Propagation: To sow seeds, to divide plants that become too leggy, and to take cuttings to make new plants or to ensure plants for the following year. See Chapter 7.

Perennial: This is a plant that lives for many years. It is sown and grows steadily to become a small shrub, or even a tree. Chapter 1.

Pests: which attack herbs such as aphids, caterpillars, earwigs, greenflies, slugs, snails, whitefly, red spider mite, scale insects. See Chapter 7.

Root rot: refers to a condition where healthy roots become pot-bound or waterlogged leading to brown, diseased roots. Healthy roots should be white or cream. See Chapter 6.

Self-seeding: is exactly as described. The plant completes its growth cycle, makes flowers, then seeds and these seeds fall on the ground so that you do not need to plant them. Once the seedlings show, you can move them easily, if you need to.

Printed in Great Britain
by Amazon

009802da-7dbf-4016-b7b6-5ac327218b6eR01

Col·lecció Busca-raons, 13
Geografia de l'oblit

Edicions Sidillà SL
La Bisbal d'Empordà 17100
info@edicionssidilla.cat
www.edicionssidilla.cat

Disseny: J. Pujadó
Correcció: Xavier Cortadellas
Primera edició: setembre 2022
Edicions Sidillà és soci protector d'Amics de la Bressola
Aquest llibre s'ha imprès a la Impremta Pagès, d'Anglès
L'edició d'aquest llibre ha rebut una subvenció de la Diputació de Girona

Diputació de Girona

ISBN: 978-84-124306-9-1
Dipòsit legal: GI 1037 2022

Eduard Niubó

Geografia de l'oblit

Exploradors i aventurers silenciats per la història

Pròleg d'Albert Bosch
Il·lustracions de David Granato

edicions
Sidillà

La Bisbal d'Empordà, 2022

Índex

8 Una espècie exploradora
12 Explorar l'exploració
16 ♣ 1. Donant forma al món
18 La descoberta del fum
18 Les estrelles
19 L'arrel dels mapes
20 La rodonesa del món
22 Les profunditats
28 ♣ 2. Amèrica
30 Alguns descobriments d'Amèrica
31 L'estret de Bering
33 El camí polinesi
36 Des d'Àsia, potser?
39 A través de l'Atlàntic
41 Els vikings i Vinlàndia
52 Dels nòrdics al segle xv
60 Cabot i Colom
64 Notícies d'ultramar
68 Els europeus al Brasil
72 I després què?
74 ♣ 3. La primera volta al món
76 Henrique de Malacca
79 Punta Gallows. De Magalhães a Drake
84 ♣ 4. L'Àrtic
86 Pitees de Massàlia. Les primeres boires
88 Cap al pas del nord-oest

90 Cap al pas del nord-est
93 Martin Frobisher. Els inuits descobreixen Europa
98 Willem Barentsz. Una porta tancada al nord-est
100 Henry Hudson. Un simple mal pas
106 Marble Island. Morir plorant
110 John Franklin. El naixement d'un mite
112 Inuits. Els humans
118 Europeus. Els Qablunaaq
122 El pes de les paraules
125 La troballa del *Terror*. Escoltar la tradició
129 Un vaixell de gel. Els eterns silenciats
132 L'obstacle del nord-est. El cap Dejniov
136 El pas del nord-oest. Ànima de fusta
144 La deriva del gel
148 Fridtjof Nansen
158 Valerian Albanov. Escriure la mort a l'Àrtic
163 El Pol Nord
163 0. De Phipps a Parry. Comença la cursa
168 1. Ni Cook ni Peary
172 2. Roald Amundsen. El nen que somiava
175 3. Els altres pols
177 4. Volant al pol nord. L'Amundsen bipolar
182 5. De Kuznetsov a Plaisted
184 5. L'ANTÀRTIDA
186 Hui-Te-Rangiora. La llegenda maori
188 James Cook. Deduir un continent
193 Dirck Gerritsz Pomp. Primers indicis
196 El pas de Drake
200 Foquers i baleners
202 Dins del cercle polar
205 Cap a l'era de l'exploració heroica

208 El pol sud 1. Congelar el moment
212 Oficis polars. Bjaaland, Lindstrøm, Rønne
216 Oscar Wisting. A l'ombra dels pols
218 El pol sud 2. Dibuixar el pol
224 La mort al Pol Sud[1]
224 1. Edgar Evans
225 2. Lawrence Oates
228 3. Wilson, Bowers I Scott
231 4. Carta a Barrie
234 Douglas Mawson. Quan res no pot ser pitjor
243 Les naus de l'oblit
250 El pol sud 3. Coses de l'aire i el vent
254 La frontera interior. Entre la il·lusió i l'obsessió
259 La solitud eterna del pol
262 6. AUSTRÀLIA
264 El temps dels somnis
269 Segle XVI
274 Uns homes blancs
276 1606. Willem Janszoon
279 1606. Torres, Quirós i el Quixot
287 Dirk Hartog. Una costa immensa
291 El naufragi del *Batavia*
297 La colònia sanguinària
303 La costa oblidada
304 1788. L'arribada dels salvatges
306 De la Pérouse. La breu presència francesa
311 D'Urville. Els viatges dels noms
314 Mary Bryant

1 Escrivim Pol Nord o Pol Sud quan indica el nom de tot un territori. En canvi, escrivim pol nord o pol sud quan fa referència només al punt geogràfic.

322 Segle XIX. Dibuixa i pinta el teu continent
327 Al final del camí més llarg
327 Yuwali
328 Yatungka i Warri
331 Els Pintupi nou
336 L'últim nòmada
338 ♣ 7. EL SOSTRE DEL MÓN
340 La conquesta individual
342 Txomolungma, Sagarmatha
344 Cap al cim
346 Els anys vint. Primers intents
351 Set xerpes oblidats i un segle de morts
354 Els anys trenta. Shipton i Norgay
357 Maurice Wilson, *El boig de Yorkshire*
362 Earl Denman. Es reprèn l'aventura
364 Els anys cinquanta. La cara sud
367 L'expedició suïssa
370 1953. El cim
376 Que ho sàpiga el món
378 Encaixada de mans
380 ♣ BIBLIOGRAFIA

Una espècie exploradora

Quan l'Eduard Niubó em va proposar prologar el seu llibre, només d'explicar-me el seu enfocament, ja em vaig emocionar. A banda de participar jo mateix en algunes aventures i de fer expedicions a llocs remots, m'apassiona llegir sobre exploradors i sobre grans gestes de la història. Per mi és com llegir una novel·la, però una novel·la que ha passat de veritat, i que és inspiradora, formativa i realment divertida. A partir d'aquí, quan vaig poder llegir tot el contingut del llibre de l'Eduard, la meva emoció va convertir-se directament en felicitat i em vaig sentir molt honorat de poder aportar el meu granet de sorra en una obra tan interessant.

L'esperit d'exploració ha estat una constant de la nostra espècie. Sempre ha format part fonamental de la nostra evolució, i sempre serà així mentre hi hagi persones curioses, imaginatives, valentes i aventureres.

Hi ha hagut molts motius que han impulsat l'home a descobrir nous llocs, a fer nous invents, a trobar noves maneres de pensar i, en definitiva, a establir noves realitats. De vegades, l'exploració ha respost a necessitats de pura supervivència; d'altres, les exploracions han estat induïdes per l'ambició de poder, pel desig de posseir més territoris, més riqueses, més recursos o més fama. Les exploracions, però també poden haver estat motivades per la passió per al coneixement, per la necessitat de trobar noves tecnologies, per la voluntat d'enriquir-se amb la connexió a noves cultures o per aconseguir millorar la vida de les persones.

Tanmateix, tant a l'antiguitat com fins a l'edat mitjana, el valor dels viatges d'exploració es mesurava més pels seus resultats en riqueses materials o per la possibilitat de dominar noves terres que per les seves aportacions a la ciència i al coneixement. Va ser, però a partir de l'edat mitjana quan es van començar a fer molts viatges d'exploració que tenien finalitats científiques, d'ampliació de coneixements o d'aconseguir més prestigi per als imperis del moment. Tota manera, encara era estrany que aquests viatges no tinguessin res a veure amb els interessos relacionats amb el poder, amb la voluntat de conquesta o amb la capacitat militar.

Va ser sobretot en els segles XIX i XX quan van anar aflorant noves motivacions per a l'activitat exploradora, motivacions com el nacionalisme o com l'ego personal d'algú o d'alguns. Fos com fos, aquestes renovades raons per explorar el nostre planeta van desfermar l'ànsia per ser el primer a col·locar una bandera en un territori sense descobrir o per alimentar el patriotisme relacionat amb la conquesta dels pols, amb els cims més alts del planeta o amb els deserts més inhòspits.

Des dels inicis de la nostra espècie, els exploradors han format part d'una petita minoria d'humans que han deixat enrere allò segur i conegut, i que s'han aventurat a descobrir el que hi havia més enllà, en una zona incerta i perillosa perquè era desconeguda, però que era també la zona de les oportunitats. I no tots ells, però sí tots els que recordem més han tingut un gran impacte en el món tal com es coneixia en el seu temps, han provocat que es fessin avenços molt importants, han accelerat l'evolució i han permès a la societat guanyar terreny i explotar les noves zones i els nous coneixements descoberts.

Per anar cap el futur s'ha de mirar sempre cap endavant, però s'ha de saber també d'on venim i com anem trepitjant i dibuixant el mapa de la història que coneixem. Fer tot això ens ajudarà a entendre millor cap on ens dirigim, quina actitud adoptem, com hi anem i, sobretot, per què val la pena que anem cap aquesta nova realitat.

És relativament fàcil explicar l'evolució de la història des d'una perspectiva lineal. Però també és força superficial si només ho fem així perquè, per entendre bé el com, el qui i el per què, cal que analitzem a fons tots els protagonistes clau en cada moment crucial, en cada decisió i en cada encreuament que es pren o que es descarta durant totes les expedicions que ens porten a descobrir i evolucionar. Fer i fer bé aquestes anàlisis ens pot aportar tanta o més informació que saber els grans titulars, que conèixer els protagonistes més famosos o fins i tot les expedicions que han fet.

En aquest sentit, *Geografia de l'oblit*, aquest llibre que teniu entre les mans, és una obra de gran valor. Llegir-lo ens ajudarà a gaudir molt més la història dels veritables aventurers i ens permetrà entendre els factors clau de l'exploració humana. També ens descobrirà personatges oblidats o no prou reconeguts, i ens enriquirà amb les grans gestes protagonitzades per moltíssimes persones, moltes d'elles ben poc conegudes, persones que ens han permès arribar al punt on som.

En el futur, l'exploració geogràfica continuarà amb més o menys pauses i amb més o menys intensitat. I si no ens hem extingit abans com espècie, l'exploració geogràfica ens portarà a descobrir i a dibuixar nous mapes, molt més enllà de la zona que ja coneixem, una zona que no és res més que una petita volva de pols a l'univers, en aquest petit planeta que anomenem *Terra.* I per continuar recorrent aquest camí és indispensable que tinguem una visió més complerta de la pel·lícula del passat a fi de no oblidar-nos de ningú i per tal de poder escollir el rumb que ens sembli millor per fer les exploracions del futur.

Amb aquest llibre de l'Eduard Niubó, magnífic i molt treballat, amb aquesta *Geografia de l'oblit* aprendrem, ens inspirarem i entendrem la necessitat d'obrir-nos més enllà de les nostres fronteres físiques i mentals. I amb una mica de sort i amb un xic d'empenta per part nostra, assumirem que, com ha passat sempre, però més encara a la nostra època, hem de tenir una actitud més exploradora, més valenta, més curiosa i més proactiva perquè gran part de les coses interessants encara estan per fer o encara són per descobrir. No ens hem d'acomodar, doncs, amb el que ja es coneix, sinó que hem d'entusiasmar-nos amb el que s'ignora. Així és com ho feien tots els protagonistes —oblidats o no— que descobrireu en aquestes pàgines, i així és com hauríem d'integrar part del seu caràcter i passió per la vida i pel món si volem que el nostre lideratge personal, professional i social sigui sòlid.

Que gaudiu, doncs, d'aquesta *Geografia de l'oblit.* I que tingueu també una apassionant exploració vital.

Albert Bosch
Aventurer i emprenedor

Explorar l'exploració

Això que teniu a les mans és gairebé una història de l'oblit. Una de les moltes possibles. Un llibre per donar veu a aquells pioners de l'exploració que han quedat arraconats a les pàgines més discretes de la història dels descobriments.

Rere el tòpic que la història l'escriuen els vencedors, massa sovint la dels descobriments es converteix en la d'una conquesta occidental, i a banda d'algun nom propi europeu ben lluent, poc més s'explica dels que han obert les portes cap a les siluetes que avui dibuixem als mapes. Per això de tant en tant es fa necessari explorar l'exploració i donar a cadascú el lloc que es mereix.

Així doncs, som a punt d'embarcar-nos amb aquells que gairebé han acabat ofegats al tinter de la història i que bé podrien ser un fil principal per estirar. Perquè la història no és només el passat, sinó el relat que se'n fa; i mentre els noms d'alguns aventurers llueixen en grans pàgines daurades, a la majoria només els han quedat les mans plenes d'oblit. Però sense ells no tindríem ni mapes, ni països, ni formes al món. I malgrat tot, sovint no els coneixem. Sabem realment qui ha descobert l'Antàrtida o Austràlia? I Amèrica? Segur? I Europa? Sabem qui ha descobert Europa? Perquè fora d'aquest petit continent, el món també té altres melics des dels quals es fan descobriments, i aquest relat sempre revisable ja no es pot reduir a la imatge ridícula i eurocèntrica d'un capità de vaixell trobant una terra que la resta d'occidentals ignoraven. Menys encara quan es tracta de terres habitades des de temps remots, amb les seves cultures riques i sorprenents, amb els seus imperis i les seves relacions comercials, amb influències de civilitzacions antigues i llunyanes... i també, és clar, amb els seus descobridors.

Aquest viatge que comencem, doncs, és ple d'aquests discrets pioners. Alguns encara rescatables de l'oblit, altres, immersos en aquest oblit a tanta fondària que ja mai més no podrem fer-los surar de nou, i molts més, encara, que senzillament ens hauran quedat escampats pel teclat sense trobar forma en les pàgines que segueixen. Perquè el ventall és amplíssim i també aquí ens toca triar en l'intent de rescatar de la foscor alguns dels que no tornen per explicar la seva fita al món.

D'una banda hi haurà els que no tornen. Difícil donar-los veu, cert, però no sempre impossible. Més fàcil hauria de ser rescatar els ignorats que senzillament acompanyen els triomfadors. Perquè rarament els exploradors s'han aventurat sols enlloc, i posar un únic nom al davant de tot un descobriment és injust i fantasiós. Més enllà dels grans noms propis, la història dels mariners morts de gana i de por és la porta d'entrada al coneixement del món. Sense ells, sense la seva desesperació, no hi ha res.

En aquestes pàgines nosaltres anirem a la recerca i rescat d'aquells que, en topar amb una terra desconeguda, més que descobrir-la i treure'n la capa que la tapava, s'hi van posar a cobert per no ser vistos mai més. Potser amb el nostre modest intent no sabrem sortir del tot d'aquella visió umbilical europea, però si més no, seria un bon primer pas entendre que més enllà del discurs establert hi ha sempre la història dels que s'ho han jugat tot per no descobrir res més que oblit. I de tant en tant ens toca a nosaltres també descobrir aquest oblit, encara que només sigui com a exercici de respecte i d'humilitat, o com a pràctica per desemmascarar mentides en un món cada cop més saturat d'informacions mal estudiades. O si es vol, encara, senzillament per fascinar-nos de la manera discreta i silenciosa com hem anat donant forma al món.

De tots aquests oblidats, en les pàgines que segueixen podrem poc més que fer-ne reflotar alguns que ja estan més o menys documentats, però que, lluny de navegar en grans velers pel mar dels llibres d'història, s'hi troben mig surant a la deriva damunt de rais improvisats. Aquests aventurers de l'oblit que gairebé són els nàufrags de la història.

30
60
80
0
N
E
S

1. Donant forma al món

La descoberta del fum

El foc. És curiós, sembla que ningú no pensi mai que abans del descobriment del foc hi hauria d'haver el del fum. Tothom queda embadalit davant del trofeu més vistós i lluent, i queden al país de l'oblit aquells que han descobert els inútils senyals irrespirables, aquells que han obert el camí, els que han guiat aquells que han vingut posteriorment —a vegades com els canaris de coves i mines, que amb la seva mort anuncien la manca d'oxigen— i que permeten recular per tornar-ho a intentar més endavant, sabent-ne més. En la descoberta del foc, cauen a l'oblit aquells que han sucumbit a les primeres flames de la humanitat, i a la fi, és erigit com a descobridor aquell que ha après posteriorment a dominar-lo i que ha sabut tornar a casa.

Però en algun lloc queden unes cendres, ossos recremats, potser encara olor de carn rostida...

Les estrelles

Esvaït el primer fum del descobriment, apareix en la nit el foc immensament llunyà i misteriós dels estels.

Caldria mirar al cel nocturn, entendre les estrelles, fer-ne un alfabet comprensible. A cada lloc del món, les mateixes constel·lacions convertides en alfabets diferents. Perquè ben mirat, allà comença tot, en el mapa celeste. Així doncs, abans de començar a aventurar-se enllà, potser calia foscor i mirar cap a una altra banda. Calia, mirar cap amunt, de nit, cap al descobriment més antic i llunyà de tots. Les estrelles. Si no haguessin existit, mai no s'hauria navegat, mai no s'hauria descobert aquest món nostre tan proper. El gran espai de l'univers ens dona la pista per moure'ns per casa nostra.

Un cop descobertes les matemàtiques i la ciència, un cop llegides les constel·lacions com un primer alfabet, els humans vam poder fer-nos a la mar i començar el viatge de descobrir casa nostra, llançar-nos a navegar, a descobrir l'oblit.

L'arrel dels mapes

Sens dubte la parla humana ve de bracet amb la imatge, el significant. Què és la paraula si no? Qui sap, doncs, a on queda el primer mapa de la humanitat? Potser va ser un efímer esquema marcat a la sorra, unes pedres indicant fites, un caçador indicant una estratègia...

A les proximitats de Montignac, a França, hi ha les coves de Lascaux, meravella pictòrica del paleolític amb quinze mil anys d'antiguitat. Entre les parets decorades amb tota mena d'animals d'un detallisme sorprenent, alguns entesos veuen els mapes celestes més antics que coneixem avui: potser el Triangle d'estiu —amb Altair, Deneb i Vega—, o les constel·lacions de Taure, Orió, les Plèiades. Qui ho sap? Tot continua lligat a les nostres hipotètiques interpretacions modernes, però, sens dubte, molt abans que els antics grecs comencessin a establir el mapa celeste que coneixem avui, molts astres han tingut ja noms i vides de mites oblidats. Mapes d'estels que són cementiris, làpides, epitafis de déus morts i esvaïts en el no-res del qual venien, succeint-se segles rere segles, potser déus que s'esfumen desenganyats dels humans que els han donat vida.

Els primers mapes del cel, potser, en la volta opaca i fosca d'una cova.

Però qui ho sap? Qui ho sap?... El dubte es va repetint troballa rere troballa, i és possible que un ullal de mamut trobat a la localitat txeca de Pavlov mostri el mapa més antic que coneixem de la humanitat. Aquest, ara sí, ens parlaria de la terra. Segons els experts, fa més de vint-i-cinc mil anys en aquest ullal de mamut algú hauria gravat la representació d'una muntanya, el curs del riu Dyje (fronterer entre Txèquia i Àustria) i les valls properes, potser també rutes i camins. És difícil desxifrar mentalitats i esquemes tan llunyans, però a poc a poc estem començant a explicar una imatge del món.

I malgrat tot, potser encara tenim mapes més antics. Passen tant per alt! Passats de generació en generació, les línies de cançons australianes són, potser sí, el mapa més antic i que ha durat més de la humanitat. Cançons repetides i invariables, qualsevol error en la memorització portaria a perdre's en el desert i a no arribar mai més enlloc. Mapes mentals, musicals; només els qui recordin les cançons i les transmetin amb total precisió trobaran aigua i aliment i arribaran al final del camí. Per una mena de llei darwinista, en el continent australià ha sigut així durant desenes de milers d'anys. Cançons que han perdurat fins avui i que potser ja eren antigues en l'època que a Pavlov algú marcava el riu Dyje en un ullal de mamut... Sens dubte la parla humana ve de bracet amb la música. Què és la paraula si no?

La rodonesa del món

Les estrelles deixen ben clara la forma de la Terra. La seva rodonesa no és un invent dels temps de Colom. Ja els antics grecs (alguns, no tots) coneixien la forma i la mida del planeta.

A l'Alexandria del segle III aC, Eratòstenes (grec, però africà) ja en calcula el perímetre amb força exactitud, igual com l'indi Āryabhata al segle V i qui sap quanta gent més de l'antiguitat, arreu del món. Perquè no sigui dit, també s'apunten a la rodonesa del món alguns referents del cristianisme com Sant Agustí (s. IV-V), Boeci (s. V-VI) o el monjo Beda (s. VII-VIII) entre altres. Una altra cosa més difícil era considerar la Terra en moviment, però també a l'antiguitat hi havia astrònoms preveient eclipsis, cosa que implica uns avançats càlculs que per força posaven la Lluna orbitant al voltant de la Terra i la Terra al voltant del Sol, com un astre més. I encara, en aquesta constel·lació de rodonistes, trobarem també tota una autoritat com Dante Alighieri, que cap al 1320, a la *Divina Comèdia*, atribueix un perímetre d'uns 33.000 quilòmetres al nostre planeta.

No està gens malament. La ciència ja fa segles que permet no suposar que la Terra té la mida de la Lluna, i això fa quasi imperdonable la pretensió de Colom d'haver arribat als antípodes amb la simple travessa de l'Atlàntic. Però encara més sorprenent serà la seva elegant sortida d'atribuir forma de pera a la Terra tot assegurant que ell ha trobat el paradís terrenal fent drecera voltant el gran mugró planetari, per un hemisferi que és «*com una teta de dona en una pilota rodona*». Així mateix ho deixa escrit aquest deliciós Cristòfor Colom, inventor d'un planeta Teta que podria haver fet passar una bona estona a Freud. Potser no hi ha tanta valentia en els seus viatges com en aquesta fantàstica teoria que es treu de la màniga el 1498, en el relat del seu tercer viatge, per justificar que ha arribat al paradís terrenal.

Alguna cosa, doncs, ha fallat amb aquells europeus. I si la ciència falla, deu ser que s'ha imposat una altra cosa. Ves que no sigui l'amenaça religiosa, que preferia la ignorància a la realitat. No és cap secret que l'església esquivava la ciència quan li convenia, sobretot per mantenir el seu poder absolut sobre el més enllà, i per tant, també sobre el més ençà.

Caldrà, doncs, anar eixamplant el món. De moment començarem mirant cap avall, sota els peus, mirant d'ubicar-nos en aquest univers encara estrany. Perquè la gran por de l'església no era la forma de la Terra, sinó el lloc que aquesta ocupava. Curiosament —detall ben mirat incomprensible— insistien a situar-la al centre del món, desplaçant-ne el seu déu i posant-hi el diable. Perquè l'infern, ja se sap, és sota terra. Fins i tot Dante situa Llucifer en aquell precís punt on coincideixen els hemisferis boreal i austral, i que esdevé punt d'atracció de la gravetat. Així s'avança, sigui dit de passada, fins i tot a Newton i a qui sap quants més.

Les profunditats

Coneixedors ja de la forma de la Terra, conscients avui que el seu cor és inaccessible, començarem per fi el nostre viatge real cap a la fondària més pregona possible de l'astre, fins allà on es pugui, per ressorgir després i començar a explorar-ne la superfície. Dominat el foc i la llum, podem començar a penetrar en la foscor de túnels i cavernes, deixar-hi petges anònimes i perennes, protegides de tota inclemència durant mil·lennis. Pintures rupestres estampades en indrets impossibles que la humanitat moderna retrobarà quan, de nou, també s'endinsi en les cavitats del món.

Però sobretot, no oblidem que explorar la foscor demana dominar el foc, la llum. Mirem si no el simplíssim exemple de Philibert Aspairt el 1793. Segons la llegenda que l'envolta, lluny encara de ser cap espeleòleg, més aviat accidental precursor d'una moderna exploració urbana, el 3 de novembre d'aquell 1793 Aspairt entra a les catacumbes de París amb una llàntia. No explicarà mai què hi buscava, potser només avança empès per la curiositat de descobrir el misteri de la foscor fins que, en la immensitat solitària dels passadissos que explora, la llàntia se li apaga i, abandonat a la negror laberíntica, el seu cos no serà trobat fins passats onze anys. Així de senzill.

Dominar la llum, la curiositat, el saber. Mentrestant, les profunditats del món subterrani són allà, esperant ser explorades fins que, per fi, amb els temps de les noves ciències, al segle XIX neixi l'espeleologia i a poc a poc es vagi entrant terra endins a la recerca de les màximes profunditats.

El francès Edouard-Alfred Martel és considerat el pare de l'espeleologia amb les seves primeres exploracions a finals de segle XIX. Però ja abans altres li han obert camí. Les entranyes de la terra sempre han tingut portes obertes. Les coves han sigut des de sempre refugi i misteri, però també font de recursos. És per això que el 1841 l'enginyer de mines Anton Friedrich Lindner es converteix en la persona coneguda que més s'ha endinsat a la terra fins aleshores. Aquell estiu, a base d'enormes esforços i dificultats, Lindner i el seu equip d'oblidats aconsegueixen obrir-se pas fins a més de tres-cents metres de profunditat vertical buscant les aigües subterrànies del riu Timavo. L'objectiu és trobar el curs a prou alçada per millorar l'abastiment de la ciutat de Trieste. El resultat és pobre. La desesperació de Lindner deu créixer a cada pou que li cal baixar: com més avall sigui el riu subterrani, més difícil serà canalitzar-lo. Finalment, aquest primer rècord mundial de profunditat no serveix per aportar l'aigua que Trieste necessita, i havent arribat massa avall, Lindner tanca la seva aventura arruïnat i amb una salut tan deteriorada pel sacrifici continuat dels últims mesos que no podrà sobreviure més enllà d'aquell mateix setembre.

Amb esforços d'aquesta categoria hem començat per fi a saber damunt de què som, i podem començar a baixar cada cop més avall. Només ens passa que en aquesta foscor sòlida no hi haurà un Everest invers que es pugui assenyalar amb el dit. A diferència de les muntanyes, netament visibles i identificables, sempre quedarà un racó per descobrir en aquestes arrels de l'aire que cal anar trobant gairebé a les palpentes. Ben mirat, per conèixer alguna cosa potser no hi hagi res millor que palpar; tot amor visual reclama després el tacte. Però en aquest món subterrani que només es deixa ser descobert en la intimitat, difícilment podrem saber qui i quan ha tocat el fons de la Terra. ¿Qui sap on és cada porta i què hi pot haver al darrere? A diferència dels mapes superficials, sota terra potser sí que sempre hi haurà un nou món per descobrir.

Mai se sap quan s'obrirà una porta impensada a tot un món de meravelles. Ben bé com una Alícia que segueix un animaló als peus d'un arbre, el setembre de 1940 un jove de disset anys, Marcel Ravidat, passeja pels afores de Montignac quan veu el seu gos, Robot, furgant a prop d'un arbre caigut per una tempesta. Empès per la curiositat, Ravidat de seguida s'adona que el petit orifici trobat pel seu gos ha de donar pas a una cavitat molt més gran, i pocs dies després torna al mateix punt amb tres amics més, Jacques Marsal, Georges Agnel i Simon Coencas.

Després d'ampliar la boca de la cova per fer-s'hi pas, aquests quatre nois d'entre tretze i disset anys comencen a descendir fins que topen amb una de les troballes més sorprenents que es podien imaginar. Autèntic museu del paleolític, les parets de les sales que acaben de descobrir són plenes de representacions pictòriques de més de quinze mil anys d'antiguitat. En pocs anys, aquesta cova de Lascaux serà coneguda com «la Capella Sixtina del Paleolític».

D'una manera semblant, a poques hores de Lascaux, el 1990 un jove espeleòleg de quinze anys, Bruno Kowalczewski, descobreix la cova de Bruniquel, que conté les restes d'activitat humana més antigues conegudes al món fins ara, un vertiginós abisme de 175.000 anys entre nosaltres i un grup de Neandertals, ancestres nostres amb els quals compartim més ADN del que pensàvem.

L'atzar ha permès trobar aquest impensable enllaç amb la prehistòria, però ¿quants secrets no ha de guardar encara la terra? La recerca subterrània ha de ser així, íntima, discreta, a cegues, sense gaire més pistes que una modestíssima porta d'entrada.

Ben bé com amb les persones.

I és que, més enllà dels atzars d'entrada, sempre volem arribar tan a prop del cor com sigui possible. El rècord de profunditat de Lindner continuarà vigent durant tot el segle XIX; al llarg del XX s'anirà davallant cada cop més, fins als 1.500 metres, i en els primers anys del XXI encara es continuarà superant aquesta fita fins que, el 2018, quatre membres de l'equip rus Perovo-speleo assoleixin els 2.212 metres de profunditat vertical a la cova Verióvkina, a Abkhàzia. Per mantenir la nostra promesa de fer reflotar noms oblidables, aquells dies de març, Pavel Demidov, Ievgenii Kuzmin, Ievgenii Rybka i Zdeněk Dvořák arriben fins al fons de la cavitat natural més profunda que es coneix en aquell moment.

Algú, tard o d'hora, arribarà encara més enllà, però de moment aquest és el límit. El cap de l'expedició, Demidov, compararia la seva aventura amb un viatge a la Lluna, però el que és sobretot aquesta exploració és una recerca laberíntica de galeries, sales, passatges i rius durant dies de fred i humitat, de risc d'inundacions sobtades i d'esllavissades de roques. És així com el mateix Demidov trobaria la mort dos anys després en una cavitat propera a la cova Veriókvina.

Però la fascinació pel desconegut és un imant irresistible. Sens dubte es continuarà arribant més avall. Sens dubte aquest no és el fons absolut de l'espai obert. Naturalment, l'impossible cor ardent de la Terra està molt lluny de ser trepitjat. Hi ha, però, altres vies per davallar més endins en les entranyes del planeta, i aquestes impliquen obrir una escletxa a través de la seva solidesa. D'això se n'encarrega sobretot la mineria, encara que amb intencions ben diferents que les dels espeleòlegs. Ben mirat, no tots els exploradors i descobridors han sigut sempre valents aventurers disposats a jugar-se la vida per gust. Sovint els oblidats dels límits són anònims com un miner. ¿Quants mariners oblidats no han naufragat en l'oblit només per culpa de la fam? En les mines més profundes del planeta tampoc no s'hi baixa per gust. I això que algunes d'aquestes profunditats farien l'enveja dels exploradors més àvids.

En aquest món subterrani, sòlid i canviant de les mines, avui les més profundes que podem trobar són a Sud-àfrica. Allà, la mina d'or de Mponeng té, en el moment d'escriure aquestes ratlles, l'honor de ser la més profunda del món amb més de quatre mil metres de profunditat vertical. Aquí no hi ha noms propis que marquin cap fita, sinó suor i patiment d'anònims treballadors esforçats. Cap explorador ha estat mai tan a prop del centre de la Terra. I malgrat tot, aquesta abismal fondària no arriba ni a la profunditat mitjana dels oceans. Tenint en compte que el radi planetari supera els 6.370 quilòmetres, amb aquests prodigiosos quatre quilòmetres endins tot just es pot començar a dir que ja queda menys... per travessar la pell de la poma.

I així, arribats al cul-de-sac d'aquestes profunditats, no tenim altre camí que allunyar-nos-en per aflorar en la superfície de la Terra i començar-la a explorar per fora.

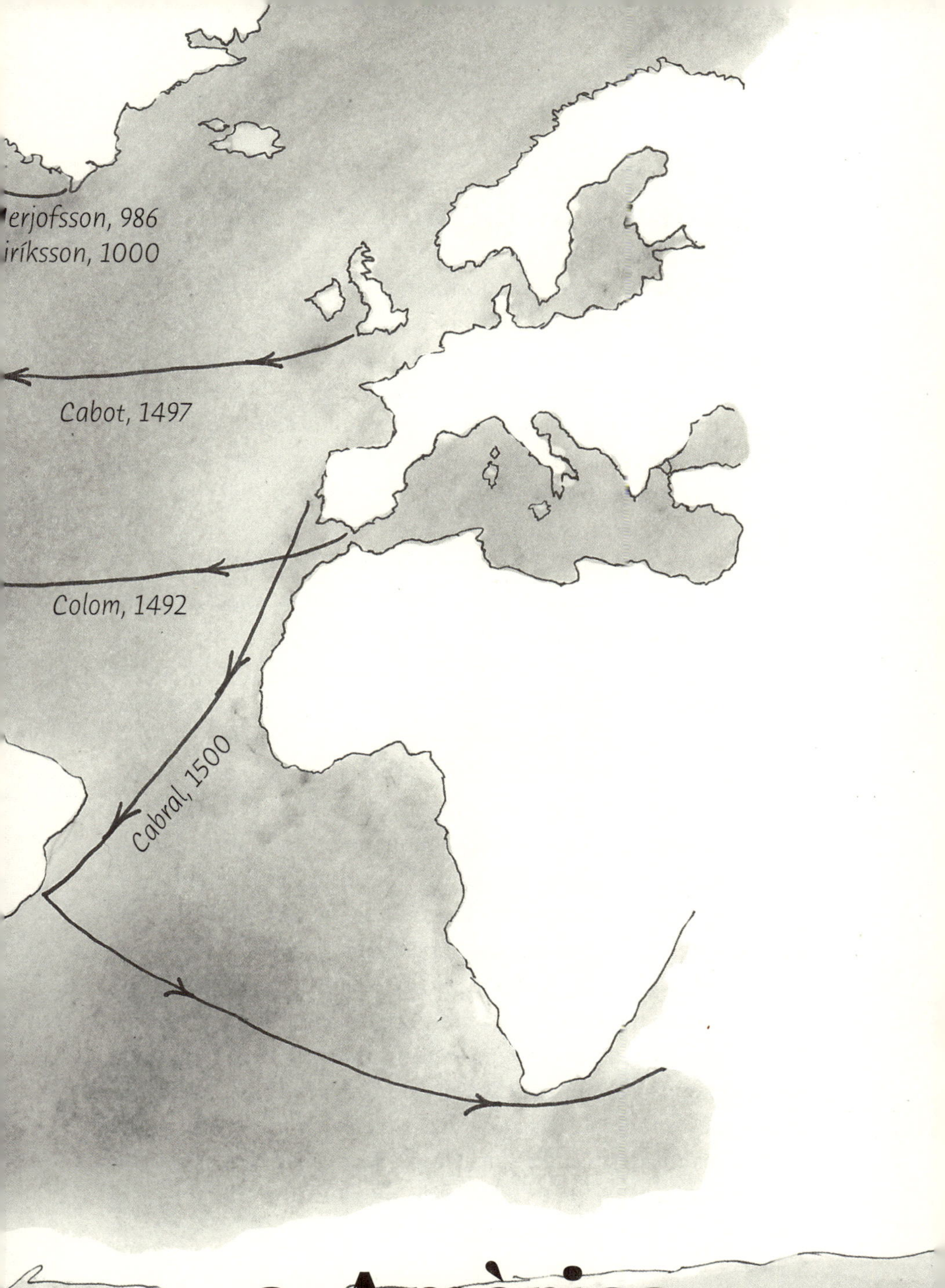
erjofsson, 986
iríksson, 1000
Cabot, 1497
Colom, 1492
Cabral, 1500

2. Amèrica

Alguns descobriments d'Amèrica

Tots fem petits descobriments cada dia. Una botiga nova, un destí de vacances, un record al fons d'un calaix, una moneda en una butxaca... Descobrir —fer visible allò que no vèiem perquè estava amagat— no és res que s'hagi de limitar a una sola vegada ni a una sola persona. Cadascú, a la seva manera, ho va descobrint tot a poc a poc. I així, si volem, tots som també descobridors d'Amèrica, cadascú a la seva manera.

Però faríem trampa si neguéssim el camí obert per altres.

Quan parlem de grans descobriments, el d'Amèrica es converteix en un d'aquells que per repetitiu quasi podríem dir que esdevé quotidià. Una altra cosa són les conseqüències de cada descobriment, i sens dubte el de Colom és d'un pes innegable per tal com canvia la història del món d'avui per demà. Però aquesta terra en realitat ha estat descoberta una pila de vegades per gent que venia d'ultramar i que topava amb ella sense saber-ne l'existència, perquè era gairebé inevitable: tal com estiren els braços de pol a pol les dues Amèriques, qualsevol navegant que es llanci oceà enllà des d'un altre continent toparà amb les seves costes. Si no naufraga abans, és clar.

I si a més en torna, podrà explicar que allà hi ha alguna cosa que... («ah, tu també?») és descoberta un cop rere l'altre. Reculem si no, reculem en el temps fins a deixar Amèrica encara sense humans i reprenem el camí de bon principi. Iniciem de nou aquest redescobrir cíclic i aturem-nos, com a mostra, en alguns d'aquests episodis que, de vegades molt propers entre ells, es donen prou aïllats perquè els puguem considerar grans descobriments d'Amèrica.

L'estret de Bering

Sens dubte algú va ser el primer a veure el continent americà; i algú el primer a trepitjar-lo. És clar que d'això ja fa trenta mil anys i avui ens sembla només —només!— un pas més de l'expansió humana pel planeta, però segurament el viatge no devia ser cap broma. Viatge de no retorn, quan encara ningú tornava per explicar al món que havia deixat enrere i que ja formava part del passat que havia descobert una nova terra.

Per això, perquè encara no surt ningú a compartir la troballa, a esbombar-la ni que sigui al ritme lent de la nostra prehistòria, de moment la descoberta d'aquests primers humans no ho serà encara de tota la humanitat. Amèrica és encara un recipient buit que xucla els seus descobridors fent el buit des del coll d'ampolla que acabem de destapar a l'estret de Bering. És encara un estómac o un pulmó que descobrim dins nostre perquè necessitem omplir-lo, però que no l'acabarem d'entendre del tot fins que no l'hàgim de buidar per primer cop.

La història de la primera petjada humana sobre Amèrica podria ben bé ser així: una vegada, un grup de gent que vivia a les terres del nord-est de la gèlida Sibèria d'aquella era glacial aprofiten la solidesa del mar de Bering per avançar en la blancor infinita i convertir-se en els primers humans que trepitgen el continent americà. Hem trobat una nova terra. Potser aspra, erma i freda, però generosa de caça i prou deshumanitzada per no témer cap guerra.

Amèrica ha descobert els humans.

Més endavant, de temps en temps, altres onades migratòries semblants continuaran arribant a Amèrica. Onades igualment sempre plenes de descobridors del continent. Sembla fàcil i quasi evident, avui que estem acostumats a veure aquestes migracions com un fet natural, però si la vida en aquells temps ja havia de ser prou dura, ¿com de dura devia ser la d'aquells que vivien en els confins més remots de l'expansió humana? Si el mar Àrtic estava permanentment glaçat, també ho havien d'estar les seves terres, ni fèrtils ni generoses.

I doncs, què hi fa un primat d'origen tropical en unes condicions com aquestes? Segur que no és el plaer el que ha empès ningú a desplaçar-se cap a territoris cada vegada més hostils. Però la vida és breu i el pas és lent, potser tant que ni els que migren s'adonen que ho fan, amb cada generació lligada al seu paisatge però encara no a cap terra prou determinada. Durant aquells mil·lennis, les migracions humanes avancen inexorablement per tot el planeta, segurament per raons diverses, i el periple asiàtic del sud cap al nord ben segur que no havia d'acabar a Sibèria.

Obligats pel que fos que empenyia aquests grups, alguns d'aquells avantpassats siberians devien seguir més al nord, cap a l'Àrtic glaçat, on devien sobreviure qui sap quant de temps, podríem apostar que ben poc, amb sort potser alguns dies. La mateixa sort devien córrer molts dels que van continuar el viatge més cap a l'est; només que algú, alguns, van tenir la sort de travessar a peu la blancor llarga i erma de l'estret de Bering. No sabem quines calamitats acompanyarien aquesta aventura, només sabem que finalment tornarien a trobar de nou la terra ferma, amb un clima igualment hostil i sense saber que algun dia els seus descendents continuarien cap al sud, mentre anirien descobrint grans prades, muntanyes, llacs, rius, selves, deserts... un continent immens, generós, un camí cap a climes tropicals, cap a climes ja oblidats moltes generacions enrere.

Allà, al blanc estret de Bering, comença un nou estadi de les migracions que va d'Alaska a la Terra del Foc, on de nou el clima torna a ser d'una exigència suprema. Allà on arriben aquests humans en el seu camí cap al sud de les Amèriques, s'estableixen uns i en marxen altres. Bering. Separar-se, fugir, marxar... Continuar avançant per no tornar mai més, fins que inclús els records deixin de passar de generació en generació, i finalment la pròpia història es vagi esborrant també en un nus d'oblit insalvable amb els ancestres.

Amèrica ha estat descoberta i poblada de nord a sud, però com un xuclador que omple el buit, ningú no en surt encara per explicar-ne res. El contacte amb la resta del món s'esborra. Des d'Amèrica, la resta del món ha deixat d'existir i tard o d'hora aquests americans hauran de descobrir tot d'altres continents oblidats i poblats per altres humans.

El camí polinesi

Continuem encara a la prehistòria, en la qual tot queda diluït com un pas més de l'expansió humana pel planeta. Com un got d'aigua abocat damunt la taula, l'ésser humà es converteix en una plaga que ocupa fins i tot les superfícies que li són menys favorables. Mirem si no el bon exemple que és el Pacífic, continent d'aigua que es vessa per damunt de mig planeta, però amb les seves illes disperses aquí i allà que en faciliten la conquesta. Igualment com en altres capítols d'aquelles migracions, podem estar segurs que molts dels primers navegants que van sortir d'algun continent cap a l'horitzó s'acomiadaven de la terra ferma per sempre més.

Però era factible, les evidències hi són: les illes de la Polinèsia estan habitades des de fa entre tres mil i cinc mil anys. La gran pregunta durant molt de temps va ser saber d'on provenien els primers pobladors d'aquelles illes tan remotes. Es tracta d'un territori incòmode conquerit, domesticat, i això vol dir que calen uns coneixements i unes tècniques molt acurades. Ja no és una qüestió d'atzar que una embarcació de cada moltes arribi a un punt concret.

Molt de temps després, el 1947, el noruec Thor Heyerdahl (amb Knut Haugland, Bengt Danielsson, Erik Hesselberg, Torstein Raaby i Herman Watzinger) farà el recorregut des del Perú fins a la Polinèsia en la memorable expedició de la *Kon-Tiki*, una embarcació feta només amb materials i tècniques antigues, i demostrarà així que el viatge entre Amèrica i la Polinèsia era possible (possible, no demostrarà pas que fos un fet) ja en una antiguitat remota. El motiu que empeny Heyerdahl a embarcar-se en una aventura tan singular és demostrar que les cultures polinèsies haurien pogut provenir d'Amèrica, però ell mateix insisteix que el seu èxit no demostra aquesta teoria, i que com a molt permet demostrar que hauria sigut factible el viatge transoceànic entre els dos continents. Res més.

Més tard sabrem que l'origen dels polinesis és sobretot asiàtic, però tot i això, semblen evidents els contactes entre pobles oceànics i d'Amèrica del sud. Potser sí, doncs, que el continent ha començat a vessar, a transpirar, a suar algunes gotes d'humanitat. Potser sí que algú en surt i va cap a una altra part del món, encara que sigui per la via més difícil i impensada. Fos com fos, però, Heyerdahl, més enllà de viure una aventura apassionant, fa el seu viatge amb una tecnologia que no sembla permetre el viatge en sentit invers, de la Polinèsia cap a Amèrica. Així doncs, la pregunta que ens planteja és evident: on s'estableix el contacte entre uns i altres?

Amb totes les llacunes que se'ns obren en aquest espai, podem imaginar diferents possibilitats: probablement de les costes d'Indonèsia o de les Filipines havien de sortir els primers pobladors polinesis que, d'illa en illa, havien d'expandir-se lentament per tot el Pacífic, avançant per un mar farcit d'illes cada vegada més distants entre elles, fins que el mur blau i llis del mar es feia infranquejable. Com sempre, alguns es devien aventurar cap a llocs més remots fins que potser la sort els va permetre contactar amb l'altra paret de l'oceà. Més difícil per a alguns i més fàcil per a altres és pensar que des de la costa andina, sense que hi hagi cap arxipèlag important a prop, algú gosés endinsar-se setmanes i setmanes de navegació sense saber què trobaria fins que va anar a topar amb alguna de les illes de la Polinèsia.

Però qui ho sap. Tenim un petit poblat a la costa americana, i des d'allà algú veu aparèixer a l'horitzó una embarcació que ve de l'est, on no hi ha constància que hi hagi res ni ningú; es tracta d'uns polinesis que s'han sorprès de la columna de fum d'una foguera humana que sortia en aquella immensa franja de terra llunyana i desconeguda. O potser és a l'inrevés i tenim uns pescadors polinesis que veuen aparèixer per l'est una embarcació de gent que deu venir d'alguna illa desconeguda, enllà, enllà. O fins i tot podríem tenir una fortuïta i providencial trobada a alta mar, ¿per què no, descobrir els habitants abans que els continents, i parlar de trobada i no de descoberta? O uns polinesis que arriben a Amèrica abans que els de l'estret de Bering. Qui ho sap? Les migracions marítimes no poden deixar els mateixos rastres que les terrestres i tot són conjectures, però tant si el contacte es va fer en una direcció com en una altra, la Polinèsia va ser sens dubte el primer territori exterior trobat per pobles americans (un cop oblidat aquell remot Bering). S'ha descobert la Polinèsia, i s'ha descobert Amèrica.

Des d'Àsia, potser?

Vet aquí una taula ben grossa i rodona al cor de la biblioteca més rica i antiga de tots els temps, amb tot d'estudiosos capficats en els seus llibres antics, mirant mapes i rellegint amb lupa paraules que el pas dels anys potser ja hauria d'haver esborrat fa molt. Al centre de la taula, tota sola i lluent, una bola del món, un mapa d'Amèrica, una medalla d'or. I també una data.

Així que ens hi acostem, silenciosos per no destorbar els seus ulls cansats, veiem que en aquestes olimpíades del descobriment d'Amèrica, de moment guanya un tal Colom (o el seu mariner Rodrigo de Triana, primer de l'expedició a veure terra) l'any 1492. Però aquests jutges de la competició no voldrien ser injustos, i de tant en tant algú s'aixeca tot seriós, de vegades fins i tot eufòric, mostrant tot de dades amb la mà per assegurar que a la Xina van descobrir Amèrica abans que Colom. Aleshores tots els altres clatells també es redrecen i tots ells riuen. Són gent de paraules precises i això els fa riure, caldrà rectificar:

—Així dieu que van trobar Amèrica a la Xina?

—Bé, no és que la descobrissin a la Xina, sinó la gent que hi vivia.

De moment, l'home intenta aconseguir la seva medalla en nom dels vells xinesos, però potser aviat se li esfondrarà l'argument, perdut en tot de lletres quasi suposades que es van esborrant a poc a poc de documents antics.

—És cert —dirà— que seguim encara sense tenir dades exactes, però tenint en compte l'antigor de la Xina i que els asiàtics de més al sud navegaven pel Pacífic des de temps remots, res no impedeix pensar que els xinesos naveguessin també pel mar que els era proper i que exploressin les aigües més enllà de l'horitzó...

—Siguem seriosos, company. La medalla serà per a qui aporti dades, no possibilitats.

I els clatells tornen a lluir cap al sostre sense que al mig de la taula ningú canviï la data de 1492.

Que el descobriment de Colom tindria unes conseqüències molt més espectaculars no ho qüestiona ningú, i qualsevol que el pugui destronar sovint només aconseguirà un rècord sense més valor que la medalla d'or pòstuma. Aquí, qualsevol recerca d'informació porta a un cúmul de dades confuses, de pretensions d'autors moderns que es voldrien descobridors de descobridors previs a Colom per prendre-li el ceptre. Però qui no ho voldria? Fins i tot aquest text ha començat per aquest camí. Novel·listes que necessiten vendre best-sellers històrics, maçons que asseguren que ells es van establir als Estats Units al segle XII, dirigents de països musulmans que proclamen que els àrabs també van vèncer Colom... Però amb la Xina hi ha una diferència: l'arribada de la Xina a Amèrica, tot i que sense conseqüències aparents per a nosaltres, és summament plausible. I amb tot, probablement molts dels descobridors de descobridors s'equivoquin.

Alguns situen el primer contacte entre xinesos i els primers americans fa més de quatre mil anys; altres, pensen que aquests contactes van començar tot just poc abans que els europeus arribessin a Amèrica, però tothom pensa que serà difícil esbrinar quin va ser el primer contacte de tots. Potser els xinesos van descobrir Amèrica diferents cops i la van oblidar altres tantes vegades, hem de creure que desencantats, o avorrits o cansats.

Imaginem un d'aquests possibles moments. La rica Xina medieval (què no dir de l'època de les primeres grans dinasties) no tenia cap necessitat d'explorar la llunyana Europa. Europa en tot cas ja es preocuparia de venir on eren ells si volien alguna cosa com ara seda o espècies. Tant és així que l'estroncament de la ruta de la seda va moure els europeus, no pas els xinesos, que amb l'economia resolta ja eren el que avui en diríem una potència mundial. Només l'accidental i providencial descoberta de l'or americà alteraria aquests rols i canviaria el destí d'Europa.

Per tant, de moment tenim una Xina que sens dubte navega, i encara que avui circulin dades errònies o poc fiables, sí que sembla raonable una certa presència seva a les costes del nord-oest d'Amèrica. En tenim poques pistes, com a molt restes puntuals potser de naufragis o d'una incipient activitat comercial mai consolidada. Poca cosa que tot just de vegades es vol reforçar amb coincidències culturals o lingüístiques que alguns estudiosos observen amb més o menys convenciment. Gairebé tot, pistes poc datades que es fonen entre els dits.

La tan evident presència xinesa a Amèrica no ha deixat rastre als ulls del món occidental, però ¿com s'explica la història a les escoles xineses? Com tantes coses de fora del món occidental, el món xinès ens resulta encara un misteri. Fins i tot en l'era de les comunicacions globals ens costa apropar-nos al món àrab o xinès (per posar un parell d'exemples) sense passar per les llengües que ens són properes, sovint per l'anglès. Cadascú explica les coses a la seva manera, i poc sabem de què es diu sobre el descobriment d'Amèrica a la Xina. I malgrat l'apropament tangencial que podem fer a la seva veu, el primer que ens crida l'atenció és que els xinesos no semblen apropiar-se de cap descoberta d'Amèrica.

Sens dubte algun xinès va ser el primer a arribar-hi. Tant se val de quan i de qui. I també, tant se val de si van trobar una ruta d'anada i tornada. Si hagués estat així, potser igual com passaria als nòrdics a la costa oposada del continent més descobert de la història, aquells territoris no els devien oferir massa res interessant que compensés els esforços d'enviar-hi navegants (una mica com amb Europa: si volen ja vindran). Així, una cosa és innegable quan parlem d'Amèrica del nord, i és que fins al segle XIX, el llunyà oest continuaria sent molt i molt llunyà, es vingués des d'on es vingués, i si hi hagués hagut riqueses hauria deixat de ser-ho. Però allà no hi havia res de bo: fins i tot Rússia es va desentendre d'Alaska el 1867 venent aquell vast territori per 7,2 milions de dòlars als Estats Units, poc abans que s'hi descobrís or i, més tard encara, petroli. Però els xinesos, fos quan fos que hi anessin (una o mil vegades), mai no van topar amb cap filó d'or, i en aquesta cursa pel podi dels grans descobriments només compta la riquesa.

A través de l'Atlàntic

Ara que ja ho sabem, potser no era tan difícil com això travessar l'Atlàntic. El 1896 els noruecs George Harbo i Frank Samuelsen es converteixen en els primers homes coneguts que travessen l'Atlàntic a rem, després de cinquanta-cinc dies fent la travessia entre Nova York i les illes Scilly, a la Gran Bretanya. També tant o més memorable es farà John Fairfax quan el 1969 es converteix en el primer a completar aquesta travessia a rem i en solitari, de les Canàries a Florida.

Però, per si algú volgués pensar que aquests agosarats remers no demostren res respecte a l'antiguitat perquè utilitzen embarcacions i coneixements que abans no eren accessibles, un cop més arriba Thor Heyerdahl per tornar a plantejar algunes coses que es donaven per inqüestionables.

Sembla que per a Heyerdahl l'important no és tant demostrar fets com plantejar possibilitats. No busca fets consumats, busca coses factibles. Així, el 1970 (amb Norman Baker, Carlo Mauri, Iuri Senkevitx, Santiago Genovés, Abdullah Djibrine i Georges Sourial) fa el recorregut entre Àfrica i Amèrica del sud a bord del *Ra II*, una petita embarcació feta amb totora. Tot i que l'any anterior ja ho havia intentat amb el *Ra*, de papir, i que l'expedició havia quedat en un intent frustrat, les dues *Ra* estaven construïdes amb materials i tècniques semblants com les que coneixien els antics egipcis. Com en altres expedicions de l'antropòleg noruec, això no demostra que aquest viatge s'hagués fet, sinó que en tot cas hauria sigut factible, i ens recorda una vegada més com l'Europa moderna té el costum de subestimar qualsevol ciència que no neixi en el seu món cultural i temporal proper. En qualsevol cas, el viatge del *Ra II* serviria per donar una possible explicació a qualsevol presència africana a les costes sud-americanes. I ja hi tornem a ser. ¿Podria ser, al final, que els europeus fossin els últims a descobrir Amèrica, i que l'últim continent descobert pels americans sigui Europa, petita i amagada en un raconet antipàtic del món, accessible només des de la costa nord-est de l'Atlàntic?

Però no, de moment, per tranquil·litat dels europeus medievals, descartarem els egipcis per falta de proves, igual com descartarem qualsevol altra cultura de l'antiguitat clàssica i anirem directament cap als que segur van travessar l'Atlàntic fins a les Amèriques. I els primers que sabem amb total certesa que se'n van sortir són, precisament, avantpassats dels nostres amics Heyerdahl, Harbo i Samuelsen: els vikings nòrdics.

Els vikings i Vinlàndia

I arribem a un dels moments més esperats de la història dels descobriments d'Amèrica. Si des de la nostra visió suposadament moderna i occidental algú pot fer ombra a Colom en aquesta cursa cap al «nou món», aquest és sens dubte Leif Eiríksson, amb el permís de Bjarni Herjolfsson, noms que a molta gent potser no els diuen res. Una altra cosa ben diferent és quan en comptes de noms propis parlem directament dels vikings. Aleshores sí que tothom afirma amb el cap, arrufant celles i morros, perquè ja se sap que els vikings van arribar a Amèrica abans que qualsevol altre europeu. El seu problema és que, una vegada més, els seus viatges no van transcendir prou clarament més enllà de la seva cultura, com un secret massa ben guardat.

Però el misteri viking no ens sorprendrà tant si tenim present les poques perspectives que tenia aquest nou territori per ells: remot, poc fèrtil i amb uns amfitrions hostils (fins i tot per als vikings). Sens dubte, aquells nòrdics no podien ni imaginar com era d'important la seva descoberta. Per a ells, que es van escampar per tot el món conegut i per conèixer, no era estrany descobrir que darrere d'una illa desconeguda n'hi havia una altra. Els seus descobriments de terres en la mar se succeïen un darrere l'altre, com una cosa tan natural com trobar llacs en terra ferma: les illes Fèroe, Islàndia, Grenlàndia, Vinlàndia (avui Terranova), Irlanda la Gran (que no Irlanda, sinó una mena de mítica terra promesa que hauria pogut ser Amèrica)... Així doncs, hi van arribar i en van tornar, i ben mirat sí que tenim els primers noms propis, noms que comencen a donar-nos més pistes de la descoberta europea del continent americà. Però fins i tot, com veurem, el campió dels vikings, Leif Eiríksson, haurà d'abaixar el cap davant d'altres precursors dels quals també tenim noms i dades precises.

Abans que res, per imaginar els nòrdics anant i tornant feliçment d'Amèrica, cal que els vegem com uns navegants fora de sèrie, amb tècniques i embarcacions molt perfeccionades que els permetien dirigir les naus a on volien, sense dependre només de vents o de corrents favorables. En això s'avancen de molt fins i tot als portuguesos del segle XV, grans dominadors de l'Atlàntic que durant molts segles encara continuaran depenent dels vents i dels corrents.

Aquest prodigi d'embarcacions nòrdiques, juntament amb la capacitat d'orientació d'aquesta gent que encara no utilitza ni brúixola ni mapes, és quasi un miracle del saber humà sota aquests cels sovint tapats on es fa difícil distingir la posició exacta del sol o de les estrelles. Evidentment, tenen eines per ubicar els astres, però també i sobretot els guia una cultura oral summament fiable, amb una memòria i capacitat per descriure costes i trajectes que converteixen els seus cervells en autèntics mapes mentals. Així com la seva cultura és oral, així com és oral la seva literatura, potser també els seus mapes són orals, i no per això menys útils o menys precisos que els utilitzats per altres pobles europeus d'aquells temps.

Gairebé n'hi ha prou d'observar qualsevol mapa europeu medieval i imaginar-se el que havia de significar fer-se a la mar refiant-se d'aquells documents. Imagineu-vos-ho. Feu-ho, imagineu-vos el mapa: es tracta d'un d'aquells mapes que avui veiem deformats per la dificultat de mesurar la longitud dels meridians, un mapa amb monstres marins i unes costes llegendàries que ningú que conegueu ha vist mai... Imagineu-vos ara que us fan embarcar cap a un Atlàntic desconegut en una embarcació de fusta i que us deixen triar entre dos capitans: el capità A, que té un d'aquests mapes medievals i confia cegament en aquell tros de paper que ha dibuixat un desconegut, o el capità B, que ha parlat amb un altre navegant de la seva confiança que ha fet el mateix recorregut un temps enrere i que, per tant, té la certesa que Grenlàndia és un país de verdor fèrtil i generosa. Amb quin dels dos us embarcareu...? Si teniu dubtes, imagineu-vos novament aquell tros de mapa amb monstres marins i penseu bé la resposta.

Plantem-nos ara a la Islàndia de, per exemple, el segle XIII. Siguem uns nens enmig de la desolació hivernal, passant les fosques setmanes a la vora del foc. Què farem? Aprendre a llegir i escriure, rellegir una vegada rere l'altra el llibre que conté la saga familiar, escoltar pares i avis com ens la reciten ja de memòria, i amb els anys, potser, ampliar-la també nosaltres i a poc a poc anar convertint la nostra cultura oral en una de les primeres cultures populars escrites d'Europa. Així, mentre la resta d'Europa s'esforça per mantenir els laics en la tenebra de la ignorància, Islàndia ensenya a llegir els seus fills durant els foscos hiverns a la vora del foc. Cap país no ha tingut mai abans tanta gent il·lustrada.

Nosaltres nens islandesos medievals, potser tindrem a casa, en pergamí o vitel·la, la *Saga d'Eirík el Roig* o la *Saga dels grenlandesos*, antics textos orals que amb els segles van saltar a la lletra escrita, i no dubtarem gens ni mica d'allò que expliquen. Però els europeus del futur què en diran? Desconfiats de mena, els del segle XXI necessiten alguna cosa més per creure'ns i els cal anar a textos erudits, com la *Gesta Hammaburgensis ecclesiae pontificum*, que un tal Adam de Bremen deixaria al voltant del 1075, o l'*Islendingabók* d'Ari Thorgilsson, més conegut amb el nom d'Ari l'Historiador o Ari el Savi, de cap a l'any 1127. I un cop revisats tots els llibres possibles, aquells del XXI poden encara anar fins al lloc a comprovar les coses palpant-les amb els dits. I aquí els tenim, els europeus del futur, mirant amb lupa els jaciments arqueològics de Terranova que demostren el pas dels nòrdics per aquí. I es miren uns als altres fent que sí amb el cap mentre de passada ens recorden que la paraula té un pes per a qui n'és mereixedor, que la cultura oral d'aquells primers islandesos és sòlida i fiable. I nosaltres, nens islandesos de segles enrere, els podrem dir «que no t'ho deia, jo?», i tornarem a enfonsar el nas a la nostra saga, al costat del nostre foc hivernal per tornar de nou a Vinlàndia amb els besavis.

Segons la *Saga d'Eirík el Roig*, Eirík Thorvaldsson el Roig s'ho passava tan bé tacant la seva espasa de sang humana que cap a l'any 985 va ser desterrat d'Islàndia i en va marxar i va endinsar-se mar enllà cap a l'oest. Això sol explicar-se com si res, però que un desterrat marxés així com així, cap a la immensitat desconeguda de l'Atlàntic nord, com a mínim hauria de fer-nos preguntar quants d'ells —desterrats o no— no devien sucumbir a tempestes, icebergs, naufragis, fred, inanició... Com sol passar, sempre hi ha algú que abans dona una pista, obre un camí, i en aquest cas Eirík senzillament es refiaria de la notícia donada per Gunbjorn Ulf-Krakason, un navegant que cap a la dècada del 920 s'havia extraviat a causa d'una tempesta i havia anat a parar davant d'una costa desconeguda. Ulf-Krakason de seguida es va adonar que havia passat de llarg en el seu camí de Noruega cap a Islàndia i va fer mitja volta per arribar a la seva destinació. De moment s'havia aplanat el camí per ocupar Grenlàndia, però durant molt de temps encara ningú no es preocuparia d'aquelles noves terres.

Pocs anys abans que Eirík emprengués la seva aventura grenlandesa, Snaebjorn Galti va intentar establir-s'hi sense èxit, però va acabar morint a mans de la seva pròpia tripulació, de manera que amb tot plegat el camí estava aplanat per al següent que ho intentés. Així, Eiríк el Roig navegaria cap a l'oest fins a topar, com esperava, amb una basta costa glaçada. Amb paciència, va anar resseguint aquella blancor desconeguda i solitària fins a trobar, ja a la costa occidental, un dels pocs racons no coberts de neu que hi devia haver en aquell tros de món oblidat. Allà va poder establir-se, refer la seva vida i fundar una colònia que ell va anomenar «Terra verda», Grenlàndia.

I vet aquí per què avui la Terra de Gel (Islàndia) és verda i la Terra Verda (Grenlàndia) és de gel. Essent potser una de les jugades propagandístiques més sonades de la història, el nom va servir de reclam per promoure un enclavament estable en aquell territori. Eirík el Roig de seguida va tornar a Islàndia a fer saber la seva troballa, i aviat se'n tornava cap al seu raconet verd amb vint-i-cinc vaixells, catorze dels quals sembla que van aconseguir arribar a Grenlàndia amb els primers quatre-cents europeus que s'establirien a l'illa.

No sabem quina cara devien fer aquells pioners en veure que la seva promesa de terra verda era d'un to tan pàl·lid que no es distingia del blanc. O bé Eirík era més salvatge del que ens podem imaginar, o bé aquells vikings eren més pacífics del que crèiem, però el cas és que la colònia va prosperar en aquell territori que de fet, segons la geografia física, ja és americà. Per tant podríem dir que Eirík el Roig hauria descobert Amèrica ja l'any 985, amb el permís de Galti que ja ho hauria fet la dècada anterior, i amb el permís de Gunbjorn Ulf-Krakason, que ja ho hauria fet cap al 925. Però com que tradicionalment s'ha considerat aquella Grenlàndia territori europeu, aquestes expedicions continuen sense entrar en els registres de descobriments d'Amèrica, i avui es considera Eirík el descobridor de Grenlàndia i el seu fill, Leif, el d'Amèrica.

No deixa de ser curiós que Colom, havent trepitjat només illes minúscules que no es poden comparar amb Grenlàndia ni de lluny, sigui considerat més descobridor d'Amèrica que Eirík el Roig. Però, per si amb el descobriment d'Eirík no n'hi hagués prou, quinze anys més tard el seu fill Leif Eiríksson s'embarcaria novament des de Grenlàndia encara més cap a l'est, on per naturalesa els nòrdics devien considerar que sempre hi havia més terres, qui sap si la tan desitjada Irlanda la Gran, i va anar a parar a unes costes, aquesta vegada sí, molt més fèrtils que Grenlàndia. Una costa que es podia seguir molt cap al sud, on el clima es feia més amable.

Sembla que això va passar l'any 1000. Però com se li va acudir a Leif endinsar-se cap a l'est si no en tenia cap necessitat especial? Tornem a enfonsar el nas a *La Saga dels grenlandesos* i fullejant-lo amb calma al llarg de l'hivern hi trobarem una pista que acostuma a passar desapercebuda en els llibres. Bjarni Herjolfsson era un comerciant escandinau que, en tornar a la seva llar familiar islandesa l'any 986, va ser informat que el seu pare s'havia embarcat amb Eirík el Roig cap a Grenlàndia. Aleshores, sense pensar-s'ho dues vegades es va fer a la mar per seguir les passes del seu progenitor. Però ja se sap que quan es viatja sense mapes en una zona desconeguda on les tempestes no perdonen, el més fàcil és perdre's, per molt viking que siguis, i això és el que va passar al nostre amic Bjarni i a la seva tripulació.

Quan la tempesta va amainar després de molts dies de navegació, van trobar-se davant d'una costa plena de boscos i turons. Curiosament, malgrat el nom verdós de la nova terra descoberta pel seu pare i companyia, i malgrat les insistències dels seus companys de viatge per baixar a terra ferma a refer-se de provisions, Bjarni Herjolfsson tenia clar que allò no podia ser Grenlàndia i va ordenar seguir la costa cap al nord. Dos dies més tard passaven per davant d'una altra costa que també descartarien trepitjar, i encara tres dies després trobarien una altra terra de muntanyes ja cobertes només de glaceres. Els estudiosos actuals especulen que aquestes tres costes vistes per Herjolfsson podrien ser respectivament Terranova, Labrador i Baffin, però aquella gent encara no ho sabia, així que Herjolfsson, veient que allò tampoc no era Grenlàndia, va decidir tornar enrere i al cap de quatre dies de navegació cap a l'est, ara sí, van topar amb una costa que coincidia amb la descripció que ell tenia de Grenlàndia, on naturalment es va retrobar amb el seu pare com si fos la cosa més normal del món.

Que Bjarni Herjolfsson arribés a Grenlàndia i anés a petar a casa del seu pare ho hem d'atribuir repartidament a la sort, a la perícia com a navegant, a les bones descripcions orals que es devien transmetre i a la seva tossuderia. Amb tot això, hem d'acceptar la simplificació del viatge que ens en fan les sagues, ja que si el seu viatge va ser realment així, no devia estar exempt de peripècies que avui signarien els millors cineastes d'aventures. O potser no, ja que en tot moment es va negar a trepitjar cap d'aquelles terres desconegudes, cosa que devia convertir el primer viatge europeu a Amèrica en una cosa summament avorrida. Però fos com fos, encara que Herjolfsson no trepitgés pròpiament sòl americà, sí que se'l pot considerar descobridor abans que Leif Eiríksson, si més no un semidescobridor que va desaprofitar una ocasió d'or, cosa que el seu entorn no va entendre mai. Tant és així que quinze anys després Leif Eiríksson compraria el vaixell de Herjolfsson per embarcar-se cap a la seva descoberta americana. Per tant, aquesta vegada sí que hem trobat un predescobridor amb nom i cognom, i quan Leif Eiríksson s'embarca cap a la descoberta d'Amèrica té molt clar on va. Mentre el nostre amic Leif, fill d'Eirík, fa el seu primer viatge cap al seu descobriment d'Amèrica, el vaixell que l'hi porta ja hi va per segona vegada. I qui sap si també algun dels seus trenta-cinc tripulants i tot.

Probablement Leif Eiríksson va seguir una ruta semblant a la del seu predecessor en aquelles aigües, batejant terres amb els noms de Helluland («Terra de pedres planes»), Markland («Terra de boscos») i Vinland («Terra de vi») tal com les anava trobant de nord a sud. Tot indica que podrien ser el que avui es coneix com l'illa de Baffin, Labrador i Terranova.

Així, encara que descoberta per Bjarni Herjolfsson, és amb Leif Eiríksson quan podem començar a parlar dels primers assentaments europeus a Amèrica. Com podem suposar, més fèrtil que Grenlàndia ho és qualsevol estepa coberta de la tundra més severa, fins i tot la majoria de deserts ho són, però per a algú avesat a Grenlàndia, la més meridional d'aquestes terres devia ser directament un jardí de possibilitats infinites que Eiríksson va anomenar «Terra de vi».

Ja veiem que eren gent imaginativa amb els noms. Sembla que aquesta vegada la inspiració va arribar per algun fruit silvestre que hi van trobar, semblant al raïm. Però, ¿coneixien aquest fruit aquells nòrdics i els nens islandesos que llegien sagues els hiverns a la vora del foc? No sabem ben bé quina planta van trobar, però per si de cas, la *Saga dels grenlandesos* ens explica que un tripulant alemany anomenat Tyrkir va descobrir els fruits tot assegurant que es tractava de raïm, i que ho sabia perquè en el seu país n'hi havia. Fos el que fos, segur que era alguna mena de fruita silvestre dolça, fàcil de fermentar i de convertir en licor. Perquè el raïm potser no el coneixien, aquells homes dels mars glaçats del nord, però el vi és indubtable que també els arribava. I segur que el celebraven com nosaltres, que només veure'l aparèixer ja ens trobem badant amb aquesta fruita. I mentre brindaríem amb ells per la troballa, gairebé ens passaria per alt un detall important: la sorpresa de trobar un alemany a Amèrica del nord a l'any 1000. Tyrkir.

Així, en aquell lloc de l'actual Terranova, a l'any 1000, se suposa que es va produir l'enèsim descobriment americà que no portaria gaire enlloc. Qui ho sap, potser si hagués transcendit, Terranova també seria avui un territori considerat tan europeu com Grenlàndia o com Islàndia, que en realitat es troba a cavall entre les dues plaques continentals. Segurament qualsevol de les illes que circumden Amèrica pel nord, com l'illa de Baffin o de Victoria per citar les més destacables, ens serien una evidentíssima porció d'Europa, i Amèrica només començaria un cop se'n trepitja la part continental. ¿Per què sinó Grenlàndia és encara avui Europa per a la majoria? Per descomptat és un tema més cultural i polític que no pas físic. Exactament igual al fet que totes les illes del Mediterrani siguin europees, rarament asiàtiques o africanes. Tan difícil és a vegades establir fronteres que en el fons aquest tros de terra islandesa on va néixer el primer descobridor europeu d'Amèrica ja és físicament a Amèrica, en la placa americana.

En tot cas, per no barallar-nos amb gaire gent i no anar al Valhalla abans d'hora, començarem acceptant l'any 1000, Leif Eiríksson i Terranova com el descobriment nòrdic d'Amèrica. I a partir d'aquí, allò de sempre per a aquests homes: continuar avançant. Segons les dues sagues que en parlen, aquells navegants haurien pogut resseguir la costa nord-americana cap al sud, fins als 41 o 42 graus de latitud nord, a les proximitats de l'actual Nova York. Però tot plegat són incursions estèrils de límits incerts que només podem suposar a partir de la vegetació que descriuen.

Com sempre, de seguida que van arribar notícies de la nova descoberta, i novament amb un nom tan llaminer, hi va haver diverses expedicions disposades a provar sort a Vinlàndia. Entre elles trobem la de l'islandès Thorfinn Karlsefni, el qual aviat intenta establir-hi una colònia i se n'hi va amb seixanta tripulants, entre ells cinc dones. Allà, en algun moment entre el 1005 i el 1013, la seva esposa Gudrid Thorbjarnardóttir donarà a llum Snorri Thorfinnsson, el primer americà d'origen europeu (o el primer europeu nascut a Amèrica, com es vulgui), títol que només pot ostentar una persona en tota la història de la humanitat, i de la qual tenim la sort de conservar el nom i una vida força documentada. I si això no és un descobriment d'Amèrica ben consolidat, ja podem plegar tots.

Diverses expedicions nòrdiques van explorar el nou país en diferents direccions, fins i tot terra endins. Malgrat tot, l'únic que en sabem del cert és la seva presència a Terranova i com a molt a la península de Labrador i a l'illa de Baffin. Encara que els nòrdics no s'hi van establir de manera estable, hi ha raons per pensar que es van mantenir contactes amb aquells territoris durant força temps. Però de vegades la memòria ens arriba amb llacunes. Coneixem l'afició dels islandesos a les sagues familiars que s'explicaven de generació en generació a la vora del foc durant aquelles interminables nits boreals, però deixar constància de la rutina diària els devia fer més mandra, i un cop explicada l'èpica dels orígens, la resta, potser per quotidiana, ja no ens arriba de la mateixa manera i ens hem de limitar a fonts més esporàdiques. Així, podem entendre que Vinlàndia no desapareix mai de l'imaginari nòrdic d'aquelles latituds, i que el contacte, encara que feble, es manté.

En aquell món d'illes perdudes i mars sòlids, ningú no té clar què és un continent, i encara que sigui d'una manera difusa Vinlàndia continua formant part de la realitat d'islandesos i grenlandesos. Com a mostra, el fet que el 1347 es documenti l'arribada a Islàndia d'un vaixell carregat de fusta de Markland (suposadament l'actual Labrador) que s'havia extraviat en el seu camí cap a Grenlàndia. Ben mirat, és raonable que la reduïda població grenlandesa pogués trobar els recursos més propers de fusta i terra fèrtil a la desconeguda terra occidental molt més fàcilment que no pas a la llunyana Europa. O sigui que Vinlàndia segueix allà, sabuda i descoberta encara que només sigui per una qüestió pràctica, no pas perquè allò sigui una mina. Durant segles aquella terra serà, fins i tot per als grenlandesos, un lloc remot on anar segurament fastiguejat a resoldre alguna manca de recursos. Res de què fer-ne bandera a la resta del món.

Com és raonable pensar, els establiments esporàdics dels nòrdics en aquelles terres van permetre els primers contactes entre pobles europeus i americans, alguns amb èxit, altres, intents fracassats gràcies a la base guerrera de tots plegats. Encara sort que tenim les sagues que ens en parlen, però ens queda lamentar que se'ns escapin detalls que podrien ser-nos deliciosos. Agafem com a exemple l'experiència de Thorvald, germà de Leif, que, explorant un territori on establir-se, va topar amb uns habitants del lloc als quals va saludar matant-los tots menys un, que va fugir i va tornar amb prou reforços per matar Thorvald i aconseguir que la resta de la seva tripulació carregués tot el raïm possible a correcuita i s'embarqués precipitadament de tornada cap a Grenlàndia.

Mirem-nos-ho des de l'altra perspectiva: ara soc un indígena americà que passeja feliçment pel bosc amb uns companys de la tribu, a veure si cacem alguna cosa per menjar. De sobte veiem aparèixer, com si fos un extraterrestre, un homenot pelut cobert de pells que, a manera de salutació, mata tots els meus companys a cops de destral i cridant com si m'hagués de disparar directament contra els budells i travessar-me l'abdomen. Davant d'aquesta inesperada carnisseria, marxo corrent amb les cames fetes un flam fins que arribo al poblat on intento fer-me entendre tot quequejant i tremolant. O no, potser resulta que no quequejo ni tremolo, potser passa que aleshores, com que no sabem que aquella bèstia ferotge és un temible viking, sinó que simplement s'ha limitat a matar els meus companys a queixalades i a cops d'espasa, ens armem empipats per aquesta situació tan molesta, ens hi arribem i el matem, fent que els seus companys s'espantin tant que carreguen el vaixell de raïm i fugen de pet cap a Grenlàndia amb els culs cagats per no tornar mai més.

Ara tornem a ser nosaltres altre cop i no ens sabem imaginar què devien fer aquells indis americans al pobret Thorvald.

Ni com devia ser de bo aquell raïm.

Anècdotes simpàtiques a banda, amb els nòrdics ha arribat el primer contacte documentat entre europeus i americans, que no sempre és violent malgrat les escasses habilitats socials que de vegades es mostren entre uns i altres.

Dels nòrdics al segle XV

A mesura que avancen els segles i anem deixant els nòrdics enrere, cada cop és més fàcil trobar suposats descobridors dels quals se sap poc o res i que potser només ens interessaran per poder-los descartar. Un dels primers que trobarem en aquesta llista es diu Abu-Bakr II. Alguns estudiosos parlen d'un possible viatge per explorar l'Atlàntic que hauria portat aquest emperador malinès a les costes del Brasil cap a l'any 1312, però del qual no hauria tornat mai. I ja hi som: per parlar d'un territori, ens cal algú que en torni, i l'opinió més general no és simplement que Abu-Bakr II no tornés, sinó que aquest viatge ni tan sols no es va fer mai.

Alguns historiadors també han volgut suposar que els germans Ugolino i Vadino Vivaldi haurien pogut arribar a Amèrica després de perdre's de vista per sempre més el 1291 a l'Atlàntic, buscant les Índies. Probablement el viatge dels Vivaldi és un dels precedents més semblants al de Colom. Quan totes les rutes cap a les Índies passaven pel nord d'Àfrica, la petita flota dels Vivaldi seria una de les primeres a buscar una alternativa per l'Àfrica Occidental. El que no queda clar és si, després de ser vistos per darrera vegada, volien descobrir un pas aleshores inimaginat pel sud d'Àfrica o si volien fer la volta cap a l'oest. Tenint en compte que en aquell temps la rodonesa de la Terra no era cap misteri, i que en canvi no se sabia si l'Atlàntic era obert al sud d'Àfrica, l'alternativa «americana» podia semblar gairebé més factible que trobar un inimaginat cap de Bona Esperança. Però tot són elucubracions que no porten enlloc, i no es pot negar res ni tampoc sobretot no es pot afirmar res del destí dels Vivaldi i companyia.

Altres autors han indicat també que els baleners bascos haurien pogut arribar cap al 1375 a Terranova o a Labrador. És cert que els baleners sempre tindrien motius per no revelar els llocs on més abundés la seva presa, i sens dubte sempre hi haurà descobridors seguint-los el solc arreu del món, de vegades fins i tot sense saber-ho i plantant banderes en terres desconegudes però trepitjades ja per compatriotes baleners. Tant de bo aquí es pogués obrir aquesta porta i posar noms als que han obert aquests camins; però sense més certeses, la versemblança sola no serveix per construir un relat històric, sinó només per qüestionar gratuïtament allò establert i, com a molt, concedir a l'historiador de torn una medalla que ja no podrà penjar-se l'autèntic descobridor. Ara mateix, doncs, no es pot parlar amb certesa de baleners bascos.

També hi ha qui defensa que el 1487 Vaz da Cunha va fer un mapa de les costes del Brasil, i que el mateix any ho va fer també Fernandes de Andrade. Primer de tot hauria de sorprendre que el mateix rei portuguès enviés dos exploradors per separat a la vegada a un lloc que ni se sabia que existís... ¿O sí que se sabia i per alguna raó els que ho sabien s'estimaven més callar-ho? Portugal, en aquell temps, ha començat a agafar el vici d'explorar aigües que per dret internacional no li pertoquen, i de vegades ha d'amagar alguns descobriments, però en tot cas sorprèn la poca incidència d'una fita tan destacada, i el fet que gairebé no se'n parli fa pensar que aquests mapes de 1487 són una invenció més en la cursa per comprar l'entrada número u a Amèrica. És cert que hi havia expedicions secretes, i també que es conserven pocs mapes portuguesos amb els seus descobriments del segle xv, ja que molts desapareixen amb el terratrèmol de Lisboa de 1755. Així, els mapes de l'època que mostren les costes explorades pels portuguesos solen ser còpies posteriors provinents d'altres ciutats europees. I ja ens trobem de cop en el fangós terreny de la reproducció i la còpia, i de nou, malgrat el domini atlàntic incontestable d'aquells portuguesos, no es pot negar res, però tampoc no es pot afirmar res.

També els francesos han intentat participar en la lliga americana gràcies al normand Jean Cousin, que hauria trepitjat el Brasil el 1488. ¿Es tracta també d'una possible invenció francesa per reclamar el Brasil? Sembla evident que sí, però per si de cas, en el seu moment, des de França també es va assegurar que nàufrags d'aquest país haurien arribat a les costes americanes el 1491. ¿I com ho saben? ¿I per què francesos sí i d'altres països no? ¿I per què només tan poc abans del 1492?...

I podríem continuar la llista de possibles descobriments que tenen poca credibilitat...

...Així que anem a parts i mirem d'anar entrant a poc a poc a aquest oceà Atlàntic, procurant sempre saber on som per poder tornar a casa quan ens interessi. Per fer això, primer de tot ens caldrà parlar de la *volta do mar*, una tècnica de navegació que descobreixen (o inventen) els portuguesos i que permet als navegants que van cap a les costes africanes tornar a la península Ibèrica. El secret consisteix a endinsar-se oceà endins direcció nord, de manera que a determinada latitud els corrents i els vents de l'oest et tornen més fàcilment cap a Portugal. Això és el que facilitaria primer de tot la descoberta de les Açores.

A diferència dels vells nòrdics, els portuguesos i en general els europeus del segle XV encara depenen dels vents i dels corrents per dirigir les seves naus. És per això que travessar les aigües somes de l'equador encara és un repte difícil a l'abast de pocs navegants, i per això també l'Atlàntic sud continuarà sent una assignatura pendent fins que no se superi aquest obstacle equatorial. Per tant, mentre no es milloren certes tècniques de navegació, tot el que poden fer els portuguesos és deixar-se portar per aquests corrents circulars tan divertits de l'Atlàntic nord com qui puja a uns cavallets de fira amb parada obligatòria a les Açores.

I malgrat tot, és curiosa la poca importància que se sol donar al descobriment d'aquestes illes, com si fos natural trobar un arxipèlag de dimensions tan reduïdes enmig d'un oceà com l'Atlàntic, aparentment tan inexplorat. I segurament no és per ganes de no donar importància a la descoberta de les Açores, sinó per la dificultat de situar la fita en una data concreta.

Amb tot, en aquell segle XV Amèrica és cada dia més a prop. Ja només és qüestió de temps i de sort. Portugal envia vaixells cada cop més enllà. Topa amb les Açores, i des d'aquí pot temptejar encara més i més enllà. Però sense haver recollit encara les tècniques que havien dut els nòrdics a dominar totes les aigües a plaer, les expedicions portugueses cap a l'oest sovint són retornades pels vents. Malgrat tot, insisteixen a perseguir illes de mite en mite. Només a tall d'exemple, el 1486 el portuguès d'origen flamenc Ferdinand van Olmen és enviat cap a l'oest des de l'illa Terceira, a la recerca de la mítica illa de les Set Ciutats. Més enllà d'aquesta ordre, poc se sap si Van Olmen va salpar realment, si va tornar rebutjat també pels vents, si va arribar a algun lloc del qual més valia no parlar... I vet aquí potser el silenci portuguès. Però sigui com sigui, al segle XV, sí, Portugal envia vaixells cap a l'oest.

Un dels artífexs de l'exploració portuguesa a l'Atlàntic va ser l'infant Enric el Navegant (1394-1460), que més que descobrir es va esforçar a promoure l'exploració portuguesa de l'Atlàntic. A partir d'aquí comencem a trobar noms destacats com el de Diogo de Silves, considerat el descobridor de les Açores el 1427, tot i que no sembla fàcil resoldre la controvèrsia dels mapes que ja dibuixen aquestes illes i Madeira al segle XIV. Madeira, considerada descoberta el 1418, ja apareix en un mapa del 1339 conservat avui, i les Açores hi comencen a aparèixer a partir del 1351. De vegades és difícil identificar les fonts dels mapes medievals, i en casos com aquests fins i tot podria tractar-se de territoris llegendaris com l'illa de sant Brandan.

Estirem aquest fil? Segons la llegenda, Brandan era un monjo irlandès que al segle VI va emprendre un viatge per mar a la recerca del paradís terrenal, i durant el seu periple per l'Atlàntic hauria trobat, entre altres llocs d'absoluta fantasia dignes del millor baró de Munchhausen, aquesta misteriosa illa-balena que apareix i desapareix, i que ningú no aconsegueix ubicar en cap lloc concret. Encara que la primera font escrita que trobem d'aquest meravellós viatge data del segle IX, és creïble que alguns cartògrafs medievals pensessin que existia i la ubiquessin en algun lloc de l'Atlàntic, fent que després qui més qui menys se la volgués apropiar: Les Canàries? Les Açores? Les Fèroe? Islàndia? Grenlàndia? Terranova? Florida?

Al més pur estil Heyerdahl, entre el 1976 i el 1977 l'historiador i aventurer Tim Severin va construir un *currach* de cuir com el que hauria utilitzat el monjo irlandès del segle VI i va fer el recorregut des d'Irlanda cap a Terranova, intentant identificar els diferents territoris que la fantasia narrativa havia convertit en impossibles (les Fèroe, Islàndia, Grenlàndia i Terranova). Així, Severin demostrava que el viatge des d'Irlanda fins a Amèrica en un *currach* de cuir i amb tècniques pròpies del segle VI era factible, però igual com en altres casos semblants, aquests viatges fascinants bàsicament obren la porta a demostrar la possibilitat d'un viatge, però no són suficients per dir que aquell Brandan va trepitjar Amèrica.

Com que, malgrat els avenços tecnològics, la fantasia entre els exploradors per explicar com era el món arriba fins al segle XVII, és fàcil entendre que per a la mentalitat cristiana medieval que creia en miracles aquesta illa podria haver existit. Avui, la llegenda de sant Brandan òbviament no té cap credibilitat, però tant si els mapes medievals dibuixaven illes a l'Atlàntic influïts per llegendes com si ho feien gràcies a descobriments poc difosos, els britànics podrien haver aprofitat l'avinentesa d'aquest sant irlandès per reclamar un possible descobriment d'Amèrica molt abans que Colom.

Els defensors d'aquest mite troben una mica de suport de l'arribada irlandesa a Amèrica en una llegenda del poble Shawnee que situa a Florida una tribu d'homes blancs vestits de llarg i que coneixien el ferro. El que no sembla clar és fins a quin punt, una vegada més, no hi ha una manipulació del recurs de les llegendes: ¿Existeix realment aquesta llegenda shawnee des del segle VI? Si fos així, ¿com es pot transmetre un relat que parla d'un material desconegut? ¿Com es pot parlar del ferro en l'idioma d'una societat que no el coneix? No seria estrany que tota referència en aquest sentit nasqués amb l'arribada ja consolidada dels europeus a Amèrica, o en el millor dels casos en la reinterpretació de mites més antics. Un cop més, qui ho pot saber? Res de tot plegat no fa factibles les fantasies relatades tres segles després del suposat mite de sant Brandan.

Per tant, sembla que el camí irlandès només ens porta a explicar que alguns cartògrafs medievals van donar per certa la llegenda de sant Brandan i van dibuixar unes illes a l'Atlàntic sense que ningú les hagués vist abans. O sigui que es refiaven de fonts errònies i que dibuixaven unes illes que només hi eren per casualitat. Però com sempre, la lectura a posteriori de la història és molt còmoda, i si les Açores no haguessin existit, alguns dirien que els mapes del segle XIV ja dibuixaven Amèrica. En qualsevol cas, el viatge de Brandan, amb tot el que tingui de cert o de fals, va ser donat per autèntic i per tant devia obrir portes a l'exploració de l'Atlàntic amb el convenciment que hi havia terres noves per trobar.

Tornem doncs on érem. La *volta do mar*, les Açores, informacions imprecises... Tot això no arriba sol en un món d'exploracions basades en la delicada tècnica d'assaig-error. Per molt inevitable que sigui topar amb les Açores seguint els vents i corrents atlàntics, als segles XIV i XV ningú no es llança al mar obert sense més ni més i torna amb unes illes cartografiades sota el braç com qui no vol la cosa. Descobrir la *volta do mar*, tan antinatural com sembla, devia tenir sens dubte un preu molt alt en vides. La *volta do mar* bàsicament són uns corrents que permeten vorejar el mar dels Sargassos, regió que ocupa una gran franja de l'Atlàntic. Aquests corrents circulars permeten apropar-se cap a les Bermudes pel sud i cap a Portugal pel nord. Colom mateix va seguir aquests corrents del mar dels Sargassos en el seu famós viatge, però no va ser el primer a navegar per aquesta regió de l'Atlàntic, sinó que seguia pistes que algú li havia donat: els navegants portuguesos.

El mar dels Sargassos i la *volta do mar*, sense tenir un nom propi ni una data, podem estar segurs que han estat descoberts a base d'intents, d'extraviaments, de naufragis... Podríem imaginar una explicació del tipus «algú que tornava de les costes africanes va topar amb un camí de tornada a casa absolutament antinatural i més fàcil». Sense més ni més sembla una explicació massa innocent. Més aviat l'explicació hauria de ser del tipus: «algú va topar amb uns corrents que el van llançar cap a l'interior de l'Atlàntic. Algú altre també. I alguns més. De tots aquells, algú va trobar la manera de tornar; altres no van trepitjar terra mai més; algú, potser, va veure una terra d'on no va poder tornar mai més». Podem estar segurs que alguns mariners extraviats han d'haver pogut arribar a Amèrica en un d'aquells descobriments sense retorn. Però descobriments al cap i a la fi. Si fos així, els americans (els Shawnees o qui sigui) haurien descobert els europeus abans que a Europa se sabés que hi havia un continent americà.

De fet és així fins i tot amb Cristòfor Colom i John Cabot: els europeus trigaran un temps a saber que allò que han descobert és un nou món, però els americans ho tenen claríssim des del moment que veuen aparèixer una vela a l'horitzó: hi ha un territori inexplorat a l'altra banda del mar.

Cabot i Colom

A poc a poc ens anem acostant a la història més coneguda de totes, al segle XV del gran campió Colom i dels seus rivals més directes. Un d'ells és John Cabot, navegant venecià —possiblement d'origen genovès o català— contractat per Enric VII d'Anglaterra perquè comenci a explorar tots els racons possibles de l'Atlàntic nord i planti la seva bandera a tot arreu on pugui. La rivalitat amb Colom és molt més que directa, ja que en aquella època Anglaterra sap que Colom ha arribat a les Índies i els anglesos volen mantenir-se en la cursa; per tant, sembla raonable dir que Cabot perd la partida abans de començar. A priori sembla que comença tard i derrotat. Però...

...Però és que si ens posem exigents com ens agrada, avui sabem que Colom no va posar pròpiament els peus al continent americà, sinó en illes properes. I si ho va fer, va ser més tard que Cabot, l'home que va trepitjar Amèrica del Nord el 1497 i en va tornar per donar comptes al rei d'Anglaterra. Vet aquí per què els anglesos van poder reclamar aquells territoris que avui són el Canadà i els Estats Units.

És cert que el punt de partida d'Enric VII és la presumpció que els castellans han arribat a les Índies, i sabent això s'espavila de seguida a buscar algú que li ofereixi una ruta encara més ràpida, inevitablement pel nord. Sense saber-ho encara, aquest serà el primer cop que algú es planteja trobar el famós pas del nord-oest. Així, el 1496 Cabot ja emprèn una primera expedició que no passa d'Islàndia, punt des del qual ha de fer mitja volta per problemes amb la tripulació. Però tot just l'any següent durà a terme l'expedició que li donarà el reconeixement més important. El maig de 1497, salpa de Bristol a bord del *Matthew*, i en només cinquanta-dos dies de navegació, el 24 de juny d'aquell mateix any (el dia del seu sant, supera això, Cristòfor!), es planta a les costes d'Amèrica del Nord, més o menys a les proximitats del riu Saint Lawrence. Es fa difícil precisar en quin punt exactament, segurament Labrador o Nova Escòcia, però el que sí que sabem del cert és que en aquells dies, Cabot es passeja per la costa americana, això sí, convençut també d'haver arribat al Japó, un país que cap europeu encara no ha trepitjat mai.

No és gaire exagerat dir que Colom primer (i els que el segueixen) i Cabot després són els primers europeus que creuen haver estat al Japó... i sense trobar ni un sol japonès. En aquest sentit, des de la nostra privilegiada i abusiva perspectiva històrica, Cabot fa un ridícul semblant al de Colom quan converteix el nostre planeta en una cosa minúscula, com si volguéssim jugar a tenis amb una pilota de ping-pong. Però encara que el seu descobriment es deu en gran part a l'encara suposat èxit de Colom, Cabot sí que passeja pel continent; també sense saber-ho, però hi passeja i en torna ben satisfet lluint ormejos de pesca locals que demostren que allà on ha anat hi ha algú, i de passada porta la notícia d'haver trobat una quantitat ingent de bacallà. Tant, diu, que s'hi pot caminar per sobre i tot. Com sempre, aquesta és una informació que pretén ser un reclam i a la vegada una medalla per penjar-se davant del rei. Segurament res massa sorprenent per als islandesos i grenlandesos d'aquelles èpoques, però en cap cas no hi ha constància que Cabot clavés la bandera britànica damunt del llom de cap bacallà.

L'any següent, el 1498, Cabot es tornarà a embarcar cap als territoris explorats, però aquesta vegada, un cop desapareix més enllà de l'horitzó europeu, el navegant sembla fondre's en la bromera de la història i no en tornem a saber res més. La història no ens deixa clar si aquest últim és un viatge sense retorn, però sigui com sigui, amb tota certesa també Cabot acabarà els seus dies sense saber que ha descobert un nou continent, sense saber que després dels nòrdics ha sigut el primer europeu a tornar a Europa havent posat els peus en el continent americà.

Amb tot plegat, el 1492 Colom encara no ha trepitjat terra continental americana, sinó només algunes illes (que de fet són, no ho qüestionarem, tan americanes com el continent), però no deixa de ser un detall interessant sobretot quan, com veurem de seguida, per a Colom i la seva reputació era d'una importància crucial trepitjar pròpiament terres continentals... asiàtiques.

I aquí ve la jugada del partit. Si realment Colom trepitja terres continentals americanes, això no succeeix fins al 1498, un any després que Cabot. En aquell any pot ser que Colom ja no trepitgi només illes, però els seus deliris de grandesa s'interposen entre ell i nosaltres, i comencem a no poder-nos-el creure del tot: per si de cas, quan arriba a Cuba fa jurar a tota la tripulació que allò que han trepitjat és una península connectada al continent asiàtic. Què ens podem creure doncs de qualsevol gesta que s'autoatribueixi el mateix Colom tot seguit?

Cal no oblidar que els exploradors europeus busquen un camí cap a les Índies, no nous territoris que n'impedeixin l'arribada. La lluita entre Cabot i Colom no és per res més que per obrir una nova ruta de comerç, i per això Colom insisteix tant que Cuba no és una nova illa, sinó una península asiàtica.

En qualsevol apropament mínimament crític al personatge, de seguida es troba una tendència als deliris de grandesa d'un navegant que va viatjar prou ben acompanyat, amb una tripulació prou eficient i fidel per permetre-li entrar a la història deixant passar desapercebuts detalls importants com ara que, entre altres coses, no sabia fer anar correctament el quadrant, segons opinen alguns autors que n'han estudiat les cartes nàutiques. Altres més tradicionals, en canvi, asseguren que Colom era un autèntic crac de la navegació i que es va avançar al seu temps per tal com va preveure una ruta perfecta tant d'anada com de tornada. Un cop més, o té una pista prèvia (detall important a tenir en compte) o hi ha un cop de sort i és, de tots els que s'han llançat al mar durant els segles XIV i XV, el que ha anat a parar al camí adequat tant d'anada com de tornada.

Tampoc no ens alarmarem ara ni li traurem tants mèrits com això. En aquells temps, de navegants brillants n'hi havia molts. Molts de brillants al fons del mar i molts de mediocres ancorant a port segur dia rere dia. Colom, sense entrar gaire més en la seva habilitat com a mariner, va ser sobretot un navegant amb sort (que també demana saber-ne), un navegant que continuarà ofuscat amb els seus aires de grandesa, però que mai més tornarà del nou món amb res de valor que superi les mostres d'or que va portar del primer viatge: aquella miqueta de metall inútil que va canviar la història del món, ben bé com si uns descobridors extraterrestres del nostre planeta hi trobessin plàstic i aquest material fos per a ells prou valuós per arrasar la Terra en cerca de les seves mines.

Notícies d'Ultramar

Bromes a banda —l'humor és una cosa molt seriosa—, no ens enganyarem: anar fins a Amèrica i tornar-ne sense saber que existeix té un punt de sort, però també has de saber el que fas. Hi ha turistes del segle XXI que encara tenen problemes per sortir-se'n amb mapes interactius i tot. Així, potser Colom i Cabot no són dos imprevisibles qualssevol. Sens dubte abans dels seus descobriments ja es plantegen quina via atlàntica cap a les Índies serà més factible. Mentre Cabot aposta per la via nòrdica amb l'argument que allà els paral·lels són més curts, Colom opta per la del sud, potser per haver temptejat ja la del nord sense èxit.

El 1495, en una carta als reis catòlics, Colom explica que el 1477 ja havia viatjat a Islàndia i havia navegat fins a cent llegües més a l'oest d'aquella illa. Hi ha qui insinua que ja aleshores hauria pogut arribar a les costes de Terranova, pensant que allò era el Japó. Però si fem cas del que ell mateix deixa escrit, com a molt devia navegar aigües endins per tornar cap a Islàndia d'alguna manera; i si hagués tocat alguna terra més enllà d'Islàndia, havent navegat cent llegües no podria ser cap altre lloc que Grenlàndia.

En qualsevol cas, si Colom va ser a Islàndia abans del seu famós viatge, potser sí que hauria sentit parlar dels vikings, de les sagues, de terres més a l'oest, qui sap si de Vinlàndia i tot... Però si en aquell món Colom va sentir parlar d'aquestes costes allunyades Reykjavík enllà, no seria l'únic. Les seves orelles eren com les de tothom; això sí que no cal demostrar-ho. I és a Islàndia, estirant el fil d'aquesta via nòrdica en què es debaten Cabot i Colom, on trobem un altre nou candidat que alguns reclamen com a presumpte descobridor d'Amèrica: Didrik Pining, un alemany que en una expedició danes o portuguesa suposadament hauria arribat a aquelles terres entre el 1470 i el 1476, acompanyat del també alemany Hans Pothorst, el portuguès Joao Vaz Corte-Real i un misteriós Johannes Scolvus que alguns han volgut relacionar amb Colom mateix però del qual no se sap res.

El problema de Pining és que ni tan sols hi ha dades segures sobre la seva expedició. Els primers documents que ens en parlen són fragmentaris i del segle XVI, quan ja massa impostors s'han apuntat al carro i no hi ha credibilitat per a ningú més. La seva expedició tant podria haver existit com ser una invenció molt ben travada i versemblant. Segons les fonts més fiables, aquesta expedició hauria arribat a una costa que alguns han volgut identificar amb Terranova, cosa que posaria també danesos i alemanys en la cursa americana. Però com tants altres, aquests es posen a jugar el partit quan la resta de jugadors ja s'estan dutxant, i els defensors de Pining no poden fer més que jugar a la versemblança: potser sí que va existir aquesta expedició, i potser sí que va arribar a Amèrica, però assegurar-ho seria fer pseudohistòria; per tant, en cap cas sembla que Pining i companyia tinguin opcions d'entrar en la lluita pel podi americà del segle XV, i sense proves concloents, si la seva expedició va existir, el seu és un descobriment no homologat.

També podria ser que aquesta expedició hagués existit realment i que senzillament hagués arribat a Grenlàndia, però no necessàriament més enllà. En aquell moment les colònies grenlandeses estaven abandonades. A principis de segle XV els gels havien avançat cap al sud, i entre el fred i els pobles inuits que havien seguit la línia del gel, els colons feia temps que havien deixat l'illa. Així que qui sap si Pining hauria redescobert Grenlàndia, convertint-se potser, això sí, en una bona font d'inspiració per a Cabot i Colom.

Així doncs, malgrat els molts candidats que haurien pogut obrir-los camí, els únics navegants del segle XV que sabem del cert que troben Amèrica cadascun pel seu costat continuen essent Cristòfor Colom i... Pedro Álvares Cabral (aviat el coneixerem). I, potser també encara, John Cabot. Però encara que aquella expedició danesa no toqués Amèrica, sí que mereix un accèssit com qualsevol altra de les que han obert camí Atlàntic enllà. Real o no, si se'n parlava bé podia donar idees.

Però no s'acaba encara el reguitzell d'expedicions que podrien haver inspirat l'aventura de Colom. Encara en trobarem una altra a les Açores, en la mateixa època en què el famós almirall es dedicava al comerç entre Islàndia i Àfrica.

Segons la llegenda, en aquells temps una caravel·la castellana s'hauria vist sorpresa per una tempesta a l'Atlàntic i hauria anat a parar a una illa caribenya. Allà, la tripulació hauria pogut reparar la nau per reprendre el camí de tornada cap a Europa. Retornats per fi a les Açores o a Madeira, moririen tots els supervivents, però l'últim encara tindria temps d'explicar la descoberta a Colom, que amb el secret ben guardat començaria a buscar finançament per a la seva aventura.

Entre la diversitat de versions d'aquesta llegenda, el nom que més fortuna ha fet com a predescobridor i informador de Colom és el d'Alonso Sánchez de Huelva, citat per primera vegada el 1609 per l'historiador peruà Inca Garcilaso de la Vega, que cent anys després dels fets, diu recordar que de petit havia sentit comentar que els vells parlaven de... I així ens perdem en una memòria indocumentable, amb aquest cronista que —mor oficialment el mateix dia i any que Shakespeare i Cervantes— viurà un segle després del descobriment. Massa temps per a una cultura que ja té tant de suport en el paper escrit.

Certament es pot pensar que al segle XV altres europeus han navegat per costes americanes. El setembre de 1492, la famosa expedició castellana ja troba restes d'un pal major a les proximitats del Carib (si Colom hagués naufragat, tampoc no en sabríem ni mitja paraula); i al cap d'un mes, ja explorant les primeres illes que han trobat, alguns mariners asseguren haver vist algú amb una moneda d'or amb lletres, objecte de possible origen europeu. Res demostrable, com sempre, però en tot cas, tant durant el seu viatge com abans d'emprendre l'aventura, hi ha indicis que Colom té una pista i que algú el pot haver precedit: la felicitat amb què s'embarca, la decisió i precisió amb què fa la ruta, les possibles cartes amb illes marcades, els miserables vidrets i claus com a mercaderia a canvi d'un or que busca des del primer moment... Si es vol, tot fa pensar que Colom sabia on anava, i això referma la llegenda del predescobridor. Però com sempre, d'aquí a la certesa hi ha un abisme difícil de salvar. Primer de tot, ha de sorprendre que de tots els supervivents de la predescoberta només un d'ells parlés a una sola persona d'aquella aventura tan singular. A més a més, d'aquest Alonso Sánchez no hi ha ni tan sols cap certesa que existís, i vet aquí una altra llegenda que s'esfuma...

I malgrat tot, ben mirat, res que tregui mèrits a Colom: si no sabia que hi havia terra a occident, va ser atrevit; i si algun desconegut li havia dit que n'hi havia i li va fer cas tan feliçment, potser més que atrevit va ser temerari, cosa encara més admirable.

Els europeus al Brasil

Si la descoberta americana de Colom no és necessàriament la primera, tampoc no cal que sigui l'última. Un dels descobriments més nets, eficaços, discrets i ben documentats que trobem avui als llibres d'història, probablement és el de Pedro Álvares Cabral al Brasil. Aquest navegant portuguès gairebé passa de puntetes pel nostre espectacle sense que ningú no li qüestioni gaire res, i si no arriba a ser per la miqueta d'or que Colom va portar del seu primer viatge, avui es podria considerar Cabral el descobridor d'Amèrica i Colom probablement s'hauria quedat en el gran grup dels misteriosos predecessors qüestionats, un altre Didrik Pining, una llegenda més en l'arribada al que els europeus anomenaven el nou món.

El 1500 Pedro Álvares Cabral és l'encarregat de capitanejar una expedició portuguesa cap a les Índies a través de la ruta que l'any abans ha obert Vasco da Gama vorejant Àfrica pel sud. Com ja sabem, en aquell temps els portuguesos tenen cada vegada menys por d'endinsar-se oceà endins per aprofitar els corrents dels Sargassos o la *volta do mar*; així, sigui per això, per les tempestes o per errors de càlcul en la navegació, en comptes d'avançar pels arriscats corrents que voregen les costes africanes, tal com indiquem en un mapa, Cabral se n'allunya i va ben cap al sud-oest per afrontar el cap de Bona Esperança encarant-lo directament per l'est. I tant s'endinsa cap a l'oest que acaba topant amb una illa que anomenarà Ilha da Vera Cruz, la qual resultarà ser un continent que a sobre, segons el tractat de Tordesillas de 1494, es banya feliçment en aigües portugueses. Això passa el 22 d'abril del 1500, tot just un mes després d'haver deixat enrere Cap Verd.

Qualsevol que es miri un mapa de l'Atlàntic i observi la longitud a què es troben les Açores i el cap de San Roque al Brasil trobaria comprensible que els portuguesos descobrissin Amèrica del Sud com qui no vol la cosa. Però no és un tema tant de distàncies com de corrents, i el secret segurament és haver superat l'equador. Un cop traspassat el paral·lel zero i empesos pels corrents i pels vents de l'hemisferi sud, el més lògic per a ells potser era, ara ja sí, descobrir el Brasil amb la mateixa naturalitat amb què havien anat descobrint (o redescobrint, amb permís de fenicis, cartaginesos i guanxes africans) totes les illes atlàntiques conegudes aleshores entre les Açores i Cap Verd, les Canàries incloses. Com que la distància entre Cap Verd i el Brasil ja no oferia gaires secrets a la navegació, van ser suficients trenta-un dies exactes perquè Cabral, sense seguir la ruta més curta de totes, es plantés a allò que va creure una illa i que aviat seria coneguda amb el nom d'illa Brasil.

O sigui que aparentment Cabral troba el Brasil sense voler, en el camí de vorejar el cap de Bona Esperança, i tot i que no hi ha cap certesa que fos el primer navegant europeu a trepitjar aquelles terres, sí que és el primer a documentar-nos-les. I a sobre hauria arribat a Amèrica sense cap referència prèvia, sense que el viatge de Colom li servís de pista per a res. Realment un descobriment de campionat.

Però de seguida que busquem una mica, també comencen a aparèixer-li competidors.

Primer de tot trobem Vicente Yáñez Pinzón, excapità de *la Niña* que acompanyava Colom en el seu primer viatge a Amèrica. Pinzón s'embarcaria per compte propi a explorar les costes de l'altra banda de l'Atlàntic en una expedició que el va portar breument a les costes del Brasil el gener del 1500, cosa que gairebé el podria convertir en el primer home a descobrir dos cops Amèrica. Tot just seguint-li les passes, el seu cosí Diego de Lepe també passejaria breument per aquelles costes poques setmanes abans que ho fes Cabral. Però per molt ben documentades que estiguin les expedicions de Pinzón i de Lepe, com que el tractat de Tordesillas donava el monopoli d'exploració d'aquelles aigües a Portugal, les seves descobertes il·legals no es devien poder fer públiques i no van tenir cap conseqüència per als que els van seguir.

També queda igualment amagat el possible descobriment del Brasil per part del portuguès Duarte Pacheco Pereira. Sembla clar que el 1498 aquest navegant portuguès va trepitjar el Brasil, o en tot cas Amèrica, i només queda el dubte que no hagués estat fent voltes més al nord, qui sap si a les Antilles o altres costes que el tractat de Tordesillas adjudicaria a la corona castellana. Ja sol passar que aquestes expedicions secretes d'espionatge entre Castella i Portugal transcendeixin poc. Si el viatge al Brasil de Pereira fos cert, entraria en el mateix grup de Pinzón i Lepe per part castellana (1500), i Vaz da Cunha i Fernandes de Andrade (1487) per part portuguesa. Si tots plegats van passar pel Brasil, bàsicament podríem dir que són incursions de reconeixement de les aigües i territoris que corresponen a cada corona. Tot plegat, descobriments que només transcendiran si no fan entrar els dos regnes en conflicte.

¿Però quin conflicte hi ha en el fet que una expedició portuguesa navegués en aigües brasileres, si aquestes li corresponien? Pereira ens deixa una llarga carta escrita per ell mateix el 1508 titulada *Esmeraldo de Situ Orbis*, on entre altres coses descriu la costa occidental de l'Atlàntic. Comptant que salpa de Cap Verd, és raonable pensar que aquella costa occidental fos la del Brasil, portuguesa amb tota regla. Però el silenci lusità sobre Pereira porta alguns historiadors a entendre que devia explorar més al nord, cap a latituds descobertes per Colom. Alguns sostenen que potser, les Antilles, altres fins i tot gosen suposar Pereira a les costes nord-americanes. Ho fonamenten en l'*Esmeraldo de Situ Orbis* i en la precisió amb què la suposadament inexplorada península de Florida apareix al planisferi de Cantino, un mapa portuguès datat el 1502. En qualsevol cas, el que ens diu aquesta confusió és que durant tota l'última dècada hi van arribant europeus que cartografien aquelles costes sense acabar de deixar petja als llibres d'història.

Una altra explicació de per què no va transcendir el descobriment de Pereira podria ser, com tants altres cops, que no sabia el que havia descobert. Sembla que molts exploradors d'aquella època (entre ells Pereira) encara tenien una visió ptolemaica del món segons la qual tot mar ha d'estar envoltat de terra, tot mar ha de tenir uns marges. Aquesta era una visió gairebé excusable per a uns pobles europeus amagats en un racó de món i que encara no han aconseguit arribar al final de la seva única costa oceànica ni pel sud ni pel nord. Fins i tot, de seguida que entenguin que a l'altra banda de l'Atlàntic no hi ha Àsia, continuaran apareixent mapamundis que mostren l'Atlàntic i l'Índic com dos mars envoltats de terra, a l'estil del Mediterrani, com una idea gairebé lògica i inalterable. Inclús Colom va mantenir-se entossudit en la seva visió ptolemaica del món que li permetia defensar que havia arribat a les Índies. Ja veiem, doncs, que Ptolomeu estava tan fortament arrelat en la visió del món, que sovint prevalia fins i tot per damunt de cartes portolanes de primera mà.

Pel que sembla, Pereira considera que es mou en aquest espai i per tant no concep la idea de moure's en un altre continent. Si això és així, encara la situació és més ridícula, si no alarmant quan veiem els europeus navegant per cinc continents abans d'haver entès com és un oceà. I més encara, el cas de Pereira no deixa de ser preocupant si pensem que el 1488 Bartolomeu Dias ja havia arribat al cap de Bona Esperança i que els europeus (i portuguesos) ja poden saber que Àfrica està envoltada de mar, que és vorejable, que l'Atlàntic i l'Índic són mars oberts...

Segons explica Heròdot (IV, 42), l'any 608 aC el faraó Nekao II ja havia enviat una expedició que va circumnavegar Àfrica abandonant Egipte des del mar Roig i tornant-hi al cap de tres anys pel Mediterrani. O sigui que quan Bartomeu Dias arriba al cap de Bona Esperança, ja fa dos mil anys que una altra expedició l'ha precedit.

Però és que el xoc no deu ser fàcil d'assumir: si els oceans són oberts i no tenen vores, si aquelles terres de l'Atlàntic occidental no són les Índies, i si tampoc no connecten amb Europa pel sud d'Àfrica, als europeus se'ls gira feina de la grossa per repensar tota la geografia mundial.

I després què?

Ara que s'ha consumat el descobriment europeu d'Amèrica, arriba la fal·lera per rastrejar-la de dalt a baix, d'ocupar-la, de portar-hi esclaus que hi treballin, de canviar-la per complet d'una manera brutalment dramàtica i cruel.

I malgrat el drama que és aquest episodi, potser una de les imatges més còmiques i patètiques del món de les exploracions ens la dona l'Amèrica del segle XVI. Si ens ho miréssim des de ben amunt, veuríem tot d'europeus voltant amunt i avall per tots dos continents buscant mines d'or, ciutats fantàstiques, tresors amagats, mars perduts... En veuríem alguns convençuts que són a Àsia o intentant convèncer-ne els altres, en trobaríem d'altres satisfent els seus aires de grandesa convertint-se o autoproclamant-se reis, emperadors, governadors... Sovint es tracta de proscrits, pàries analfabets que imitaven personatges de novel·la cavalleresca per enaltir-se posant de passada noms tan novel·lescos com Califòrnia o El Dorado. Mai més, des d'aleshores, tantes llegendes sense fonament han generat un deliri col·lectiu tan gran: n'hi ha que passen vint-i-cinc anys buscant la mítica Ciutat dels Cèsars, que se suposava plena d'or i plata; altres busquen o bategen llocs com Isla Brasil, Saguenay al Quebec, Amazones, Cíbola, Quiriva... I probablement, el més hilarant o sarcàstic de tot això, si ens ho mirem amb una certa perspectiva, és la bogeria que arribaria segles més tard, quan ja ningú no buscava riqueses ni paradisos sinó una terra fèrtil on cultivar i sobreviure i va arribar, més per casualitat que altra cosa, el descobriment de l'or i del petroli. De sobte, amb la febre de l'or al segle XIX renaixerien tots els mites i els delirants desplaçaments en massa cap a terres inhòspites. Però com se sol dir, aquesta ja és una altra història.

MALACCA
HENRICUS
1519
Puerto
San Julián
Estret de Magalhães

3. La primera volta al món

Viatge d'Henrique de Malacca

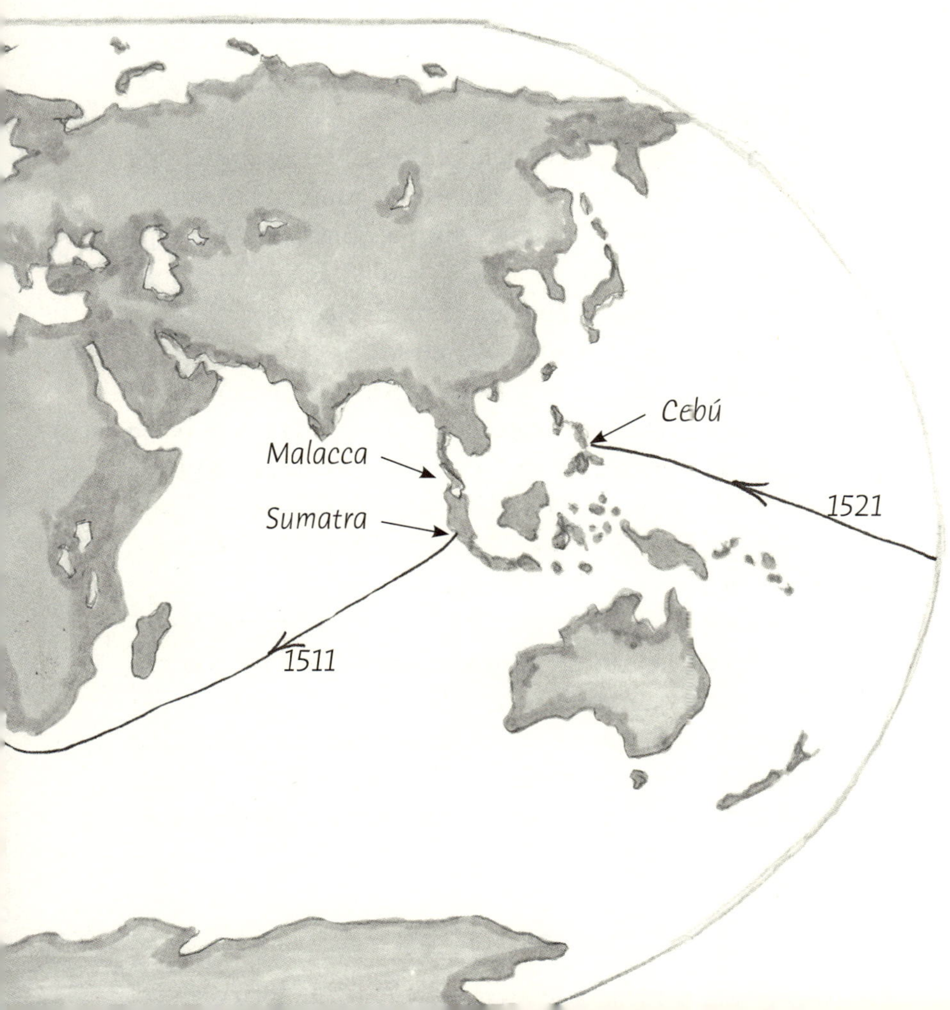

Henrique de Malacca

L'arribada a les Índies per la via del cap de Bona Esperança oberta per Vasco da Gama el 1499 permet als portuguesos fer-se els amos de l'Índic. Entre les activitats que hi duen a terme hi ha, com per desgràcia sol passar, la de proveir-se d'esclaus, i és així com el 1511 a Sumatra els portuguesos capturen un noi malai d'entre dotze i divuit anys, conegut amb el nom d'Henrique de Malacca, que es convertirà en l'esclau més memorable d'aquest episodi històric. Allà mateix el compra un navegant anomenat Fernão Magalhães que se l'emportarà cap a Portugal. Un cop a la seva nova llar, el noi aconseguirà guanyar-se la confiança del seu nou amo fins al punt que, quan vuit anys més tard Magalhães emprengui una de les aventures més sonades de la història de la navegació, s'hi emportarà Henrique per tal que els serveixi d'intèrpret quan arribin a les Moluques des de l'est. Tal és la confiança que Magalhães té en Henrique que fins i tot al testament que farà abans de marxar de Sevilla li concedeix la llibertat i 10.000 maravedisos.

Dir que Magalhães no és la primera persona a completar la volta al món no serà cap sorpresa per a ningú. Ja hi era ben a prop, quan el dissabte 27 d'abril de 1521 mor en un combat a Mactán, a l'illa de Cebú, no gaire lluny de les illes on anys enrere havia adquirit l'esclau Henrique; així que per poc, però Magalhães no és el primer, això segur.

El que sí que és segur és que amb la mort del portuguès els fets es precipiten. Una de les primeres conseqüències és el primer d'uns quants canvis de comandament de l'expedició, que acabarà tornant a Sevilla capitanejada per Juan Sebastián Elcano. Una altra de les conseqüències, i la que més ens interessa ara, és que segons el testament de Magalhães, Henrique de

Malacca, que en aquests moments té entre vint-i-dos i vint-i-vuit anys, torna a ser un home lliure.

Les hostilitats d'aquests últims dies, culminades amb la mort de Magalhães, han deixat l'expedició clarament afectada, i segons alguns testimonis, aquell dia Henrique es queda a la nau perquè està lleument ferit. Duarte de Barbosa, el primer a prendre el relleu de Magalhães al capdavant de l'expedició, li reprèn aquesta passivitat, l'amenaça de fuetejar-lo i li assegura que ell mateix s'encarregarà que no recuperi la llibertat quan tornin a Castella. Aleshores l'esclau s'aixeca i aparentment amb tota naturalitat se'n va cap a terra a fer la seva tasca d'intèrpret amb el rajà local.

No tenim cap testimoni directe dels tractes que Henrique fa amb el rajà, però sembla que deu ordir un complot amb ell. Sigui com sigui, veient el tracte que li ofereix Duarte de Barbosa, de motius no li'n falten. En qualsevol cas, l'esclau torna al vaixell com qui res, amb la mateixa tranquil·litat taciturna amb què ha desembarcat i assegurant que ha tancat un tracte comercial amb el rajà.

Més tard, uns quants homes baixen a fer l'intercanvi comercial establert, l'intèrpret Henrique entre ells, és clar. I poca estona després, des del vaixell s'adonen que alguna cosa no va bé. Des de coberta només aconsegueixen veure un dels seus homes a terra, João Serrão, ferit i cridant que tots els altres homes són morts, excepte Henrique.

Òbviament, el fins ara esclau i probablement l'home que podrà completar la primera volta al món decideix quedar-se a la seva terra —illa més, illa menys— abans que no pas seguir el seu camí cap a l'esclavitud amb un capità que no li promet res de bo. Molt millor això que continuar en una expedició que per allà on passa, si no pot comerciar, mata i roba, de vegades directament sense preguntar, segons gustos i necessitats. En molts episodis, i cada vegada més, l'expedició magallànica adquireix trets propis dels corsaris, saquejant en nom de la corona de Castella.

En tot cas, quan veuen João Serrão cridant a la platja, els supervivents de l'expedició castellana tenen clar que el millor que poden fer és fugir immediatament, així que l'última notícia que tenim d'Henrique de Malacca és en veu d'aquest dissortat João Serrão demanant ajuda, ferit i cridant que el mataran, un João Serrão cada vegada més lluny i més petit en aquella illa on Henrique de Malacca amb tota probabilitat ha recuperat la llibertat. Res més no se sap d'ell, no sabem si viurà unes hores més o unes quantes dècades, com tampoc no podem saber si mai arribarà a trepitjar aquella imaginària línia precisa que els moderns com nosaltres necessitem per dir si va completar o no la volta al món. I segurament a ell li serà ben igual (és més, probablement s'estimarà més no tornar al lloc on els portuguesos el van capturar uns anys enrere), però el cas és que Henrique havia sortit de la seva terra natal cap a l'oest, i cap a l'oest ha tornat a les illes on es parla la seva llengua i on ha pogut conxorxar-se amb un rei per salvar la seva vida i la dels habitants de l'illa, lluitant contra aquells que l'havien esclavitzat.

A Magalhães li ha faltat molt poc per completar la volta al món, però tenim la certesa que en cap cas no ho ha aconseguit. D'Henrique, en podem tenir la seguretat que ni que sigui per poc té ocasió de superar el portuguès. Situades a banda i banda de l'illa de Borneo, el trobem per primer cop a Sumatra i l'abandonem a Cebú. No està gens malament. I qui ho sap, potser venia de més a l'est de Sumatra, o potser algun dia l'atzar el porti més a l'oest de Cebú.

Però anem a les certeses. Tot i que per aquelles terres Henrique ja s'està comunicant en la seva llengua, és possible que sovint ho faci a través d'altres intèrprets malais de les zones que parlen les llengües locals. Sembla que és així com es comunica amb el rajà de Mactan, a través d'un altre intèrpret que havia estat a la terra natal d'Henrique, de manera que la qüestió de l'idioma tampoc no ens serveix per concloure totalment que fos el primer. Per tant, doncs, si d'una cosa no hi ha dubte, és que el malai, la llengua d'Henrique, és la primera a fer la volta al món. Quan Henrique torna a utilitzar la seva llengua materna en arribar a les actuals Filipines, per primer cop una creació humana ha fet la volta al món.

Pensem en la primera paraula, la primera salutació que Henrique intercanvia amb algú altre a les Filipines. En aquell precís instant, ara sí, aquella paraula intercanviada per dues persones ha sortit del mateix país en dues direccions oposades guardada en el cap dels dos homes. Alguna cosa humana ha fet la volta al món abans que Magalhães, evidentment, i abans que el *Victoria* no arribi a Cap Verd el 9 de juliol de 1522, on la trentena de supervivents que hi ha podran ja dir que han completat la gesta...

Però per sempre més, abans que cap persona, una paraula haurà fet la volta al món.

Punta Gallows. De Magalhães a Drake

Entre el 31 de març i el 24 d'agost de 1520, l'expedició de Magalhães que protagonitza la primera volta al món passa l'hivern a Puerto San Julián, un lloc solitari on, a mesura que s'avança cap al sud, la vegetació va cedint terreny per oferir-lo al fred i a la desolació. Malgrat tot, durant aquesta escala els homes de Magalhães tenen l'oportunitat d'entrar en contacte amb alguns dels habitants locals, tehuelches, els quals anomenaran patagons.

No deu ser un hivern fàcil, aquest de 1520. La llunyania, l'hostilitat creixent del paisatge, el fred, la incertesa, les rancúnies i desconfiances entre castellans i portuguesos, i també el contacte amb els tehuelches, a vegades pacífic, a vegades hostil fins a la mort, tant per un costat com per l'altre, fan d'aquest un dels episodis més intensos de l'expedició de Magalhães.

A la cruesa d'aquells difícils dies hivernals, cal afegir-hi encara els inevitables motins que acabaran amb la vida d'uns quants expedicionaris. Tot i que entre altres mesures Magalhães condemna quaranta homes a morir a la forca a causa d'un motí, finalment entén que és excessiu i un cop sufocat el complot sembla que es desdiu d'aquesta sentència tan excessiva. Però de totes maneres l'escala a l'actual Puerto San Julián deixa algunes víctimes de l'expedició; entre les més destacades hi ha Luis de Mendoza i Gaspar de Quesada, que moren a ganivetades i després són esquarterats, mentre que Juan de Cartagena i el capellà Pedro Sánchez de la Reina seran abandonats allà en salpar l'expedició més cap al sud, a finals d'agost.

La sort de Cartagena i de Sánchez de la Reina sembla evident ateses les poques opcions que tenen. En aquells temps l'abandonament dels amotinats és una pràctica que acostuma a fer-se en un illot on les possibilitats de sobreviure solen ser escasses a causa de la set, la gana, el fred o qualsevol altre perill, entre els quals pot haver-hi fins i tot l'ofegament en pujar la marea. En aquests casos de vegades es deixa els abandonats amb una arma i una bala per tal que puguin resoldre el seu destí per la via més ràpida.

Si Cartagena i Sánchez de la Reina realment són abandonats en un illot, molt probablement la seva vida no durarà més d'uns dies. Si no, en el millor dels casos, els podem imaginar en terra ferma, on difícilment podran integrar-se en la societat tehuelche, especialment després d'algunes de les hostilitats que han tingut durant els pocs contactes que hi han fet. Així doncs, si han quedat abandonats en terra ferma, és fàcil creure que no els espera altre destí que interceptar una fletxa dels patagons.

Si per aquelles coses ens equivoquéssim en aquestes conjectures i han tingut la sort de sobreviure fins al novembre, és possible que la nau *San Antonio*, en abandonar sobtadament l'expedició per tornar cap a Europa els hagi recollit, però no hi ha cap certesa d'aquest fet i per tant podem comptar que els seus dies acaben a les proximitats de Puerto San Julián amb l'únic consol que el seu patiment segurament serà breu.

Potser si tinguéssim un testimoni que ens en pogués parlar...

Potser sí que el tindrem... perquè no és cap d'aquestes quatre víctimes tan sonades qui deixarà petja en la toponímia d'aquest solitari racó de món, sinó un altre desconegut de l'expedició que tampoc no seguirà el seu viatge cap a la descoberta de l'estret de Magalhães.

De moment, tot el que podem saber és que quan l'últim vaixell de l'expedició deixa enrere aquest lloc, deixen balancejant-se un cos en una forca en un cap visible a l'interior de la badia. Ningú no s'hi acostarà per baixar aquest pèndol humà. Ni cap dels indígenes ni els abandonats Cartagena i Sánchez, que sens dubte li haurien donat cristiana sepultura si haguessin pogut arribar fins allà (vet aquí el detall que ens permet pensar que no van sobreviure). Passaran hiverns freds i ventosos, hores de sol i de nits... i el macabre pèndol humà seguirà bellugant braços i peus a mercè del vent i de la pluja fins que un dia les inclemències faran caure el pal de la forca i les restes humanes quedaran desmanegades per terra.

És així com reposa aquest pacient esquelet quan el juny de 1578, cinquanta-vuit anys després dels fets, torna a aparèixer una vela a l'horitzó patagònic. Aquesta segona vegada l'expedició de Francis Drake, la segona a circumnavegar el planeta, també entrarà a la badia de Puerto San Julián i trobarà l'escena en aturar-se exactament en aquest mateix punt, al qual donaran el nom de Punta Gallows («punta de la forca»).

D'això se'n diu una mort solitària de debò, deuen pensar els cinc homes que troben les corprenedores restes de la forca. Però així que veuen aquesta escena premonitòria, un d'aquests cinc primers homes que baixen a fer un reconeixement a terra és ferit per una fletxa. Potser no és tan solitari el lloc. De sobte sembla com si sempre hi hagués algú a la solitària Patagònia, uns habitants que en tot cas mai no han tingut la intenció de profanar aquest mausoleu tan singular que van deixar els visitants de fa més de mig segle i als quals sembla que hagin estat esperant durant dècades pacientment amagats rere una roca.

Més enllà de les vicissituds del viatge de Drake, molt probablement aquest esquelet sigui l'únic testimoni humà que comparteixen les dues primeres expedicions que circumnaveguen la Terra. Així, gràcies a la macabra troballa del navegant britànic, aquest mariner oblidat s'haurà convertit, involuntàriament i sense desitjar-ho ni poder-ho sospitar mai, en l'únic secundari de les dues primeres voltes al món.

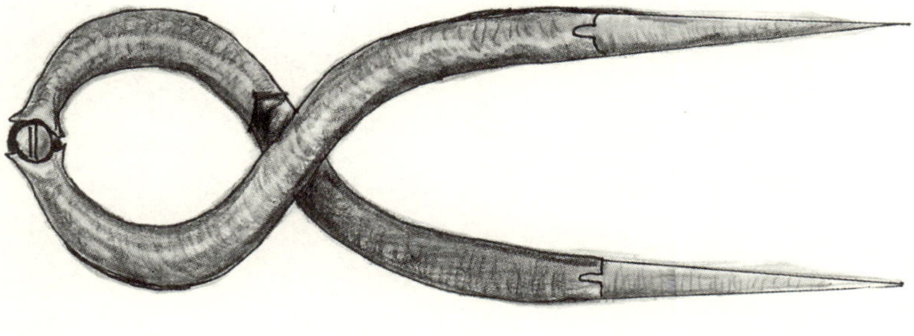

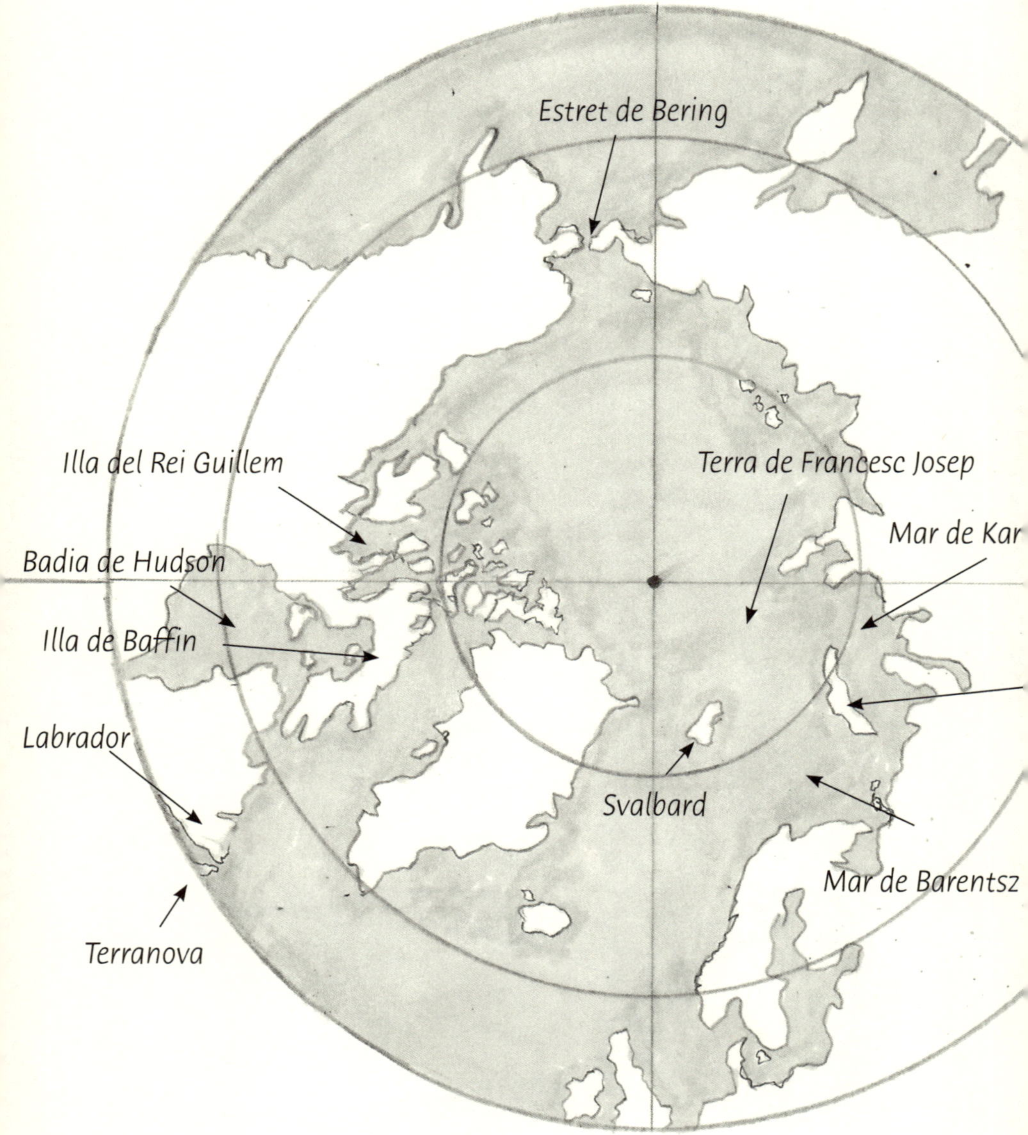

Estret de Bering
Illa del Rei Guillem
Terra de Francesc Josep
Mar de Kar
Badia de Hudson
Illa de Baffin
Labrador
Svalbard
Mar de Barentsz
Terranova

4. L'Àrtic

Pitees de Massàlia. Les primeres boires

Artos: ursus: os. Àrtikos s'ha de dir la terra de l'Ossa Major. Ja els grecs han posat nom a aquella terra mirant cap al cel negre que la cobreix. I així el nom d'Àrtikos només podia néixer de nit perquè fa referència a la constel·lació de l'Ossa Major.

Ja sabem que la Terra és rodona, ja sabem que gira, ja sabem que hi ha d'haver doncs dos pols i que a sota d'aquella gran ossa còsmica hi ha d'haver una terra o un mar que ara ja té nom. Però Àrtikos neix sense ser res més que un nom sense un significat gaire clar. Per a un poble tan lligat al mar com el grec, aquell Àrtikos és massa enllà a través del continent. Per als grecs, ja ho sabem, la mar és el camí predilecte. I si aquest camí per mar cap al nord existeix en algun lloc, ha de ser un camí massa absurdament llarg. I no hi ha cap necessitat d'anar-hi. Per això ens deu costar tant trobar algú que s'hi aventuri.

Fins que apareix Pitees de Massàlia.

Sabem ben poc de Pitees. La seva és una obra perduda entre les flames de la biblioteca d'Alexandria i només ens n'arriba notícia de segona mà, a través d'altres autors que el poden citar. Malgrat tot, el seu viatge a la costa atlàntica europea ens és un punt de partida per al coneixement d'aquest continent, i també per començar a posar una primera tènue llum sobre aquella negror absorbent de l'Àrtic. Al segle IV aC, aquest navegant marsellès d'origen grec ens donarà no només les primeres descripcions escrites de les costes occidentals europees, sinó també d'altres elements com les marees, les aurores boreals o el cercle polar.

Algun dia d'aquell segle IV aC, Pitees emprèn un viatge més enllà de les columnes d'Hèrcules tot resseguint la costa cap al nord. Sabem que passa per les illes Britàniques i que continua navegant encara més lluny. I més enllà de la fi del seu món, en l'extrem final del nebulós misteri nocturn que envolta el seu viatge, Pitees arriba fins a una desconeguda illa que anomena Thule. No sabem on és exactament aquesta terra perduda en la penombra boirosa i callada del nord profund, i mai més no podrem tornar a posar aquella Thule al mapa sense por d'equivocar-nos. Avui alguns diuen que es podria tractar de les illes Shetland o de Dinamarca; altres, que Thule podria ser Noruega, i encara n'hi ha, els més atrevits, que diuen que Thule podria ser Islàndia.

L'opció d'una Thule islandesa de Pitees és molt més que improbable, però durant un temps serà la que farà més fortuna: molts segles després, les illes misterioses acostumaran a reclamar un lloc equivalent als mapes medievals ¿i quina illa més misteriosa que Islàndia podrem trobar en aquells segles i en aquelles latituds de foscor?

D'alguna manera encara relliscosa, Pitees ens ha començat a posar l'Àrtic al mapa. Però és encara un àrtic així, relliscós, un àrtic fantasmal i sense rostre que se'ns esmuny d'entre els dits en plena nit, que ens cau tan sordament enteri en algun lloc al voltant dels nostres peus que no en sentim cap so quan toca a terra i que no sabem encara on l'hem d'anar a collir, perquè, en abaixar el cap, ens adonem que tenim les cames encara ben enfonsades en la fosca. I així aquell Àrtic relliscós que teníem entre els dits s'esvaeix.

Confusos, ens mirem les mans obertes, les cames perdent-se'ns avall en la negror, i ja no estem segurs de si havíem tingut una cosa àrtica entre els dits o de si només ho hem somiat. Arrufem les celles amb un imperceptible tremolor de mirada buida, provant de fer memòria de no sabem què, fins que finalment ja només sabem que hi ha algun lloc on no hi ha res; i aleshores, mig desconcertats, ho deixem estar.

Si almenys algú ens en digués alguna cosa... Perquè a l'Àrtic ja hi viu gent des de fa segles, però ningú no ens en parla encara. Els camins encara no són traçats i el nostre Àrtic llunyà ens és encara silenciós, misteriós, mut.

Per a nosaltres, amb Pitees neix el misteri àrtic, i amb ell mateix mor també durant molts segles.

Cap al pas del nord-oest

Sense anar més enllà de tímides i borroses incursions, per als forasters, l'Àrtic ha sigut quasi sempre un misteri innecessari: poc benefici s'ha esperat mai d'un entorn tan estèril i inhòspit, i només quan ha calgut trobar noves vies de comunicació entre continents ha nascut un cert interès per conèixer aquesta part del planeta.

Un camí, doncs, és la primera riquesa que s'hi espera trobar. Però aviat es veurà que l'Àrtic és un botí car i escàs. Només molt més endavant, quan arribi l'era daurada dels exploradors, la seva riquesa serà ja l'aventura, el camí en si. Però de primer, encara, darrere el camí hi ha d'haver alguna cosa més que atipi les butxaques dels poderosos. Cal trobar una ruta comercial entre Europa i Àsia.

Ja ho sabem, si no hi ha or ni societats riques amb qui comerciar, a cap europeu li interessa ni l'Àrtic ni cap altre lloc del món. I molt menys encara l'absurditat d'arribar a l'esterilíssim pol nord. L'únic que volen els europeus és esquivar aquesta nosa de continent americà que bloqueja el pas cap a la rica Àsia de les espècies i de la seda. Res més. I vist que la ruta pel sud és poc més que impracticable, cal trobar el pas del nord-oest sigui com sigui.

Des que Cabot ha topat amb l'obstacle d'Amèrica del Nord el 1497, cada cop més navegants es desvien a latituds més elevades buscant l'anhelat camí. El 1508 prova sort el seu fill, Sebastian Cabot, que potser enganyat per l'immens atzucac de la badia de Hudson assegura haver trobat el camí a Catai (l'actual Xina). El 1524 Giovanni da Verrazzano s'interna pel riu Hudson també convençut que ha trobat el pas. I tres anys després, John Rut s'aventura cap al nord de la costa canadenca, hi ha qui diu que potser seguint la pista d'un suposat monjo del segle XIV que ja hauria fet un viatge semblant cap al pol, però no hi ha res documentat clarament. Les notícies confuses ens diuen que Rut arriba entre el paral·lel 53 i el 64 i que torna enrere a causa del gel. Aquell és encara un món de descobriments casuals, de provatures i d'errors, de llegendes marineres que es prenen per certes, d'informacions imprecises i difícils de contrastar...

L'Àrtic és encara un misteri en el qual els únics estrangers que semblen trobar-se com a casa només deuen ser els baleners. De fet, segueixen els descobridors de tan a prop que a vegades sembla que ja hi eren abans. Si no és que ja hi eren i que amagaven discretament el secret de l'abundància de l'Àrtic.

Però no és aquesta riquesa del mar el que busquen els grans apoderats europeus, i com una herència dels grecs, continuen buscant el mar com un camí, mirant d'esquivar la terra.

Cap al pas del nord-est

Des que la ruta de la seda es va fer inviable, tots els possibles camins europeus cap a Àsia han sigut portes tancades. Pel Mediterrani, res; vorejant Àfrica, llarg i complicat; per l'Atlàntic sud, de bojos; directament per l'oest, el mur americà; més al nord, un laberint de gel... i finalment, acabant aquesta volta de compàs, ja només queda provar sort pel nord-est siberià.

Això deu tenir al cap el vell Sebastian Cabot quan el 1551 juntament amb Richard Chancellor, Hugh Willoughby i un gruix de més de dos-cents inversors funden una companyia per explorar i per fer comerç amb nous territoris. Nascuda amb el deliciós nom de *Company of Merchant Adventurers for the Discovery of Regions, Dominions, Islands, and Places unknown* (Companyia de comerciants aventurers per al descobriment de regions, dominis, illes i llocs desconeguts), la primera missió d'aquesta nova empresa serà precisament explorar les possibilitats d'un encara inexistent pas del nord-est. Així, a la primavera del 1553 Willoughby i Chancellor salpen de Londres al capdavant del *Bona Esperanza*, el *Bona Confidentia* i l'*Edward Bonaventure.* Aquestes naus, però, tot i que construïdes expressament per a l'ocasió, encara no tenen prou domini contra els capricis dels elements, i el viatge no anirà com estava previst. Sotmesa a vents desfavorables des de ben principi, l'expedició dedicarà massa temps a recórrer la costa noruega, i no podrà encarar la costa siberiana abans que el breu estiu àrtic comenci a declinar.

Amb prou feines estan començant a encarar el repte per aquest mar desconegut quan una tempesta separa les naus i l'*Edward Bonaventure* de Chancellor es perd de vista amb els seus quaranta-nou tripulants a bord. Potser els convé més així;

la sort acabarà portant aquests mariners a port rus i de retorn cap a casa, mentre que les altres dues naus es trobaran perdudes per l'Àrtic. Així, apartats de la ruta per la tempesta, sense referents geogràfics ni eines per poder-se ubicar amb precisió, el *Bona Esperanza* i el *Bona Confidentia* continuen fent rumb a cegues cap a l'est fins que el 14 d'agost topen amb la costa hostil i desconeguda del que probablement avui coneixem com Nova Zembla.

Fins aleshores, aquest arxipèlag només ha sigut visitat des del segle XI per caçadors pomors arribats esporàdicament des del continent. Cap notícia d'aquest lloc ha sortit mai cap al món, i lluny de qualsevol cosa que poguessin desitjar aquests exploradors anglesos, aquesta terra no només no ofereix cap opció de comerç amb la Xina, sinó que ni tan sols els convida a passar-hi l'hivern. Davant d'aquesta costa impracticable a on no poden ni desembarcar, l'única opció de Willoughby és ordenar el retorn cap a l'oest abans que el gel no els atrapi.

Però van tard, tot just un poc massa tard, i un mes després d'haver deixat enrere el seu descobriment, els vaixells queden atrapats a les proximitats de la península de Kola. Varats a la desembocadura del riu Varzina, envien homes a l'est, al sud, a l'oest d'aquesta terra, però tots tornen sense haver trobat cap indici de presència humana i decideixen hivernar en aquest racó perdut.

Tota manera, calma, no és qüestió de deixar-se vèncer pel pànic; aquests exploradors estan preparats per a tot i tenen provisions. Com a molt, potser només els deu faltar saber encarar aquest fred tan cru que amenaça matar-los a tots. Però malgrat la duresa de les condicions, van trobant la manera de sobreviure, i encabits els seixanta-tres supervivents dins del *Bona Esperanza*, van passant les llargues i negres hores hivernals.

Potser aquesta placidesa immòbil aguditza la imaginació i l'enginy, eines sense les quals no hi pot haver cap mena d'exploració. I potser és així, amb llargues hores de pensament quiet, que apareixen solucions contra aquest fred que, penetrant per escletxes i finestres, cada cop deu tenallar més el grup. I deu ser lluitant contra aquesta última escletxa de fred, que decideixen fer el seu refugi tan hermètic com puguin perquè no se n'escapi ni el fum. La idea deu ser d'allò més reconfortant, perquè així d'arraulits és com els trobaran a la primavera vinent uns pescadors locals.

Quan aquell 1554 el bon temps torna a convidar els pescadors a la mar, un grup d'aquests troben els dos vaixells, silenciosos i tranquils com qui hiberna sense preocupacions. Sens dubte encuriosits, hi entren a veure si hi ha algú o si en poden treure res de profit. Un, fantasmagòricament buit. De l'altre, la llegenda s'encarregarà d'exagerar més o menys els detalls de l'espectacle, però el retrat que ens n'arriba no deixa lloc al dubte. Es dirà que els cossos són trobats en les posicions més quotidianes, escrivint llapis en mà, menjant cullera en boca o en tasques d'allò més trivials. En qualsevol cas, potser sí que estaven més preparats del que ens pensàvem, res de morts violentes ni de llargues agonies. Cap senyal d'escorbut ni de baixes nombroses abans d'aquesta escena congelada en el temps, cap signe de patiment dramàtic. Tot plegat, una silenciosa escena de museu, com un macabre diorama fet expressament per impressionar els visitants, ben bé com si la mort hagués entrat d'un cop de porta i hagués esculpit un grapat d'estàtues per anar-se'n sense mirar, tot a una velocitat fotogràfica.

És cert que aquests cossos estan congelats, però la mort per congelació no pot arribar mai amb aquesta rapidesa. Alguna cosa més que el fred ha passat al *Bona Esperanza*. Més aviat, potser ha passat el contrari: s'havien protegit tan bé de les inclemències glacials aquests exploradors, que més que pel fred o per l'escorbut probablement hagin mort intoxicats pel monòxid de carboni del fum que tampoc no trobava sortida a l'exterior.

Ets aquí dins, tot calentó, escrivint o xarrupant una sopa, quan de sobte t'envaeix un endormiscament, voldries pensar alguna cosa i així us troben després de l'hivern, amb la sopa congelada sense acabar, a mig posar el punt d'una i. Oi que fàcil?

En aquesta estranya troballa, només la paraula escrita es manté viva, i només amb el seu diari ens podrà Willoughby posar Nova Zembla al mapa abans que ningú n'hagi tornat viu.

D'aquesta manera, començant a donar forma al pas del nord-est, tanquem el cercle de possibles camins cap a la Xina descobrint que no n'hi ha cap de fàcil. I de passada, amb aquest efímer museu congelat, la llegenda del fred àrtic està servida.

Martin Frobisher. Els inuits descobreixen Europa

La primera expedició cap al pas del nord-est no ha anat del tot com imaginaven. D'una banda, Willoughby i companyia sucumbeixen al fum de l'oblit, i mentrestant hem perdut la pista de Chancellor, apartat massa aviat de la ruta a les costes del mar Blanc. Però que les coses no siguin com s'imaginen no vol dir que vagin malament del tot, i aquí Chancellor tindrà més sort que el seu soci.

Un cop passada la tempesta que dividia l'expedició, els tripulants de l'*Edward Bonaventure* es troben en ple estiu a les costes de la península de Kola, on contacten fàcilment amb pescadors i pobladors locals que, sens dubte sorpresos, els van guiant per aquesta costa de port en port. Aviat les notícies d'aquests misteriosos visitants arriben terra endins fins a les orelles d'un encuriosit tsar Ivan IV. Més endavant conegut com a Ivan el Terrible, aquest és el tsar d'un incipient regne rus en plena expansió, i per tant també un interessant filó comercial. D'aquesta manera, gràcies a l'atzar d'una tempesta àrtica, s'estableix un primer contacte entre Chancellor i Ivan IV; i a partir d'aquest moment, les relacions comercials anglo-russes quedaran sota el monopoli de la companyia que representa el britànic, rebatejada des d'ara amb el nom de *Muscovy Company* (Companyia de Moscòvia).

Potser sí, doncs, que el projecte ha tingut la seva part exitosa: durant els segles següents, aquesta serà una de les més grans corporacions comercials del món perquè tenir el monopoli del comerç amb Moscou també vol dir, de retruc, tenir-lo amb Àsia en general.

Però malgrat aquest monopoli, el camí marítim cap a Catai continua essent una prioritat, sigui per l'est o per l'oest. I veient els problemes de la via siberiana, el 1576 apareix Martin Frobisher per tornar a posar sobre la taula la recerca d'un pas pel nord d'Amèrica, entre Grenlàndia i el Labrador.

Així de decidit, el 7 de juny d'aquell 1576, l'expedició de Frobisher salpa del Tàmesi amb tres embarcacions i trenta-cinc tripulants. Passen per les illes Shetland i per Grenlàndia (la qual confonen amb Frislàndia, illa imaginària que apareix en els mapes que duen, conseqüència dels viatges també ficticis dels germans Zeno), i després de patir tempestes, avaries, el naufragi de l'embarcació més petita i el retorn del vaixell *Michael*, Frobisher continua endavant amb el *Gabriel* fins que el 20 juliol veuen una terra que anomenen *Meta Incognita*, avui l'illa de Baffin.

Després de dues setmanes entre gels, a 63° N, passen per un estret que creuen que separa Àsia i Amèrica. Tres-cents quilòmetres més endavant veuen la sortida al Pacífic, Catai i les Índies Orientals, i amb això ja en tenen prou per celebrar l'èxit de l'expedició. Així de fàcil. L'únic inconvenient és que avui aquell seu oceà Pacífic ha quedat reduït a la ignorada badia de Frobisher. Fins aquí, doncs, quin desengany, res especialment memorable que canviï massa el món, encara que ells no ho saben.

Estan passant peripècies en aquelles latituds quan, el 26 d'agost, després d'haver sigut atacats pels inuits i amb ja només tretze mariners a bord, Frobisher i companyia decideixen tornar cap a Londres, on expliquen la feliç troballa geogràfica i de passada porten un inuit (potser tres, segons alguna font) que molt probablement sigui el primer del seu país a descobrir Europa. Aquest dissortat inuit morirà aviat a causa d'una malaltia pulmonar, però la seva presència a Londres genera una gran expectació, alimentada entre altres coses per la seva semblança amb els asiàtics. ¿Quina millor prova podria haver-hi per demostrar que el que s'ha descobert pel nord-oest és Àsia? Així doncs, si fins aquí no hi havia massa res que canviés el món, encara sembla que reculem un xic més: gairebé cent anys després de la flagrant confusió de Colom, a finals del segle XVI encara hi ha gent que arriba a Amèrica pensant que és a Àsia.

Però si allò que s'ha descobert és o no és el pas del nordoest, és una qüestió que de seguida passarà a segon terme perquè entre les curiositats que ha portat Frobisher de la seva Meta Incognita hi ha un tros de roca negra i pesant que crida l'atenció a Michael Lok, un dels fundadors de la Companyia de Moscòvia. En principi sembla que no es tracta de res més que de pirita de ferro, però un dels experts a qui Lok fa analitzar aquest mineral, l'italià Giovanni Battista Agnello, diu que pot contenir or. Possiblement sigui un error, o potser una mentida dita expressament perquè es financin noves expedicions, però en qualsevol cas tornarà a quedar clar que en els descobriments a l'europea sempre interessa més el contingut que el continent. I aquí és on l'expedició finançada per la Companyia de Moscòvia farà que passin coses interessants que podrien canviar el món.

El març de 1577, el mateix Michael Lok funda la Companyia de Catai, que de seguida reuneix capital suficient per posar en marxa allò que possiblement sigui la primera febre de l'or de l'Àrtic americà, encara que molt lluny de les de finals del segle XIX. De moment, aquesta incipient febre de l'or es limita a l'aportació de cinc mil lliures per part de la reina, nobles i mercaders.

La nova expedició, que salpa cap a aquelles terres amb el *Gabriel*, el *Michael* i el buc reial *Aid*, amb cent trenta-quatre homes (miners inclosos), planta la bandera a l'actual illa de Loks Land el 17 de juliol de 1577. Estan tan absolutament convençuts que es troben a Àsia que ni tan sols es molesten a dubtar-ho o a verificar-ho. Un cop allà, mentre es barallen amb els inuits de les terres properes, es dediquen a extreure dues-centes tones d'aquella roca negra que als seus ulls és autèntic or. Sens dubte la febre de l'or és la que provoca més deliris, sobretot si són deliris col·lectius. La seva singular recollecta dura fins que a mitjans d'agost el gel comença a avançar cap al sud, i abans de quedar-hi atrapats es veuen obligats a tornar cap a Londres, on el seu botí generarà una expectació tan gran que en qüestió d'un any el capital de la nova companyia ja supera les vint mil lliures.

Empès per l'entusiasme i per l'èxit, l'any següent Frobisher torna a salpar cap a la seva mina d'or negre, aquest cop amb un estol de quinze vaixells. A aquest ritme, si la flota es quintuplica d'any en any, probablement els constructors de vaixells s'haurien d'estar fregant les mans i haurien ja començat a talar tots els arbres d'Anglaterra per construir la següent flota de 75 vaixells per a l'any 1579, 375 per al següent, 1.875 vaixells més per... i així anar fent, que és com funcionen aquestes febres dels castells de vent.

Però no ens avancem encara. De moment el 1578 Frobisher salpa amb quinze vaixells, té les ordres de desembarcar un centenar d'homes que passaran l'hivern a la seva mina. Aquesta vegada, el mal temps d'aquell estiu, la boira i el gel obliguen Frobisher a entrar en un estret diferent —que després serà anomenat de Hudson— on les inclemències i la pèrdua de material fan impossible construir el fort per hivernar, de manera que es limiten a deixar una cabana amb algunes coses que només podran ser aprofitades pels inuits. No està gens malament el resultat per a una expedició d'aquestes dimensions.

En qualsevol cas, durant cinc anys es porten a Anglaterra més de 1.300 tones de roca negra sense que se'n pugui treure ni un sol gram d'or ni cap mena de metall preciós, la Companyia de Catai s'enfonsa el 1579. Com si no hagués passat res, Anglaterra comença a oblidar-se de cap mena de riquesa mineral, es torna a pensar realment en Catai i en el pas del nord-oest i es torna a posar el nas als mapes per dibuixar una via marítima a la mida perfecta dels anglesos.

De moment Frobisher no ha aconseguit el que buscava, però ha obert el camí de la recerca d'un pas pel nord-oest que trigarà encara uns quants segles a trobar-se. I mentrestant, amb tot plegat, la pirita més cara de la història servirà finalment per arreglar també els camins del sud d'Anglaterra, cosa que com a mínim algú devia agrair.

Willem Barentsz. Una porta tancada al nord-est

Al llarg del segle XVI, Europa ha començat la recerca d'una sortida pel nord tot topant un cop i un altre amb obstacles que només alguns han pogut convertir en oportunitats. És el cas dels que es freguen les mans amb el naixement de la Companyia de Moscòvia. Però l'Àrtic, al seu ritme gèlid, continuarà atraient aquells que no es donen per vençuts o que voldran esquivar el nou monopoli moscovita. Entre els que reprendran la difícil recerca del pas del nord-est, trobarem l'holandès Willem Barentsz, el qual, després de dos intents topant amb Nova Zembla, salpa d'Amsterdam per tercera vegada el maig de 1596 novament disposat a obrir aquesta ruta.

Aquest cop, els dos vaixells de l'expedició començaran buscant un pas més al nord, on toparan amb unes illes fins llavors desconegudes, les Svalbard. Però Barentsz, que no ho veu prou clar, dividirà l'expedició en dos i emproarà la seva nau cap a l'est fins a la seva ja coneguda Nova Zembla. Per tercer any consecutiu s'hi planta, i per tercer cop el gel li barra el pas, ara ja no per arribar a terra, sinó per tornar enrere, cosa que obliga els disset tripulants a hivernar a aquesta latitud extrema de 76 graus.

Hivern calamitós, aquests exploradors aviat es veuen obligats a desmantellar la nau per fer-se un refugi i tenir combustible. A més a més, els manca el pa, les botes de cervesa rebenten en congelar-se i es perd bona part de la beguda, i des d'aleshores també han d'anar descongelant un vi molt més que racionat. Però malgrat les penalitats, sobreviuen al fred i a l'escorbut gràcies a les provisions que duen per al comerç i a una prou generosa caça. Poc més que esperar es pot fer contra el caprici del gel, que, en aquesta contesa, no deixa lloc a la mar oberta fins al juny següent.

Quan per fi, després de tants mesos, la mar es torna a fer navegable, els supervivents. abandonen Nova Zembla en dos bots. I com que aquest viatge tampoc no sembla gaire prometedor, per si de cas no tornen mai al món, abans d'abandonar per sempre el seu refugi, Barentsz hi deixa una nota explicant l'aventura hivernal que acaben de superar.

No s'equivoca de gaire quan pensa que potser no tornarà mai més a la seva Holanda perquè al cap d'una setmana Barentsz mor sense tornar a trepitjar terra ferma. El mateix destí correran altres quatre dels exploradors. Finalment, després de dos mesos més de periple, dotze d'ells tindran la sort de posar els peus a la península de Kola i ser rescatats per l'altre vaixell de l'expedició que van abandonar l'any passat. I així, amb aquest cop d'efecte de l'atzar, podran tornar a Holanda i commoure el món amb l'aventura dels primers supervivents hivernals en aquelles latituds tan extremes.

Poc els ha faltat per ser uns més dels perduts en l'oblit del no retorn, i costa tan poques línies recordar-ne els noms (Jacob van Heemskerck, Gerrit de Veer, Pieter Pietersz, Lenaert Heyndricksz, Laurens Willemsz, Pieter Cornelisz, Jan Hillebrantsz, Jan van Buysen Reyniersz, Jacob Evertsz, Jacob Jansz

Hooghwout, Jacob Jansz Sterrenburgh i un mig anònim amb cognom de Hans Vos) que, abans no els oblidem per sempre, prou mereixen també de tant en tant el seu raconet en una pàgina de llibre.

Mentrestant, per si algú volgués dubtar del testimoni d'aquests primers hivernants àrtics, queden les proves a Nova Zembla. Les restes del refugi i la nota de Barentsz continuaran allà esperant... I no es pot negar que devien ser uns homes de fiar, metòdics i meticulosos (segurament qualitats imprescindibles per sobreviure en aquelles condicions) perquè, quan el 1871 el noruec Elling Carlsen sigui el primer a retrobar el refugi de Barentsz, comprovarà que es manté encara dempeus, exactament tal com el van descriure els supervivents. I comprovarà també que encara hi ha tot el seu aixovar d'incomptables objectes esperant a dins, com una silenciosa taula parada des de fa tres segles.

Henry Hudson. Un simple mal pas

Un altre dels europeus que en aquells temps es dedica a buscar un pas pel nord serà Henry Hudson, que devia ser un navegant ben tossut. Això es pot deduir de la seva insistent recerca d'aquesta ruta. El 1607 el trobem provant sort pel litoral oriental de Grenlàndia i avançant fins a Spitsbergen, Svalbard, on es veu obligat a tornar cap a Anglaterra. L'any següent intenta trobar el pas més cap a l'est, entre Spitsbergen i Nova Zembla, però també en aquelles illes del nord de Sibèria es veu obligat a retrocedir a causa del gel. Finalment, descartada la via nord-oriental, el 1609 comença a buscar el pas del nord-oest per Amèrica, entrant primer de tot pel riu Hudson, cosa que tampoc li obre encara el camí cap a Àsia però que li permetrà donar nom a aquest riu descobert ja per Giovanni da Verrazzano el 1524. I ja de passada, a banda d'alguns redescobriments, sobretot després d'aquest tercer intent frustrat, Hudson comença a mostrar també una singular habilitat social, una estranya bel·ligerància contra els habitants que troba a les terres que explora, amb els quals tant es pot barallar a mort com establir relacions comercials.

Realment Hudson ha de ser un explorador tossut i constant. Així, després de tres intents, el 1610 encara el tornem a trobar en una nova i definitiva expedició amb el mateix propòsit d'obrir una ruta cap a Àsia.

El 17 d'abril d'aquell 1610, Hudson salpa d'Anglaterra a bord del *Discovery* amb vint-i-tres homes i provisions per poc més de mig any. Passen per les Òrcades, les illes Shetland, les Fèroe, Islàndia, Grenlàndia, i el 3 d'agost de 1610 travessen l'estret que dona entrada a la badia de Hudson i que Frobisher ja havia batejat amb el nom de Mistaken Straits («estrets equivocats»). Fa de mal dir, però gairebé aquí el més encertat seria equivocar-se. La badia de Hudson és tan gran (tant com mig Mediterrani) que qualsevol que hi entri buscant un mar obert tindrà la certesa d'haver-lo trobat. Per això gairebé sorprèn que Frobisher en digués «estret equivocat» i no pensés que hi havia trobat el pas cap al Pacífic. Que Frobisher l'encertés i digués que allò era un estret equivocat gairebé sembla un error incomprensible, i per això Hudson no dubta a travessar aquest pas que a partir d'ara anomenarem estret de Hudson per endinsar-se en aquest mar obert, en realitat una immensa badia tancada de la qual ja mai més no sortirà i que portarà també per sempre més el seu nom. Ell que només volia donar nom al pas. Vet aquí el dissortat descobridor d'un autèntic cul-de-sac.

Potser si Hudson pogués tornar enrere demanaria recuperar el nom de Mistaken Straits a la porta de la badia, reconeixeria el seu error i posaria algunes coses a lloc. Però de totes maneres el descobriment de la badia de Hudson no serà poca cosa, obrirà l'entrada fins al remot cor del continent nord-americà i a partir d'aquesta nova ruta naixerà aviat la *Hudson's Bay Company*, una empresa de dimensions incalculables que es farà amb grans quantitats de pells després d'acabar amb molts animals en els segles següents.

Ateses aquestes noves riqueses, aviat el vell somni europeu del pas cap a Àsia anirà perdent sentit. Però de moment tenim Hudson endinsant-se per aquest suposat mar obert que podria ben bé ser el Pacífic. Fins aquí tot bé (si es pot dir així), però a la sempre difícil convivència de l'expedició s'afegeixen les inevitables tensions amb alguns inuits que troben per la zona, cosa que acaba amb uns quants tripulants morts. Més endavant, el 10 de setembre, el primer oficial Robert Juet és jutjat per instigar un motí i acaba substituït per Robert Bylot; i al novembre, per si s'ho estaven passant massa bé, l'arribada de l'hivern els obliga a treure el vaixell de l'aigua per evitar que el gel l'esclafi, situació que els mantindrà encallats fins que puguin tornar a embarcar de nou el 18 de juny, quan després de tot l'hivern es troben ja debilitats per la fam, afectats per l'escorbut i amb encara més fortes tensions entre la tripulació.

Fins aquí ja no tot va bé, però sí que va dins d'allò previsible. No oblidéssim que el món de l'exploració implica tancar un grup reduït d'*homo sapiens* en un espai comprimit durant un temps indefinit, amb recursos limitats i en situacions extremes enmig d'una immensitat hostil i desconeguda de la qual potser no es tornarà mai més. I si alguna cosa falla, n'hi ha un que és responsable de tot plegat.

Tot i que ens falten detalls prou exactes, és possible que Hudson volgués seguir les exploracions durant aquell estiu de 1611; o és possible que senzillament pensés a tornar, però sigui com sigui les provisions ja fa temps que són summament escasses i caldrà prendre decisions desagradables o córrer riscos insalvables. Les versions que ens arribin del que passarà aquell juny seran sempre parcials, però no hi ha res que ens impedeixi imaginar la duresa a què s'enfronten aquests exploradors. Segons la versió dels supervivents, la fam i l'escorbut els obliga a abandonar un grup d'homes malalts en una xalupa per tal que les provisions del *Discovery*, que es calcula que no duraran més de dues setmanes, permetin tornar els sans a Anglaterra. Aquesta és la versió oficial, que no sempre vol dir la veritat. Però el cert és que aquell 22 de juny, nou homes són abandonats així a la seva sort, entre ells Hudson i el seu fill adolescent.

No consta enlloc que l'escorbut es transmeti per simpatia de pares a fills o entre amics, i per tant cal atribuir aquest contagi selectiu a una casualitat. Tanmateix, segons la versió dels supervivents, en aquest cas el destí ha sigut tan benvolent que només els bons se salven de la malaltia, mentre que precisament la mala gent ha sucumbit a l'escorbut. Evidentment podem suposar que els abandonats ens donarien una altra versió dels fets i fins i tot que, potser, ens parlarien d'un motí. Però dels abandonats mai més no se'n sabrà res i quedaran allà oblidats, en un racó de la badia de James, al sud de la badia de Hudson, remotament lluny de qualsevol possibilitat de retorn o comunicació.

Qui sap si potser encara viuran un temps, si potser algun supervivent serà trobat per alguns inuits, però, sabent l'amistositat que han tingut amb els nadius d'aquestes latituds, poc ajut en poden esperar.

Mentrestant, el *Discovery* reprèn el seu camí de retorn cap a Anglaterra, però, ni tan sols havent abandonat els malalts, els supervivents tindran garantit el retorn a casa, a poc a poc i per diferents motius aniran morint ara uns ara altres. El 29 de juliol, quatre homes més són morts pels inuits mentre buscaven aliment prop de la sortida de la badia de Hudson. Poca cosa devien recollir, perquè la travessia de retorn encara s'enduria més vides; l'última, la de Robert Juet, de gana, i ja a prop de la costa d'Irlanda.

Un cop a Anglaterra, en el judici per haver abandonat el capità i els malalts, els vuit supervivents coincideixen a culpar Juet i les quatre últimes víctimes dels inuits. Si això fos cert, per una vegada la sort hauria sigut honesta i s'haurien salvat tots aquells que podien tenir la consciència tranquil·la. Sempre és un bon recurs culpar els morts, sobretot si l'atzar ha sigut així de benèvol... I ja no és cosa nostra jutjar els supervivents. Oi que no?

De fet, ni tan sols la justícia anglesa s'arriscarà a condemnar-los. Si realment hi ha hagut un motí i un abandonament, caldria penjar aquests supervivents amotinats, com mana la llei. Però com s'hauria d'arriscar la corona britànica a perdre la valuosa clau del pas del nord-oest? Als ulls de l'imperi, aquests homes són els únics que coneixen la drecera cap a Àsia, així que cap problema: l'atzar ha sigut amable amb els bons, i ara aquests senyors seran també tan amables de tornar cap a aquelles aigües i acabar d'obrir el pas cap a Àsia. Oi que sí?

Així, com que sembla que al segle XVII els europeus encara continuen sense tenir clar on acaba Amèrica i on comença Àsia, el 16 d'abril de 1615 el *Discovery* torna a salpar amb divuit homes a la recerca del pas del nord-oest, aquest cop capitanejat des del principi per Bylot i pilotat per William Baffin. Aquesta vegada l'expedició de reconeixement tornarà al complet, satisfeta i amb noves pistes per on buscar el desitjat pas cap a Àsia. De moment, Baffin podrà estar content de deixar el seu nom als mapes; des que torni amb la seva detallada narració, l'illa més gran de la regió explorada portarà el seu nom. A més a més, Baffin deixa clar que el pas del nord-oest ha de ser més al nord de l'estret de Hudson.

Mentrestant, per la seva banda i ben calladet, Bylot pot estar content que no s'hagi sabut fins ara que l'estret de Hudson no era la porta cap a l'Índia. Amb tot plegat, per molt que l'esforç sigui compartit, Baffin s'emporta el mèrit, però Bylot no es pot queixar d'haver tornat viu de l'expedició amb Hudson i d'haver-se estalviat la forca per amotinament, així que potser ja li va bé passar discretament pels llibres d'història. El 1616 els mateixos homes tornen a embarcar-se al *Discovery*, recorren la costa oest de Grenlàndia fins a prop d'Upernavik, aconsegueixen contactar amistosament amb els inuits i això els permet continuar més al nord, fins als 77° 45', latitud considerada rècord fins al segle XIX. Certament fa de mal precisar un rècord de latitud entre expedicions que es mouen cada cop més sovint per aquestes gèlides aigües perquè en aquells anys ja hi ha navegants que estan explorant el nord del Canadà, Grenlàndia, Spitsbergen... Fins i tot Baffin mateix ja ha estat en aquestes exigents latituds en expedicions anteriors, i a més a més n'hi ha alguns que no en tornen mai més potser perquè precisament han arribat massa més enllà.

Marble Island. Morir plorant

Al nord-oest de la badia de Hudson, a uns trenta quilòmetres del continent, hi ha l'illa de Marble, blanca i erma, amb un paisatge dominat per la quarsita d'aspecte marmori, que li dona nom. En una badia arraconada d'aquesta solitària illa, les restes d'una casa buida, abandonada des de fa mig segle. Aquí i allà, deixalles de carbó, eines, armes, cables, maons; i no gaire lluny, una cinquantena de tombes. I enmig d'aquesta desolació oblidada i silenciosa, dos esquelets damunt del terra blanc. Un, el de l'últim home que estava a punt de ser-hi enterrat; l'altre, el de l'home que va morir, plorant tot sol i cavant l'última tomba, sabent que ell ja no seria mai enterrat per ningú.

Com ha de ser l'últim esforç de qui mor cavant una tomba? No pot ser més crua i aspra aquí, la mort. Com si aquest fos l'últim cementiri del món i el d'enterramorts l'últim ofici, mai més ningú ha tornat a plorar davant d'aquestes tombes sense làpides. No hi ha marbre a l'illa de marbre, i tan precari és aquest cementiri anònim que no hi ha ni làpides ni qui vingui a plorar-hi.

El 1767, Samuel Hearne navega per aquestes aigües perdudes en què la *Hudson's Bay Company* es dedica al comerç de pells amb els habitants locals. Aquí, Hearne troba les restes d'aquest refugi abandonat i l'escampall d'objectes europeus que en el seu dia els inuits no es van endur; i ben a prop, a la badia, troba el buc de dues naus a uns deu metres de fondària. Sens dubte són l'*Albany* i el *Discovery* de James Knight, en silenci sota el seu llit de mar des de feia cinc dècades. Ningú no ha tingut notícies de la seva tripulació des que l'octogenari James Knight se'n va anar a buscar el pas del nord-oest el 1719.

Nascut el 1640, no hi ha dubte que per a James Knight el sol fet d'aventurar-se a l'Àrtic amb quasi vuitanta anys ja implicava tota una gesta. Segurament tenia una edat en què ja havia perdut la por de morir, i més que un futur, Knight ja només es jugava un lloc a la posteritat si tenia la sort de trobar el pas del nord-oest. I de passada, si tot anava bé, l'expedició també volia localitzar mines d'or i de coure, i fins i tot establir una indústria balenera per a la companyia.

L'ambiciós Knight devia saber el que feia. El 1719 ja feia temps que era tot un expert en l'Àrtic. El 1676 (amb trenta-cinc anyets de res) havia entrat a treballar de fuster a la *Hudson's Bay Company*, i a poc a poc, a força d'assumir responsabilitats i experiència, finalment aquell James Knight octogenari estava ja preparat per dirigir la seva ambiciosa expedició.

El juny d'aquell 1719, Knight i cinquanta homes més s'embarquen amb l'*Albany* i el *Discovery* amb la intenció d'anar directament cap als 64° N sense ni tan sols aturar-se a cap dels forts d'aquesta companyia per a la qual treballa —tan gran és la seva convicció—. La següent cosa que en sabem és que el 1721 Henry Kelsey troba pals i veles de vaixells europeus que són utilitzats com a tendes d'un campament inuit a Marble Island. Però de moment Kelsey no acaba d'aclarir el destí de Knight i dels seus homes, i fins i tot s'especula que potser hagin trobat el pas cap al Pacífic i s'hagin perdut en algun lloc de camí a Califòrnia. Serà John Scroggs, l'any següent, el 1722, qui trobarà les restes enfonsades dels vaixells i semblarà resoldre la desaparició de Knight i companyia. Han naufragat i ja ningú no farà cap més esforç per trobar-los; no té sentit fer-ho.

Així, el destí d'aquells homes queda en el silenci fins que Samuel Hearne fa la seva troballa el 1767. De moment només ha trobat el mateix derelicte de l'*Albany* i el *Discovery* que ja va trobar Scroggs el 1722, però durant els anys vinents, Hearne, movent-se encara per aquesta zona, aconsegueix parlar amb dos vells inuits a qui pregunta per les restes trobades. Segons el seu testimoni, aquells vaixells havien encallat ben avançada la tardor, mentre la tripulació provava de trobar port. Eren uns cinquanta europeus que van construir una casa per passar-hi l'hivern. A l'estiu següent, el 1720, els inuits van tornar a veure els europeus, però aleshores ja n'hi havia molts menys, i els supervivents estaven greument malalts. Malgrat l'aliment que els van anar oferint els inuits quan tenien excedent, a l'estiu de 1721 ja només hi havia cinc europeus vius, tres dels quals estaven a punt de morir. Segons els vells testimonis inuits, els dos últims supervivents van fer esforços per enterrar els seus tres últims companys, i durant dies encara van continuar buscant una salvació. Passaven llargues hores mirant a l'horitzó des de dalt d'una roca elevada. El relat dels testimonis inuits en lletra de Hearne ens mostra aquests dos supervivents asseguts junts damunt el promontori, plorant amargament de desesperació.

Amargament, diuen. No tenim costum de veure els nàufrags plorant. Calia que ens ho expliqués algú? Els nàufrags ploren. I amargament. Durant anys. I sols.

Finalment, sempre segons el relat dels vells inuits, l'últim dels dos supervivents va morir mentre intentava enterrar el seu company a les proximitats del refugi.

I allà van quedar els seus esquelets, tal com els troba Hearne cinquanta anys després.

Així ho expliquen aquests inuits que, si van ser testimonis d'aquelles últimes morts el 1721, bé devien ser també la mateixa gent que es protegien amb els pals i les veles que trobaria Kelsey, potser pocs dies després que morís l'últim supervivent.

I doncs, ¿com no va rebre Kelsey aquest relat tan recent aleshores? De sobte, amb Kelsey entremig, tot plegat comença a enfonsar-se encara més en una mena de misteri líquid i sord, en una mena de silenci estrany, de paraules no dites: la distància del no parlar.

És ben misteriós, l'Àrtic, amb aquest seu silenci opac amb què s'ho empassa tot. Encara que ho veiem, encara que ens ho expliquin, de vegades tot sembla tan irreal... Un home morint cavant una tomba, els esquelets abandonats durant mig segle... Però d'una cosa no hi ha dubte: els nàufrags ploren amargament. No hi ha misteri ni dubte en el plor amarg dels nàufrags.

Els llibres d'història, com cròniques heroiques, rarament ens parlen del plor, i, si en parlen, ho fan des de la llar: les famílies que esperen el retorn del nàufrag ploren tristament, desconsoladament, fins i tot confiadament; i ploren només una sola cosa: la pèrdua de l'heroi estimat, que no és poc. Però els nàufrags, els perduts, ploren, amargament, la pèrdua de tot. Ho ploren tot. Absolutament tot. Per a nosaltres, hereus de cròniques heroiques, aquests inuits que ens ho expliquen han d'haver vist un nàufrag de veritat. Plorant de veritat el pitjor de tots els plors.

Avui, de tot allò que reposava sobre l'illa de Marble ja no queda res, però tres segles després del desastre, no gaire lluny d'aquesta badia encara es poden trobar sota la superfície del mar les restes del doble naufragi de l'*Albany* i el *Discovery*.

John Franklin. El naixement d'un mite

Segurament una de les fites que han perseguit més tossudament els exploradors europeus durant més temps és el pas del nord-oest entre l'Atlàntic i el Pacífic. Al llarg dels segles que van del XVI al XX, una pila d'expedicions s'endinsaran en el laberint d'illes i de gel del nord d'Amèrica sense trobar el camí, de vegades ni tan sols el de tornada. Entre aquests últims, potser un dels casos més coneguts sigui l'expedició dels *HMS Erebus* i *Terror* que, comandada per John Franklin, el 1845 s'acomiada d'Anglaterra per ser engolida misteriosament per les aigües de l'Àrtic, aparentment sense deixar cap rastre. Després que uns baleners els hagin vist per última vegada a la badia de Baffin, l'*Erebus* i el *Terror* semblen esborrar-se del món com si no haguessin existit mai.

No deixar rastre és segurament una de les morts menys reconfortants que es pot tenir en una expedició d'aquesta mena, sobretot també per als que n'esperen inútilment el retorn o bé, quan això ja no és possible, per als que confien que en tot cas la mort dels desapareguts hagi estat sense patiment. Potser va ser el cas dels cent vint-i-nou tripulants d'aquesta expedició.

El 1850 ja fa temps que a Anglaterra ningú no sap res d'aquesta gent, i les esperances s'esvaeixen igual com s'ha esvaït tota l'expedició sencera. Però el país sencer sembla abocar-se al seu rescat. No només per la insistència de Lady Jane Franklin, l'esposa de John Franklin, sinó perquè som davant d'autèntics mites vivents de l'època.

En aquells moments, l'*Erebus* i el *Terror* ja són dos mites de la marina britànica i de l'exploració polar. El *Terror*, avarat el

1813, ja ha servit intensament a la corona britànica abans de començar una carrera d'exploració científica, ha sobreviscut a guerres, a un huracà que el va deixar encallat a la costa de Lisboa el 1828, vuit anys després ha passat un hivern atrapat al gel de l'Àrtic canadenc, i encara el 1837 ha aconseguit tornar a Europa malgrat les ferides de l'atac d'un iceberg.

Després, ja amb el seu inseparable germà *Erebus,* avarat el 1826, els dos vaixells han assumit les ordres de James Clark Ross en diferents expedicions: des d'Austràlia fins a l'Antàrtida. En aquest continent, entre 1840 i 1843, més d'un cop s'escapen miraculosament dels gels d'aquelles latituds mentre Ross va batejant llocs com l'illa de Ross, el mont Erebus, el mont Terror o la barrera de gel de Ross. I quan es prepara l'expedició de Franklin no hi ha dubte que el *Terror* i *l'Erebus* són els vaixells que necessita.

I si memorables són l'*Erebus* i el *Terror*, no és menys memorable John Franklin, mite vivent després que, durant la tardor del 1821, va tornar d'una expedició al riu Coppermine (a l'Àrtic canadenc), una de les aventures de supervivència més impressionants del seu temps. En aquesta aventura onze dels vint exploradors que hi havia van sobreviure a una llarguíssima caminada, en la qual van suportar neus, tempestes, incendis, van travessar rius quasi infranquejables, glaçats o torrencials, i van superar tensions internes, tot sense aliments i quasi sense forces. Van ser tan a les portes de la mort que la fam els va portar fins i tot a cuinar les botes de recanvi, restes de pells, líquens diarreics, restes podrides d'animals morts, i encara, si més no un cop, van menjar una carn estranya aconseguida per un dels homes. Suposadament, era carn de llop, qui sap, però, si van menjar carn humana d'algú que havia estat assassinat. Van passar per tot això, mentre provaven d'arribar a Fort Enterprise, un racó de món abandonat on no els esperaven ni les provisions que pensaven que hi trobarien. Quan ja només estaven esperant la mort, Franklin i els seus homes van ser rescatats in extremis per un grup d'indis Yellowknife a les ordres del seu cabdill Akaitcho.

Des d'aleshores, per molt que tots ells haguessin compartit aquell àpat, només va ser Franklin qui va entrar a formar part de l'imaginari col·lectiu britànic com l'home que es va menjar unes botes. En això caldrà esperar cosa d'un segle perquè arribi Charles Chaplin per fer-li ombra.

Mentrestant, en la memòria popular anglesa trobem l'escena d'un grup d'homes famèlics enmig del no-res i del fred, tots al voltant del foc, fent bullir pacientment unes botes de pell... cuinant a poc a poc el mite de John Franklin.

Inuits. Els humans

Mentre els europeus descobreixen nous territoris, els habitants d'aquests llocs van descobrint els europeus. Però rarament els inuits descobreixen Europa i rarament els europeus van gaire a fons quan descobreixen els habitants nadius.

Esquimal, mot probablement d'origen algonquià, suposadament vol dir «menjadors de carn crua». Els que despectivament els donen aquest nom potser haurien fet bé de saber que la carn crua és una font de vitamina C que ajuda a evitar l'escorbut. Altres diuen que el mot *esquimal* potser vol dir «els que fan raquetes de neu», menys despectiu, però és estrany que un costum o un ofici serveixi per donar nom a tota una societat. Quin ofici o costum triaríem nosaltres per donar nom a la nostra? No ens posaríem d'acord. Ells senzillament són *inuit*, «la gent» (plural d'*inuk*, «home» o «persona» en inuktitut)[2]. Ells són *gent* i els que venen de fora són altra cosa, estrangers, de vegades blancs. I força estranys. En la seva llengua, *qablunaaq*.

Des que aquests *qablunaaq* comencen a aparèixer per les terres dels inuits, cada cop s'expliquen més històries de com venen de lluny amb grans barques. De vegades es perden o naufraguen i han de passar un temps en aquestes terres afortunades, però que, tanmateix són tan difícils, que ben fàcilment aquests *qablunaaq* europeus acaben perdent la vida.

Se n'expliquen coses, però molt pocs els han vist mai, i si no fos perquè de vegades algú troba senyals que en demostren la seva existència, gairebé diríem que això dels blancs és una invenció llegendària. Però els pobles que tenen costum d'escoltar, prou bé saben distingir la llegenda de la realitat. I tot això és veritat.

Som a finals d'estiu, un grup d'inuits estan pescant foques a la zona que ells anomenen Ootloo-lik, en un oblidat racó de l'illa de Qikiqtaq, quan veuen un vaixell unes tres milles endins del gel. Un d'ells, Nuk-kee-che-uk, és l'únic que gosa apropar-s'hi. El vaixell, sense cap senyal de vida, està totalment malmès al gel. És evident que alguns homes blancs hi van viure l'hivern passat. Segons les petjades que hi ha a la neu del voltant, fins fa poc allà probablement hi havia quatre homes que devien sobreviure caçant. Però ara mateix no hi ha ningú i Nuk-kee-che-uk s'emporta algunes coses que troba fàcilment al seu abast. Un cop de retorn al seu campament d'iglús, de seguida que els altres veuen el benefici que n'ha tret Nuk-kee-che-uk, no triguen gaire a anar-hi i a fer el mateix.

2 Tanmateix, en català inuit és una paraula singular. El plural és inuits.

Aviat al voltant del vaixell hi ha tot de gent que està mirant-lo encuriosida. Molts d'ells és el primer cop que veuen una cosa com aquesta, i com que no saben obrir les portes fins i tot foraden el buc de la nau per poder entrar al seu interior. És aleshores quan descobreixen en una llitera el cos sense vida d'un home molt alt. Vet aquí que les petjades indiquen que dels quatre homes que han viscut darrerament al vaixell, tres d'ells n'han marxat. L'altre, que no ha pogut sobreviure, per a molts d'aquests inuits és el primer *qablunaaq* que han vist en la seva vida.

Un d'aquests inuits, Ikiunelikpatolok, explica que de petit, potser trenta anys abans, ja havia vist *qablunaaq*. Va ser una vegada que estava pescant al riu Back. Va aparèixer una barca amb un grup d'homes que el van saludar. Aquest és el següent blanc que veu. No serà l'últim. Algun dia Ikiunelikpatolok encara tindrà l'oportunitat d'explicar aquesta troballa.

Però a banda d'aquest cos i de les petjades a la neu del voltant, al vaixell hi ha més senyals que algú hi ha passat l'hivern: restes de menjar, llaunes obertes, algunes de tancades, i també un munt d'objectes desconeguts, als quals els inuits no troben gaire utilitat. Un d'aquests objectes són llibres. De tot plegat, el que de moment veuen més útil és emportar-se'n la coberteria i els pots de cuina.

Després d'això, quan arribi el nou desglaç i l'aigua torni a envoltar el vaixell, part d'aquesta aigua s'escolarà pel forat que els inuits han fet per entrar-hi. La nau s'enfonsarà, deixant només al descobert, damunt la superfície, la part superior de tres dels quatre pals que encara manté sencers. Al voltant, hi haurà tot de restes surant. Alguns inuits encara podran aprofitar-les de tant en tant. Aquest vaixell és l'*Erebus*. L'illa de Qikiqtaq per a molts és l'illa del Rei Guillem, o de King William, i el cos llargarut que jeu en una llitera dins del vaixell ha perdut el nom. Mai més ningú no ens en sabrà explicar res més.

No és l'única troballa que faran en aquests anys. Un altre dia, en aquesta mateixa zona, els inuits també troben un segon vaixell enfonsat. Està tan ensota que no podran accedir-hi per aprofitar-ne res. Un altre dia, In-nook-poo-zhe-jook, troba uns bots al lloc avui conegut com a Erebus Bay. Com que viuen en un entorn tan poc generós, aquests caçadors i pescadors inuits aprofiten tot allò que l'atzar els ofereix. A les naus europees que apareixen de tant en tant a les seves costes hi ha fusta i metalls com ferro i coure, uns materials valuosos i difícils de trobar a l'Àrtic. Per als inuits, acaben essent com unes mines plenes de recursos. Quan localitzen una d'aquestes naus, no els costa gens dedicar uns dies a anar dels seus campaments a aquestes naus per recollir-hi i aprofitar-ne tot el que poden, com aquell que esprem un recurs fins a exhaurir-lo. Els primers que hi arribin s'emportaran el trofeu de les eines i de les armes, però sempre quedarà alguna cosa més per aprofitar. Ben fàcilment, els inuits trobaran alguna utilitat a tots aquests nous objectes. A vegades, els utilitzaran com a fites per orientar-los; més sovint els serviran d'eines, de pals per a les seves tendes, com a llances, arpons, arcs, fletxes, mànecs de ganivets... Ho aprofitaran tot: des de la peça més gran fins al clau més petit per fer hams. Fins i tot allò que en un primer moment no els sembla útil, com els passa amb el paper, pot servir perquè els nens hi juguin. Tot s'aprofita i algú treu benefici de la desgràcia dels europeus. Així doncs, qui sap si aquest recurs com caigut del cel no salva més vides de les que ha costat...

També en aquells mateixos anys, a la primavera de 1850, un grup de famílies inuits que està caçant foques a les proximitats de l'illa de Qikiqtaq troba una quarantena d'estrangers desnodrits i famèlics que arrosseguen penosament damunt la neu barques i trineus. Només es podran comunicar amb signes, tot just el mínim necessari per entendre que aquests forasters han naufragat en el gel i que es dirigeixen cap al sud per caçar alguna presa. Si és així, després que se'ls enfonsessin els vaixells, aquests homes han estat dos anys arrossegant absurdament aquestes barques i trineus sense haver avançat gaire. Potser anirien més lleugers si, en comptes de ser de fusta, aquestes barques fossin fetes amb pell de morsa, com fa tothom a l'Àrtic. I sobretot també, si els inuits sabessin què duen a les barques, potser entendrien per què han decidit anar tan feixugament lents.

Poc temps més tard, els inuits ja no troben quaranta homes, sinó un camí d'esquelets que porta a una mena de campament macabre amb un munt de cossos escampats arreu. Alguns han sigut enterrats, altres han quedat sense cap més tomba que l'interior d'una tenda abandonada o que el sota d'una barca capgirada. Encara, uns últims han quedat senzillament abandonats allà on devien caure per últim cop. Potser només alguns pocs han seguit el seu camí. Però no és l'escampall de morts el que dona a aquest lloc un aspecte dantesc, sinó alguna cosa molt més esgarrifosa. La presència de cossos mutilats fa evident que a manca de cap altra presa que els alimentés, els últims supervivents han aprofitat l'únic recurs que tenien a l'abast per resistir una mica més. Ells mateixos.

És innegable la seva lluita extrema per sobreviure fins al final de tot, però potser haurien fet bé, aquests salvatges estrangers, d'aprendre a viure com els inuits, com les persones.

De fet, així haurà de ser durant algun temps. Tres o quatre d'aquests supervivents (entre ells potser el capità del *Terror*, Francis Crozier) passaran l'hivern amb un grup d'inuits que ignoren bona part de l'infern que han viscut aquests *qablunaaq*, però amb el final de l'hivern àrtic aquests estrangers reprendran el seu camí cap al sud. See-gar, un dels inuits que ha conviscut amb ells, molts anys després tornarà a trobar alguns blancs que li preguntaran precisament per aquella gent, i els explicarà com van seguir el seu camí cap a la terra dels Kin-na-pa-too, a la badia de Hudson. Ningú més no ens n'ha sabut dir res i aquí se'n perd la pista per última vegada.

Aquesta mena d'històries sobre els estrangers *qablunaaq* circulen sense gaires distorsions per l'entramat nòmada dels inuits durant anys. En una societat nòmada, en una terra perillosa i poc generosa, cal ser precís amb els detalls. Què, qui, on. Equivocar-se per poca distància a l'hora de trobar un recurs o una persona pot ser definitiu. No hi ha vida sense explicacions clares, sense paraula, sense escoltar. Per als blancs, la veritat viu molt estretament lligada a la paraula escrita, al paper, però els nòmades tenen un mapa i uns fets gravats a la memòria i no es poden permetre fallar.

Quan anys després arribin altres blancs i preguntin per aquells supervivents, alguns inuits els sabran donar explicacions prou precises i convincents. Sempre que es puguin permetre el luxe de donar detalls, és clar. Als blancs no els indicaran amb precisió el lloc on hi ha el naufragi, una mina que val moltes vides per als inuits. Més val protegir aquest recurs. Però no dubtaran a explicar amb precisió allò que puguin dir. In-nook-poo-zhe-jook serà el primer a explicar a John Rae com els supervivents de l'*Erebus* i el *Terror* van haver de recórrer al canibalisme, notícia que —sense botes cuinades que ens distreguin del drama— causarà una gran commoció a Anglaterra.

Canibalisme? És fàcil imaginar l'impacte mediàtic del relat de Rae en la societat britànica de l'època. Des del moment que es constata la desaparició de l'*Erebus* i el *Terror*, i sobretot després de la impactant notícia que ha portat Rae, a Anglaterra es posen en marxa més expedicions de rescat de les que mai hi havia hagut navegant per l'Àrtic. Moltes d'aquestes expedicions són promogudes per Lady Jane Franklin, també exploradora i esposa del capità de l'*Erebus*, que, per descomptat, es nega a creure Rae, a qui acusa de calúmnies. Poc s'imagina Lady Jane que el seu marit no ha tingut prou temps per arribar a aquell macabre extrem. Sigui com sigui, mentre hi ha esperances de trobar supervivents, es desencadena una febre tan gran per trobar-los que es perdran més vides buscant l'expedició de Franklin que les que s'han perdut en aquesta expedició. Les primeres dècades de recerca seran especialment intenses i, tot i que no se'n troba cap supervivent, sobretot John Rae (1854), Francis McClintock (1859) i Charles Francis Hall (al llarg de la dècada de 1860) recolliran força testimonis directes dels inuits sobre els supervivents de l'expedició de Franklin. Poc se'n pot aclarir durant els primers anys de recerca, però és tan gran l'impacte d'aquesta desaparició que encara en el segle XXI hi ha qui en busca restes. A poc a poc es van reconstruint alguns fets.

Un dels primers rastres que trobem dels dissortats de l'*Erebus* són tres solitàries tombes congelades a l'illa canadenca de Beechey, a 74° Nord. Allà, enmig del no-res, reposen tres làpides datades entre gener i abril de 1846 amb els noms de John Torrington, John Hartnell i William Braine. Costa d'imaginar quins esforços cal fer per excavar una tomba en aquelles condicions hivernals de fred i foscor absoluta. I, atès que els homes que caven aquestes tombes saben què els passarà després, és just considerar que van fer un esforç sobrehumà.

Després que aquestes tombes quedessin oblidades durant un segle i mig, en els anys 1984 i 1986 un equip dirigit per Owen Beattie exhuma els tres cossos que hi ha en un intent de donar una mica més de llum als fets. Perfectament momificats al permafrost, l'autòpsia revela que aquests tres homes estaven malalts de tuberculosi i que probablement van morir de pneumònia, però sobretot es detecta que tenien una alta intoxicació de plom. Fins allà on sabem, no deuen ser els únics exploradors que moren intoxicats per les soldadures de les llaunes de menjar en conserva que els haurien d'haver salvat la vida, però per als tripulants de l'expedició deu ser una experiència terrible veure l'agonia d'aquests homes sense entendre'n els motius, i més terrorífic deu ser continuar veient altres companys que pateixen i moren misteriosament, un rere l'altre, mentre cadascun d'ells espera el teu torn sense saber què pot fer per esquivar aquell inexplicable mal.

Sigui com sigui, la intoxicació i les dures condicions de vida debiliten la salut i obren la porta a malalties com la tuberculosi, l'escorbut o la pneumònia. El juny de 1847 John Franklin mor als seixanta-un anys d'edat, i a l'abril de 1848 l'expedició ja té vint-i-quatre baixes. En aquell moment, per algun motiu desconegut, els cent cinc supervivents decideixen abandonar els vaixells a l'illa del Rei Guillem per intentar arribar a peu a la badia de Hudson, mil milles al sud, i salvar-se; però pel camí van deixant rastres que a poc a poc van essent pistes del seu destí. Un d'aquests rastres són restes humanes abandonades, cosa que ens ajuda a traçar la ruta que seguien. Un altre, és el testimoni d'alguns inuits amb qui es troben mentre avancen cap al sud. El 1854, l'expedició de rescat de John Rae troba uns inuits que els donaran una pista definitiva. El seu interlocutor, In-nook-poo-zhe-jook, li assegura que pocs anys enrere van veure alguns homes de l'expedició de Franklin, potser uns trenta-cinc o quaranta, empenyent un trineu i una barca per la costa de l'illa del Rei Guillem, i que van ser trobats morts un temps més tard. Per si algú vol posar en dubte aquest testimoni, Rae compra a aquests inuits algunes relíquies (plats i coberts) amb el nom de l'expedició de l'*Erebus* gravat, cosa que els inuits només poden haver aconseguit d'un lloc.

Fins aquí, la història de supervivència s'assembla a molts altres pitjors viatges del món, però els inuits també asseguren que els cossos tenien evidents senyals de canibalisme. És cert que per part de Rae tornar a Europa amb aquest testimoni és molt atrevit, però els inuits no són mentiders. Per ells sabem que els supervivents anaven morint mentre avançaven, i, per les restes d'ossos que es van trobant dels exploradors perduts, podem confirmar que efectivament van haver de recórrer al canibalisme per mirar de no morir de fam. Segons els experts, hi ha senyals de ganivet (ganivets europeus) en els ossos i a les extremitats. Van serrar-les sense cap mena de dubte.

Per molt angoixant que sigui, no és el primer cop que algú ha de recórrer al canibalisme per sobreviure perquè, malgrat la desesperació, quan el grup és nombrós, sempre sembla més fàcil tenir possibilitats de continuar viu. D'alguna manera, menjar la carn dels teus companys morts és creure en la supervivència, però fins i tot en els pitjors viatges del món sempre hi ha coses que poden ser pitjors: aquella carn humana és una carn malalta, potser intoxicada de plom. I cada cop n'hi ha menys. I si no sobreviu ningú, vol dir que ha mort l'últim. I abans, el penúltim. Alguns moren caminant, drets, caient a mig fer la seva última passa, i per a cada supervivent que veu morir un company, el viatge es fa pitjor. Costa posar-se a la pell dels dos últims supervivents mirant-se per últim cop. Completament animalitzats i sabent-se morts, un dels dos viurà una mica més que l'altre, menjarà uns dies més que l'altre. Si els veiéssim, segurament no els reconeixeríem com a humans; només veuríem dos éssers demacrats a les portes de la mort, al final d'un interminable infern en vida.

I l'últim queda sol. Ja sense res per menjar. Potser només avançant per oblidar-ho tot una mica abans de caure definitivament lluny de tot i de tothom. O potser ni avançant, jaient al costat del company per morir al seu costat i no quedar eternament sols.

Des de la desaparició de l'*Erebus* i del *Terror*, mai no s'han deixat de trobar noves peces del trencaclosques. El 1859 l'expedició de McClintock troba dos cadàvers en un bot salvavides a la costa de l'illa del Rei Guillem, i des d'aleshores de tant en tant aniran apareixent cossos amb senyals de dents o de serres i de ganivets. Però abans d'arribar a aquest extrem han passat coses que els equips de recerca miraran d'anar aclarint, i ben aviat, l'any següent, el 1860, a la mateixa illa del Rei Guillem es localitza una fita de pedres amb objectes de l'expedició perduda i amb un parell de notes escrites.

El primer missatge, datat el 28 de maig de 1847, resumeix el recorregut fet fins aleshores per l'expedició i no denota cap desesperació especial, però la segona nota ja és més alarmant. Datada a 25 d'abril de 1848, un any més tard, explica que fa tres dies els cent cinc tripulants de l'*Erebus* i el *Terror* han abandonat les naus. De passada, aclareix la mort de John Franklin l'11 de juny de 1847 i que els supervivents tenen la intenció de marxar aviat cap al riu Back, de camí a la badia de Hudson, on mai no arribarien.

No gaire lluny d'aquesta troballa, una barca mig enterrada a la neu amb restes humanes ajuda a explicar per què no van sobreviure. Rellotges d'or, coberteria de plata, llibres... Només el munt d'objectes absurdament innecessaris que hi ha a la barca que arrossegaven a força de braços ja són un sobrepès mortal quan la vida penja d'un fil.

El pes de les paraules

Or. Plata. Aquest és el drama. Que vivim en un món contaminat més que de plom, del valor de l'or i de la plata. El drama d'aquells homes és que en abandonar el vaixell encara no han descobert que ja no formen part del nostre món. Mentre els inuits busquen ferro i coure, aquests homes ja sense món arrosseguen or i plata per descobrir quin és el preu de la vida. Massa tard deuran fer el seu terrible descobriment oblidat: que el ferro i el coure marquen el preu de la vida; i l'or i la plata el del canibalisme, el de l'infern.

I llibres. Paraula escrita. Vet aquí també el pes de les paraules. Però per als inuits el paper no resisteix res, no serveix per a fer reparacions, ni eines, ni armes de caça. Només els nens hi troben utilitat com a joguina i deixen aquells llibres esmicolats damunt la neu.

Vet aquí, en canvi, el poder de la paraula dita.

La xarxa comunicativa oral dels inuits és de grans forats i pocs nusos, però de cordes necessàriament fortes, fiable, com exigeix el solitari i inhòspit entorn en què viuen. Potser per una qüestió de supervivència, en les històries que s'expliquen els inuits no hi ha gaire lloc per a la distorsió; qualsevol mentida o imprecisió sobre els fets i els llocs importants pot costar vides. Per això podem saber que el que expliquen dels *qablunaaq* és cert. Una altra cosa són les dates, els anys; el passat és passat i prou, però els fets no canvien.

Quan Charles Francis Hall a partir de 1860 emprèn diferents expedicions a la recerca de Franklin, començarà veient-se obligat a passar dos anys entre els inuits, als quals escolta i dels quals aprèn. Durant aquest temps establirà una forta amistat amb el matrimoni format per Ipirvik (1837-1881) i Taqulittuq (1838-1876) (coneguts també com a Joe i Hannah per facilitar les coses als blancs), que li faran de guia i d'intèrpret i que li seran sempre uns grans amics i un ajut primordial en les seves exploracions.

Probablement una de les primeres sorpreses que tindrà davant d'Ipirvik i Taqulittuq a Hall serà sentir que el conviden parlant en un anglès perfecte a prendre el te al seu iglú, on Taqulittuq es dedica a fer mitja al més pur estil britànic. Però és que, igual com passa als *qablunaaq* occidentals, ser inuit no està renyit amb el coneixement d'altres cultures i idiomes, ni amb el fet de viatjar. A principis dels anys 1850 un balener anglès els havia portat a Europa, on Ipirvik i Taqulittuq van ser exposats gairebé com una atracció de circ. Farien tanta sensació que fins i tot van ser presentats a la reina Victòria. Així doncs, quan aquesta parella coneixen Hall, ja han passat un parell d'anys a Anglaterra i dominen suficientment l'idioma. Sense esverar-nos massa podem entendre que aquests visitants fan allò d'aprendre la cultura del lloc on van, però, a més, sense perdre la pròpia (de veritat que aquestes coses passen). I amb aquesta bona entesa des del primer dia, l'amistat de Hall amb Ipirvik i Taqulittuq serà tan forta que ja l'acompanyaran en totes les expedicions de l'explorador, fins i tot en la del seu intent per arribar al pol nord amb l'expedició del *Polaris*, durant la qual Hall morirà el 1871.

Ipirvik i Taqulittuq continuaran viatjant durant la resta de la seva vida. Exploraran l'Àrtic amb els *qablunaaq*, i també, les terres d'aquests, sobretot els Estats Units, on el 1876 morirà Taqulittuq, precisament lluny de la seva terra, igual com tants altres exploradors de tot el món. Ipirvik viurà encara uns pocs anys més i morirà en algun lloc de l'Àrtic. Al final dels seus dies, tots dos s'hauran convertit ja en uns dels inuits exploradors més cèlebres, curiosament pel fet de conèixer l'anglès i per haver pogut portar els *qablunaaq* pel territori que aquells estrangers venen a explorar.

I és que per molt que coneguin altres mons, els inuits viuen arrelats a la seva terra i a la seva cultura, i això inclou que la transmeten amb força.

Quan el 1860 Hall arriba a l'illa de Baffin, encara té esperances de trobar algun supervivent de l'expedició de Franklin entre els inuits, però de seguida veurà que no és així, i en tot cas serà ell qui es veurà obligat a conviure-hi més temps del que esperava. El primer hivern ha de quedar-se amb la comunitat de baleners (aquells que sempre sembla que hi siguin abans que els exploradors, i aquells que efectivament mantenen un contacte més viu i proper amb els inuits). És aleshores quan Hall aprofita per començar a entrar al cor de la cultura inuit. És aleshores quan coneix Ipirvik i Taqulittuq, i també és aleshores quan de boca de la gent més gran comença a recollir històries sobre anteriors exploradors blancs. Sorprenentment, una de les històries que Hall recull dels inuits correspon a la d'uns *qablunaaq* que van arribar durant tres anys seguits, cada cop amb més vaixells, i que van intentar excavar una mina a l'illa de Kodlunarn. Li expliquen també com aquesta història va acabar amb baralles, amb morts i amb inuits segrestats i portats cap al país dels *qablunaaq*. No sabem amb quina cara d'estupefacció Hall rep aquest relat, sobretot quan s'adona que la tradició oral el porta directament a les tres expedicions de Frobisher de tres segles enrere (1576-78). Sorprès per la precisió amb què s'han transmès els fets, pregunta com s'ho fan els inuits per mantenir aquestes històries tan intactes. L'explicació que rep no pot ser més eloqüent:

«Quan els nostres fills petits són prou grans els expliquem tot sobre vosaltres i els *qablunaaq* que van portar totxos, ferro i carbó al lloc on has estat, i dels *qablunaaq* que van construir un vaixell a l'illa de Kodlunarn; quan el nen arriba a ser un vell inuit ho explica a altres inuits, i així tots els inuits sabran el que ara sabem.»

Fàcil, oi?

La troballa del *Terror*. Escoltar la tradició

De l'expedició de Franklin, doncs, desapareguda misteriosament, a poc a poc n'anem sabent coses. Sabem que molts tripulants van morir als vaixells, possiblement intoxicats pel plom de les soldadures de les llaunes, que altres van avançar carregant un llast absurd, que van anar morint pel camí, que es van alimentar d'ells mateixos... Ningú no ha trobat encara la tomba de Franklin, però a poc a poc es va tancant el cercle de la desaparició dels seus vaixells. El 2014 un equip canadenc trobarà l'*Erebus*, i el 2016 el *Terror*, enfonsats i abandonats en les condicions que els testimonis dels inuits feien pensar. Ara sabem del cert que els vaixells encallats al gel han sigut abandonats abans d'enfonsar-se, i a partir d'aquell moment potser encara devien avançar en una deriva fantasmal sobre el gel abans de fer el seu darrer viatge cap al fons.

Però l'Àrtic deu ser ple de naufragis i, per cert, no ha sigut fàcil localitzar aquests vaixells en comptes d'uns altres.

Les troballes i contalles dels inuits no semblen tenir fi. El 2009 Sammy Kogvik i James Klungnatuk, dos inuits de la comunitat de Gjoa Haven, surten a pescar com de costum. Mentre avancen amb les seves motos de neu per la solitària costa sud de l'illa del Rei Guillem, Kogvik s'atura un moment per esperar el seu company, i aleshores, mirant a l'horitzó, s'adona d'alguna cosa dreta damunt del gel en la llunyania. Massa lluny perquè cap dels dos ho pugui identificar, decideixen acostar-s'hi, i un cop al lloc es troben davant la punta del pal d'un vaixell que sobresurt sobre el gel en l'alçada d'una persona. En apropar-s'hi, Kogvik ja transmet a Klungnatuk la sospita que es tracta del *Terror*, un dels vaixells de Franklin abandonats l'abril de 1848, i Klungnatuk fins i tot fa a Kogvik una foto al costat del pal, però la foto només és paper, pesa, i a més a més, per mala sort Kogvik perdrà la càmera en el camí de tornada a Gjoa Haven i mai ningú no veurà aquesta imatge.

Tot i que el descobriment és interessant, la importància que els dos amics li donen de moment és relativa, potser perquè tampoc no són els primers inuits que localitzen aquest vaixell. Qui més qui menys entre els inuits de la zona ha sentit parlar de les restes del *Terror*. Potser no és tan estrany, doncs, que un cop perduda la foto, Kogvik decideixi desar aquest record en el terreny de l'anècdota; ells només són uns més dels que han trobat el *Terror*. A més a més, l'any següent Klungnatuk patirà un accident que li costarà la vida, i sense ningú amb qui compartir el record, Kogvik semblarà oblidar la troballa feta amb el seu amic.

Així doncs, mentre els inuits ja fa temps que expliquen que allà es veuen restes del que podria ser el *Terror*, curiosament tots els operatius de recerca segueixen pistes més científiques que no pas les contalles d'aquesta gent del nord que segurament mai no han perdut del tot la pista del naufragi. Perquè la modernitat és imparable. Fotos aèries, sonars, radars... Pocs anys després que Kogvik es fes una foto amb el *Terror*, el govern canadenc reprèn el projecte de localitzar els dos naufragis. El setembre del 2014, les noves tecnologies permeten finalment localitzar l'*Erebus*, i quan el 2016 el govern canadenc comença un nou operatiu de recerca, Kogvik decideix explicar el que sap a Adrian Schimnowski, en qui confia prou. Schimnowski, director d'operacions de l'Artic Research Foundation, és algú que a més de mirar, escolta. Escolta què diuen els ancestrals habitants d'aquest territori, i encara que les pistes de Kogvik el porten a buscar a cent quilòmetres d'on se suposa que reposa el *Terror*, decideix fer-li cas. Així, el setembre d'aquell any, en menys de tres hores de recerca troben el que ningú no ha sabut trobar en cent setanta anys. Així de fàcil era. Escoltar.

En paraules del mateix Schimnowski, «els inuits coneixen el territori millor que ningú més i jo en soc un visitant. Soc a casa seva i em faria vergonya no escoltar-los, perquè realment això va de la vida i la mort a l'Àrtic». I encara ens recordarà, després del descobriment, que «això ensenyarà a la gent que potser el petit gest d'escoltar és més important que tota la tecnologia i l'equipament que es pot portar a bord d'un vaixell per buscar alguna cosa». Segurament si els primers exploradors haguessin pogut escoltar i aprendre més dels inuits, alguns dels cent vint-i-nou dissortats de l'expedició de Franklin haurien pogut explicar el seu pitjor viatge del món. Però com dirà encara Schimnowski, «he sentit massa històries que no han sigut escoltades, així que ja era hora de començar a fer-ho.»

Així, escoltant, sembla que per fi es posa punt final a una recerca de segle i mig que ha costat més vides de les que van desaparèixer en el moment del desastre. Destruïts els dos vaixells entre l'agost i el setembre de 1848, l'*Erebus* apareix especialment malmès, enfonsat a causa del forat que hi van fer els primers inuits per entrar-hi i, de moment, sense pistes del cos que se suposa que reposava en una llitera. Qui sap si algú, abans que el vaixell s'enfonsés, el va treure i el va enterrar, potser inuits, potser companys que per algun motiu van tornar al vaixell i en van tornar a marxar en veure'l més malmès encara. I pel que fa al *Terror*, és trobat reposant dignament dret i intacte a vint-i-quatre metres de profunditat. A banda dels tres pals trencats, es manté tan intacte que es diria que no hi ha passat absolutament res. Senzillament es diria que el vaixell, un cop abandonat, ha decidit descendir beatíficament cap al fons sense desendreçar res del que hi ha als seus prestatges, igual com hauria pogut decidir volar plàcidament com un fantasma o continuar navegant i acabar de creuar el pas del nord-oest, a les portes del qual ja no es troba gaire lluny.

L'expedició de Franklin ha sigut engolida per l'Àrtic, però ja no misteriosament.

Un vaixell de gel. Els eterns silenciats

Rarament els llibres donaran protagonisme als inuits Ipirvik i Taqulittuq. Sovint a aquest matrimoni només se li reconeixerà un paper secundari darrere la figura de Charles Francis Hall. Però en canvi, si es vol, se'ls pot considerar protagonistes del primer intent d'arribar al pol nord. Segurament aquests inuits són dels pocs que surten ben parats d'aquella expedició, perquè poques vegades es deu haver organitzat i dirigit una expedició d'una manera tan maldestra com aquella del Polaris el 1871.

Aquell any, Ipirvik i Taqulittuq s'embarquen amb el seu vell amic Hall, el qual dirigeix l'expedició juntament amb Sidney Budington i George Tyson, un triumvirat de relacions tenses en el qual tots tres mai no es posaran d'acord. Serà la perdició de l'expedició. L'octubre d'aquell any, amb el *Polaris* a 82° de latitud a la costa nord de Grenlàndia, un grup de quatre homes marxa en trineus per explorar aquella regió que els ha d'obrir el camí cap al pol; són els inuits Ipirvik i Hendrik, a més dels estrangers Hall i Hubbard Chester. Després de dues setmanes en condicions extremes, ja de nou al *Polaris*, Hall emmalaltirà de sobte, i entre nàusees, vòmits, paràlisis i deliris no pararà de queixar-se d'haver estat enverinat. N'acusarà sobretot Budington o algú proper a ell. Durant la seva agonia, només els remeis de Taqulittuq li alleujaran els símptomes, però la insistència del metge de l'expedició per ajudar-lo farà que de nou reprengui el tractament científic, que empitjori de nou i que acabi morint en qüestió de dies. El seu últim llegat serà una solitària tomba al nord de Grenlàndia, on reposa prou ben congelat perquè cent anys després, el 1968, se'n puguin analitzar mostres que permetran refermar la possibilitat de l'enverinament. En cap cas, però, es pot assegurar això amb tota la certesa, i sobre Budington planejarà sempre més l'ombra del dubte.

Sigui per malaltia o per enverinament, des de la mort de Hall, la vida al *Polaris* a les ordres de Budington es regeix per una organització cada cop més caòtica: hi ha un ús excessiu de l'alcohol, primer per part de Budington mateix i després per part de cada cop més tripulants, a més d'un malbaratament dels recursos i de cap mena de planificació seriosa. Així, sense previsió dels riscos, a l'estiu de 1872 es fan dos intents d'avançar cap al pol nord amb l'únic resultat de destruir tres bots de l'expedició a tot just pocs quilòmetres del *Polaris*.

Després del fracàs, aprofitant que el *Polaris* s'allibera del gel, reprenen rumb cap al sud, però el seu progrés és molt lent i s'hauran d'aturar de nou a l'octubre després de topar contra un iceberg. En aquest moment comença a entrar aigua al vaixell. Per alleugerir la nau, Budington ordena treure'n tota la càrrega que puguin i manen que la deixin damunt del gel. Sense cap mena de delicadesa, gran part del carregament és destruït en ser llançat per la borda, però afortunadament per a alguns homes, no tot serà malmès. A la nit, durant la feina de descarregar el vaixell, la banquisa de gel s'esquerda i un grup de dinou persones queden separats del *Polaris*. Són nou inuits, entre ells Ipirvik i Taqulittuq, i deu estrangers. Quan torni la llum del dia, la distància entre el bloc de gel a la deriva i el *Polaris* serà d'uns quants quilòmetres i ja ningú no anirà a ajudar-los.

Els catorze tripulants que queden al *Polaris* veuen com allà lluny, al gel, s'esfumen a la deriva dinou persones amb bona part de les provisions. Efectivament, el *Polaris* ha alleugerit el seu pes, però ara, pràcticament no duu res més que el que porten a sobre. Als catorze tripulants del vaixell ja només els queda confiar en la sort. Després d'aquesta maniobra tan absurda de buidar el *Polaris*, embarranquen la nau a la costa nord de Grenlàndia, prop d'Etah, on construeixen uns refugis i on sobreviuen a l'hivern amb l'ajut dels inuits de la zona. Passat l'hivern, aquests supervivents construiran una barca amb el que els queda de fusta del *Polaris* i emprendran un complicat viatge cap al sud fins que seran rescatats per un balener i tornats de nou al país dels estrangers. Una història més que els inuits d'Etah tenen per explicar als seus descendents.

Mentrestant, aquell hivern, en algun lloc enmig de la foscor tempestuosa de l'Àrtic, hi ha un bloc de gel navegant a la deriva amb dinou persones al damunt. Mentre els inuits preparen iglús com a refugi, els sempre tan hàbils estrangers s'escalfen cremant un dels bots que tenen al gel (no era aquesta la idea de *cremar les naus*, si tinguessin més hàbit de llegir potser ho sabrien, però aquests estrangers semblen encallats a mig camí entre la paraula oral i l'escrita). Mentre els inuits cacen foques, els estrangers malbaraten les reserves d'aliments i d'alcohol que han salvat del *Polaris*. Res més a dir. Durant els pròxims sis mesos, nou inuits (amb deu estrangers més) viuran en aquest bloc de gel a la deriva cada cop més amenaçadorament petit, dormint en iglús improvisats, caçant foques i aprofitant el que els estrangers no malbaraten.

Sense els inuits, aquests deu estrangers serien encara més uns descobridors de l'oblit. Però tenen uns bons amfitrions, Ipirvik i Taqulittuq entre ells, i amb ells, gràcies a ells, sobreviuran mig any al gel navegant gairebé tres mil quilòmetres a la deriva en aquesta misteriosa embarcació minvant. Finalment, l'abril de 1873, aquests deu estrangers seran rescatats (ah, sí, i amb un grup d'inuits sense nom) a la badia de Baffin pel *USS Tigress* en la seva expedició de rescat del *Polaris*. I així aquests homes seran reconeguts per tots els mitjans periodístics del món després d'una sorprenent aventura de supervivència. Un cop més, els inuits que també han viscut aquesta aventura passaran de puntetes per damunt de la paraula escrita.

L'obstacle del nord-est. El cap Dejniov

Mentre en el somni d'arribar a Àsia els europeus occidentals s'estavellen un cop rere l'altre contra el mur americà, per l'altra banda l'imperi rus creix i creix cap a l'est fins al cor del continent, fins a les portes de la Xina i Mongòlia, fins al mar del Japó. A poc a poc, els pobles europeus van tancant el cercle per banda i banda, i el 1639-40 Ivan Iurèvitx Moskvitin arriba fins a la desembocadura del riu Amur, al mar d'Okhotsk.

Semblava que no passaria mai, però en la seva infinita expansió estepària l'imperi rus ha arribat al Pacífic, i cada cop es fa més necessària una ruta des de la metròpoli fins a aquelles costes llunyanes. Així, mentre el transsiberià és encara inconcebible, cada cop pren més forma la idea d'un pas del nord-est cap al Pacífic. Però per a això encara cal saber si Amèrica i Àsia són un sol cos, si hi ha un pont terrestre (en aquest cas un mur) entre els dos continents o si hi ha una via navegable. Cal resseguir les costes fins a dibuixar els últims extrems del continent als mapes.

I aquí és on trobem Vitus Bering, un danès que segons els llibres el 1728 travessa per primer cop l'estret que ara duu el seu nom.

Avui el mapa és molt clar amb els seus noms tan ben escrits i amb el de Bering fins i tot als mapes mundials; però apropem-nos-hi una mica més, ampliem el mapa i disposem-nos a buscar amb lupa els noms dels accidents geogràfics més petits. Agafem aquest estret de Bering, mirem-nos bé el continent asiàtic i enfoquem la vista en el punt de contacte entre aquests dos elements: a la punta de tot de la península de Txukotka, a l'extrem més oriental d'Euràsia apareix, destacat i discret, un raconet anomenat cap Dejniov.

El nom de cap Dejniov és posterior a Bering, potser com una mena de reparació històrica, però Semion Dejniov, que és d'on prové aquest nom, va córrer un gran risc de ser un autèntic oblidat vuitanta anys abans que Bering es guanyés un lloc als mapes del món.

Sigui especulació o sigui coneixement, ja en el segle XVII hi ha mapes que mostren Europa i Àsia separades per mar. Per tant, és creïble que Bering segueixi els passos d'altres exploradors que ja s'hi han aventurat abans. De tots aquells altres exploradors, amb prou feines coneixem el nom de Semion Dejniov.

Tota ruta àrtica cap a Àsia implicaria vorejar l'agitat braç de mar glaçat que hi ha per entrar al Pacífic. El primer intent conegut el farà Isai Ignatii Mezenets el 1646 en intentar vorejar la península de Txukotka. Després del seu fracàs, el 1647 Fedot Aleksèiev Popov i Semion Dejniov ho tornen a provar, però també topen amb l'obstacle del gel. No serà fins l'any següent quan els mateixos Popov i Dejniov dirigiran l'expedició que els posarà, encara que sigui amb lletra petita, als llibres d'història.

En aquell 1648, set vaixells i un centenar d'homes formen part de l'expedició dirigida per Popov. Entren a l'Àrtic des del riu Kolimà, naveguen cap a l'est, i gràcies a un estiu especialment calorós, aconsegueixen superar l'obstacle del gel i entrar a l'oceà Pacífic. Finalment, ja més al sud, després de moltes dificultats i de sobreviure un hivern a les portes del riu Anadir, els supervivents s'endinsen de nou cap al continent en una última odissea terrestre a través d'aquest riu per mirar de tornar a poc a poc i penosament, a la civilització. Només en tornen dotze.

I ja està. De seguida està explicat. Però ja veiem que no és un viatge fàcil. Entremig, en el seu periple per aquestes aigües mai navegades per ningú conegut, alguns dels set vaixells de l'expedició naufraguen sota les tempestes, i altres senzillament desapareixen també arrossegats per les inclemències sense deixar cap rastre. Un d'aquests vaixells és el de Popov, el cap de l'expedició. Popov és l'oblidat dels oblidats.

Un naufragi rarament porta mai gaires dubtes, però una desaparició misteriosa sempre ens porta la il·lusió de la supervivència. És, en certa manera, una bona manera d'aferrar-se a la memòria des de l'oblit. Amb les ungles clavades al caire de la memòria i amb el cos penjant xuclat pel precipici de l'oblit, aquests mariners desapareguts alimentaran encara algunes llegendes segons les quals haurien arribat a Alaska i s'haurien establert en una colònia que ningú no ha vist mai. Altres, en canvi, diran que els desapareguts han sigut rescatats pels inuits i que s'haurien adaptat a les seves comunitats. No se'n sap res, i, com que el món del mar és ple de llegendes, sempre hi ha exploradors i mariners que senten, que diuen, que asseguren que han vist... però mai no se sap res de prou sòlid. De fet, poques opcions més quedarien a aquells desapareguts llevat de la mort immediata. La més probable.

Sigui com sigui, el periple de l'expedició no es va acabar ràpidament. Sembla que es devien endinsar força cap a Alaska perquè fins i tot van arribar a descobrir un parell d'illes que probablement eren les Diomedes, dues petites illes rocoses separades per quatre quilòmetres de mar. Una d'aquestes illes avui és territori rus; l'altra, dels Estats Units. Com que han quedat a banda i banda de la línia de canvi de data, a l'hivern queden separades per quatre quilòmetres de gel i per gairebé un dia sencer del calendari. D'aquesta manera, si mai voleu repetir una data d'hivern n'hi ha prou a fer aquests quatre quilòmetres a peu cap a l'est, sempre sabent que en tornar cap a l'oest deixareu de viure una altra data concreta. Si sou prou hàbils, esquivareu, doncs, aquella que us porti mals records.

Però el 1648 aquests viatges no són tan fàcils. Finalment, dels líders de l'expedició només Dejniov sobreviu per explicar la història, cosa que amb prou feines va fer. Com si la seva aventura fos poc més que un tràmit burocràtic, Dejniov no deixarà cap més registre del seu viatge que una nota oficial redactada anys després. Amb això, tot i la certesa que no va ser el primer humà a navegar aquestes aigües, sí que és el primer nom avui conegut d'algú que va fer aquest viatge. De la resta de l'expedició, tanmateix, no en sabem res. Moltes gràcies, doncs. Apa! A descansar també sota la manta de l'oblit parada per aquest discret explorador!

Així, per molt que en alguns mapes de l'època ja es comença a dibuixar una Alaska i una Àsia separades, per algun motiu el descobriment del 1648 no serà prou conegut o reconegut. Durant les dècades següents, per molt que s'intenti, ningú més aconseguirà repetir aquest viatge. No serà fins al 1728 que arribarà Vitus Bering i s'emportarà el nom d'aquest braç de mar. Per a Dejniov va quedar només la punteta del final del continent, un cap que probablement no va ni tan sols arribar a veure. I per a Popov, el principal cap de l'expedició, només va quedar l'oblit sota les aigües gèlides. Si ja és difícil trobar el nom de Dejniov en llibres i mapes, què podem dir de Fedot Aleksèiev Popov?

Però l'Àrtic continua guardant encara molts secrets. Que els continents americà i eurasiàtic estan realment separats no ho demostrarà del tot ningú fins a l'any 1879, quan Adolf Erik Nordenskiöld completi per primer cop el pas del nord-est. És veritat que ja ho sabíem, però amb Nordenskiöld quedarà clar que allò que ja buscava la Rússia de Dejniov era factible, si bé no era viable com a ruta comercial.

El pas del nord-oest. Ànima de fusta

Haurà calgut esperar molt, massa. Després de quatre segles llargs buscant la ruta comercial del pas del nord-oest, entre el 1903 i el 1906 una reduïda expedició dirigida per Roald Amundsen a bord del *Gjøa* aconsegueix navegar per aquest lloc per primera vegada en la història, una gesta que el mateix Amundsen deixarà també clar que no té cap utilitat comercial.

Amb Amundsen, a bord del *Gjøa*, també viatgen sis homes que tenen uns noms avui pràcticament oblidats: Godfred Hansen, Helmer Hanssen, Anton Lund, Peder Ristvedt, Gustav Juel Riik i Adolf Lindstrøm. Aquest últim era un entranyable cuiner que anirem trobant incansablement en altres expedicions polars, un oblidat que gairebé sense proposar-s'ho es convertirà en la primera persona a circumnavegar completament les dues Amèriques, la del nord i la del sud.

Però de moment, perquè aquests noruecs puguin travessar el pas del nord-oest, cal que abans algú l'hagi localitzat. I per això cal retrocedir mig segle i no perdre de vista els primers anys de recerca de l'expedició de Franklin. La tasca d'exploració que fan els possibles rescatadors del *Terror* i de l'*Erebus* aporta uns coneixements tan grans sobre l'Àrtic que, per dramàtic que sigui, gairebé es diria que si Franklin no s'arriba a perdre, l'Àrtic hauria sigut un misteri profundíssim durant encara molts anys més.

De moment una d'aquestes expedicions que s'aventuren al gel nòrdic serà la que localitzarà el pas del nord-oest. I ja que entre els oblidats hi ha cuiners, començarem per la cuina d'aquell vaixell.

Ens plantem a l'abril de 1850 a l'estret de Magallanes, a mig camí entre Anglaterra i l'estret de Bering, en un vaixell britànic anomenat *Investigator* capitanejat per un home de caràcter tirànic i iracund, Robert McClure. Hi ha una tripulació de seixanta-sis homes més, tots ells bàsicament tenen fama d'indisciplinats i conflictius. Un d'aquests homes és Henry Sugden, oficial de cuina.

Aquell abril de 1850, Sugden rep quaranta-vuit fuetades amb un fuet de nou cues. Els que no n'hem patit mai cap no ens podem imaginar la tortura que deu ser això. L'esquena en carn viva rebent les nou puntes del fuet quaranta-vuit vegades sobre una carn cada cop més viva, sobre una pell que ja no hi és. No sabem què ha dit exactament Henry Sugden, però aquest és el càstig que imposa McClure al cuiner per haver dit paraules inapropiades.

Però l'*Investigator* no va sol. De fet el vaixell principal de l'expedició és l'*Enterprise*, comandat per Richard Collinson, un home que tampoc es queda curt en el seu autoritarisme delirant i que serà capaç de tenir arrestats bona part dels oficials de bord durant els tres anys vinents que durarà la seva aventura àrtica. Si mai hem tingut somnis romàntics d'haver participat en aquelles expedicions polars del segle XIX, definitivament aquesta expedició no hauria sigut la millor.

Com en tantes altres expedicions d'aquelles dates, el pretext de Collinson i McClure és mirar de localitzar el *Terror* i l'*Erebus* de Franklin. Però sobretot, més enllà d'aquest pretext, hi ha la possibilitat de cartografiar costes desconegudes, i potser també de fer una incursió cap al pol nord, i qui sap si fins i tot de trobar el pas del nord-oest tan buscat.

¿Com posar d'acord dues mentalitats autoritàries com les de McClure i Collinson? Segurament només allunyant-los l'un de l'altre. Deu ser per això que l'*Enterprise* no espera l'*Investigator* a Hawaii i s'avança pel seu compte cap a l'estret de Bering. I és aleshores quan el colèric McClure decideix avançar Collinson per una ruta més directa a través de les illes Aleutianes i, desobeint les ordres, entrar a l'Àrtic en solitari.

Tres hiverns després, quan siguin rescatats, McClure i els moribunds supervivents de l'*Investigator* seran els primers a poder explicar que hi ha un pas del nord-oest. No és navegable, però, després de descobrir l'illa de Victòria i l'estret del Príncep de Gal·les, poden demostrar que hi ha una frontera marítima al nord del continent nord-americà.

I de Franklin, tampoc res de res, malgrat que, sense saber-ho, en alguns moments es poden haver trobat a pocs quilòmetres de distància. Quin ajut més absurd s'haurien donat dues expedicions exposades a la deriva àrtica!

La improvisada recerca de McClure porta l'*Investigator* a passar el temps resistint l'embat de l'Àrtic, intentant obsessivament avançar cap a l'est, si cal provocant explosions al gel, suportant tempestes que el porten amunt i avall a la deriva, mig perseguit per l'*Enterprise* del crispadíssim Collinson i mig buscant el *Terror* i l'*Erebus*. I mentrestant, per gaudir millor, ha d'anar paint les tensions humanes internes. Només com a exemple de la disciplina que es viu a bord, des de ben principi, ja amb les primeres setmanes de tempestes àrtiques, els homes de l'*Investigator* buiden tot el rom del rebost, no fos cas que la mort segura que els espera els enxampés més sobris del que cal. Per molt que McClure s'indigni davant d'això, no consta que fuetegi de nou cap oficial, segurament perquè si tothom es passa dies absolutament begut, ¿qui podria fuetejar a qui en aquestes condicions?

Tota manera, i durant els propers hiverns, ni el retruny del gel, ni la fam, ni l'escorbut, ni la foscor absoluta per manca de combustible, ni la manca de caça, ni les temperatures que arriben a baixar dels setanta sota zero no són impediment perquè el delirant McClure s'aventuri cada cop més en un camí de no retorn cap al pas del nord-oest. Encallats al gel durant tres anys, envia homes malalts a fer incursions impossibles, de vegades més amb la intenció de minvar la tripulació i repartir millor les provisions escasses que no pas d'aconseguir cap avenç real. I tot i això, la tripulació resisteix tossudament. Només cinc dels seixanta-set tripulants moriran sense tornar a casa.

És així com a la primavera de 1853, després de tres anys a l'Àrtic, un grup d'homes malalts d'escorbut i afeblits es troben vagarejant en trineus per les solituds àrtiques intentant arribar miraculosament a algun lloc on demanar ajut. Mentrestant, McClure i alguns dels homes menys debilitats, convençuts que els que han marxat no tornaran si no és amb l'ajuda d'algú, veuen com ara els queden més provisions per a cadascú i continuen confiant que l'estiu vinent s'obri una escletxa cap a l'Atlàntic nord.

Només un miracle els pot salvar.

I així va ser.

En aquells moments de la primavera de 1853, a uns doscents cinquanta quilòmetres més a l'est hi ha el *Resolute*, comandat per Henry Kellett, un dels quatre vaixells de l'expedició (de rescat de Franklin, no cal ni dir-ho) que dirigeix un tal Edward Belcher. Belcher! Aquesta sola paraula hauria fet tremolar qualsevol mariner de l'època. Belcher probablement sigui un dels homes més odiats i temuts del món de l'exploració polar, té una fama tant treballada d'estúpid, autoritari, incompetent i arrogant que fa semblar innocents i infantils els iracunds McClure i Collinson. Però, per sort dels homes de l'*Investigator*, Belcher encara queda prou lluny. Abans que res, la salvació és en el *Resolute* de Kellett, encallat també al gel tal com sembla que correspon a una bona expedició àrtica. Això sí, de moment, el *Resolute* de Keller està en una situació millor que l'*Investigator* de McClure i els seus homes.

Una cosa a l'horitzó.

Una silueta humana a l'horitzó blanc.

No pot ser cert el que veu McClure...

Finalment, d'una manera gairebé misteriosa, el 6 d'abril d'aquell 1853 un dels tripulants del *Resolute*, el tinent Bedford Pim (amb William Domville, Robert Hoyle i Thomas Bidgood), arriba fins a l'*Investigator* i hi troba un grup d'homes cadavèrics. McClure, entre ells. L'arribada de Pim a l'*Investigator* sembla tancar, per fi, el camí entre l'est i l'oest de l'Àrtic americà. L'ésser humà ha traçat el camí del pas del nord-oest.

Però què hi fa una silueta humana buscant McClure en un racó de l'Àrtic?

Tot sembla tan estrany i incomprensible que, com si fos un misteri més de les regions polars, la casual semblança de noms

—Pim i Pym— ens podria submergir en un aiguabarreig encara més profund de fantasia i realitat que inquietaria el mateix Edgar Allan Poe. A la seva *Narració d'Arthur Gordon Pym*, de 1838, Poe envia el seu protagonista a fondre's en les proximitats oníriques d'un pol sud aleshores absolutament inconegut. I de sobte, misteriosament també, com si el Pym fictici reaparegués materialitzat a l'Àrtic quinze anys després, aquest Pim –i no pas Pym— de carn i ossos sembla tancar també un llaç entre els dos pols, i també entre la fantasia i la realitat.

Pym, fantasia i desaparició a l'extrem Sud. Pim, realitat i aparició a l'extrem nord...

Tot són maneres de veure-ho, però el que és innegable és que l'oblidat Pim (real) i els encara més oblidats Domville, Hoyle i Bidgood van ser els que, tancant aquest cercle en contactar amb l'expedició de l'*Investigator*, van fer una passa que és una nova petita descoberta de l'oblit. No l'han navegat encara, de moment cal travessar-lo amb trineus, però el pas del nord-oest existeix.

Un cop Pim arriba a l'*Investigator*, explica a McClure que a cent seixanta milles hi ha el *Resolute*, a càrrec del capità Henry Kellett, també encallat al gel però òbviament en molt millors condicions. A partir d'aquí vindran encara uns quants viatges més de trineus fins al *Resolute*, on el capità Henry Kellett escoltarà incrèdul com McClure li assegura que tot va bé, que l'*Investigator* pot continuar endavant en la seva comesa de ser el primer a navegar pel pas del nord-oest. Tots els supervivents de l'*Investigator* estan malalts, desnodrits, congelats o cecs i gairebé viuen en una mena de deliri. Ningú no se salva de l'escorbut i McClure continua mantenint-hi un severíssim règim tirànic i unes dietes molt rigoroses, fins i tot per als més malalts. Kellett no s'ho pot ni creure. Tot va bé, segons el delirant McClure.

Afortunadament, Kellett aconsegueix fer portar tots els homes de McClure cap al *Resolute* i rescatar-los d'una mort inevitable. I un cop abandonat definitivament l'*Investigator*, des del *Resolute* McClure encara enviarà un grup d'homes més cap a l'est, al *HMS Phoenix* (en aquests anys, l'Àrtic canadenc està tan ple d'expedicions de rescat que gairebé sembla difícil no trobar-ne cap). Aquest reduït grup que es desplaça fins al *Phoenix* seran els únics de l'expedició de McClure que aquell mateix any podran trobar mar obert i salpar de nou cap a Europa per explicar que han trobat el pas del nord-oest. Així, el 1853 Samuel Gurney Cresswell i Robert Wynniat seran els primers homes a completar el viatge al voltant de les Amèriques (en vaixell i trineu...). Mentrestant, McClure i la resta de supervivents hauran d'esperar encara un altre any més a ser alliberats del gel i de Belcher per tornar a un món civilitzat que ja fa temps tenien oblidat.

Amb McClure, doncs, s'ha fet la volta a Amèrica, s'ha trobat el pas del nord-oest i ara ja només queda navegar-lo. Per a això últim caldrà esperar que el 1906 arribi Amundsen amb el seu cuiner Adolf Lindstrøm, el primer home que circumnavegarà (navegant) el doble continent americà, el del nord i el del sud, abans que ningú altre, gairebé es diria que sense voler, sense sortir de la cuina del vaixell, com qui perpetra una mena de venjança dels cuiners maltractats en tantes anteriors expedicions àrtiques.

Mentrestant, a McClure, després d'haver abandonat Collinson i l'*Enterprise* i de no haver buscat Franklin, a Anglaterra, l'espera un judici per la pèrdua del vaixell. Tot plegat abans que rebi la recompensa de deu mil lliures gràcies al seu descobriment. I això malgrat que aquest descobriment va ser com a conseqüència del seu caràcter tirànic i d'haver desobeït les ordres de Collinson. Collinson, és clar, no es prendrà gens bé els mèrits que ara atorguen a McClure.

Però Collinson on és? Què se n'ha fet? Després d'anys perseguint-se amb McClure, jugant al gat i la rata per l'Àrtic, Collinson haurà de desistir, farà mitja volta i tornarà a Anglaterra el 1855. De fet, si l'*Enterprise* i l'*Investigator* haguessin estat sota un comandament més humà i menys aïrat, probablement els dos vaixells haurien continuat junts i haurien tingut moltes més possibilitats de trobar el pas del nord-oest i l'expedició de Franklin. Vet aquí alguna cosa que ens permet pensar en l'essència de l'ésser humà.

Finalment, obeint tot d'ordres incomprensibles de Belcher, els homes que passen l'últim hivern al *Resolute* abandonen la nau el maig de 1854 i tornen cap a Anglaterra amb una nova expedició de rescat. Però aquest no és encara el final del vaixell. En una decisió molt criticada, l'inepte Belcher mana que s'abandonin els quatre vaixells de la seva expedició. A partir d'aquest moment, sembla que la natura es relaxi. El gel que aturava el *Resolute* comença a fondre's. Gràcies a això, fent honor al seu nom, tot resolut, aquest vaixell, alliberat del gel i de qualsevol persona, navegarà calmosament cap al sud fins que el setembre de 1855 el balener nord-americà *George Henry* capitanejat per James Buddington el troba a uns dos mil quilòmetres del punt on va ser abandonat.

El *Resolute*, aleshores, retrobat com un vaixell fantasma a les portes de l'Àrtic, és portat als Estats Units i, finalment, de nou, a Anglaterra. Després d'uns quants anys més de servei, part de la seva fusta serà reutilitzada per construir uns escriptoris. Però naturalment, després d'una aventura com aquesta, no es pot tractar d'uns escriptoris qualssevol, sinó d'uns escriptoris que serveixin per prendre grans resolucions: un d'aquests mobles anirà a parar al palau de Buckingham. Un altre serà un regal que la reina Victòria farà el 1880 al president dels Estats Units, Rutherford B. Hayes. Encara avui presideix la Sala Oval de la Casa Blanca.

La deriva del gel

1

Ets la solitud del gel àrtic, vasta i infinita, estèril, buida. Ets la solitud i no coneixes ningú ni res més que gel, només el so del vent i el cruixir del gel on no ha arribat mai ningú. Així ets i així has sigut sempre. I ara, enmig d'aquesta buidor, per primer cop des de fa milers o potser milions d'anys, des de l'inici dels temps i de la teva solitària existència glacial, alguna cosa pràcticament imperceptible sembla que et pugui posar en dubte: en la blancor del gel, uns taulons de fusta, una caixa, papers, roba vella. Com si tinguessin vida pròpia, aquests objectes han arribat sols fins aquí i marxaran impassibles seguint el seu camí com si res.

Són fora del món i del temps.

Ningú no en sap res, i no en sabrem mai el seu camí exacte, però probablement aquests objectes avançaran tot sols uns cinc quilòmetres diaris empesos per aquest món del gel. Això vol dir potser uns dos-cents metres cada hora. Uns tres o quatre metres cada minut. Potser cinc o sis centímetres cada segon.

Aquesta diminuta escala d'uns pocs dits per segon és la que ens permet veure avançar aquests misteriosos objectes pel solitari gel àrtic. Pacientment, a ritme de formiga, durant tres anys, durant més de mil dies.

Llargues nits, llargs dies, tempestes, ventades, milers de quilòmetres de vasta solitud, però la caixa de fusta, els pantalons, la llibreta, angoixosament lents, metòdics i impassibles, gairebé com fantasmes somnàmbuls, avancen i avancen.

2

El 18 de juny de 1884, a la població del sud de Grenlàndia de Qaqortoq (aleshores amb el nom danès de Julianehåb), uns pescadors inuits troben uns estranys objectes enmig del gel. Avui, per a nosaltres, gent del futur, habituats com estem a la nostra petja per tot arreu, aquests objectes potser serien considerats deixalles, però per a aquest grup de pescadors trobar res que no sigui gel i foques a la seva costa és encara massa estrany, totalment nou. És per això que ho recullen tot i que ho fan arribar a terra, on la troballa cridarà l'atenció de Carl Lytzen, el governador danès de la zona. Entre els objectes apareix el nom d'un vaixell, *USS Jeannette*, alguns noms de la seva tripulació i també el del seu capità, George De Long. Vet aquí les restes d'un naufragi d'un vaixell que mai no ha passat per aquí.

3

El 12 de juny de 1881, després de dos anys embarcats, els trenta-tres tripulants de l'expedició del *Jeannette* abandonen el vaixell en tres bots salvavides a les proximitats de l'illa siberiana de Wrangel, encara coneguda només per ells, que en són els descobridors.

Fa dos anys que van sortir de San Francisco. Des d'allà van travessar l'estret de Bering per comprovar si realment al Pol Nord hi ha un mar obert, potser d'aigües càlides, però de seguida van ser atrapats pel gel i empesos cap al nord-oest.

En aquell moment encara ningú no sap com és exactament el Pol Nord. Hi ha diferents teories. Des d'antic n'hi ha hagut moltes i algunes d'especialment imaginatives, hipòtesis que han parlat de continents habitats, de mars oberts i càlids, d'una gran illa de ferro o fins i tot d'un gran forat que condueix al centre de la Terra o qui sap si al Pol Sud. La ciència del segle XIX ja descarta les teories més inversemblants, però el cas és que ningú no sap del cert com és el Pol Nord. Probablement fixant-se en la direcció que pren el corrent càlid del Golf de Mèxic, la possibilitat de trobar aigües temperades a l'Àrtic sembla prou sòlida. Amb aquesta convicció De Long emprèn la seva aventura el 1879.

Al principi la vida a bord és prou tranquil·la i, tot i que han quedat encallats al gel poc després de travessar l'estret de Bering, el gel els fa avançar. Com que tenen prou provisions, resisteixen al vaixell durant prop de dos anys. Malgrat tot, en aquestes circumstàncies el gel és una força vivent, es mou, cruix sorollosament, esclafa constantment la carcassa del vaixell i la fa espetegar sense que hi hagi ni un segon de silenci durant aquests anys. Un sol d'aquests cruixits faria creure al més valent que el vaixell s'acaba de partir en dos, i cada cop sembla més evident que la pressió del gel tard o d'hora destruirà aquesta closca de nou.

Estan totalment aïllats del món. A l'estiu de 1881, però, es comencen a organitzar expedicions de rescat del *Jeannette.* Precisament, en aquests mateixos dies, quan són a prop de l'illa de Wrangel que acaben de descobrir, De Long dona l'ordre d'abandonar el vaixell. Això passa el dia 12 de juny. La tripulació carrega tres bots salvavides amb el que és més imprescindible i, abans de poder-se'n allunyar, veuen com el *Jeannette* es parteix en dues meitats sota les mandíbules blanques de l'Àrtic.

L'autèntica aventura de De Long gairebé comença ara. Però també en comencen moltes altres. De moment, repartits en tres bots salvavides, s'inicien tres aventures diferents de supervivència. De la més curta se'n sap poc: un dels bots no triga a desaparèixer sense deixar rastre, engolit també per la natura. De les altres dues, sabem que els supervivents, després de tres mesos arrossegant els bots pel gel, arribaran a mar obert i acabaran a la desembocadura del riu Lena, on la majoria dels expedicionaris moriran abans de ser rescatats. Finalment, només tretze d'ells tornaran a casa seva.

Una quarta aventura que començarà aquí serà la dels objectes que pacientment travessaran l'Àrtic fins al sud de Grenlàndia. Una aventura muda i cega. I arran d'això, encara hi haurà una cinquena aventura: la del jove Fridtjof Nansen, un noruec de vint-i-tres anys que el 1884 llegirà un article escrit per Carl Lytzen sobre els objectes del *Jeannette* trobats a Grenlàndia. En aquest article, Lytzen explica la possible deriva del gel, i aquí és on Nansen començarà a pensar en la construcció del *Fram* per fer-se encallar expressament en el gel i mirar d'arribar així al pol nord. Nansen no arribarà al pol nord, però les seves expedicions a bord del *Fram* seran entre les més memorables de l'era de l'exploració polar.

Amb l'aventura de Nansen hi haurà un abans i un després en l'exploració polar i en el coneixement del món.

Però això serà més endavant. De moment, uns pocs objectes han fet el camí de Wrangel a Qaqortoq, uns cinc mil quilòmetres per l'Àrtic. Mai no sabrem si aquests objectes van ser la primera presència humana al pol nord. Potser les restes del

Jeannette han passat tot soles pel mateix pol nord geogràfic abans que cap persona, i han tornat a la civilització com qui res. Potser així el pol nord ha conegut l'existència dels humans abans que hi arribessin. Seria molta casualitat, però ningú no ho sap. En qualsevol cas, aquestes restes del *Jeannette* han descobert la deriva del gel i han donat una idea a Nansen.

Així és com ens coneix el fons del mar. Abans que nosaltres a ell: en forma de deixalles i naufragis.

També aquest és un descobriment.

Potser el pol nord ha descobert els humans abans que els humans a ell. Sempre anem tard.

Fridtjof Nansen

L'armador noruec d'origen escocès Colin Archer és l'escollit per construir un vaixell capaç de resistir el viatge que ha imaginat Nansen. Segurament rep l'encàrrec sense poder evitar una mirada escèptica, però el projecte és molt temptador: cal que el vaixell pugui resistir un viatge que per a qualsevol altra nau seria un viatge sense retorn. Cal que es pugui deixar encallar en el gel de l'Àrtic fins que la deriva el retorni a les aigües lliures en algun punt de l'altra banda d'aquell l'oceà desconegut. Potser, amb sort, el gel els portarà al mateix pol nord, o prou a prop per poder-hi arribar esquiant. Entre altres coses cal, sobretot, que el buc del vaixell sigui prou resistent per no rebentar amb la pressió del gel, o millor encara, que el vaixell s'aixequi per sobre d'aquest element i no rebi tanta pressió.

Tothom considera que el projecte de Nansen és un suïcidi, però després del cas *Jeannette*, la seva idea és treballar amb les forces de la natura, no contra elles, i insisteix: «Poseu-nos sobre el gel». La resta és responsabilitat d'ell.

Només algú com Fridtjof Nansen podia convèncer les autoritats a emprendre una aventura com aquesta. El seu prestigi com a explorador és inqüestionable des que el 1888 culminava la primera travessa de Grenlàndia esquiant, juntament amb Samuel Balto, Ole Nielsen Ravna, Otto Sverdrup, Oluf Christian Dietrichson i Kristian Kristiansen (salut als oblidats). Ja aleshores, molts creien que aquells sis aventurers emprenien un viatge cap a la mort. I de ben poc va anar, atesa la quantitat d'accidents i de trampes mortals que van haver d'esquivar en el desert de gel. A més a més, tots aquests contratemps van impedir que acabessin la travessa de Grenlàndia en les dates previstes. No els va quedar cap més solució que haver d'hivernar amb els inuits. Però Nansen aprofitaria aquells mesos per aprendre'n les tècniques de caça, d'abric, de menjar, de transport... Fins i tot va aprendre l'ús del caiac, llavors encara molt desconegut a Europa. Per estrany que avui ens pugui semblar, coses ara tan elementals com els esquís i el caiac no entren de ple en el món de l'exploració polar fins que Nansen els posa damunt la taula. I mentrestant, també aquell mateix hivern, ja comença a rondar-li pel cap la idea d'una nau capaç de navegar per l'aigua i pel gel.

Nansen és l'explorador de moda a Noruega, l'heroi nacional que des de les seves primeres aventures ha recollit l'experiència dels samis i dels inuits, que ha adoptat la seva forma de vida quan ha fet falta, que ha escrit llibres sobre ells per difondre'n l'estil de vida i els valors... Nansen no és un aventurer qualsevol. Gairebé es diria que la geografia que explora és l'excusa damunt la qual es dona la vida humana. I això és el que descobrim en Nansen: la humanitat que va tenir durant tota la seva vida. El món occidental està descobrint el nord gràcies a ell, que n'és una autoritat indiscutible. És per això que, quan parla d'aprofitar les forces de la natura, té molt clar que ningú no tindrà arguments prou sòlids per dur-li la contrària.

Això ho sabem avui. Però aleshores, quan deia que volia fer-se encallar al gel polar, també l'hauríem titllat de boig.

Finalment, el *Fram* («Endavant») és construït i varat per salpar l'estiu de 1893. Té una tripulació de tretze persones i porta provisions per a cinc anys. Entre aquestes persones, per cert —una casualitat de noms ben curiosa—, l'atzar voldrà que hi hagi dos discrets oblidats anomenats Sigurd Scott-Hansen i Anton Amundsen. Un Scott i un Amundsen que, és veritat, no tenen res a veure amb els futurs conqueridors del pol sud, però que una mena de premonició sembla que ja vol ajuntar aquests dos noms als límits polars del planeta. La resta de la tripulació està formada per Henrik Greve Blessing, Theodor Claudius Jacobsen, Adolf Juell, Lars Pettersen, Fredrik Hjalmar Johansen, Peder Leonhard Henriksen, Bernhard Nordahl, Ivar Otto Irgens Mogstad, Bernt Bentsen i, sobretot, per Otto Sverdrup, capità del *Fram,* vell conegut de Nansen i supervisor d'Archer en la construcció del vaixell.

Mentre molts continuen pensant que l'expedició d'aquests tretze homes és un suïcidi, Nansen té clar que ell no vol ser un màrtir, sinó que vol tornar a casa. Des del primer moment que emproa cap al nord, no deixa de somiar mai en el sud, en la seva filla Liv de tot just uns mesos de vida i en la seva esposa, Eva Sars, a qui ha promès tornar. ¿Però qui no faria aquesta promesa? En aquestes aventures extremes, sempre ens oblidem de la gent que pateix a casa. Sembla que costi massa pensar què representa, al segle XIX, tenir un marit disposat a fer-se encallar al gel àrtic amb provisions per a cinc anys. Al *Fram* hi ha tretze persones amb tretze famílies esperant-los a casa. Nansen jura que tornarà. Però això, explicat mirant enrere és molt fàcil. Tothom qui no ha tornat havia jurat fer-ho.

Durant aquell estiu, el *Fram* recorre la costa siberiana fins a l'extrem oriental. El mes de setembre queda atrapat pel gel. De seguida es comprova que la feina d'Archer compleix a la perfecció el que havien previst: ben bé com uns llavis sense dents, les mandíbules del gel no aconsegueixen queixalar el buc arrodonit del *Fram*, que llisca i s'aixeca damunt la capa sòlida que se li va formant a sota.

Durant els primers dos anys encallats al casquet polar, la tripulació viu en condicions prou bones. La vida a bord gairebé es podria comparar a unes vacances de creuer. A més a més, fins a l'hivern de 1895 la deriva els acosta força cap al pol. Però quan sembla que la ruta glacial ja no els hi ha d'apropar gaire més, Nansen pren la decisió definitiva i aquell 14 de març ell i Hjalmar Johansen deixen el *Fram* disposats a arribar al pol esquiant amb tres trineus, dos caiacs i vint-i-vuit gossos de tir.

Aquell dia saben que probablement no tornaran a veure mai més ni el *Fram* ni els seus amics. I malgrat tot, Nansen està tan segur d'ell mateix, que només el rosega la recança d'estar abandonant l'expedició a la seva sort. Mentre el vaixell continuarà la seva deriva a cavall del gel, Johansen i ell hauran de trobar la manera de tornar al món amb els seus propis mitjans.

Les dures condicions que han d'afrontar no trigaran gaire a posar a prova Nansen i Johansen. Mentre encara estan avançant cap al nord, es veuen obligats a sacrificar algun dels gossos més dèbils per alimentar els altres. La llei de la supervivència ho dicta així. En el mes següent arriben a la latitud 86° 14';

mai ningú no ha arribat tan al nord, però continuar endavant seria massa arriscat i Nansen sempre pensa en el retorn. En la gent. En la seva petita Liv, que sigui com sigui creixerà amb un pare. Aquests 86 graus de latitud nord, doncs, seran el seu punt de retorn. Aquí és on començaria per a ells el suïcidi, i aquí comença segurament una de les aventures més sorprenents de supervivència de l'exploració polar, si és que són comparables unes i altres.

Des d'aquest punt, Johansen i Nansen comencen a dirigir-se de nou cap al sud. Lentament, cansats, amb provisions escasses i amb el material deteriorat, durant tres mesos els dos exploradors es mouen perduts per aquest impracticable desert de gel. La llei de la supervivència continua dictant les seves normes. Quan es queden sense provisions es veuen obligats a alimentar-se ells també dels seus propis gossos. D'un en un, primer són motor, després carn fresca. Vet aquí que els gossos són, encara més, els grans herois forçosos i els més oblidats de tots de l'exploració polar.

Durant mesos, Johansen i Nansen es mouen per la boteruda capa glaçada de l'Àrtic sense trobar res que els pugui ubicar en cap mena de mapa. Així avancen fins que finalment, el 6 d'agost arriben a una illa. Per primer cop en més de dos anys trepitgen terra ferma. Durant les setmanes següents avancen per aquest arxipèlag desconegut fins que el final de l'estiu els obliga a construir-se un petit refugi entre roques i gel per encabir-se tots dos a dins d'un mateix sac. Construït pràcticament sense eines ni material, aquest refugi serà la seva llar durant l'hivern vinent. Sobreviuran alimentant-se de carn d'os i de morsa. Vet aquí que haver après aquestes coses dels inuits els permet sobreviure en unes condicions tan extremes com la interminable nit àrtica.

No es pot imaginar un hivern més cru. Però Nansen té un optimisme tan indestructible que és capaç de tancar el 1895 escrivint al seu diari: «Conclòs aquest any singular. Després de tot, no ha sigut molt dolent». Qui més podria escriure una cosa així després de nou mesos caminant pel gel sense repòs?

Només el fet de sobreviure un hivern en unes condicions semblants ja seria suficient per considerar aquesta una de les aventures més dures viscudes mai a les regions polars. Almenys entre les que s'han pogut explicar. I per explicar-ho, aquests dos homes només poden comptar amb un rescat, però aquest racó oblidat de món no és un lloc on ningú pugui esperar aquest miracle impossible. A la primavera següent reprenen el viatge cap al sud amb la intenció d'arribar a Spitsbergen i ser rescatats. L'única alternativa és topar amb alguna expedició, potser la de Frederick Jackson, un anglès a qui Nansen no va contractar per al *Fram* i que a hores d'ara podria ser a l'Àrtic, a la Terra de Francesc Josep, amb la seva pròpia expedició.

Quinze mesos passaran Nansen i Johansen fent voltes i perduts per aquest desolat desert de gel. Quinze mesos de solitud absoluta, de no saber on són, de paisatge repetit incansablement. De silenci. Només les pròpies veus, les pròpies petjades, la pròpia respiració. I el vent. I el cruixir o l'estrèpit del gel. I l'aigua. Gairebé cap altre so.

Només, de tant en tant, algun animal. Guineus, morses, ossos, ocells i algun tret, sempre comptant les bales que els queden. I en l'avenç cap al sud, un atac de morsa que et fa aturar a reparar el caiac. De nou t'has salvat per pèls, però aquesta vegada el poc que tenies queda malmès per l'aigua i les opcions de sobreviure gairebé s'esvaeixen. Així són les coses quan, el 17 de juny de 1896, Nansen aprofita un moment que s'aixeca la boira per enfilar-se a un monticle i observar l'horitzó per provar d'ubicar-se. Aquesta illa que tenen davant, quina deu ser? És en algun mapa? ¿Forma part de la Terra de Francesc Josep? O són en un arxipèlag desconegut?

Un lladruc imaginat a la llunyania.

El cor de Nansen fa un bot. Pot ser?

Més lladrucs, li sembla, i de sobte tot es precipita. Corre a avisar el seu company, que no sap si creure'l. Una mica més tard, mentre camina en direcció a aquests suposats lladrucs, Nansen veu petjades de gos o de llop. Un punt negre que podria ser l'animal. I un altre punt que sembla una silueta humana. Ho són de veritat. S'acosten. I finalment, un cop cara a cara, Nansen sent per primera vegada en més d'un any una altra veu que no és la de Johansen. És algú que, després de saludar-lo cordialment, li diu en anglès:

—*Aren't you Nansen?*

—*Yes, I am Nansen.*

Tres anys a l'Àrtic lluny del món, quinze mesos abandonat a la sort del gel, i de sobte un ésser com caigut d'un altre planeta et pregunta si tu ets Nansen.

Efectivament, Nansen ha reconegut de seguida Frederick Jackson, l'anglès a qui ja havia conegut quatre anys enrere a Londres. De fet, gairebé confiava trobar-lo en algun moment. Jackson, però, està encara més sorprès en trobar aquesta mena de troglodita i descobrir, darrere les pells i la barba ennegrida per les capes de greix acumulades, la mirada de Nansen, aquest noruec a qui tothom dona per mort. I malgrat tot, Jackson també comptava amb aquesta possibilitat. Fins i tot, un cop al seu vaixell, el *Winward*, li lliurarà algunes cartes que li duia per si es trobaven. ¿Quantes possibilitats de topar amb algú poden tenir dos homes perduts en un lloc tan deshabitat? I de sobte algú et pregunta pel teu nom i et lliura un grapat de cartes.

El gir entre la ficció i la realitat de vegades pot ser molt sorprenent. Molt més encara. Gairebé cent anys abans, Mary Shelley havia creat l'home que naixia del retorn de la mort, el monstre de Frankenstein, i el feia perdre's a l'Àrtic en una de les escenes més misterioses i oníriques de la seva novel·la epistolar. Es diria que, gairebé de la mateixa manera que el monstre de Frankenstein, Johansen i Nansen tornen de la mort a l'Àrtic. Ningú no podia imaginar que encara fossin vius.

O potser sí?

Potser només la tripulació del *Fram* confia que els seus dos amics continuen vius. I aquesta és la pregunta de Nansen a Jackson. Algú en sap res del *Fram*?

No, res.

Això no li és, doncs, encara cap retorn a la vida. Però si més no, les coses es comencen a resoldre. Sense notícies de la resta de l'expedició, els dos supervivents tornen a Noruega, a Vardø, aquell mateix agost de 1896, tot just els mateixos dies en què el *Fram*, comandat per Otto Sverdrup, ha estat finalment alliberat del gel a prop de Svalbard i torna a navegar en aigües lliures cap al sud.

En arribar a Svalbard, els del *Fram* topen amb l'expedició de Salomon August Andrée, que es prepara per anar al pol nord en globus. Com que venen del món, els del *Fram* pensen que potser tindran notícies de Nansen, però els expedicionaris de Salomon August Andrée no els en poden dir res. Sembla que Nansen s'hagi fos en el gel. Als onze del *Fram* només els queda confiar que Jackson els hagi trobat. Si no és així, de tan convençuts com estan que tot ha anat bé, estan decidits a anar ells mateixos a buscar els seus dos companys a la Terra de Francesc Josep, on suposen que deuen ser. Deuen ser les úniques persones del món que no els donen per morts, però és que és aquesta confiança total el que els farà sobreviure. Mai no s'abandona un amic.

Sense notícies a Svalbard, tornen a Noruega amb el neguit de si els caldrà recular i anar a rescatar Nansen i Johansen. A Noruega, però, s'assabenten que els seus dos companys han tornat. Són camí de Tromsø, hi arriben tan sols un dia més tard que Nansen i Johansen. Els espera un retorn triomfal a Oslo, tota la tripulació de *Fram* s'ha salvat.

L'èxit és absolut. Nansen no ha arribat al pol nord, però s'ha complert el principal objectiu de l'expedició: explorar la conca polar i els corrents de la deriva del gel. En aquest sentit, Johansen i Nansen han tornat de l'aventura més difícil de totes, però abans que en el que han fet ells, l'èxit científic de l'expedició és en els onze del *Fram*, que han tornat cap a casa després de travessar l'Àrtic a cavall del gel tal com havien previst.

Promesa complerta.

El desig era arribar al pol nord; la promesa, com en tot viatge, era tornar. Perquè per a Nansen, quan ets tan al nord, desig i promesa són el mateix: anar cap al sud.

I amb tot plegat, l'expedició de Frederick Jackson —aparentment poc important— es converteix potser en una de les més transcendentals de l'època. I s'hi converteix senzillament perquè haver trobat Nansen en ple Àrtic és molt més que un fet: Nansen encara té moltes coses a dir al món.

Per fer-se'n una idea, només cal veure de quina manera el noruec passarà el ceptre de rei polar a Roald Amundsen. Quan anys més tard Amundsen comença a planejar la seva expedició al pol nord (que després en secret redirigirà al pol sud), Nansen està pensant en la seva pròpia expedició antàrtica amb el

Fram. Aparentment els dos exploradors estan preparant expedicions diferents, però Amundsen, que encara no coneix els plans de Nansen, té clar que necessita el *Fram* per a la seva expedició àrtica i li demana permís per utilitzar-lo. L'atracció polar és sens dubte una de les forces més difícils contra les quals lluitar, i sovint es converteix en una obsessió invencible per a aquells que s'hi han jugat la vida, però en aquell moment Nansen té clar que li toca renunciar per sempre més al seu somni polar i cedir el *Fram* perquè Amundsen culmini l'arribada al pol nord que ell mateix va haver de deixar a mitges. Que finalment Amundsen canviï de plans en secret i el *Fram* s'acabi dirigint cap al sud ja serà una altra història. Potser, en cas d'haver-ho pogut preveure, hauríem tingut una arribada al pol sud amb Nansen i Amundsen junts. Però Nansen ja té clar que és moment de començar una altra vida. I Amundsen està fet d'una altra pasta, no vol ombres, vol la glòria per a ell sol.

Així, tot i que Nansen no arribarà mai a cap pol, la seva experiència serà clau per al coneixement de l'Àrtic, i tots els grans exploradors polars es faran aconsellar per ell. Gràcies a ell (i companyia) ja sabem que l'Àrtic és un oceà amb molt poca terra ferma. Els seus mapes seran la primera imatge fiable que té la humanitat d'aquest gran nord desconegut.

Però, a més de continuar participant en diferents expedicions, Nansen iniciarà també una carrera diplomàtica que el convertirà en el primer representant noruec a la Societat de Nacions. Des de la Societat de Nacions la seva tasca serà clau per resoldre el problema dels presoners de guerra després de la Primera Guerra Mundial. Nansen tindrà, doncs, un paper decisiu en el retorn a les seves llars de centenars de milers de persones i en l'ajut a refugiats de diferents països. Tot plegat, el farà mereixedor del premi Nobel de la Pau el 1922.

Centenars de milers de vides.

Si per alguna cosa el món és millor gràcies a Nansen, no és perquè sobrevisqués a la gran aventura polar, sinó, sobretot, perquè el seu retorn permetrà salvar i reconstruir les vides de tanta gent.

¿Quantes vides no se salven o es perden només per un seguit de petits cúmuls de casualitats? Si en el seu dia Frederick Jackson hagués estat acceptat al *Fram* i no hagués fet la seva pròpia expedició, si aquell dia una morsa no hagués atacat el caiac de Nansen, si el 17 de juny de 1896 no s'hagués obert la boira uns moments i Nansen no s'hagués enfilat a un monticle de gel per saber on era, si el gos de Jackson en aquell moment no hagués bordat, potser els dos exploradors noruecs no haurien tornat d'aquella infinita presó blanca i avui el món seria encara una mica pitjor.

Valerian Albanov. Escriure la mort a l'Àrtic

L'estiu del 2010 una expedició russa trobarà restes humanes a la remotíssima i desolada Terra de Francesc Josep. Al costat d'uns ossos humans, hi haurà objectes com una llibreta de notes, un rellotge de butxaca, un xiulet, una mena d'esquís o sabates de neu, un ganivet, una cullera amb les inicials P.S. gravades, unes ulleres de sol fetes a mà amb culs d'ampolla, una tassa, cartutxos de rifle, restes d'un cubell... i també roba esquinçada per les urpes d'un os, possible causa de mort del dissortat, si no és que abans ha sucumbit al fred, a la fam, a l'escorbut o a un accident i l'animal ha aprofitat la presa inerta i fàcil per fer un banquet.

Vet aquí una misteriosa troballa en un lloc tan remot, unes restes que estan esperant de fa un segle. Per fer memòria d'un altre dels oblidats, podem dir que aquella llibreta pertanyia a Vladimir Gubanov, i el rellotge i la cullera a Pavel Smirennikov, dos dels vint-i-dos desapareguts el 1912 amb l'expedició russa del *Santa Anna*. Les restes del cos trobat, després d'un segle al gel, encara trigarem a saber de qui són exactament.

Hi ha històries de supervivència que es fan més conegudes i populars que altres, però no és la gent qui fa l'èpica sinó que els fets mateixos i l'esforç per sobreviure de qui es troba immers en cada aventura. També és cert que el segle XX té també els seus mites ben repartits. Aquesta història serà especialment coneguda a la Unió Soviètica, popularitzada allà encara més per Veniamin Kaverin a la seva novel·la *Els dos capitans*. Però no és la novel·la el que ara ens interessa.

Així, tot just després de la cursa pel pol sud entre Scott i Amundsen, i mentre Shackleton prepara la seva famosa expedició a l'Antàrtida, a l'Àrtic s'està vivint aquesta altra aventura de dimensions igualment èpiques. Més dramàtica i menys mediàtica per a nosaltres, però no per això menys memorable.

El 1912 la goleta *Santa Anna* salpa de Sant Petersburg cap a l'Àrtic amb la intenció de fer la travessa cap a Àsia a través d'un nord tan poc cartografiat que ni tan sols porten mapes prou fiables. L'expedició és capitanejada per Gueorgui Brusilov, el seu segon és Valerian Albanov i en total hi ha vint-i-quatre persones que en menys de dos mesos es trobaran encallades pel gel en el mar de Kara.

Igual com havia passat al *Jeannette* tres dècades abans, durant l'any i mig vinent el *Santa Anna* serà arrossegat a la deriva per la seva presó de gel. Això durarà fins a l'abril de 1914, quan amb el *Santa Anna* cada cop més malmès, a prop de l'enfonsament i amb tensions entre Brusilov i Albanov, aquest últim decideix abandonar el vaixell per provar d'arribar a peu a l'extrem nord de la Terra de Francesc Josep. Si encerta en la distància i en la direcció, i si hi arriba, confia trobar el refugi que va deixar-hi l'expedició de Frederick Jackson (1894-97) i, per tant, potser una eventual opció de rescat. Albanov sap que aquesta barreja de casualitats quasi improbables és l'única opció. Única i minúscula. Bàsicament sap que la mort és inevitable i sembla que s'estima més morir lluitant que no pas esperant-la en la inanició dalt del *Santa Anna*. Segurament, saber-se sense opcions allibera de pressió, permet mantenir la calma i el cap clar.

A Albanov el seguiran deu homes més igualment desesperats, mentre que els altres es quedaran a bord del que queda del *Santa Anna*, escalfant-se tot cremant el que poden del mateix vaixell i convençuts que a fora només hi ha la mort. Per a aquells l'única esperança és que el que queda de la nau, ja pràcticament sense combustible ni aliments, torni a navegar lliurement o que el gel els porti a alguna salvació.

Del *Santa Anna* i dels que s'hi van quedar mai més se n'ha sabut res.

Mentrestant, el grup d'Albanov emprèn aquesta nova aventura sense saber ben bé on són, sense mapes adequats ni mitjans per situar-se amb precisió. Tenen al davant centenars de quilòmetres per recórrer en un gel en moviment. Des d'aquest moment s'enfronten a tota mena de perills: ossos polars, morses, tempestes, fam, escorbut i fins i tot a tensions que acaben en motí.

Durant els tres mesos vinents el grup es va reduint, de tant en tant l'extenuant gel s'empassa misteriosament algun dels aventurers sense deixar-ne rastre, els precaris trineus i caiacs improvisats es perden amb la senzillesa més angoixant. Avances pel laberint de gel i t'atures per esperar els companys que has deixat enrere fa uns minuts. Esperes. Tornes enrere i res. Per molt que esperis o reculis a buscar-los mai més no els trobaràs i tornes a seguir endavant. Aquesta mort blanca és per tot arreu i només després d'una precisa combinació d'innombrables contratemps i de cops de sort, únicament Albanov i Alexander Konrad arriben a terra ferma, on finalment troben el refugi que buscaven. Molt pocs dies després seran rescatats per una expedició que casualment passa per la zona.

Però qui pot passar per una costa tan remota a efectuar un rescat? Només algú semblant a tu. El rescat ve de la mà del *Saint Foka*, un vaixell que, havent salpat el mateix estiu de 1912 amb la intenció d'arribar al pol nord, també fa dos anys que està aïllat del món intentant tornar al continent com sigui. Sense combustible i justos d'aliments, de fet els del *Saint Foka* havien decidit anar al refugi on han trobat Albanov i Konrad a buscar la fusta, precisament perquè la fusta d'aquest refugi era l'única que podien trobar en tota aquesta zona. La seva única salvació és cremar el refugi a les calderes del *Saint Foka* per avançar una mica més cap al sud. Si Albanov, doncs, s'hagués decidit uns dies més tard o el *Saint Foka* hagués arribat abans, tot hauria estat inútil.

Així, després de l'eufòria en veure el *Saint Foka*, Albanov i Konrad es troben a bord d'un vaixell mig enfonsat, amb una tripulació malalta, amb escassetat d'aliments i de combustible... Segurament ells dos són els únics que es poden sentir feliços i acollits en un entorn com aquest. Per a ells tot és escalfor, aliments, salut i companyia. Què més es pot demanar?

Finalment el *Saint Foka* tornarà a la civilització amb grans dificultats, i Albanov i Konrad seran els dos únics supervivents de l'aventura del *Santa Anna*, immortalitzada de primera mà pel mateix Albanov en el seu llibre *En el país de la mort blanca* (1917).

I vet aquí, doncs, el detall que pot passar desapercebut: que tot això ho sabem gràcies al diari que Albanov va escrivint durant tota la seva aventura i que després li servirà de base per al seu estremidor llibre. Tant Albanov com Konrad mantenen el costum d'escriure un diari. No són els únics a fer-ho: és un costum estès entre tots els aventurers de l'inconegut.

Escriure és un esforç. Fer-ho en determinades condicions es converteix en una autèntica èpica. Per això, i com que el final de la història ja el sabem des de bon principi, en llegir la narració dels únics supervivents del *Santa Anna*, gairebé tan dolorós com la pèrdua d'un company ens sembla la pèrdua d'una part dels diaris en el gel. Evidentment res és pitjor que veure desaparèixer un company, però veure engolides per l'aigua glaçada aquestes pàgines escrites és també com morir una mica un mateix. De tota la dificultat i esforç que implica deixar negre sobre blanc en aquelles circumstàncies, Albanov no ens en parla, però ho percebem quan relata la pèrdua d'alguns dels seus diaris. És una pèrdua que vivim amb dolor.

Qualsevol detall que explica Albanov és fascinant. En qualsevol d'ells hi ha sempre un esforç titànic, però com sol passar, Albanov ens parla de tot menys del moment d'escriure. És admirable que amb tota la càrrega que han de suportar aquests pioners de l'Àrtic, amb el ritme esgotador que implica córrer més que la mort, amb les forces al límit i amb una necessitat absoluta de descans, trobin encara al final de la jornada un moment i prou energies per escriure, per arrossegar paper blanc o escrit, tinta i ploma o llapis.

Però un cop es troben el moment i l'energia per fer-ho, ¿com és escriure mentre s'intenta sobreviure perdut a les regions polars? Primer de tot cal fer-ho sense guants, breument, de pressa, aturant-se tot sovint per tornar a escalfar els dits embalbits o ja quasi congelats. Després sol haver-hi el problema de la tinta congelada en cas que s'escrigui amb ploma, o la feina de fer punta al llapis si s'escriu amb llapis. En aquest últim cas, a més, el baf de la respiració a baixes temperatures pot crear una finíssima capa de glaç al paper que en dificulta el traç. Costaria trobar un exemple millor per recordar que escriure sempre és un esforç.

Igual com coneixem el pitjor viatge del món de Scott a l'Antàrtida explicat per ell mateix in situ en el seu diari —l'única veu d'ell que ens torna del Pol Sud—, sabem també d'un altre de tants pitjors viatges del món, en aquest cas en la mateixa època i als antípodes boreals. Scott, Albanov i tants altres saben que tan important com sobreviure és rescatar la memòria. Sense això no té sentit l'exploració: es convertirien en descobridors de l'oblit. Que n'hi ha, i aquells sí que han fet el pitjor viatge del món, però mai no ho sabrà ningú.

El Pol Nord

0. De Phipps a Parry. Comença la cursa

Després que els europeus provessin d'esquivar el continent americà que s'interposava en el seu camí cap a Àsia, a poc a poc han anat girant el rumb cap al pol que volien evitar i s'hi han acabat plantant de cara.

Desviant la proa cap al nord, el primer que apunta clarament cap al pol és Constantine Phipps, quan el 1773 dirigeix l'enèsima expedició britànica a la recerca d'un pas cap al Pacífic. Aquesta vegada, les ordres que rep Phipps de l'almirallat britànic no són exactament les de trobar una ruta cap al Pacífic, sinó explorar cap al nord entre Spitsbergen i Grenlàndia i avançar en direcció al pol tant com sigui possible, mantenint-se sempre en mar oberta, sense posar en risc la tripulació i, en cas d'arribar al pol, tornar-ne per explicar-ho. És més aviat una expedició científica i d'exploració geogràfica per temptejar el terreny. Cal saber què hi ha allà i si s'hi pot passar. La ciència necessita avançar sempre.

Perdoni, mantenint-se sempre en mar oberta, diu? Al pol, diu també? Sí, la ciència necessita avançar. Com sol passar tantes vegades amb la ciència antiga, i amb tot el que sabem ara, aquesta idea d'un mar obert a l'Àrtic del segle XVIII avui fa riure, però en aquells temps es dona gairebé per cert que a prop del pol les aigües seran més càlides i navegables del que han trobat fins aleshores els exploradors àrtics.

No és cap notícia que Phipps no arribés al pol. Avui la seva expedició gairebé només és recordada per alguns detalls anecdòtics, com, per exemple, la primera descripció científica d'un os polar o la presència d'un jove guardiamarina de catorze anys anomenat Horatio Nelson (aquell futur almirall Nelson que el 1805 moriria a la batalla de Trafalgar). En tot cas, però, ja tenim la primera expedició del món en direcció al pol nord.

Durant l'estiu de 1773, Phipps i companyia es passegen pel nord de Spitsbergen, però res de mar obert; el gel els atura a poc més dels 80° N. Més enllà només poden descriure el paisatge d'un mar glaçat i cobert de neu fins a l'horitzó, una mena de llisor blanca, perfecta i sòlida trencada només per alguns corrents d'aigua. Un paisatge que per al lector de l'època sens dubte semblaria idíl·lic, sobretot amb l'afegit del bon temps que descriu Phipps i de la cacera abundant que hi troben.

I això és tot. I a finals d'agost faran mitja volta cap a Anglaterra per meravellar el públic amb el seu relat del viatge cap al pol nord.

I aquí ens quedem glaçats durant mig segle. Perquè allò de Phipps no era ja l'inici de la cursa cap al pol per arribar al pol, sinó encara cap al Pacífic per al comerç. En realitat la recerca del pol haurà d'esperar encara fins que arribi William Parry.

El 1827, William Edward Parry ja és tot un expert en l'Àrtic: ha participat en diferents expedicions a la tossuda recerca del pas del nord-oest, coneix de prop l'Àrtic i els inuits, i si llavors hi ha algú preparat per dirigir una expedició cap al pol, sens dubte és ell.

Naturalment, Parry partirà de la descripció de Phipps, que, altrament, ja podria haver fet qualsevol dels nombrosos baleners que hi ha a Spitsbergen. Però als baleners, aquells oblidats que semblen haver-hi sigut sempre abans que els exploradors i els científics, ningú no els pregunta mai gaire res. Si es preguntés més als baleners i als inuits!

En tot cas, l'expedició de Parry és la primera expedició polar plantejada seriosament. És per això que ja no volen anar cap al pol nord només amb vaixell. Això hem après de Phipps (i dels baleners, i dels inuits). A l'abril de 1827 Parry s'embarca amb el *Hecla* cap a Hammerfest, on el gruix d'homes de l'expedició aprofiten per fer un ràpid primer contacte amb la neu, per aprendre a moure-s'hi amb els esquís i amb els rens que compren allà mateix i que hauran de tirar els trineus quan arribin a Spitsbergen i encarin la gran pista de gel i de neu promesa per Phipps.

Sí, és així: es pot ser un dels primers buscadors del pol sense abans haver-se posat mai uns esquís, ni haver portat mai un trineu, ni haver vist mai cap ren. Bàsicament es pot dir que molts descobreixen la neu un cop ja ha començat l'expedició. Però és que els del futur estem molt ben acostumats: allò són plantejaments nous, moderns; algun dia ho havien de ser. I amb aquesta experiència de dos o tres dies a Hammerfest, es planten a Spitsbergen disposats a provar també per primer cop un dels artefactes més raonables i absurds que s'han vist mai per aquelles latituds: uns bots de sis metres d'eslora, amb espai per a catorze persones cadascun, adaptats amb rodes i patins; un híbrid pretesament triterreny aigua-terra-gel que hauria de ser tirat per rens.

El pla és ben senzill: avançar fàcilment en aquests trineus navegables tirats per rens, arribar al mar càlid del Pol Nord, que ningú no ha vist mai però que tothom té clar que hi ha de ser, aturar els rens allà i fer navegant el que quedi fins al pol. Parry ho veu d'allò més fàcil.

Finalment, arriba el moment de posar els vehicles en marxa. Un cop els bots tunejats (*Enterprise* i *Endeavour*) són damunt la neu, les rodes s'hi enfonsen, els rens comencen a tibar, els homes empenyen després amb els rens. I això és tot. Davant l'abruptesa d'un antipàtic paisatge gelat, les rodes dels trineus, ancorades en la neu, s'entossudeixen a mantenir-los clavats al mateix punt on han caigut el primer cop.

Mirat des del nostre temps, gairebé és entranyable. Damunt la neu, al costat del vaixell, una mena de vehicle a la vegada barca, carro i trineu; un tir de rens tibant i un grup d'homes empenyent sense que hi hagi res que avanci ni un dit.

I malgrat tot, calia provar-ho. És així com se sumen progressos i com s'aprèn a fer el pas següent. Lliçó apresa. Cal refer els plans. Oblidar-se dels rens i de les rodes i alleugerir la càrrega: durant els propers mesos cada home de l'expedició al pol nord arrossegarà una càrrega equivalent a més de cent quilos.

Amb tot plegat, ridículament tard pel que sabem avui, ja a finals de juny, quan el gel de l'Àrtic comença a ser més fràgil i traïdor, un petit grup d'homes inicien el seu camí cap al pol nord. Porten ja només uns trineus més convencionals, de tracció humana. Mai ningú no ha provat abans d'arribar al pol nord d'una manera tan seriosa. Hi ha William Parry, James Ross, Edward Bird, Charles Beverly i Francis Crozier. Poca broma amb aquests noms si poguéssiu parlar de l'Àrtic amb gent del segle XIX.

¿I aquella deliciosa pista de patinatge que prometien les paraules de Phipps? Res a veure amb un gel que canvia dia a dia, any rere any. Aquell 1827, mig segle després de Phipps, l'oceà és un mar de pannes de gel impracticables, una crosta boteruda i antipàtica mig barrejada amb esquerdes obertes sobre aquest mar que tenen sota els peus. Res més. Gairebé sorprèn descobrir que cal que faci fred. En un estiu més calorós del previsible, aquests cinc homes avancen esforçadament amb temperatures per sobre dels zero graus. Això vol dir que hi ha gel fonent-se, pluges que deixen una pàtina perillosament relliscosa i tallant, i que han de posar i treure constantment els feixucs trineus. Ara a l'aigua! Ara al gel! De vegades, ho han de fer només per poder superar obstacles d'uns pocs metres cada pocs metres. I així fins qui sap on.

A més a més, enmig d'aquest paisatge misteriós i confús, hi ha la broma d'un sol constantment present al cel. No hi ha dies ni nits. No hi ha hores. I el sol no para de fer voltes desconcertants al voltant d'aquests homes cansats damunt d'un gel d'horitzons monòtons, en constant moviment. Amb això últim no hi comptaven. No és un bon lloc per perdre el nord.

A finals de juliol, Parry comprèn que el gel sobre el qual avancen és viu, que es mou i que recula a un ritme cada cop més vertiginós. Fins al punt que hi ha dies que tots els esforços per caminar han servit només perquè reculessin una mica menys.

Camines deu hores cap endavant i estàs uns quilòmetres més enrere. Ben absurd. Camines per tornar al punt de sortida com quan llegint un llibre tornes a la mateixa línia, com quan llegint un llibre tornes a la mateixa línia, com quan llegint un llibre tornes i no saps com.

Més absurd encara és que calgui esperar setanta anys perquè Nansen s'adoni de la deriva del gel. Res que no sàpiguen tots els que s'hi han encallat abans.

En qualsevol cas, aquell 26 de juliol, per sobre dels 82° de latitud, a vuit-cents quilòmetres de l'objectiu, només queda tornar cap al *Hecla*, camí que serà més fàcil. Que se sàpiga, ningú no ha estat mai tan al nord.

I així ha començat la cursa cap al pol.

Cap a un pol que continuarà esperant i esperant, misteriós i sol.

1. Ni Cook ni Peary

Després d'una llarga història de solitud, arriba un dia que la cursa pels pols es precipita. A poc a poc l'ésser humà va avançant cap al nord. Després d'algunes expedicions fracassades, l'abril de 1908 Frederick Cook és el primer a assegurar que ha arribat al pol nord acompanyat pels inuits Ahpellah i Etukishook.

Quan l'any següent Robert Peary torni de l'Àrtic assegurant també que ha arribat al pol i descobreixi que mentrestant Cook s'està proclamant vencedor d'aquesta cursa, començarà la disputa per desmentir la proesa de Cook. Encara avui, segons els entesos, amb dades a la mà, el viatge de Cook era impossible i per tant, durant unes dècades, semblarà que Peary i companyia hagin estat els primers a haver trepitjat aquest pol de la Terra.

El 1909, doncs, els nord-americans Robert Peary i Matthew Henson, i els quatre inuits Ooqeah, Ootah, Eginwah i Seeglo, tornen de la seva expedició assegurant haver assolit la fita. Durant molts anys es donarà la seva expedició per bona, però avui també sabem que les seves dades de navegació eren errònies o imprecises i que com a molt devien arribar a unes desenes de quilòmetres del pol, cosa que, d'altra banda, no està gens malament. Però més enllà d'això, la seva expedició ja ens diu alguna cosa interessant, o més que l'expedició, la llegenda que deixen, especialment pel que fa a Henson, que era afroamericà.

La història parla dels que tenen una obsessió i es fan acompanyar per assolir-la. Però no existiria cap èxit d'aquestes persones obsessives sense que hi hagués també uns oblidats, escollits gràcies als seus mèrits. Aquesta vegada, la història sembla voler donar un protagonisme especial a Henson. El fet que el primer home a arribar en un dels dos pols fos d'origen africà es converteix gairebé en una mena de reivindicació multiracial, o d'agermanament de cultures, o de classes, o del que es vulgui. Sigui com sigui, tot i que per motius diferents, la llegenda queda ben repartida entre Henson i l'euroamericà Peary. Sembla que això deixa molts narradors tranquils. Però per què un afroamericà és sovint encara considerat menys americà que un euroamericà? I per què aquests dos haurien de ser més americans que els inuits? Igual com passarà amb els xerpes de l'Himàlaia, ni tan sols quan es reivindica l'origen de Henson, rarament algú destaca els noms dels quatre inuits que van amb ells. Potser la història faria més justícia si ho digués així: Ooqeah, Ootah, Eginwah i Seeglo haurien pogut ser els primers homes a arribar al pol, acompanyats d'un africà i d'un europeu, però els errors d'aquest últim els van fer tornar amb les mans buides.

De fet —ells no ho saben ni ho sabran mai—, hi han estat tan a prop que durant dècades el gel que han portat sembla ben bé del mateix pol, però tard o d'hora la seva gesta s'acabarà fonent en no-res. I malgrat tot, són els primers humans a pensar que han assolit un dels pols. Per molt equivocats que estiguessin, van poder explicar l'emoció que van sentir en arribar-hi. I aquesta és la diferència entre equivocar-se i mentir. El que menteix no pot explicar què se sent en triomfar: el que s'equivoca, sí. El primer està obligat a inventar, el segon a recordar. No és ben bé el mateix enganyar-se que enganyar, i mentre Peary (1909) sembla més a prop de l'error, Cook (1908) sembla més a prop de la mentida. I decidir què pesa més a cada plat de cada balança ja és cosa de cadascun d'ells.

Quan el 1908 Peary afronta la seva enèsima aventura polar, ja té cinquanta-dos anys. Sap que és la seva última oportunitat, que és o ara o l'oblit. I realment hi està tan a prop que fins i tot pot ser que estigués convençut que hi havia arribat. Encara molts avui pensen que va ser el primer home d'arribar a un dels pols. Fins i tot a la seva tomba hi ha aquest epitafi: «Descobridor del pol nord». Segurament més d'un es deu plantejar què cal fer en aquests casos. Es pot esmenar un epitafi? S'hi pot posar un asterisc i una nota al peu?

Cook, d'altra banda, arrossega una treballada fama de falsificador de dades, sobretot en destapar-se la mentida amb què pretenia ser el primer a haver pujat el Denali, sostre d'Amèrica del Nord, el 1906. D'aquesta manera i amb la seva pròpia trampa del pol, Cook evita l'oblit de la pitjor manera que hauria desitjat: l'evita perquè passa com un mentider. Segur que s'hauria estimat més ser oblidat que no pas ser recordat per això.

Però ni un ni l'altre no hi van arribar. La veritat és que, mentre el món celebra l'arribada al pol nord de Peary, sembla que no és així, que el pol continua sense haver estat trepitjat per cap humà...

Si en el món dels descobriments anem veient que sempre hi ha algú abans que ha obert el camí al primer descobridor, en el cas del pol nord gairebé es diria que passa a l'inrevés. Així de misteriós i esquiu és el lloc. En la història del pol nord sembla que cada cop que algú hi arriba torni a ser el primer, que l'anterior sempre s'hagi equivocat o hagi mentit. Sempre sembla que abans no hi ha hagut mai ningú. Quan hi arribes, el pol sempre s'ha empassat l'última aventura com si no hagués existit. Et mira amb l'aire sorprès de qui no sap de què va la cosa, però també impassible, com qui xiula dissimulant i sabent que també s'empassarà la teva aventura. No a tu, però sí la visita que li has fet. Tornaràs d'allà i no hi hauràs estat mai.

Una cosa és descobrir un territori inconegut, inimaginat, i una altra, el pol. Perquè el pol tothom sap que hi és. No cal que hi hagi anat ningú abans per saber que hi és. És per això que de vegades sembla possible tornar del gran buit àrtic i jurar que has estat en un punt determinat d'aquella immensitat. Però no, finalment se saben coses. En un lloc tan fràgil i hostil a la vegada, les falsedats pesen, cremen, fonen el gel i, finalment, un dia cauen, s'enfonsen en el gel que elles mateixes han fos.

2. Roald Amundsen. El nen que somiava

Ni Cook el 1908, ni Peary el 1909. Per tant, veient la controvertida descoberta del pol nord, i per posar ordre a les curses polars en general, farem bé d'obrir un parèntesi i anar a veure de moment un dels reis indiscutibles de l'exploració polar.

El 1872 neix a Noruega un nen anomenat Roald Amundsen. Per a un nen noruec del segle XIX, mirar el món és veure gairebé un planeta sencer al sud i tenir una gran buidor al nord, un gran forat boirós on es concentren tots els herois nacionals i estrangers, on creixen les fantasies del que pot haver passat a Franklin i a les expedicions que els busquen. Tal com correspon al món en què neix, no és estrany que el petit Roald admiri dels exploradors polars i que la seva il·lusió sigui des de sempre arribar un dia al pol nord. Segurament fins aquí l'imaginari infantil del petit Amundsen coincideix amb el de tants altres petits noruecs del seu temps. Però en el seu cas el somni va més enllà d'una mera il·lusió infantil. Viurà tota la seva vida, fins a l'últim moment, amb les mateixes passions que ja va tenir de nen. Tan clar té el petit Roald quin és el seu gran desig, que ja des de ben menut, durant els llargs hiverns escandinaus, agafa el costum de dormir amb la finestra oberta per habituar-se al fred. Aprenent a suportar aquests hiverns gèlids, és com aquest nen està dient que el seu somni és de debò.

Des de petit somia en el pol nord. El pol nord. El pol nord. El pol nord...

I de jove...

I d'adult...

Des que comença la seva carrera polar, ja no deixarem de trobar-lo capficat en una expedició o altra. Entre els 1897 i 1899 participa en la del belga Adrien de Gerlache, que va amb el *Belgica* a la recerca del pol sud magnètic. Com que l'expedició és atrapada pel gel seran els primers a resistir la llarga nit antàrtica. En aquest lloc, Amundsen coincidirà amb Frederick Cook, un altre dels grans exploradors polars de l'època. (Serà el primer a proclamar-se campió de la cursa al pol nord el 1908). La imprudència obsessiva d'Adrien de Gerlache per apropar-se cada cop més al sud els obligarà a passar l'hivern encallats al cinturó de gel que envolta el continent austral. Mentre la tripulació es desespera, Amundsen i Cook comparteixen coneixements i aprenen. Sobretot, Amundsen.

Més endavant, entre el 1903 i el 1906, trobarem Amundsen embarcat en el *Gjøa,* fent la primera travessa del pas del nord-oest. Entre altres descobriments científics i geogràfics, com la confirmació que el pol nord magnètic es desplaça, durant aquesta travessa Amundsen aconsegueix obrir el pas del nord-oest, la ruta que s'havia començat a imaginar quatre segles abans. El 1903, quan el *Gjøa* era a punt de salpar, l'expedició va estar a punt d'aturar-se per manca de recursos, però Amundsen va ordenar salpar de nit i d'amagat cap a Grenlàndia. Des d'aquí, s'endinsen en el laberint d'illes i canals del nord d'Amèrica. Durant tres anys de solitud, ningú, fora d'alguns inuits, ningú no tindrà notícies de l'expedició. Finalment, arriba un telegrama des de Nome, Alaska, en el qual Amundsen confirma la gesta. L'impacte internacional d'aquest viatge tindrà unes dimensions imprevisibles a tot el món. Ha calgut quasi mig mil·lenni d'espera, des que John Cabot va començar l'any 1497 el somni d'arribar a Àsia per l'Atlàntic nord, perquè algú arribi a fer el pas del nord-oest.

D'una manera semblant a com es comportava Nansen, durant aquests anys Amundsen no para d'aprendre. Aprèn tant dels exploradors que l'acompanyen com sobretot dels inuits amb qui conviu tan sovint. ¿Pot ser que això encara no sigui el més normal del món? Igual com Nansen ha fet unes dècades abans, Amundsen també veu la importància d'aprendre del poble inuit. Que això sigui encara una notícia ens permet explicar la tossuderia occidental de no voler aprendre de ningú altre, de no voler veure la perspectiva del món de cap altra cultura. La tossuderia de no aprendre ha sigut la norma del món europeu. D'aquesta tossuderia se n'escapen uns pocs que saben el que fan: Nansen, Amundsen o, força més tard, Edmund Hillary.

Finalment, ja convertit en un explorador llegendari, Amundsen comença a preparar per al 1910 la que seria la primera expedició al pol nord. A hores d'ara ja porta acumulats uns quants hiverns polars i és un explorador d'un nivell indiscutible. Però no és l'únic que somia a arribar al pol nord. Quan finalment ho té tot preparat, reben les notícies de l'èxit de Cook i de Peary. En un principi, tothom creurà que Cook i Peary se n'havien sortit: havien estat els primers d'arribar al pol nord. Això fa que Amundsen canviï el seu objectiu. Canviarà de direcció. La seva expedició, doncs, amb el mític *Fram* de Nansen girarà rumb cap al pol sud, el punt on també està intentant arribar el britànic Robert Falcon Scott. A partir d'aquí, s'ha escrit aquesta història moltes vegades. No diem res que no se sàpiga si escrivim que Amundsen (amb els seus acompanyants) es convertirà el desembre de l'any 1911 en el primer humà que va arribar al pol sud. Entre altres coses escriurà aquesta observació ben curiosa:

«Mai no he conegut ningú que es trobés en un lloc tan diametralment oposat als seus desitjos. Des de petit he somiat arribar al pol nord i ara soc aquí, al pol sud. Es pot imaginar un contrast més gran?»

S'han dit moltes coses d'aquesta cursa entre Scott i Amundsen. Si algú no podria dir que és un oblidat en l'exploració polar és qualsevol d'ells dos. I tampoc no es pot dir que sigui un oblidat Shackleton. Però el que Amundsen no sabrà mai és que curiosament es va arribar abans al pol sud que al pol nord. No es va imaginar mai que la seva expedició va ser la primera en què uns humans van trepitjar un dels pols terrestres.

Vet aquí, doncs, perquè la gesta més celebrada del més gran dels exploradors polars, la mítica arribada al pol sud, mereix encara més reconeixement de la que ja té. Va ser el primer pol dels dos on van arribar els humans. Ben mirat des que es comença a trepitjar regularment l'Antàrtida fins que s'arriba al pol austral amb prou feines si han passat unes poques dècades. En canvi, el pol nord continua essent un punt escorredís enmig d'un mar glaçat sobre seracs de gel en constant moviment. És tan escorredís que fins i tot es fa difícil saber quan s'hi arriba finalment.

3. Els altres pols

En l'època que va a cavall entre els segles XIX i XX, acabar de conèixer tots els racons del món aixeca tantes passions com avui qualsevol esport de masses. Ser el primer a aconseguir una fita és gairebé una qüestió nacional en molts països occidentals. El 1911 tenim la controvertida cursa entre Amundsen i

Scott per arribar al pol sud, aventura en què el noruec i un equip d'homes sovint oblidats (Helmer Hanssen, Sverre Hassel, Oscar Wisting i Olav Bjaaland) s'avancen als britànics per pocs dies, una aventura que acaba dramàticament i que costa la vida de Scott i els seus acompanyants (homes també amb nom i cognom, Henry Bowers, Edward Wilson, Edgar Evans i Lawrence Oates), a pocs quilòmetres del dipòsit d'aliments que els hauria salvat.

Segurament, una de les fotos més memorables i corprenedores de l'exploració polar és la de Robert Falcon Scott i companyia retratats al pol sud el gener del 1912, en el punt on han trobat la bandera noruega i un missatge de Roald Amundsen. Mai un èxit ha sigut tan amarg com aquest, i les cares d'aquells herois abatuts ho diuen tot, molt lluny —als antípodes precisament— de la solemnitat amb què Amundsen i els seus es retrataven al mateix punt un mes abans. (Sense ànims de desprestigiar aquests exploradors britànics, Scott no és, ni tampoc cap dels seus acompanyants, el segon a arribar al pol sud, sinó en tot cas el sisè, després dels cinc noruecs.)

Poc després, durant la Primera Guerra Mundial, també a l'Antàrtida, hi ha Shackleton i els seus homes. La seva lluita es convertirà en una de les aventures de supervivència polar més memorables de la història. I als seus antípodes —terrestres—, exactament en els mateixos anys, tot i que el fet sigui força menys mediàtic a l'Europa occidental, tenim a l'Àrtic l'aventura de Valerian Albanov resistint en una lluita equiparable a la de Shackleton i els seus.

El cas és que al voltant dels dos pols terrestres trobem exploradors que es juguen la pell en un lloc on ja no es busca cap riquesa econòmica. I ja de passada, això dels pols està tan de moda, que sembla que no n'hi hagi prou amb dos. Potser per això, en aquelles dècades hi ha també la lluita per ser el primer a arribar a allò que alguns anomenen «el tercer pol», la lluita per fer el cim de l'Everest, una muntanya on George Mallory i Andrew Irvine deixaran la vida el 1924.

Però d'aquests tres pols, i per molt que hàgim d'esperar fins al 1953 perquè algú arribi al cim de l'Everest, el més controvertit serà precisament el pol nord, el primer on es va intentar arribar, el pol on hi haurà més persones que diran que hi han arribat. Mentre que a l'Antàrtida i a l'Everest els expedicionaris es mouen sobre terra ferma, l'aventura àrtica exigeix saber-se moure sobre un oceà de gel canviant. Avançar sobre grans plaques de gel a la deriva no és un repte fàcil, i menys quan avances lentament cap al nord sobre els interminables seracs d'una placa de gel irregular i canviant que recula cap al sud; plaques que s'esquerden, que s'ajunten, que se separen, que obren escletxes de mar...

Si t'atures, retrocedeixes, si vas massa lent també. Només serveix avançar, de pressa i sense repòs. L'objectiu sempre fuig...

4. Volant al pol nord. L'Amundsen bipolar

Que algú hi hagi arribat abans no és raó perquè Amundsen renunciï al seu desig d'anar algun dia al pol nord. I amb tot plegat, recordem que el pol continua esperant.

Com que la superfície àrtica és un obstacle per avançar fins al punt del pol, i com que es comença a dominar el cel, arribarà un dia que la cursa, fins ara marítima, guanyarà alçada i esdevindrà aèria.

De moment, per tenir certeses irrefutables sobre l'arribada al pol nord, caldrà esperar pacientment fins al 1926, quan la fita podrà abordar-se ja des del cel, cosa que tampoc no és fàcil. I tot i això, aquell 1926 encara hi haurà uns intents controvertits i unes falses conquestes.

El maig de 1926, Richard Byrd i Floyd Bennett asseguren haver sobrevolat el pol nord, però igual com ha passat amb les anteriors expedicions terrestres, tampoc ells no aconsegueixen demostrar convincentment les seves dades de vol. Fins i tot, més endavant, reconeixeran errors en els seus mesuraments. Així és com un mes més tard l'incansable Roald Amundsen entrarà definitivament en aquesta escena i farà callar a tothom.

En aquell moment Amundsen ja és una llegenda viva (encara) de l'exploració polar. Entre altres coses ha sigut el primer a trepitjar el pol sud, ha completat la primera navegació del pas del nord-oest i ha localitzat el pol nord magnètic. A tot plegat s'hi podrà afegir, sense que ell ho sàpiga, la gesta de ser el primer que se situa sobre el pol nord, ja que l'èxit de Peary s'acabarà desmentint molts anys després de la mort d'Amundsen. Així, el noruec no sabrà mai que potser va ser el primer que va arribar als dos pols. Ell i Oscar Wisting, un d'aquells oblidats amb nom i cognom.

L'aventura aèria al pol nord tampoc no serà una gesta fàcil. Entre alguns intents memorables, trobem el dels malaurats Salomon August Andrée, Knut Fraenkel i Nils Strindberg, tres homes que el 1897 han fet l'intent d'arribar al pol nord amb un globus fet especialment a París per a l'expedició. Però estaven tan convençuts d'ells mateixos que no van comprovar ni tan sols que no hi hagués errors de funcionament en les condicions especialment adverses que haurien d'afrontar. Els hauria convingut fer-ho. Gràcies als seus diaris i a les seves fotografies, sabem que, després de dos dies de vol accidentat des de Svalbard, Andrée i companyia van haver de fer un aterratge forçós enmig del gel i que van abandonar el globus i que van caminar de tornada, durant tres mesos, fins que van morir a la petita illa de Kvitøya, al nord de les Svalbard. Les seves restes hi seran trobades per casualitat el 1930, un terç de segle després.

Durant dècades, doncs, no es va saber res de l'expedició d'Andrée, Fraenkel i Strindberg. I tampoc de les seves restes. I, mentrestant, Amundsen continua tossudament amb el seu repte vital. El 1925 fa un intent seriós en avió que el porta a aterrar a pocs quilòmetres del pol nord, però no aconseguirà anar més enllà. Encallats en el gel, després de molts dies d'esforços per alliberar l'avió, aconsegueixen enlairar de nou l'aparell i recular cap a la salvació. De moment, els seus 87° 44' Nord del 1925 són la latitud màxima a què ha arribat mai cap aparell volador. Però Amundsen ho vol tot.

Finalment, l'any següent, el 1926, emprèn una nova expedició. Aquesta vegada, va amb l'italià Umberto Nobile. Els acompanyen Lincoln Ellsworth, Hjalmar Riiser-Larsen i Oscar Wisting. I aquesta vegada sí, el juny d'aquell mateix any, a bord del dirigible *Norge,* sobrevolen el pol nord en el trajecte des de Ny-Ålesund (a Svalbard) cap a Alaska. Ells seran els primers a demostrar irrefutablement que realment, ara sí, han assolit la fita d'ubicar-se sobre el paral·lel 90 Nord.

És cert que sobrevolar en comptes de trepitjar un lloc té un cert aire d'haver fet trampa, però en aquells temps volar no és cap broma. Mai ningú abans no ha deixat tan ben demostrada l'arribada al pol nord geogràfic. A més a més, sense saber-ho, Amundsen i Wisting s'han convertit en les primeres persones a visitar tant el pol sud com el pol nord. Però com que els errors de Peary no se sabran fins anys després de la mort d'Amundsen i de Wisting, els dos noruecs moriran sense conèixer aquest doble èxit.

I l'aventura tampoc s'acaba aquí.

Com sol passar massa sovint, tot i que en aquell memorable vol hi hagi cinc tripulants, els reconeixements han de ser per a una sola persona. És allò que sempre costa d'entendre. A més, Amundsen i Nobile es discutiran sobre qui té el principal mèrit de l'expedició. I és així que, com que Amundsen rep més reconeixement que Nobile, l'any 1928, Nobile farà la seva expedició personal amb el dirigible *Italia* cap al pol nord. Ara sense Amundsen. Un cop hi ha arribat, en el camí de tornada Nobile tindrà un accident. Es mobilitzen molta gent i molts de recursos per rescatar-lo. Països com Noruega, Suècia, Itàlia, França, Finlàndia i la Unió Soviètica organitzen equips per trobar Nobile. Entre tota aquesta gent hi ha Amundsen. No s'ho pensa dues vegades a l'hora de rescatar el seu antic company d'aventures i ara rival. Quan arriba l'hora que l'esquadró de tres avions en què Amundsen ha de participar s'enlairi de Tromsø, el mal temps obliga a ajornar l'operació. Tanmateix, ell decideix tirar pel dret. Tres hores després, Amundsen desapareix al fons de l'Àrtic, probablement a prop de l'illa de Bjørnøya, la més meridional i solitària de l'arxipèlag de Svalbard. Precisament pocs dies abans havia deixat dit en una entrevista que així és com li agradaria morir. Volant. I complint una gran missió, amb una mort digna, ràpida i sense dolor. Potser és arriscat afirmar-ho, però gairebé es pot dir que no hauria pogut tenir més sort. Una mort encertada i feta a mida.

Finalment, gràcies al fet que hi ha dues operacions de rescat a la vegada, es troba l'expedició de Nobile. Són rescatats després d'una llarga i tràgica espera perquè, entretant, ha mort bona part de la tripulació de l'*Italia.* D'Amundsen, en canvi, no se'n trobarà res. Només algunes restes del seu hidroavió.

Mirant-ho amb la perspectiva dels fets consumats, sabent que Nobile seria rescatat igualment, és inevitable pensar que potser Amundsen s'hauria pogut estalviar el tràngol que el va portar a la mort. Però amb quina cara hauria mirat després als ulls d'algú? L'exploració àrtica, igual com l'alta muntanya o com tantes d'altres, és una lluita de superació, però també de solidaritat. Mai no es pot negar l'ajut a ningú. I encara menys en un lloc tan remot i perillós com és l'Àrtic. En la seva última acció, Amundsen resumeix d'alguna manera els valors d'aquells exploradors, al capdavall sempre solidaris entre ells. Segurament si ell i Scott s'haguessin trobat al pol sud el mateix dia, s'haurien donat la mà i s'haurien ofert ajut en cas de necessitat, malgrat la rivalitat que tenien.

Entre els que cerquen Amundsen, per cert, hi ha també el francès Jean-Baptiste Charcot, un dels grans exploradors polars. Fins ara, Charcot sempre ha tingut la sort d'anar esquivant la mort, aquella tragèdia heroica tan temptadora per als llibres. Sempre disposat a avantposar el salvament d'una vida al motiu de la seva expedició, Charcot, no obstant, trobarà anys més tard també a l'Àrtic una mort potser més romàntica que èpica. El 16 de setembre de 1936, el seu *Pourquoi-Pas? IV* serà atrapat per una tempesta a les proximitats de Reykjavík. Aleshores, quan el naufragi fatal sigui ja inevitable, Charcot alliberarà la gavina Rita que tenen en una gàbia com a mascota. Només sobreviuen a aquest naufragi el timoner Eugène Godinec, que arriba nedant a la costa, i Rita, que emprèn el vol després de rebre una última carícia de Charcot. Vet aquí un gest altruista i d'amor. Lluny de la imatge d'un Noè alliberant un colom per trobar la terra ferma i la seva salvació, en el seu últim gest, Charcot allibera una gavina perquè se salvi. Gest inevitable dels grans exploradors, salvar tot allò que pugui.

5. De Kuznetsov a Plaisted

Mentrestant, el pol nord espera impassible que algú hi arribi i el trepitgi. Ha vist acostar-se gent que s'hi han quedat a prop, ha vist passar avions i dirigibles per damunt del seu cap, però no serà fins a l'any 1948 quan podrem tenir la certesa que algú hi ha posat els peus per primera vegada. Serà quan hi aterrarà l'expedició soviètica liderada per Aleksander Kuznetsov. En aquestes alçades de la història, l'avió ha fet deixar enrere les grans epopeies àrtiques. Sembla que quasi ningú no fa cas d'aquesta fita. Kuznetsov i els seus homes no arriben fins aquí moguts per fer una gesta esportiva, sinó per treballar... En aquell moment l'URSS ja ha aixecat diferents bases científiques a l'Àrtic. En l'arribada d'aquests homes a aquesta intersecció de meridians gairebé sembla que no hi hagi cap mena d'èpica. Quasi podríem dir que l'aterratge al pol nord té un aire rutinari: cal baixar de l'avió i posar-se a organitzar la base.

I com que són els temps de la Guerra Freda, perquè no volen ser menys, veient l'avantatge que els soviètics tenen en aquesta època en la cursa espacial, l'any 1958 els Estats Units fan una demostració de força tecnològica i visiten el pol nord per l'únic racó on encara no hi ha fites. Hi arriben submergits per sota del gel amb el submarí *Nautilus*, el primer submarí nuclear.

Ningú no pot tenir cap dubte, doncs, que el pol nord ha estat dominat. Ja no espanta, no emociona, no aixeca passions... L'època de les grans exploracions polars ha quedat enrere, però malgrat tot, el pol nord mira endavant cap a l'horitzó, mira cap a aquest sud que l'envolta per tots costats i continua encara sense veure res ni ningú que se li acosti passant per sobre la glaçada superfície de l'Àrtic...

És ben curiosa aquesta cursa cap al pol nord, una cursa en què sembla que es recorda gairebé només els intents fracassats previs. Els primers d'arribar-hi, en canvi, fa l'efecte que passen de puntetes per la història. De fet, els primers a aconseguir-ho per la via terrestre (o marítima) seran els nord-americans Ralph Plaisted, Walt Pederson, Gerry Pitzl i Jean-Luc Bombardier, que hi arribaran amb motos de neu l'any 1968. Fins aleshores, el misteriós camí cap al pol nord ha sigut, sense cap mena de dubte, el que s'ha fet esperar més. Qui es recorda d'ells? L'arribada de Plaisted i companyia serà gairebé cent anys després que aquell petit noruec anomenat Roald Amundsen hi somiés amb la finestra oberta, durant les fredes nits d'hivern...

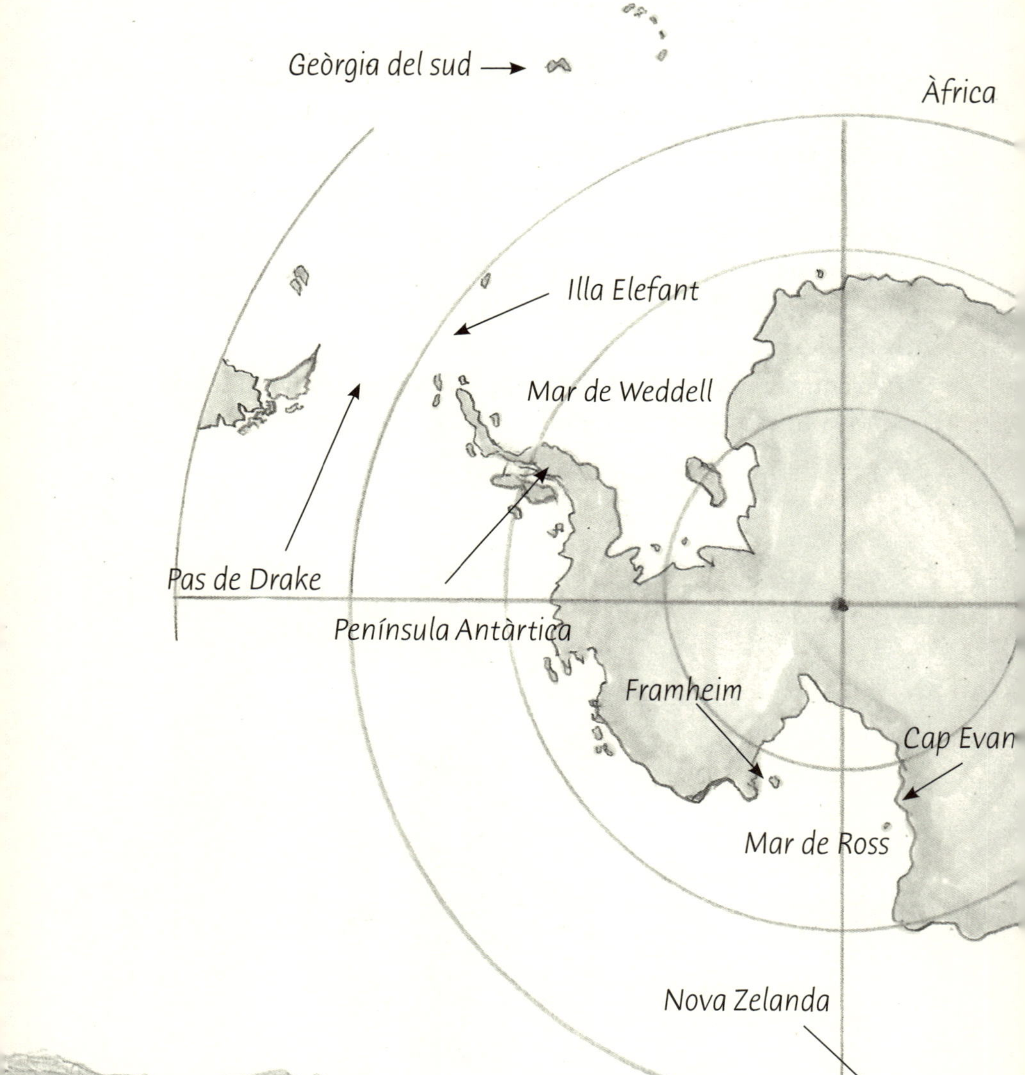
Geòrgia del sud
Àfrica
Illa Elefant
Mar de Weddell
Pas de Drake
Península Antàrtica
Framheim
Cap Evan
Mar de Ross
Nova Zelanda

5. L'Antàrtida

Hui-Te-Rangiora. La llegenda maori

Extensions infinites de gel, gairebé eternes, solitàries, lluny de tot. L'Antàrtida despoblada de tota vegetació està quieta i silenciosa des de sempre i mai ningú no hi ha posat els peus. Ningú no sap que existeixi. Tot el que hi ha de vida són algunes aus ben adaptades, poc més que pingüins i algun mamífer marí, tot just un finíssim cinturó de vida a les vores del continent. I res més. Gel blanc i interminable sobre una terra erma i desolada.

Des de l'interior del continent, on el mar seria una cosa inimaginable si hi hagués algú per imaginar, el gel perpetu llisca lentament per les glaceres, sempre, sense parar, a un ritme tossudament imperceptible. Les glaceres llisquen, mil·límetre a mil·límetre, immenses i imparables. I un dia, tu que ets un bloc de gel impertorbable, havent avançat des de fa mil·lennis, notes com l'últim bloc de gel que et precedia cau al mar amb un estrèpit que seria eixordador si hi hagués algú que pogués sentir-lo. I de sobte et trobes desprotegit, convertit en penya-segat davant la sorpresa del mar. La teva solidesa que ha estat lliscant des de l'interior del continent fins a la seva vora es converteix ara de sobte en un majestuós i imponent penya-segat de gel enmig de la solitud blanca i blava.

Però encara no ets res, encara no ets ni el bloc de gel que anunciàvem, simplement formes part del caire cantellut del continent. I així et quedes, desproveït de protecció, empès imperceptiblement però implacable pels milions i milions de tones mudes de gel com tu que venen del teu mateix origen i que demanen pas, fins que de sobte, un dia, després de molts avisos fets també pel mar amb les seves envestides, cedeixes, t'alliberes d'aquell tot continental del qual tu també formaves part i amb un estrèpit descomunal que se sentiria també a centenars de quilòmetres si hi hagués algú que pogués sentir res, et converteixes en una muntanya flotant.

Ets un iceberg immens.

A partir d'aquest moment, ets. Ja no formes part del continent.

A partir d'aquest moment hi ha vida al teu voltant, fins i tot sota l'aigua, i avances a la deriva envoltat de milers d'icebergs com tu, muntanyes de gel que mai no ha vist ningú. I empès pels corrents, t'allunyes del continent cap a aigües menys fredes que a poc a poc t'aniran fonent, empetitint-te fins que desapareguis sense que mai ningú no sàpiga res de tu.

Com més lluny del continent, menys icebergs i més petits, més mar blau, més horitzó sota el cel. I discretament, un dia, quan davant teu ja no hi ha res més que aigua apareix un punt a la ratlla entre el cel i el mar. Alguna cosa s'obre pas en aquella silenciosa escletxa aixafada de l'horitzó, una cosa que s'acosta com un iceberg d'un color que no s'ha vist mai, que no existia fins ara. Una textura nova, una cosa que es mou per si sola sobre la superfície ondulant de l'aigua, uns rems que xipollegen suaument, unes mans fermes, uns braços sobre una canoa, uns rostres humans.

Potser has anat molt al nord, o potser la canoa ha navegat molt al sud de casa seva, però aquesta primera trobada entre els gels antàrtics i l'ésser humà porta el nom de Hui-Te-Rangiora, el navegant polinesi que per alguna raó, qui sap si extraviat, ha arribat fins aquí amb la seva canoa *Nga-Iwi-o-Aotea*. A partir d'aquest dia del segle VII o VIII, els maoris, navegants experts, sabran que hi ha unes muntanyes de gel flotant molt al sud de les seves aigües. A partir d'aquest encontre, tindran raons per pensar que més enllà de la creu del sud hi pot haver alguna cosa.

Potser passaran més de mil anys abans no torni a acostar-se algú cap a aquestes latituds. O potser són certes algunes llegendes maoris que parlen de navegants com Tamarereti, que s'aventura cap al sud per descobrir el secret de les aurores australs, però els nostres llibres d'història ignoraran els polinesis i saltaran de les hipòtesis dels antics grecs fins al 1773 per parlar-nos directament de James Cook, un home que no va arribar ni a veure l'Antàrtida però que gairebé va començar a dibuixar-la al mapa. Tan misteriosa és l'Antàrtida que tothom sembla conèixer-la, intuir-la, parlar-ne, però gairebé costa saber qui la va descobrir primer. Un continent tan buit que sembla no tenir ni descobridor.

James Cook. Deduir un continent

Avui no ens hauria de sorprendre parlar de descobridors que no hagin vist el seu descobriment. En plena era de la tecnologia n'hi ha prou a aportar proves de l'existència d'un exoplaneta sense necessitat d'haver-lo observat directament, o a aplicar un model que funcioni en el diminut món de la física quàntica per entendre com funciona un electró, per posar exemples dels més grans i dels més petits de la ciència actual.

En el camp dels descobriments geogràfics, de vegades també trobem exemples d'enginy científic que permeten deduir la presència de terres no descobertes, com és el cas de James Cook amb l'Antàrtida. Aquí, probablement Cook s'emporta el mèrit de la descoberta més audaç quan entre 1772 i 1775 s'aventura cap al sud fins al cercle polar per comprovar si hi ha realment la *Terra Australis Incognita* que les llegendes i les teories científiques indiquen, o si bàsicament a les latituds antàrtiques hi predomina només l'aigua. Serà durant aquest viatge, el 17 de gener de 1773, quan el *HMS Resolution* de James Cook portarà els primers humans a travessar el cercle polar antàrtic. I encara dos anys després hi tornarà per circumnavegar aquestes aigües, però sense aconseguir veure l'Antàrtida ni un sol cop. I malgrat tot, segons Cook és inqüestionable que més al sud hi ha d'haver un continent; d'una altra manera no es podrien explicar alguns fenòmens que ell observa, com els icebergs, que segons ell i la ciència del seu temps només es poden formar a terra ferma.

Però és això realment un descobriment? Avui, a posteriori, hi ha qui gairebé el donaria per descobert, però en el seu temps continuarà havent-hi el dubte. Els exoplanetes o el bosó de Higgs avui ens són irrefutables encara que no els hàgim vist, però al segle XVIII, l'Antàrtida de Cook continua essent una hipòtesi de la qual no es podrà alliberar ni ell mateix, i el misteriós continent continuarà amagat, inexistent als ulls humans.

No és estrany que la gent de mar dedueixi la presència de terra a partir de certs elements, com la presència d'aus que no solen allunyar-se gaire de la terra ferma, algues, fauna marina, els vents, els corrents, el gel... En aquells mateixos temps, John Byron, avi del famós escriptor romàntic, buscant les illes Salomon l'any 1765 veu bandades d'ocells que volen cap al sud i ja dedueix que hi deu haver una Terra Australis Incognita. Fins aleshores, detalls com aquests han empès algunes expedicions a l'estèril cerca d'aquesta terra misteriosa sense més botí que illes disperses aquí i allà, algunes de ben localitzades, altres que semblen aparèixer i desaparèixer o desplaçar-se, convertint-se en llegenda o veritat segons si es retroben o no. Tenim per exemple l'illa de Bouvet, a 54° S, considerada la més remota del món, descoberta el 1739 i que no es torna a localitzar fins al 1808. I tenim també la descoberta de grans icebergs, com el localitzat per l'astrònom Edmond Halley (el del cometa) l'any 1700. I la descoberta d'illes que ha resultat que eren icebergs i al revés, cosa comprensible en unes aigües boiroses, amenaçadores i glaçades on tota superfície terrestre sol quedar permanentment sota gruixos de neu immesurables. Bàsicament un mar de confusió.

Aus, algues, fauna marina... No faltaran elements a Cook per persistir en la seva recerca cap al sud. I sobretot, el gel. Mentre troba icebergs i extensions de gel de difícil navegació, dedueix que hi ha d'haver una gran terra més al sud. Segons la forma i dimensió d'alguna d'aquestes grans illes flotants, Cook suposa que han d'haver-se desprès recentment d'una massa molt més gran. Així, l'1 de febrer de 1775, en descriure la forma i la mida d'un iceberg, dedueix «*que no feia gaire que s'havia allunyat de terra, i que podia venir d'una badia de la costa, on s'hauria format.*»

És clar que Cook no inventa res tot sol. Altres autors del seu temps defensen el mateix, com Mikhaïl Lomonóssov o Alexander Dalrymple, però tot plegat és encara una ciència massa confusa i no deu ser fàcil la seva recerca. L'optimisme i el pessimisme es van alternant en la seva exploració, només pocs dies abans, el 27 de gener, està cansat de les latituds meridionals i anota que «*em sembla que em puc aventurar a dir que l'extensa costa, indicada a la carta de Mr. Dalrymple de l'oceà entre Àfrica i Amèrica, i el Golf de Sant Sebastià, no existeix.*»

Però Cook no es deixa vèncer. Mentre la presència del gel li indica que hi ha terra, procura anar més enllà tant en l'espai com en les seves deduccions i extreu informació de tot el que pot en el seu llarg periple. Una dada definitiva per a ell serà la latitud a què es troba el gel: si no hi hagués més element que aigua, tot el gel es formaria a una latitud semblant, però a mesura que circumnavega el cercle polar i es troba obligat a remuntar cap al nord per esquivar les aigües innavegables que, en altres punts, li permeten avançar més cap al sud, dedueix que aquest gel no es forma a alta mar, sinó que es desprèn d'una gran terra de contorns irregulars. I des del moment que el traçat de la seva circumnavegació antàrtica coincideix força amb la silueta del continent, hem d'acceptar que té prou raó quan aquell 6 de febrer anota:

> «*Crec fermament que a prop del pol hi ha una extensió de terra d'on surt bona part del gel cap al vast oceà. També em sembla probable que s'estengui més enllà cap al nord per la banda oposada en els oceans Atlàntic i Índic, perquè sempre hem trobat gel més al nord en aquells oceans que en qualsevol altre lloc, cosa que em sembla que no podria ser si no hi hagués terra al sud; vull dir una terra d'extensió considerable. Perquè, si suposem que no hi ha aquesta terra i que el gel es pot formar sense ella, es dedueix que la temperatura ha de ser semblant gairebé a tot arreu al voltant del pol a 70° o 60° de latitud* (...)*; per tant hauríem de veure gel quasi sempre sota el mateix paral·lel, o a prop d'aquest; i en canvi passa el contrari.*»

Fascinant deducció davant la qual gairebé podríem donar el continent per descobert i reconèixer que Cook té raó.

Menys raó té el mateix dia quan, en aquell laberint de gel que només empresona un continent on no s'espera trobar altra cosa que gel i ports innavegables, dedueix també que aquest territori continuarà inexplorat per sempre més i que mai ningú no arribarà tan al sud com ell. Tan convençut n'estarà que, més endavant, quan en les seves reflexions finals torni a la possibilitat que algú altre vagi més enllà que ell, es refermarà amb un «*no li envejaré l'honor del descobriment; però m'atreviré a dir que el món no se'n beneficiarà.*»

Sorprèn l'arrogància tan humana de no adonar-se que ell, com tots els que l'han precedit, només és un pas més cap a la descoberta del món. Bé és cert que Cook i la seva oblidada tripulació han sigut molt probablement els primers a travessar el cercle polar antàrtic i els primers a fer saber al món que hi ha d'haver un continent al Pol Sud; però també és veritat que aquest quasi descobriment que continua essent una suposició eclipsarà fins i tot el nom d'aquells que realment seran els primers a trepitjar-lo o a veure'l per primer cop. Paradoxalment, ni abans ni després del no-descobriment de James Cook, els descobriments de l'Antàrtida no seran mai tan clars com amb ell.

Si Colom descobreix el continent americà sense saber-ho mai i sense ni tan sols trepitjar-ne més que illes, aquí la pregunta se'ns fa inevitable: ¿Què és descobrir un continent: saber com és, o n'hi ha prou amb saber que hi és (com els exoplanetes i el bosó de Higgs)? Perquè les apreciacions de Cook són extraordinàries, però potser abans que ell l'expliqui sense veure'l, algú ja hi ha estat sense saber-ho... ¿Hauria sigut allò un descobriment?

Quan Cook navega pel cercle polar antàrtic sap que és el primer; coneix bé tots els que l'han precedit als mars del sud, i els consulta i els cita sempre que li convé en els seus llibres, però no esmenta en cap moment ni Gerritsz Pomp ni Gabriel de Castilla, dos homes del voltant del 1600 que avui donen nom a dues bases científiques de l'Antàrtida. Com han aparegut aquests noms en aquell racó de món?

Dirck Gerritsz Pomp. Primers indicis

Fent una passejada per l'actual Antàrtida trobaríem avui a les Shetland del Sud un parell d'estacions científiques amb noms que ens portaran encara més enrere en la possible història del continent. D'una banda, el laboratori Dirck Gerritsz Pomp, dels Països Baixos, i de l'altra, la base antàrtica Gabriel de Castilla, espanyola. Tots dos són noms de pretesos descobridors de l'Antàrtida, curiosament coetanis i ben allunyats en el temps respecte a qualsevol altre descobridor que coneguem d'aquestes terres. Sempre amb informacions de segona mà, amb fonts difícils de contrastar, ens arriben notícies que Gerritsz Pomp el 1599 i Gabriel de Castilla el 1603 es van desviar de la seva ruta al pas de Drake i que van arribar a la latitud 64° Sud.

Segons un document aparegut a Holanda cap al 1620 i que potser es podria atribuir a Willem Schouten o Jacob Le Maire —descobridors del cap d'Hornos—, per sota del paral·lel 64 hi hauria una terra amb tot de muntanyes nevades i rocoses comparables a les de Noruega. D'on traurien Le Maire i Schouten això sense haver navegat mai tan al sud? Probablement de Dirck Gerritsz Pomp.

Pel que sabem, Gerritsz Pomp el 1599 estava navegant per aquelles aigües a bord del *Blijde Boodschap* («Anunciació») quan, potser havent-se desviat de la seva ruta, cosa fàcil al pas de Drake, hauria pogut trobar aquelles terres que més endavant descriuria tal com hem vist, comparant-les amb Noruega. Però sense més dades és difícil aclarir si el seu relat és cert o imaginari, ja que al cap i a la fi, de quina altra manera es podria imaginar algú una terra en aquelles latituds? Plana, verda i plàcida com Holanda, segurament no. En tot cas, sens dubte semblant a les del cap d'Hornos, és a dir, semblant a Noruega, amb tot de muntanyes rocoses i nevades. Però com que la informació encaixa prou bé amb el que podrien ser les illes Shetland del Sud, alguns ja les donaran per descobertes. Altres s'estimaran més posar-ho en dubte; i algú més, encara, ho negarà rotundament.

Entre els que no ho veuen clar, també hi ha els que creuen que Le Maire hauria pogut recollir aquesta descripció de Gabriel de Castilla, qui el 1603 hauria fet un periple semblant al que s'atribueix a Gerritsz Pomp. Per saber-ho és tan fàcil com anar a les fonts més primàries possibles... i altre cop també difícils de contrastar: segons una declaració signada cap al 1607 per Laurenz Claesz (que hauria navegat amb Gabriel de Castilla el 1603), en aquell viatge haurien arribat fins al paral·lel 64, on «van tenir molta neu». Això és tota la referència de Claesz a aquelles latituds, per a alguns ja és prou per explicar un descobriment de l'Antàrtida per part de Gabriel de Castilla. Però un parell de coses criden l'atenció d'aquesta frase de Claesz: primera, que sigui en tercera persona quan se suposa que és la veu d'un dels protagonistes; i segona i la més important, que cita literalment la neu, però Claesz en cap cas no parla de terra. I la neu, segur, també pot caure perfectament damunt dels mariners a alta mar. Amb això hi haurà qui ja gosi atribuir la descoberta de l'últim continent a aquest navegant castellà, però en qualsevol cas, les coincidències entre Gerritsz Pomp i de Castilla són evidents i les preguntes inevitables. ¿Pot ser que en tan poc temps dues naus es desviessin exactament fins a la mateixa latitud, topessin per primer cop amb les Shetland del Sud i tornessin relatant el seu descobriment sense que se'ls fes més cas? Perquè, si en pocs anys s'hi arriba un parell de cops i se'n torna, ¿podem pensar que van ser els únics?

¿O potser no van anar ben bé així aquests viatges? Tornem a Gerritsz Pomp, que navegava per unes aigües que li eren estranyes. Sembla que l'holandès, un cop al Pacífic, va arribar a Valparaíso, on va ser detingut per les autoritats castellanes i va ser pres durant cinc anys, després dels quals seria alliberat. Moriria al mar el 1608, sense tornar a casa. En aquella època Flandes i Castella estaven immersos en la Guerra dels vuitanta anys (1568-1648) i Gabriel de Castilla era a Xile lluitant contra els corsaris holandesos, de manera que és fàcil imaginar alguna topada entre aquests dos mariners.

Comptant que Gerritsz Pomp no era benvingut en aquelles aigües, podríem estar davant d'un cas semblant al dels portuguesos, molt previnguts a l'hora de difondre certs descobriments en aigües castellanes. És creïble, doncs, que Gerritsz Pomp no fes gaire ostentació dels seus periples per aquelles latituds (tampoc no en va tenir gaires oportunitats: va morir massa aviat), igual com podria ser que la corona de Castella es fes seva tota la informació de les seves aigües aportada pels corsaris estrangers detinguts.

Fos com fos, amb un Gerritsz Pomp que moria sense tornar al seu país, moria també el seu relat de primera mà. Només ens en queden narracions de segona veu. En canvi, Gabriel de Castilla sí que tindria l'oportunitat de reportar el seu descobriment... cosa que de fet no va fer mai. Per tant hauríem de creure que de Castilla no es fa seu cap relat de Gerritsz Pomp, sinó que senzillament no va veure terra en cas d'haver navegat a la mateixa latitud en què ho hauria fet l'holandès quatre anys abans. I per tant, posem-hi un xic de sentit comú, si algú va veure les Shetland del Sud, amb tota probabilitat devia ser Gerritsz Pomp el 1599.

Però com que no hi ha documents sòlids del que van trobar ni l'holandès ni el castellà, no podem fer res més que conjecturar i quedar-nos amb aquesta incertesa que alguns van agafar per bona. Fos com fos (i malgrat no ser referents ni per a Cook), és veritat que la terra descrita al relat de Le Maire existia i sembla que al segle XVII aquesta informació corria i que es prenia com a certa. I així, tant si és certa com si no, Gerritsz Pomp es converteix en un autèntic precursor de la descoberta del continent més inhòspit del planeta.

I malgrat tot, no sembla que el relat de Le Maire creï cap efecte boom cap a aquelles terres del sud. Només a la primera meitat del segle XIX aquestes latituds despertaran interès, mentre la pesca i la caça siguin un filó d'or.

El pas de Drake

Des de fa segles, el pas del sud entre l'Atlàntic i el Pacífic ha sigut una gesta que qualsevol navegant ha somiat i temut, igual com també l'han temut els que els esperaven des de terra. Tant si es tracta de l'estret de Magallanes, al nord de la Tierra del Fuego, com del pas de Drake, al sud del cap d'Hornos, el navegant que s'aventura per aquestes aigües s'exposa a tempestes implacables, temperatures gèlides, entramats de laberints de roques escarpades i esmolades i falsos passos convertits en túnels de vents impetuosos que arrosseguen les veles incontroladament, que rebenten pals i que estavellen les carcasses dels vaixells contra les roques com si fossin un ou. En qualsevol moment, sigui de dia o en la negror de la nit, una tempesta pot arrossegar el buc d'un vaixell contra uns esculls amagats sota les ones o pot enviar les naus més enllà, cap a alta mar, i deixar-les exposades en unes aigües obertes on els vents i els corrents joguinejaran amb elles amb un odi furibund, per molt grans que aquestes naus siguin.

En el decurs de la història, molts de vaixells han lluitat, de vegades durant mesos seguits, per travessar el pas de Drake i centenars d'ells han desaparegut estavellats contra les roques, contra blocs de gel a la deriva o engolits sota ones de desenes de metres d'alçada que deixen una buidor de vertigen entre una onada i la que ve al darrere. Un infern líquid en el qual, fins i tot avui, grans embarcacions modernes tenen grans dificultats a superar. Durant segles, aquestes aigües eren les més meridionals que la humanitat coneixia. Van anar engolint naus i vides amb una facilitat tan angoixant que, de sobte, va semblar que s'esvaïa la necessitat de creure en terribles monstres marins. El mar sempre ha estat un monstre que ha devorat molts de valents. Les llegendes sobre monstres van néixer per recordar-ho i per recordar que calia tenir-ho present si no es volia morir. En el pas de Drake, però, trobem unes aigües que converteixen, més que pràcticament a cap altre lloc, els monstres marins de dents esmolades en unes bèsties fetes d'aigua i de vent, i el buit immens entre dues onades molt més altes que el pal major d'una nau esdevé la boca perfecta del gran monstre que pot arribar a ser l'oceà. No és cap casualitat que els mariners que aconseguien creuar el cap d'Hornos o el de Bona Esperança es guanyessin el dret a portar una arracada d'or.

Davant d'una mar tan indomable, doncs, no cal ni dir que moltes i moltes naus van ser arrossegades al fons o cap a aigües desconegudes. A vegades, hi va haver supervivents; altres, no.

Un dels casos més ben documentats en la nostra descoberta de descobridors antàrtics és el del *San Telmo*, un vaixell que l'any 1819 va desaparèixer en aquestes aigües durant un temporal. Diferents testimonis d'altres naus de l'expedició asseguren que van veure com perdia el rumb, però ningú no va poder testimoniar-ne el naufragi fins que, l'any vinent, un mercant britànic capitanejat per William Smith, que va desviar-se de la seva ruta per culpa del mal temps, va arribar fins a les llavors encara inexplorades terres de les Shetland del Sud. Smith va trobar-hi les restes d'un naufragi. Molt probablement eren les del *San Telmo*. I és també per això que, tal com fan sovint aquells que es volen apropiar o adjudicar descobriments que no estan documentats, no falta tampoc qui va atribuir la descoberta de l'Antàrtida al *San Telmo* o al capità William Smith.

En tot cas, quan al *San Telmo*, segur que els seus supervivents —mentre n'hi va haver si és que n'hi va haver algun— van estar molt lluny de veure's com uns descobridors perquè no hi deu haver gaires coses pitjors per a un nàufrag que anar a parar a una terra desconeguda, inexplorada, hostil, inhòspita i allunyada de tot arreu. Per tant, si el *San Telmo* va anar a estavellar-se a les Shetland del Sud, tant si algun dels seus tripulants va aconseguir ser el primer humà a posar un peu a l'Antàrtida com si no, aquest possible descobriment queda en no-res. Ni tan sols, és clar, cap d'ells no va arribar a saber mai res del descobriment posterior de William Smith, un descobriment, d'altra banda, tràgic i estèril en el qual ningú no s'emporta cap premi. Més aviat passa al contrari: és el mar qui descobreix uns intrusos i se'ls emporta cap al fons o aigües enllà com tants altres cops ha fet o farà amb tants altres intrusos i amb tantes altres naus.

Potser sí, però, que William Smith tingui dret a considerar-se el descobridor de l'Antàrtida. Per primer cop, trobem documentada una terra al sud del cap d'Hornos. I, malgrat això, justament per això, encara avui ens sorprèn que el seu descobriment passés gairebé desapercebut. I hem escrit *gairebé* perquè la descoberta de Smith sí que va tenir un efecte immediat entre aquells foquers i baleners que buscaven, trobaven i amagaven els seus caladors secrets, tal com avui fan encara molts bons boletaires.

Però anem als fets posteriors. A principis del 1820, diferents expedicions de diferents països arriben a l'Antàrtida. Primer de tot, hi ha l'expedició russa de Fabian Von Bellingshausen, que es convertirà en el segon grup de persones que van creuar el cercle polar antàrtic i que van circumnavegar el continent. Suposadament, van ser els primers que van veure terra en aquelles latituds. Però la línia imaginària d'un paral·lel no hauria de ser mai una frontera més evident que la que separa mar i terra: sovint, els llibres d'història obliden que, malgrat que les Shetland del Sud trobades per Smith siguin més al nord del cercle polar, són tan antàrtiques com són americanes les illes on va arribar Colom, que —recordem-ho un cop més— no va trepitjar mai el continent americà.

En aquells mateixos dies de gener que Bellingshausen va veure l'Antàrtida sense arribar a desembarcar-hi, el nord-americà Nathaniel Palmer, que era un caçador de foques, voltava per aquelles aigües mirant de trobar un botí. També hi havia el britànic Edward Bransfield, que hi feia una expedició científica i, encara, John Davis, un altre foquer nord-americà. En el seu quadern de bitàcola Davis va anotar que el 7 de febrer d'aquell 1820 alguns dels seus homes van baixar a terra durant més o menys una hora cercant foques. Si això fos cert, probablement els peus d'aquests homes van ser els primers que van deixar les seves petjades damunt del continent antàrtic. Però una vegada més, la referència és tan vaga que es fa difícil saber on van desembarcar si és que ho van fer de debò. Alguns historiadors, ben mirat, ho posen en dubte.

En resum, doncs: després de milers i milers d'anys de l'expansió humana pel planeta, milers i milers d'anys en els quals l'Antàrtida ha passat absolutament desapercebuda, de sobte, en qüestió de pocs mesos, trobem tot un seguit d'expedicions fent voltes per les seves costes sense que sigui segur que cap dels seus homes arribés a anar-hi. La tripulació del *San Telmo*, Smith, von Bellingshausen, Bransfield, Palmer, Davis... Tots ells descobridors del continent. Tot depèn del melic que cadascú miri.

Foquers i baleners

Sembla clar que alguna cosa estranya passa al voltant d'aquest misteriós territori, però és que també sembla com si el continent s'hagués proveït d'un parell de bones defenses. Primer de tot, gràcies a les seves foques i a les seves balenes, ja en fa prou amb la immensa riquesa que donen les seves aigües. Però després hi ha els abruptes penya-segats del gel antàrtic que protegeixen el continent i que és com si fossin una muralla infranquejable, sempre que s'hagin pogut esquivar abans, és clar, la banquisa i els icebergs escampats per tot el seu perímetre. O sigui, que el continent està protegit en un primer perímetre per un mur de gel, després per un camp de mines de blocs que s'ajunten i se separen com una trampa mortal en canals imprevisibles, i encara més enllà, la millor protecció de totes, una riquesa infinita de pesca que distreu tota altra activitat humana.

Els icebergs tabulars que es desprenen de l'Antàrtida són autèntiques illes flotants a la deriva, amb immenses parets llises que empetiteixen els vaixells que s'hi apropen i que fan impossible desembarcar-hi. Per què caldria prendre possessió d'una illa de gel estèril destinada a fondre's en un mar hostil i violent? L'acció humana té una altra cosa al cap: foques, foques, foques! Les Shetland del Sud són un edèn de foques i de balenes i, per tant, no cal anar més lluny per enriquir-se.

Amb un efecte totalment magnètic, des que el 1820 es descobreix aquest botí, tot de foquers d'arreu del món arriben a les Shetland del Sud. Es calcula que en quatre anys se n'emporten unes 800.000 pells i que hi deixen l'espècie al límit de l'extinció. De manera totalment sobtada ha començat una autèntica carnisseria anònima de flotes que s'escampen per aquestes aigües; i encara que aquestes illes ja són prou generoses i el continent es continua mostrant hostil, és probable que alguns d'aquests foquers trepitgin terra continental, però només Davis ens en deixa constància, i encara quan ni tan sols se sap si allò és un continent o un arxipèlag. Aquestes expedicions són purament comercials, no estan gens interessades a plantar banderes, sinó que només volen recollir un botí suculent i gratuït en aquestes latituds sense llei i marxar-ne amb les butxaques plenes de sang.

Descobriments, tensions, rivalitats, pirateria, naufragis... tots els ingredients que podrien inspirar el petit Herman Melville que el 1819 naixia a Nova York es troben ja en aquestes aigües. Fins i tot —i això és una elegant casualitat— un dels últims vaixells a naufragar en aquestes latituds abans de l'hivern de 1821 es diu precisament *Lord Melville.* Abandonat i sense opció de rescat deixa deu supervivents en una illa on suportaran el primer hivern antàrtic (encara no polar) que coneixem en la nostra història.

Dins del cercle polar

L'infern per on passen les foques de les Shetland del Sud durarà només alguns anys. De seguida que la seva matança deixi de ser un negoci tornaran temps de silenci i tranquil·litat en aquestes illes. Finalment, doncs, els exploradors podran venir a les costes que suposadament descobreixen sense trobar, astorats, caçadors que hi hagin arribat abans que ells. Ara, tot just s'acosta de tant en tant a aquestes illes algun foquer que prova sort sense gaire èxit. I de tant en tant, també, alguna expedició científica.

Per part nostra, sembla que comencem a deixar enrere els descobridors oblidats del cercle antàrtic. Ha arribat el moment de desembarcar-hi i posar el peu en terra ferma. És el que farà el 1839 l'expedició de John Balleny, que hi arriba a bord de l'*Eliza Scott* i del *Sabrina.*

Aquestes dues naus van sortir de Londres el 16 de juliol de 1838. Balleny decideix fer el mínim d'escales possibles per no perdre temps. Per recuperar ànims i forces i per assegurar-se algunes pells de foca per vendre a la tornada, però, l'expedició fa una escala a la solitària illa Amsterdam, a mig camí entre Madagascar i Austràlia. Més endavant, s'aturen al sud de Nova Zelanda i, encara, uns set-cents quilòmetres més al sud, ja de camí cap a la desconeguda Antàrtida, fan un tercer desembarcament a l'illa de Campbell,

L'illa Amsterdam ja els va semblar un lloc solitari. La petita illa de Campbell, però, totalment fora de qualsevol ruta del món, els ho sembla encara molt més. Pocs anys abans havia atret molts caçadors de foques, tanmateix, d'ençà que l'espècie ha quedat pràcticament extingida, ja no s'acosta ningú a aquesta illa. L'últim vaixell que hi va arribar va ser el *New Zealander*, que havia salpat de Sydney el març de 1835 i que va aprofitar la seva parada a Campbell per abandonar-hi tres homes i una dona. No en sabem els motius, ni els noms, però, quatre anys després, aquests desafortunats continuen aquí. El 10 de gener de 1839 veuen aparèixer les veles de l'*Eliza Scott* i el *Sabrina* a l'horitzó. Segur que, en un primer moment, salten d'alegria quan veuen les dues naus que s'acosten. Pensen que podran tornar a la civilització. Però aquestes illes no són un lloc per tenir gaires eufòries: aviat sabran que el camí d'aquests dos vaixells és anar precisament encara més lluny del món. Malgrat això, és la seva única opció per sortir d'aquest tros de terra.

Però el destí té sovint algun caprici. Durant la setmana que l'*Eliza Scott* i el *Sabrina* ancoraran a Campbell, arriba també l'*Emma* de John Biscoe, un altre foquer i explorador, que va també cap al sud. Biscoe, justament, és un dels pocs que en aquell moment ha circumnavegat l'Antàrtida. O sigui, que després de quatre anys de misèria i solitud, l'atzar ha fet que dues expedicions coincideixin a Campbell. Tanmateix, l'única sortida per a aquells tres homes i aquella dona continua essent anar cap al lloc més deshabitat del planeta, d'on sembla que el més fàcil és no tornar. Si aquests quatre supervivents anònims estiguessin per bromes, segur que trobarien que aquesta broma és de molt mal gust.

Però no, no deuen estar per bromes, i després de quatre anys esperant, qualsevol accepta la proposta que sigui. És així com, el 17 de gener, l'expedició de Balleny reprèn el seu rumb cap al sud amb dos d'aquests dissortats a cada nau.

I ja hi som, mar enllà, dues naus cap al cercle polar.

Més enllà d'aquest cercle imaginari.

I encara més al sud malgrat l'amenaça dels gels.

I poques setmanes més tard, un dia veuen terra.

Enmig del gel i de la boira opaca, unes illes de costes abruptes i d'accés difícil. Són les illes Balleny.

Després de fer un reconeixement ràpid de les seves costes amb un parell de bots, el capità del *Sabrina*, Thomas Freeman, aconsegueix baixar a una minúscula platja d'aquestes illes. S'hi està poc temps. Amb prou feines hi ha espai per encabir-se dret en aquest racó, al peu d'unes parets rocoses. Freeman hi recull algunes mostres minerals i torna al bot. Res gaire majestuós, més emocionant que espectacular, com solen ser tantes primeres experiències, però aquest 12 de febrer de 1839, a les illes Balleny, algú ha trepitjat terra ferma per primer cop més al sud del cercle polar.

Però de foques, res. I el lloc és inhòspit, el temps no s'atura i els fets es precipiten, com si es trepitgessin uns als altres. Com en les millors llegendes, a Freeman tot just li durarà quaranta dies la satisfacció de ser el primer a trepitjar terra ferma en aquelles latituds. El 24 de març, l'*Eliza Scott* se salvarà d'una tempesta, quan molts dels seus mariners ja pensaven que naufragaria. Entretant, el *Sabrina* s'enfonsa i es perd sota les aigües.

Les illes Balleny, doncs, serien l'última terra ferma que trepitjaria Freeman. Per als altres mariners del *Sabrina* haurà sigut l'illa de Campbell. I així, coses de l'atzar, dos dels abandonats i retrobats en aquell racó de món podran tornar a la civilització, mentre que als altres dos els haurà anat de ben poc: potser sí que van saltar d'alegria quan van descobrir l'*Eliza Scott* i el *Sabrina* a l'horitzó... no sabran mai que, mentre uns d'ells naufraguen i als altres els va de ben poc, l'*Emma* de Biscoe va de retorn cap a la seguretat d'Austràlia.

Cap a l'era de l'exploració heroica

Per algun estrany motiu, abans no s'hi desembarca, l'Antàrtida es converteix en el continent més observat, circumnavegat i predescobert del món. La seva història arrenca amb una confusa llista de noms i de suposicions, de naufragis, de desembarcaments accidentals o indocumentats, qui sap si n'hi ha d'altres d'involuntaris, de mariners que potser ignoraven on eren... Amb tot plegat es fa difícil assenyalar un descobridor de l'Antàrtida. Potser n'hi ha molts. Com ha de ser.

De moment, illes a banda, només els homes de Davis semblen haver trepitjat el continent el 1820. I que se sàpiga, no hi trobarem ningú més fins al 1853, quan un altre foquer, Mercator Cooper, assegura, ara sí amb tota certesa, que ha posat els peus en aquell misteriós continent glaçat. Però un cop comprovat que aquell eldorado de foques ja no existeix, i amb els governs novament abocats a la recerca del pas del nord-oest, aquestes aigües tornen a quedar, encara més, mig oblidades i tranquil·les.

De moment només algunes expedicions s'hi apropen i a poc a poc van posant les costes del continent als mapes. James Clark Ross, James Weddell, Charles Wilkes, Dumont d'Urville... Però per molt recordats que siguin els seus viatges, cap d'ells no hi desembarca, i després de Davis i Cooper encara caldrà esperar quaranta anys més perquè algú altre hi torni a posar els peus. Serà el gener de 1895, quan el capità Leonard Kristenssen i un petit grup d'homes desembarcaran al cap Adare. Segons alguns, Kristenssen serà, una vegada més, el primer, segur, segur, segur, ara sí que sí que sí, a desembarcar a l'Antàrtida.

En qualsevol cas, amb Kristenssen viatja un tal Carsten Egeberg Borchgrevink, l'home que en trobar líquens a l'Antàrtida es convertirà en el primer a documentar-hi vida vegetal. Per fi hem establert contacte amb els nadius més arrelats al territori (més que pingüins i foques), i encara que l'home que els ha localitzat tindrà un paper destacat en la història antàrtica, el seu caràcter controvertit farà que no es guanyi mai el respecte de la comunitat científica i exploradora del seu temps.

Malgrat tot, quatre anys més tard, el 1899, Borchgrevink aconseguirà organitzar la seva pròpia expedició amb l'objectiu de ser els primers a passar l'hivern al continent antàrtic. És cert que a aquestes latituds polars ja hi ha passat l'hivern anterior l'expedició belga del *Belgica* (en què Amundsen s'estrenava a l'Antàrtida) accidentalment encallada a la banquisa, però això no fa enrere Borchgrevink, que ja ho té tot a punt. Aquesta vegada seran deu homes amb setanta-cinc gossos en una expedició bàsicament científica. El principal inconvenient que trobaran serà el lloc escollit: el cap Adare, una incomunicada platja rocosa que, a més a més, resultarà que és una de les zones més colonitzades pel vent i pels pingüins, cosa que els condicionarà totes les exploracions previstes.

De totes maneres, com que no podran triar cap altre lloc, aquell hivern es construiran en aquest solitari racó les primeres construccions humanes del continent. Encara es conserven avui. Cap altre continent del món pot avui mostrar-nos les seves primeres edificacions humanes. En aquest cas es tracta d'unes modestes barraques de fusta amb tot el mobiliari i material necessari per hivernar en les pitjors condicions possibles, fuetejades constantment pel vent, enmig de l'aspror d'un terreny erm i nevat.

És difícil saber si aquelles petites cabanes on havien de viure aquells primers hivernants antàrtics eren un lloc precari o més aviat confortable. En qualsevol cas, la seva història no és gaire diferent de, per exemple, la del refugi de l'expedició de Robert Falcon Scott, que també es conserva intacta en aquest mateix continent. I segurament, la mateixa història passa amb altres refugis que hi pot haver escampats per l'Antàrtida: es porten aquests refugis prefabricats en vaixell, es munten al lloc, s'utilitzen i s'abandonen tot deixant-hi tot allò que no sigui imprescindible per al retorn. (Si és que se'n torna).

Però això no és tot el que van deixar els homes de Borchgrevink al cap Adare. Va ser també allà, també aquell hivern, després d'una llarga malaltia, quan el dissortat Nicolai Hanson es va convertir en la primera persona que mor a l'Antàrtida. La seva tomba tindrà el mèrit estrany de ser la més solitària que haurà existit mai.

En aquell moment, la tomba més propera a la de Hanson és la d'Émile Danco, tripulant del *Belgica* que el juny de 1898 moria a la banquisa i que va ser enterrat en un gel que a poc a poc anirà allunyant-se del continent i fonent-se per acabar lliurant el malaurat Danco a les profunditats.

Mentrestant en terra ferma, algun dia, potser d'aquí a molt de temps, les inclemències arrencaran definitivament les últimes restes d'aquells primers refugis i els faran desaparèixer del tot i per sempre. També desapareixerà la creu que indica la tomba de Hanson, dalt d'un promontori exposat al vent. Però una creu no és una tomba, la tomba és sota terra, i Nicolai

Hanson sí que continuarà allà per sempre, en el lloc on, de fet, va demanar ser enterrat.

El pol sud 1. Congelar el moment

Cinc persones el desembre de 1911 i cinc més el gener de 1912. Amb cinc setmanes de diferència entre elles —que no és res després d'una espera eterna—, el pol sud veu arribar els primers éssers humans, i qui sap si els primers éssers vius que se li han acostat mai per terra. Arriben tan a prop entre ells en el temps, que fins i tot al glaçat i immòbil pol sud se li fa difícil dir qui és el primer que el trepitja, qui és el primer que trenca la seva impecable solitud. I, ben mirat, tant li fa. Com que cap dels dos grups seguia el camí obert per l'altre, en certa manera tots li semblen que són els primers. De fet, l'única cosa que aquest pol sud pot saber és que per primera vegada la neu que hi caigui esborrarà unes petjades.

Com que es fa difícil identificar qui és el primer o el desè en aquesta arribada tan atapeïda, els posarem per ordre alfabètic de nom. Es diuen Edgar Evans, Edward Wilson, Helmer Hanssen, Henry Bowers, Lawrence Oates, Olav Bjaaland, Oscar Wisting, Roald Amundsen, Robert Scott i Sverre Hassel. Els hauríem pogut posar, absurdament, ordenats també per l'edat i saber quin vencedor d'aquesta estranya cursa va arribar abans a la vida, o els hauríem pogut ordenar de qualsevol altra manera. Sempre l'encertaríem més que si volguéssim saber qui ha sigut exactament, precisant al centímetre, el primer que ha marcat amb la seva petjada la neu del pol sud. Són deu persones, totes amb el mateix mèrit inqüestionable. Arriben-miren-marxen-arriben-miren-marxen. Dues d'elles seran les que menys oblit s'emportaran del pol sud; les altres vuit se sabran algunes vencedores d'una cursa èpica, altres vencedors d'una derrota èpica. La meitat d'aquests deu homes no tornaran mai més enlloc.

Resumint és així. Res que no sàpiga tothom. Probablement és tan èpic com absurd. I extraordinàriament admirable. Però amb tota l'èpica que acompanya la famosa cursa pel pol sud entre Scott i Amundsen, oblidem que en alguns punts aquesta cursa es fa amb una sabata i una espardenya. És així. No en tots els seus aspectes, naturalment, però sí amb prou detalls per pensar que hi va haver més d'un cop de sort abans d'arribar al desenllaç tràgic que tothom coneix.

Comencem per Scott, la cara tràgica de la moneda. Que els exploradors britànics arribessin fins al pol gairebé sorprèn quan descobrim que, per molt preparats que estiguessin, mentre prepara l'expedició, Scott té dubtes sobre la utilitat dels esquís. Poc acostumats a la neu, el 1909 els britànics es troben a Noruega experimentant amb un prototip de motos de neu que havia de ser molt més útil que els esquís, però una avaria de l'aparell i la necessitat d'un recanvi ràpid aquell mateix dia permetrà al noruec Tryggve Gran demostrar la utilitat de saber esquiar. Aquesta trivial demostració improvisada farà rumiar Scott. I és per això que Gran — recomanat per Nansen— es convertirà en l'expert en esquí de l'expedició. Tindrà sobretot la tasca d'ensenyar a millorar la tècnica als homes que aniran a l'Antàrtida.

Ningú no es plantejaria avui una empresa d'aquestes dimensions sense dominar els esquís. Sorprenentment, però, la gent de l'expedició encara no té prou experiència perquè ni tan sols no acabi de ser conscient de la necessitat de saber ser ràpid i de poder ser autònom damunt la neu. Tampoc no té prou experiència per saber que és millor dur gossos que cavalls o que uns trineus motoritzats en fase experimental no són cap garantia de res.

Segurament, doncs, l'única garantia de fons de l'expedició britànica és la grandesa de l'imperi que li dona suport, el fet de saber que podran comptar amb un gran desplegament de recursos. Aquests homes n'estan tan convençuts que el seu convenciment passa pel damunt de la seva ignorància sobre alguns punts bàsics de supervivència polar. Sabent això, és gairebé un miracle que l'expedició arribés tan lluny. Perquè, tampoc no ens enganyem, efectivament tot estava molt ben preparat, però un únic petit error pot ser —ho serà— definitiu.

Els exploradors noruecs, en canvi, estan tècnicament molt més ben preparats. Tanmateix, Amundsen porta els seus plans tan en secret que fins i tot la seva reduïda tripulació salpa convençuda que marxen cap al pol nord i no cap al pol sud. No se'ls informarà del seu destí fins el dia abans de salpar de Madeira, l'últim port que trepitjaran abans de posar rumb a l'Antàrtida. Molt fàcilment algun dels tripulants hauria pogut desistir, fer-se enrere i deixar l'expedició mancada. Sense cap mena de dubte, els noruecs estan tan convençuts d'aquesta expedició com els britànics de la seva. Dominen, però, molt més l'entorn que trobaran malgrat que els seus recursos siguin molt més escassos. Què hauria passat si haguessin sabut unir els seus esforços? Però la cursa, l'obsessió per la victòria, sembla fer-los oblidar que en aquesta empresa es juguen la vida, que, en cas de reeixir-hi, el gran beneficiat serà la humanitat sencera i que, si se'n surten, tots ells seran prou famosos. La història ens ho ha demostrat així a posteriori. Avui, en el pol sud hi ha la base científica Amundsen-Scott, amb el nom dels dos líders d'aquelles expedicions.

Però l'obsessió per la glòria sovint encega la gent. La recerca d'aquesta glòria convertirà aquesta cursa en una cursa massa improvisada, molt més del que caldria esperar per poder assolir una fita d'aquesta magnitud. Scott ni tan sols no sabrà que els noruecs volen arribar també al pol sud fins que, un cop ja a l'Antàrtida, quan estan convençuts que són els únics habitants del continent, un grup dels seus homes trobaran el famós *Fram* atracat en una badia del continent. A partir d'aquí, els nervis estan servits perquè accelerin la cursa.

Però el gran protagonista de l'exploració és sempre el paisatge. En aquest cas, més que el paisatge, un punt diminut, inapreciable enmig de l'extensió més buida i desolada que es coneix. L'exploració és paisatge desconegut, i per molt que se suposi que el pol sud queda a l'altiplà antàrtic, quan noruecs i britànics comencen la seva cursa, tot són conjectures. Res no els fa pensar que el pol no es trobi, per exemple, en un punt inaccessible enmig d'una serralada impracticable. Només Shackleton s'hi ha aproximat uns quants anys abans i ho ha fet amb més sort que no pas coneixement del terreny, tal com correspon a una exploració. N'ha tornat i ha tingut prou sort per no convertir-se en un descobridor oblidat. De moment, els 88° 23' S d'Ernest Shackleton, Frank Wild, Eric Marshall i Jameson Adams el gener de 1909 són tot el que sabem d'aquell punt que es troba (només o encara) cent vuitanta quilòmetres més enllà d'on l'ésser humà ha estat mai.

És prou conegut el que passarà després: el desembre de 1911 l'equip noruec serà el primer a arribar al pol sud i en tornaran victoriosos, i el gener de 1912 l'equip britànic hi arribarà, però cinc homes moriran durant el retorn. Però fins i tot aquí hi ha oblidats. És cert que seria feixuc que la base científica del pol sud es digués alguna cosa com Hanssen-Hassel-Wisting-Bjaaland-Amundsen-Bowers-Wilson-Evans-Oates-Scott, però en aquesta cursa cap d'ells no va escatimar esforços.

Oficis polars. Bjaaland, Lindstrøm, Rønne

En una expedició polar hi ha sempre un munt de petites feines imprescindibles i incòmodes que passen inevitablement desapercebudes. Amundsen, de fet, es va preocupar prou d'estar ben cobert en tots els aspectes.

L'atzar fa que el 1909, mentre prepara la seva famosa expedició al pol sud, coincideixi casualment amb el campió d'esquí Olav Bjaaland en el vaixell de tornada a Oslo. Arran d'aquesta trobada fortuïta, l'explorador convidarà Bjaaland a participar en la seva propera expedició al pol nord. Els motius d'Amundsen són diversos, van més enllà de la possibilitat de comptar amb un dels millors esquiadors del moment perquè Bjaaland és, a més, un fuster expert que es fa els seus propis esquís. Serà una ajuda vital. I, per postres, sap tocar el violí.

Una habilitat aparentment tan poc important com tocar el violí pot ser una gran ajuda en la reduïda i aïllada comunitat d'una expedició polar de mesos de solitud, fred i foscor. Segurament una de les coses més difícils en aquelles circumstàncies és poder mantenir un bon estat d'ànim. I si Bjaaland és un dels primers cinc homes a trepitjar el pol sud, és, sense cap mena de dubte, perquè és un gran esquiador i un bon fuster, però potser, si no hagués sabut tocar el violí, Amundsen no hauria corregut a convidar-lo a la seva expedició i avui seria un desconegut.

Igual com va passar amb Bjaaland, l'èxit de qualsevol expedició depèn de la tasca imprescindible i discreta de professionals mig oblidats a l'ombra. El cuiner, per exemple. Amundsen no s'estarà mai de comptar amb qui considera la persona que ha fet més per l'exploració polar a Noruega, Adolf Lindstrøm (1866-1939), segurament el cuiner més cèlebre de l'era de les grans expedicions polars. Un home que, sense baixar pràcticament mai del vaixell, fora de quan li calia caçar alguna peça, va fer més passadores les llargues expedicions, cuinant sovint plats extraordinaris en les condicions més dures i amb ben pocs ingredients. Si més no, això és el que diu la seva llegenda. Però segurament al costat de la gana dels comensals també s'hi suma un tema de caràcter: hi ha gent que és capaç, amb la seva sola presència, de crear una atmosfera d'optimisme i d'alegria especialment vital per sobreviure els llargs hiverns polars en el reduït espai d'aquells vaixells i refugis. I Lindstrøm sembla que tenia el do dificilíssim de saber transmetre optimisme.

Encara que la seva tasca no sigui jugar-se la pell dia a dia damunt dels laberints de gel, Lindstrøm passarà llarguíssimes temporades en expedicions al voltant dels dos pols. Entre el 1898 i el 1902 el trobem embarcat al *Fram* a les ordres d'Otto Sverdrup, i entre 1903 i 1906, al *Gjøa* amb Amundsen en la primera travessa del pas del nord-oest. Malgrat no sortir gaire del vaixell, Lindstrøm devia ser un home molt inquiet, perquè un cop de retorn a Noruega, el mateix 1906 el trobem embarcat de nou a la costa oest americana, on arriba a través del cap d'Hornos, cosa que el converteix en la primera persona a circumnavegar les Amèriques. S'estarà allà fins el 1910, quan s'embarcarà de nou al *Fram*, aquest cop en l'expedició antàrtica d'Amundsen. Viurà en el *Fram* fins al seu retorn a Noruega l'any 1914. Durant aquests anys, mentre els altres vuit exploradors es juguen la vida al continent blanc, Lindstrøm passarà tres mesos llargs completament sol, confiant que els seus companys tornaran. És una espera que tampoc no devia ser gens fàcil.

Encara no cansat amb tot això, el mateix any 1914, només tres dies després d'haver arribat a Noruega, Lindstrøm decideix embarcar a l'*Eklips* cap a Sibèria, de nou sota el comandament de Sverdrup en l'operatiu de rescat de dos vaixells russos perduts a l'Àrtic des de fa temps, el *Santa Ana* i el *Gerkules*. La recerca no tindrà el resultat que buscaven. De les dues expedicions perdudes només se salvaran Albanov i Konrad (del *Santa Ana*) després d'una epopeia personal especialment dura. En tot cas, però l'expedició de l'*Eklips* servirà per rescatar la tripulació del *Taymyr* i del *Vaygach*, dos trencagels en perill de naufragar, mentre estaven provant d'obrir una ruta practicable pel nord de Sibèria.

I ja que és a Sibèria, el 1916 Lindstrøm participarà encara en una expedició al riu Ienissei, abans de tornar aquell any a Noruega, on, després d'un repòs que se li deu fer massa llarg, el 1918 decideix enrolar-se de nou amb Amundsen al *Maud* en l'expedició cap al pas del nord-est. Aquesta vegada, però, ja no podrà tornar a embarcar a causa d'un vessament cerebral just abans de salpar.

Encara més homes d'ofici. Al costat de fusters, músics i cuiners, també cal que algú domini bé el fil i l'agulla. Durant la primavera del 1909, abans d'emprendre la seva primera expedició amb el *Fram*, al més pur estil de l'antiga Xina, Amundsen aprèn a fer volar estels. Saber això a l'Antàrtida li servirà per poder fer observacions del gel. Guanyar alçada i perspectiva des del vaixell li permetria preveure rutes en les desconegudes aigües polars i li facilitaria l'avenç cap al pol. Durant els experiments que duen a terme a Horten, al sud d'Oslo, enlairen i aterren amb èxit alguns homes damunt dels estels. Però també tindran alguns accidents. En un, mor Ole Engelstad, després de ser tocat per un llamp durant un dels vols. Segurament va ser per això que van desestimar continuar endavant amb aquests experiments.

Però és aquí, a Horten, mentre aprèn a fer volar estels, on Amundsen coneix alguns dels homes que l'acompanyaran en les seves expedicions. Un d'ells és Martin Rønne (1861-1932), mariner expert i cosidor de veles que treballa en els estels amb què experimenten aquests dies. Lleuger com és, Rønne també és escollit per fer alguns dels enlairaments. Té gairebé cinquanta anys, però es guanya la confiança d'Amundsen i és per això que participarà en les seves grans expedicions a l'Antàrtida amb el *Fram* i al pas del nord-est amb el *Maud*. I encara, anys més tard, viatjarà amb ell a Svalbard per treballar en la confecció de material per a l'expedició del *Norge*. En una expedició polar cal que la petita comunitat sigui autosuficient. La roba d'abrigar, les tendes o les veles són essencials, sobretot en un entorn en què un descosit en un guant et pot deixar sense mà i de retruc sense vida.

Avui ningú no faria una expedició, per senzilla que fos, sense mirar bé la marca esportiva del material que s'emporta. La qualitat del material és bàsica i Amundsen s'assegura tant com pot de la qualitat del seu material. Mentre el *Fram* es balanceja en la lluita incòmoda de l'oceà antàrtic, a Amundsen l'admira veure Rønne hores i hores a la màquina de cosir, envoltat d'un centenar de gossos que no paren de bordar i de fer voltes al seu voltant. I això que els gossos li fan més aviat por. Els sastres, igual com tants altres treballadors, no solen ser gaire reconeguts en les expedicions polars. Més aviat formen part del gran club dels oblidats, i per això està bé recordar alguns d'aquells homes que, amb el seu ofici discret, fan que una exploració vagi endavant. Segurament Rønne sigui el sastre polar més il·lustre del món. El dia que Scott arriba al pol sud, troba una tenda cosida per Rønne. Aquesta tenda fa cinc setmanes que resisteix en solitari exposada en aquella hostilitat gèlida de vent i de neu.

Oscar Wisting. A l'ombra dels pols

Però tornem a Horten el 1909. Que Rønne sigui un bon sastre i que els experiments amb estels humans funcionin durant un temps, fa que, en aquelles dates, Amundsen conegui també el que potser serà l'il·lustre més oblidat de l'exploració polar. Estem parlant d'Oscar Wisting (1871-1936), l'home que acompanyarà Amundsen en totes les seves expedicions, sobretot en les dues arribades als pols.

D'ençà que es coneixen, Amundsen proposa a Wisting formar part de l'expedició al pol nord (que després es redirigirà cap al sud). Gràcies a això, Wisting es convertirà en la persona que ha passat més temps en alguna expedició polar: setze anys pràcticament ininterromputs que el mantindran lluny de la seva esposa, Elise Marie Johansen, i de la resta de la família. El 1910 Oscar Wisting s'embarca amb el *Fram* cap al pol sud. És pare de cinc fills. Elise està embarassada de dos bessons que moriran abans que Oscar els pugui conèixer. Entremig, també morirà Ruth, la seva única filla. No deu ser fàcil la vida d'Elise Marie durant aquells anys. Mentre omplim pàgines d'èpica oblidada als confins del món, sovint ens passa per alt que els grans oblidats de totes aquelles exploracions són les famílies que es queden a casa esperant notícies que de vegades no arriben mai més.

Durant aquests setze anys, Wisting passarà molt més temps amb Amundsen que amb els seus fills i Elise, la seva esposa. L'amistat entre els dos exploradors serà tan profunda que gairebé els convertirà en una família. Fins i tot, durant l'expedició del *Maud,* Amundsen adopta a Sibèria dues nenes inuits, Camilla Carpendale i Nita Kakot Amundsen (Kakonita). Les portarà cap a Noruega, on seran acollides per Elise durant dos anys.

Durant la seva llarga trajectòria polar, Wisting serà una peça important en totes les expedicions d'Amundsen. A bord del *Fram,* a l'Antàrtida, i amb el *Norge,* al Pol Nord, però també en la llarga expedició del *Maud* al pas del nord-est, en què Wisting agafarà el comandament des del 1922, després que Amundsen deixi el *Maud* perquè divideix l'expedició en dos grups: el d'Amundsen, que comença a preparar l'atac al pol nord en avió, i el de Wisting, que es quedarà al *Maud* i continuarà amb el pla original de seguir la deriva del gel, potser també cap al pol. Així Wisting serà ininterrompudament al *Maud* entre 1918 i 1925. Només durant una llarga escala de reparació a Seattle tindrà l'oportunitat d'estar cinc mesos amb Elise. Entremig, haurà fet també el primer vol àrtic de la història, l'any 1923. De tornada a casa, passarà poc temps amb la família perquè s'embarca de nou en l'aventura del *Norge* al Pol Nord.

Segurament, l'única expedició en què Wisting no acompanyarà Amundsen serà en la de la recerca de Nobile. De seguida que arriben notícies de la desaparició de l'expedició italiana, Amundsen proposa a Wisting afegir-se a aquesta recerca. Wisting no dubta a dir-li que sí, però no hi podrà participar perquè no hi ha prou espai a l'hidroavió. Sembla que aquest atzar haurà salvat Wisting, però ¿qui pot assegurar que no és això el que ha condemnat Amundsen a caure al mar? Potser amb Wisting tot hauria anat bé.

Finalment, després d'una llarga carrera polar, Oscar Wisting retorna a la vida familiar de Noruega. En els seus últims anys es dedica a cuidar feliçment el jardí de casa seva amb Elise. Des d'aleshores, el seu últim viatge serà només el 1938 per portar el *Fram* cap a Oslo. Aquí Wisting treballarà per a convertir en una peça de museu aquest mític vaixell. Encara avui es pot visitar al fiord de la capital noruega. Qualsevol de nosaltres, doncs, pot passejar pels racons del mític *Fram* i fer-se la idea del que devia ser viure anys seguits en un espai tan reduït enmig del gel... O potser no, no és tan fàcil fer-se'n una idea...

En qualsevol cas, l'últim viatge de Wisting és també l'últim viatge del *Fram*. Finalment, mentre s'ultimen els preparatius per al museu i es preparen les celebracions del vint-i-cinquè aniversari de l'arribada al pol sud, el 4 de desembre de 1938 es troba Wisting mort per causes naturals a la seva antiga cabina del *Fram*, presumiblement un infart.

L'home que ha sigut l'ombra d'Amundsen als dos pols, l'altre únic bipolar del planeta, ha dit prou i se'n va a reposar amb el *Fram*.

El pol sud 2. Dibuixar el pol

El 2016, durant la restauració de les cabanes de Borchgrevink al cap Adare, l'equip que treballa en la classificació i conservació dels més de mil cinc-cents objectes que hi han deixat diferents expedicions, troba un munt de papers recoberts de guano de pingüí. Entre aquests papers reposa, amagat des de fa més d'un segle, l'aquarel·la d'un ocell perfectament dibuixat amb la inscripció «Tree Creeper» (crespinell) i la data «March 1899» en un racó. Veient l'ocell que s'hi representa, sense gaire por d'equivocar-nos podem assegurar que aquesta obra va ser feta a Europa i que d'alguna manera va fer el viatge fins a aquest remotíssim racó de món. Però com? Naturalment no hi ha gaire gent que l'hi hagi pogut portar. Totes les pistes apunten cap a un jove científic i artista britànic anomenat Edward Wilson que el 1899 era a l'Europa continental recuperant-se d'una tuberculosi, però que més endavant tindrà una relació molt estreta amb l'Antàrtida.

El 1902, durant l'expedició del *Discovery* (1901-1904), Wilson ha participat en la primera aproximació al pol sud amb Shackleton i Scott. Més tard, quan el 1909 Scott prepari la seva expedició definitiva a l'Antàrtida, proposarà a Wilson que en dirigeixi l'equip científic, cosa que ell acceptarà i que el portarà a convertir-se en una de les deu primeres persones a trepitjar el pol sud.

Naturista de formació i amb evidents habilitats artístiques, Wilson destaca (entre altres coses) en el dibuix científic. A l'Antàrtida es dedicarà intensament a aquesta tasca malgrat les dificultats de dibuixar a causa d'un fred que enravena els dits i d'una llum que, o bé és artificial i dificulta treballar adequadament els colors, o bé és excessiva i pràcticament no permet ni obrir els ulls.

Quan és al cap Evans, on els britànics tenen la base principal, durant la llarga nit austral, Wilson es dedica a pintar i dibuixar, com de fet farà durant tota l'expedició. Fins i tot serà la primera persona a dibuixar el pol sud tal com el troben, amb una bandera negra onejant en un esquí vell dels noruecs. Al pol sud, la fotografia hi ha arribat poc abans que el dibuix, però Wilson és el primer dibuixant del pol sud, amb tota la dificultat que implica l'esforç d'afinar el traç i dominar els estris en unes condicions com aquelles: la inclemència del temps i el desànim en descobrir que has perdut una cursa de dimensions planetàries.

Una bandera negra que els noruecs utilitzaven per marcar-se el camí. El primer dibuix del pol sud és el de la pròpia derrota. Per què doncs fer-lo? Potser només per mer cientifisme: hem anat al pol i hi hem trobat això. Però potser també perquè al cap i a la fi aquesta bandera segurament és la primera cosa que trenca inesperadament el paisatge des de fa mesos: hem anat a un lloc on no hi ha res i hi havia això. Aquí hem après alguna cosa. Potser fins i tot ens hem adonat de quin és el límit de l'absurditat. Davant d'aquesta bandera hem arribat al fons de tot de nosaltres mateixos... I segur que mil pensaments més que no sabrem mai passen pel cap de Wilson quan dibuixa el pol sud.

O potser només hi ha la necessitat de dibuixar. La necessitat de dibuixar la primera cosa diferent que troben en molt de temps. Per fi alguna cosa diferent per dibuixar. És difícil decidir si és una necessitat científica o artística. Potser sigui, senzillament, la necessitat de dir quelcom.

Sigui durant el periple cap al pol o en el confort de la base, durant tot el temps que dura l'expedició a l'Antàrtida, Wilson fa centenars de dibuixos i aquarel·les. Fauna, des de la més gran fins a la més microscòpica; accidents geogràfics i naturals, des de muntanyes, volcans i icebergs fins a minúsculs cristalls de gel; fenòmens naturals com aurores australs, corones lunars, postes de sol, paraselenes, cels de núvols rogencs, negres, blaus, blancs... Qui diu que l'Antàrtida no és un món de colors? Pot plasmar qualsevol element de la natura o de l'expedició a les seves obres. I, naturalment, també els esforços dels seus companys. De vegades els esforços són més obvis en el traç humà damunt del paper que no pas en la calculada fredor tècnica de la fotografia (sobretot quan el protagonista de la imatge sap que el fotografien), i segurament sense els dibuixos i aquarel·les de Wilson la nostra percepció del que van ser aquelles expedicions seria encara més difusa.

No hi ha dubte que tot hi ajuda. I tant de bo tinguéssim imatges de vídeo sonor i en color, i per què no?, olfactiu i tot, però cap tecnologia moderna podrà suplir la visió personal d'un dibuix o d'una frase que retratin l'interior de qui ens parla.

Durant l'hivern antàrtic de 1911, Wilson publica dibuixos al *South Polar Times*, butlletí editat a la base per Apsley Cherry-Garrard, sens dubte la publicació més austral de la història fins aleshores. Però no només es dedica a dibuixar feliçment. Durant l'hivern, Wilson, Bowers i Cherry-Garrard fan una expedició fins al cap Crozier per estudiar una colònia de pingüins emperador que tenen localitzada des del 1902. Aquest viatge es convertirà en «el pitjor viatge del món». Està immortalitzat en el llibre de Cherry-Garrard del mateix títol, que recull tot el que va ser l'expedició de Scott de principi a final.

Aquest pitjor viatge del món de Bowers, Wilson i Cherry-Garrard és un periple hivernal impulsat per Wilson amb l'objectiu d'arribar fins a una colònia de pingüins emperadors en època de cria. El periple és tan dur que costa d'imaginar. Durant sis setmanes aquests homes viuran en una foscor total i estaran sotmesos a temperatures que arriben a baixar dels 60 graus sota zero. El problema ja no és només el fred, sinó la constància d'aquest fred. Durant aquestes setmanes, per a Wilson, Bowers i Cherry-Garrard sembla que no hi ha res més confortable que la calidesa dels 40 sota zero. Sota aquest imperi del fred, els sacs de dormir es converteixen en autèntics sarcòfags de gel. Voler entrar-hi a descansar és passar per un suplici d'una hora d'esforços dolorosos només per passar-hi unes poques hores garratibat i desitjant que acabi el temps de repòs per tornar a sortir del sac i reprendre la marxa. En quina mena de viatge es pot témer el repòs? Igual com passa amb els sacs, els abrics són una armadura que cal descongelar abans de posar-se'ls. Cal, a més, fer ràpidament la posició més bona per estirar el trineu abans l'abric no es congeli en una postura incòmoda. I després d'hores desparant el campament, cal començar a avançar a cegues per l'hivern antàrtic, entre esquerdes de gel.

I tot això ho fan per la ciència. No hi ha territoris a reclamar ni banderes a clavar enlloc, ni tan sols rutes comercials per descobrir. El principal objectiu del viatge proposat per Wilson és tan senzill com aconseguir ous i embrions de pingüí emperador per poder-ne estudiar l'evolució. Però, quan arriben al cap Crozier descobreixen que la colònia que anys enrere tenia dos mil individus ara amb prou feines en té un centenar, cosa que pràcticament fa perdre el sentit de l'aventura. I per si les condicions fossin poca cosa, mentre són al lloc una forta ventada se'ls emporta la lona de la tenda. No la trobaran fins força dies després.

Tan malament ho passen aquests tres exploradors, tan a prop de la mort es trobaran, que, un cop de retorn a la base del cap Evans, els seus companys s'espantaran en veure el deplorable aspecte que tenen. Els tres homes estan totalment extenuats i demacrats per la crua duresa a què el continent blanc els ha sotmès durant setmanes. Poc s'imaginen Edward Wilson i

Henry Bowers que encara els espera un viatge pitjor cap al pol sud.

Finalment, dels tres ous que recullen, només un arribarà sencer a la base de l'expedició, i dels tres homes, només Cherry-Garrard tornarà amb vida a Europa. Wilson, el científic artífex d'aquesta aventura, no podrà portar el petit tresor de l'emperador a la comunitat científica d'Anglaterra. I per a Cherry-Garrard potser és allà a Anglaterra, el 1913, on culminarà la duresa del pitjor viatge del món: el dia que es planta al Museu d'Història Natural de South Kensington amb l'ou de pingüí emperador i és rebut amb una barreja d'ignorància i de menyspreu.

Caldria dir alguna cosa sobre la ciència, la ignorància, l'esforç, l'agraïment... O millor, caldria aturar la lectura uns moments i pensar: és rebut amb una barreja d'ignorància i de menyspreu.

Costarà esforços perquè la tossuderia de Cherry-Garrard i la intercessió de la germana de Scott aconsegueixin que es faci l'estudi dels embrions que va proposar Wilson abans de morir. Gràcies a aquest estudi la ciència farà un pas endavant. Un pas més. Un pas més. Com sempre, cada pas és tot un esforç que valia la pena.

Sabem moltes coses d'aquestes expedicions. Tothom deixa diaris escrits, fotografies, dibuixos científics, es recullen mostres... Però no acabem de saber com és que Wilson porta un dibuix fet a Europa tants anys abans i el deixa a la cabana de Borchgrevink. Però sigui com sigui, un ocell sense vida estirat sobre el no-res de panxa enlaire, de proporcions i detalls exactíssims, igual com la coloració i la textura del plomatge, tot plegat amb uns traços impecables i deliciosos és l'obra d'art més misteriosa i antiga trobada mai al continent blanc.

La mort al Pol Sud

1. Edgar Evans

Helmer Hanssen, Sverre Hassel, Oscar Wisting, Olav Bjaaland, Roald Amundsen. Aquests són els noms de les primeres cinc persones que van arribar al pol sud. Qualsevol d'ells pot haver sigut el primer. Tots, amb els seus esforços al límit, hi arriben el 14 de desembre de 1911. El 17 de gener, un mes després, hi arriben el sisè, setè, vuitè, novè i desè. Són els britànics Henry Bowers, Edward Wilson, Edgar Evans, Lawrence Oates i Robert Scott. Per a aquests, l'arribada al pol sud davant la bandera noruega és un dels èxits més amargs que puguem imaginar. I a més, ja hem canviat d'any: del 1911 al 1912. Aquest canvi deixarà el dit de la història posat a la llaga per sempre més.

Encara no fa vint anys, l'anglès Frederick Jackson rescatava Nansen a l'Àrtic. Sembla una broma macabra que els pols atreguin els anglesos per topar amb els noruecs del *Fram*.

A partir d'aquí, a Bowers, Evans, Wilson, Oates i el seu acompanyant només els queda tornar. I si pot ser, ser els primers a explicar al món que han arribat al pol per emportar-se, com a mínim, un reconeixement provisional. Però amb un mes de desavantatge sobre Hanssen, Hassel, Wisting, Bjaaland i el seu acompanyant, poc s'imaginen aquests britànics que la seva entrada a la glòria serà precisament perquè no retornen. La seva gesta no se sabrà fins un any més tard, després d'un altre hivern antàrtic de l'expedició.

En aquests moments ja fa més de dos anys que han deixat el món enrere. L'últim arbre, l'últim carrer, l'última dona, l'últim nen, l'últim vell... Es van acomiadar de tot, per sempre, el 29 de novembre de 1910 en salpar de Port Chalmers, Nova Zelanda. Aquell dia encara no ho sabien, però per a ells el món moria i ja no seria mai més altra cosa que un record.

Mentre els britànics que han arribat al pol intenten tornar, mentre moren en el camí de retorn, mentre la nit antàrtica cau de nou sobre el continent blanc, a la base del cap Evans el seu vaixell de suport, el *Terra Nova*, se'n torna cap a Londres sense notícies del pol. Serà el segon hivern antàrtic consecutiu per a l'expedició britànica. I en aquest cas, a banda d'aprovisionar la base principal, el *Terra Nova* marxa sense poder anar a rescatar un altre grup d'homes desplaçats a un solitari racó del cap Adare, on han anat a fer estudis científics. Aquest grup d'oblidats tenen també nom i cognoms, són Victor Campbell, Raymond Priestley, George Murray Levick, George Abbot, Harry Dickason i Frank Browning. Hauran de sobreviure un infernal hivern polar amb els pocs recursos que els dona aquest racó de món, bàsicament carn de foca. Passaran l'hivern entaforats en una diminuta cova excavada al gel on amb prou feines caben. Quan l'estiu següent el gel torni a obrir les aigües de la badia i un equip de rescat vagi a buscar els seus cadàvers, descobriran que continuen vius. Gairebé un miracle que no podrà celebrar l'equip que s'endinsa cap al continent a buscar els homes que han arribat al pol.

Però tornem a principis de 1912. Poques setmanes després d'haver arribat al desolador pol sud, Oates, Evans, Scott, Bowers i Wilson continuen la seva feixuga marxa de retorn pel gel arrossegant el trineu a força de braços. El més debilitat de moment és Evans, que a més fa temps que té una ferida a la mà que li està portant complicacions. Durant la marxa, el 16 de febrer l'afeblit Evans caurà a terra. Aquell dia ja no tindrà forces ni per aguantar-se dret damunt dels esquís. Cal reposar i acampen allà mateix, al peu de la glacera de Beardmore.

L'endemà, més descansat, Evans es lleva amb més energia, explica que es troba bé i l'optimisme torna al grup. Comencen la seva marxa i poc després Evans es veu obligat a aturar-se per lligar-se millor les fixacions de les botes amb els esquís. Un cop resolt el problema, no triga a atrapar de nou els seus companys que empenyen el trineu. Però l'episodi de les botes es repeteix un cop i un altre, Evans s'ha d'aturar diferents vegades per lligar-se-les de nou fins que li demanen que s'asseguri bé les fixacions i ja els atraparà. Evans obeeix i s'atura a cordar-se bé les botes. Però passa l'estona i no els atrapa, els seus companys ni tan sols el veuen acostar-se. Finalment decideixen recular per veure què li passa.

Damunt la immensitat de la neu, un home de genolls, sense guants, mostrant les mans ferides i congelades. Aixecar-lo. Unes passes i caure de nou. Els quatre companys van a buscar el trineu, calen quatre homes per arrossegar el vehicle prou de pressa. En tornar, el troben pràcticament inconscient. Només els queda posar-lo a la tenda i confiar en un canvi del destí, però Evans ja no es despertarà mai més. Mai ningú ha deixat la vida tan al sud.

L'exploració de les terres més inhòspites és també l'exploració del més profund i inhòspit de l'ésser humà. A partir de quan es pot desitjar la mort d'algú? Els quatre supervivents han fet tot el possible per ajudar Evans, s'hi han jugat la vida, i la perdran. La salut d'Evans els ha fet avançar des de fa dies més lentament del que havien previst. Finalment la seva agonia els ha tingut dos dies pràcticament aturats. Provant d'ajudar Evans han dedicat el temps que hauria salvat potser Wilson, Scott i Bowers, qui sap si també Oates. És inevitable pensar que si Evans hagués passat uns dies menys d'agonia, si hagués tingut una mort més ràpida, potser quatre homes amb quatre famílies s'haurien salvat. És inevitable pensar-ho, però una altra cosa és decidir si és un pensament just. El racó més profund i inhòspit de l'ésser humà és un lloc fràgil i perillós com el pol.

El cas d'Evans no obre un debat sobre la mort digna —aquests cinc homes tenen tots una mort digna com poques—, sinó un debat sobre el desig de viure i sobre la solidaritat. Oates, Wilson, Bowers i Scott es juguen la vida, i la perdran, per ajudar un moribund. Això és la solidaritat, l'amistat, l'ésser humà que potser pocs arriben a trobar en el fons d'un mateix.

2. Lawrence Oates

Més endavant, també l'esgotament i les congelacions de peus i mans portaran Oates al límit. O és al revés: Oates porta al límit l'esgotament i les congelacions. Els seus últims dies, l'estat cada cop més greu d'Oates alenteix també el ritme dels seus tres companys, que de fet també saben que amb cada home menys tenen també una possibilitat menys de sobreviure.

La situació és evident i no s'estan de parlar-ne obertament, però prendre una decisió dràstica en aquest sentit és cosa del mateix Oates, que ja sap que és més un llast que no pas un ajut. Oates sap que es morirà, però una cosa és saber que es morirà i una altra estar mort. Mentre saps que et moriràs, per força ets viu, i, mentre Oates sigui viu, sap que serà un llast insalvable per als seus companys. Però els companys no poden fer res més que animar-lo a aguantar mentre pugui.

El 16 de març, Oates demana que l'abandonin en el seu sac de dormir per tal que els seus tres companys continuïn sense ell i puguin arribar al dipòsit d'aliments següent, cosa a la qual Wilson, Bowers i Scott es neguen. A la nit, però, en un últim i corprenedor esforç, Oates surt del sac i de la tenda. Mentre va cap a la tempesta diu: «Només surto a fora, potser trigaré una estona». Ningú no l'aturarà. Ningú no el tornarà a veure mai més. En les condicions en què es trobava no pot haver anat gaire lluny, potser uns pocs metres, o potser ens sorpren-dríem de la seva última caminada cap al final de tot en les pitjors condicions imaginables. Tant se val. Encara avui, aquesta estona que trigarà continua allargant-se i Oates conti-nua allà a fora, en un lloc remot i desconegut, intacte sota la blancor antàrtica on ningú no el podrà anar a trobar mai més.

3. Wilson, Bowers i Scott

El 12 de novembre de 1912, l'equip de rescat continua el camí cap al sud en cerca dels cossos dels cinc homes que van arribar al pol a principis d'any. Enmig de la blancor llisa im-maculada, Charles Wright intueix, allà lluny, alguna cosa que no hauria de formar part del paisatge. S'acosta a allò descone-gut. Tot just sobresurt uns pocs centímetres per sobre de la blancor, però s'adona que és la punta de la tenda que busquen.

No podria ser més a prop de la porta de l'oblit, gairebé se-gellada per sempre.

Enmig d'aquell silenci quasi sagrat, Wright no pot ni cridar i tot just troba la manera d'avisar els seus companys movent els braços. Li semblaria un sacrilegi cridar. Ningú no crida als cementiris. A Wright, l'Antàrtida sencera li deu semblar en aquell moment el cementiri més gran i buit del món. Miris on miris tot és blanc i llis fins més enllà de l'horitzó.

Desenterrar la tenda de la neu per després enterrar els cossos de nou allà mateix, a dins de la mateixa tenda, en la mateixa posició que els han trobat, intactes des de fa mesos. Com si fos una escena assajada, Bowers i Wilson, un a cada banda, aparentment tranquils; Scott al mig clarament agitat, possiblement l'últim a morir, amb un braç fora del sac damunt del seu amic Wilson. A banda de la pell esgrogueïda pels mesos de congelació, els cossos tenen encara el mateix aspecte que devien tenir l'últim dia de la seva vida, amagrits fins a la mort, barbes de mesos i amb les cares agredides per la intempèrie polar durant mesos i mesos d'una marxa duríssima d'anada al pol i de tornada, plenes de ferides.

Recollir allò que cal: els equips fotogràfics i, sobretot, els escrits. Sempre les paraules. Deixem imatges. Deixem paraules. Records. Memòria. Mentre li queda una mica d'energia, Scott deixa paraules fins al final. Fins i tot porta un record únic, quasi sarcàstic, del pol sud: una carta d'Amundsen per al rei de Noruega recollida al mateix pol, com un carter que hagués anat fins allà només a buidar una macabra bústia amb una sola carta.

Definitivament, l'última missió de Scott és una missió de paraules: sobretot les que li queden per dir. I sabent que és a punt de morir, assumeix aquesta seva última missió de deixar dites aquestes paraules, gairebé com la culminació d'una vida, com si la seva gran obra, l'arribada al pol sud, ara buida de sentit, s'hagués de reomplir de nou amb les paraules. Estranyament, mai abans Scott s'ha mostrat tan humà al món. En les seves últimes pàgines hi aboca tota la humanitat possible, com si necessités marxar buit i net. Sens dubte sap que en aquestes pàgines està deixant un llegat tan gran com la conquesta del pol. No és la conquesta, sinó les paraules més dures del pol sud el que ens deixa Scott. Des de casa nostra, la majoria dels humans en traurem més de les seves paraules que de la conquesta del pol.

Salvar doncs les paraules d'aquests homes tan sacrificats, sense ni tan sols treure'ls de la seva mortalla que són els sacs de dormir. Treure les canyes de la tenda, deixar reposar la lona damunt dels tres cossos, i tot seguit segellar la tomba erigint un monticle de gel amb una creu al damunt feta amb uns esquís.

Després, aquests homes de l'equip de rescat marxaran d'allà amb la intenció de no revelar mai la ubicació exacta del lloc per tal que ningú no els busqui i en pertorbi la pau. Allà deixaran aquella porta de l'oblit, definitivament segellada, ara sí, però en forma de memòria.

Segurament en el cap de cadascun d'aquests homes, d'una manera o altra, es passeja la confusa idea que tots havien desitjat, l'any anterior, ser en aquest grup que ara jeu sota la neu. I molt probablement cadascú es deu dir que si hi haguessin sigut, les coses haurien anat d'una altra manera. Qui sap si qualsevol d'aquells homes seria ara sota una creu feta amb uns esquís. És difícil saber què passa pel cap i pel cor d'algú que havent posat totes les il·lusions en un projecte se'n veu apartat de sobte. La majoria dels que participen en una expedició d'aquesta mena passen per aquesta situació. Només uns pocs arribaran fins al final. I quan van mal dades, és difícil entendre la barreja de sentiments que es congria a dins de cadascú. Al vell disgust per no haver estat escollit, s'hi barreja un estrany alleujament per no haver-hi anat i un convenciment que tot hauria sigut d'una altra manera. Però s'expliquin com s'expliquin, per moltes històries que hi hagi, al final només hi ha sempre uns fets.

S'expliqui com s'expliqui, Bowers, Wilson i Scott reposaran impertorbables per sempre més en un lloc que ja ningú no podrà dir on és. Mentrestant la tomba d'Evans continuarà perduda més al sud que cap altra. I entremig, Oates continua allargant el seu retorn a la tenda pel país de Mai Més.

4. Carta a Barrie

Durant els seus últims dies de vida a l'Antàrtida, Scott escriu no només el seu diari habitual, sinó també un seguit de cartes plenes d'agraïments, disculpes i peticions que no sap si arribaran mai als seus destinataris, però que estan carregades d'una humanitat que les convertirà segurament en el seu llegat més colpidor. Entre les set persones a qui escriu directament Scott mentre fa els seus últims esforços, hi ha un gran amic seu anomenat James Matthew Barrie, amb qui mantenen una admiració mútua i a qui resumeix la situació d'una manera així de serena:

> «*Estem en una situació desesperada, amb els peus congelats, sense fuel i lluny del menjar, però et reconfortaria ser a la nostra tenda, sentir les nostres cançons i les agradables converses sobre què farem quan arribem a Hut Point.*»

Tot i que la seva amistat ha sigut curta —amb Barrie s'han conegut el 1906, i el 1910 Scott s'ha acomiadat dels seus per última vegada—, també ha estat intensa i sobretot sincera. De fet, aquells anys hauran sigut especialment intensos en la vida de Scott. El 1908 es casaria amb l'escultora Kathleen Bruce i el 1909 naixeria el seu fill Peter. Però aquesta amistat amb Barrie, el matrimoni amb Kathleen i la paternitat de Peter es convertiran per a Scott en una experiència massa breu.

Quan Barrie i Scott es coneixen el 1906, ja fa dos anys que hi ha motius perquè tots dos siguin cèlebres. El 1904, l'any en què Robert Falcon Scott tornava de la seva primera expedició a l'Antàrtida amb el *Discovery*, és també l'any que James Matthew Barrie estrenava una obra de teatre titulada *Peter Pan*, que, després del seu gran èxit, tindrà una versió novel·lada a partir de 1911. Scott no podrà mai llegir la versió novel·lada d'aquesta obra, però quan l'explorador abandona el món civilitzat per marxar al seu particular país de Mai Més, el personatge de Barrie ja és prou cèlebre perquè el 1909 Scott posi el nom de Peter al seu fill i el converteixi en fillol de l'escriptor.

Ja que Barrie és el padrí del seu fill, a la seva última carta escrita des de l'Antàrtida, Scott demana al seu amic que es preocupi per la seva esposa Kathleen i pel petit Peter. I prou que Peter tindrà la vida que potser hauria desitjat el seu pare. Durant els anys següents a la tragèdia, abans d'un segon matrimoni, Kathleen dedicarà part de la seva tasca d'escultora a la memòria del seu difunt marit, mentre també es preocuparà de transmetre al seu fill els valors que Robert ha volgut per a ell. Així, al llarg de la seva vida, Peter Scott efectivament destacarà com a ornitòleg, pintor i esportista (ciència, art i esport; ment, cor i cos), i a més es convertirà en un mediàtic defensor de la natura. A banda de ser medallista olímpic en vela el 1936 i de convertir-se en un habitual en programes de ràdio i televisió sobre natura i vida salvatge, Peter Scott serà també un destacat dibuixant científic. I aquí sembla tancar-se un misteriós cercle; les seves pintures d'ocells no poden fer més que retornar-nos a una sorprenent aquarel·la apareguda precisament a l'Antàrtida el 2016, atribuïda a Edward Wilson, l'amic amb qui el seu pare moriria abraçat, i de la qual Peter Scott no podia saber res.

Pel que fa a la carta que Scott escriu a Barrie, va trigar un any a arribar a les mans d'ell. Barrie en va quedar tan profundament impressionat que el juny de 1937, el dia que moriria, encara la tenia guardada en una butxaca. Sempre, amb ell.

Ben mirat, quanta gent pot rebre algun cop a la vida una carta amb un comiat semblant d'una persona estimada?

«*Mai en la meva vida he conegut un home a qui admirés i estimés més que a tu, però mai t'he pogut mostrar tot el que significava per mi la teva amistat, ja que tu tenies molt per oferir i jo res.*»

És el final d'una persona des de la fi del món. En aquestes circumstàncies, es fa difícil saber en qui pensaríem nosaltres, o si algú pensaria en nosaltres.

I pel que fa a Peter Pan, més enllà de la lectura del nen que no volia créixer, segurament en podem trobar moltes altres. El país de Mai Més és el país de Peter Pan: ell hi dicta les normes, des de la més trivial fins a la més sobrenatural. En alguns moments fins i tot, en aquell món, Peter fa por. És tan capaç de qualsevol cosa per satisfer els seus desitjos que en alguns moments arriba a ser angoixosament dèspota i egoista. Però és que és el seu món i és només seu. És per això que qualsevol que vagi al país de Mai Més estarà perillosament sotmès als seus capricis, fins i tot per entrar-hi o per sortir-ne.

I qui no diria que l'Antàrtida és ben bé l'illa de Mai Més?

Douglas Mawson. Quan res no pot ser pitjor

Algú ha dit res del pitjor viatge del món? Ha existit realment, o sempre n'hi pot haver un de més terrible? Per estrany que sembli, sí, sempre és possible que les coses vagin més malament.

Pràcticament tothom del 1912, i també molta gent que viurà més endavant sembla que estigui molt pendent d'aquell raconet de l'Antàrtida on un grup d'homes han viscut el pitjor viatge del món. Però ara que aquells exploradors tenen l'escalf, per més dubtós que sigui, de tantes pàgines escrites, un cop aquell 12 de novembre han tancat l'episodi de la troballa dels cossos de Bowers, Wilson i Scott, podem començar a aixecar la vista d'aquest lloc, començar a sobrevolar amb el cap la immensitat del continent blanc i allunyar-nos d'ells encara més, deixar-los, doncs, enrere i endinsar-nos de nou en aquesta buidor glaçada. Podem volar i volar per damunt de la vastitud fins que en un altre racó oblidat de l'Antàrtida descobrim, espetegant i bufetejada histèricament pel vent, una misteriosa tenda enmig del no-res. Sembla que hi ha algú més al continent. A dins d'aquesta tenda, tres homes, encara més oblidats pel món, es protegeixen de la fortíssima ventada que els assetjarà durant cinc dies. Douglas Mawson, Belgrave Ninnis i Xavier Mertz encara no tenen notícies de l'arribada al pol sud de noruecs i anglesos. Tan solitària és l'Antàrtida del 1912 que aquest triomf és sabut a tot el món, llevat del mateix continent.

Aquests tres homes formen part d'una expedició australiana que té la base a dos dies de camí, en un punt de la costa anomenat Commonwealth Bay. Porten gairebé un any al continent, des del gener d'aquest mateix 1912. Dirigeix l'expedició Douglas Mawson, el geòleg de trenta anys que està a punt de fer un viatge encara més espantós que el viatge pitjor del món.

A hores d'ara Mawson ja és un veterà de l'Antàrtida. El 1908 ja va participar a l'expedició del *Nimrod*, la primera que provava d'arribar al pol sud, dirigida per Shackleton i on hi havia també Robert Scott. Aquell cop, el dia 16 de gener de 1909, Mawson, Alistair Mackay i Edgeworth David van ser els primers a trepitjar el pol sud magnètic. Llavors, encara era sobre sòl continental. I encara el 10 de març de 1908, aquells mateixos tres homes havien coronat la primera ascensió al cim de l'Erebus, seguits immediatament per Jameson Adams i Eric Marshall, i amb el suport de Phillip Brocklehurst, que els hauria d'esperar a la meitat del descens.

Per tant, si de Mawson no en sabem gran cosa és perquè en part, com aquells seus companys, ja és un descobridor de l'oblit. Tota manera, ja sap també el que és patir a l'Antàrtida. Però res que permeti imaginar l'aventura que està a punt de començar aquest novembre de 1912.

De moment, Douglas Mawson es troba dins d'aquesta solitària tenda amb els seus amics Belgrave Ninnis i Xavier Mertz.

El 10 de novembre de 1912 (dos dies abans que es trobin les restes de Wilson, Bowers i Scott), aquests tres homes han deixat els companys de la base de Commonwealth Bay per fer una exploració que els portarà uns cinc-cents quilòmetres cap a l'interior del continent. Durant un mes, fins al 14 de desembre, avançaran més de quinze quilòmetres diaris amb l'ajut de setze gossos, herois obligats i oblidats; gossos també amb noms: Basilisk, Shackleton, Ginger Bitch, Franklin, John Bull, Mary, Haldane, Pavlova, Fusilier, Jappy, Ginger, George, Johnson, Castor, Betli i Blizzard.

Durant aquest mes, l'exploració avançarà sense més contratemps que els que havien previst. Estan descobrint la zona més assetjada pel vent que es coneix en tot el planeta. Lluny del que es podria pensar, en aquesta infinitud blanca la llisor de la neu i del gel és inexistent. L'embat incansable dels vents modela la superfície i deixa les glaceres plenes de zastruguis, diminutes dunes de neu congelades i esmolades que dificulten qualsevol avenç. Durant dies, els tres exploradors travessen extensions quasi impracticables d'aquestes formacions, esquiven constantment un laberint d'esquerdes en el gel i s'enfronten a la força del torb. Molts matins es lleven amb el campament colgat per la neu. En aquest entorn perden alguns gossos mentre altres no poden ajudar-los tant com caldria. És el cas de la husky Ginger Bitch, que pareix uns cadells que no sobreviuran al viatge. Però tot plegat entra encara dins del que era d'esperar atesa la duresa de l'exploració polar.

Així, un mes de monotonia i d'esforços extenuants està explicat —més que no pas imaginat— de seguida.

Les coses es comencen a complicar una mica, només, quan els arriben els primers mals, com les primeres cegueres de neu i les primeres congelacions. Malgrat tot, tot això encara és el que havien pogut preveure. No hi ha res, doncs, que els privi de continuar avançant.

Però hi ha patiment. I l'Antàrtida no perdona. De moment qui ho està passant més malament és Ninnis, que durant dies pateix una infecció en un dit que el torturarà tant que acabarà demanant a Mawson que li talli la part infectada. Cal fer-ho en viu amb un ganivet. Mawson li tallarà aquesta part infectada de dit el matí del 13 de desembre. Aquella nit Ninnis dormirà bé per primer cop en molts dies.

Mentre Ninnis es recupera, preveient que l'endemà es llevarà encara afeblit, per alleugerir la marxa Mertz i Mawson buiden el trineu més malmès perquè volen continuar avançant només amb dos vehicles. Sortosament, però, l'endemà Ninnis es llevarà prou bé. Tot fa pensar, doncs, que podran continuar l'exploració al ritme que havien previst.

I ja hi som de nou. Un esquiador i dos trineus de gossos al darrere. Esquivant esquerdes i avançant lentament en la vastitud blanca.

Mentre aquest mateix 14 de desembre en el món civilitzat cinc noruecs deuen estar celebrant el primer aniversari de la seva arribada al pol sud, Mertz obre camí esquiant. El segueix Mawson amb un trineu. Tanca el grup Ninnis amb l'altre. És obvi que obrir pas és jugar-se la vida. Hi ha el perill de caure en una esquerda camuflada sota la neu. Per això bona part de provisions i els millors gossos van amb l'últim trineu.

El terreny és perillós, però les coses van prou bé. En algun moment d'aquest 14 de desembre, mentre es troben en una zona d'esquerdes, Mawson mira enrere per comprovar com està Ninnis. Atura els gossos, es gira, i aleshores veu darrere seu les traces del seu trineu sobre la blancor de la neu. Res més. Ninnis s'ha fos.

A l'hemisferi nord, un brindis innocentment macabre per la conquesta del pol.

Aquestes coses no avisen. És així. Mawson i Mertz es giren i Ninnis no hi és. Ha caigut en una esquerda. Reculen fins al lloc on ha desaparegut el seu company, aboquen els caps a la foscor del buit i en un replà, a potser cinquanta metres de fondària, només poden identificar el cos d'un gos mort. Més avall, la negror absoluta. Malgrat l'evidència dels fets, Mertz i Mawson criden el seu company durant hores, abocats a la gola de l'abisme, però la resposta de Ninnis no arribarà mai més. La nit passada, Ninnis ha dormit bé per primer cop en molts dies. I per últim cop també. Allà mateix, finalment, en una modesta cerimònia, el donen per enterrat. Belgrave Ninnis ja ha fet el seu pitjor viatge del món.

I tot seguit, Mawson i Mertz miren al seu voltant i es donen per enterrats ells també. Cal tornar enrere, però la base és a un mes de distància per a un equip de tres trineus en bones condicions. Ara són dos, i en el trineu perdut hi havia quasi totes les provisions i la tenda, a més dels gossos més forts (Basilisk, Ginger Bitch, Shackleton, Castor, Franklin i John Bull). Això deixa Mertz i Mawson a cinc-cents quilòmetres de la salvació, sense cap més refugi que una petita tenda improvisada on amb prou feines es podran encabir. Tenen aliments per només deu dies, sense comptar els gossos, que també cal alimentar.

En aquests casos extrems, aliment i transport són la mateixa cosa; és l'única opció de salvar-se ells i alguns dels animals, si tenen sort. Aviat sacrifiquen el gos més dèbil, George, el cuinen com poden amb el fogó de querosè que conserven per casualitat i se'n reparteixen la carn immastegable entre ells dos i els cinc gossos que queden vius.

Així avancen penosament de tornada durant deu dies, cada cop més afeblits. Com ja podem imaginar-nos, la marxa és feixuga. Cal afegir-hi, a més a més, els llargs esforços que han de fer per plantar el campament. Un cop muntat, quasi no aconseguiran dormir. Tots dos estan entaforats en l'espai que hauria d'ocupar una persona. En aquestes condicions, després de sobreviure a la nit sense haver descansat prou, coses aparentment tan senzilles com tornar a desparar el precari campament els exigeix encara dues o tres hores d'esforç. No de temps: d'esforç.

Però continuen avançant com poden. A centenars de quilòmetres de l'ajut més proper, sense aixopluc ni aliment adequats, Mertz i Mawson avancen envoltats només per la grisor, pràcticament cecs i desorientats. Cecs per dins i per fora: patint la ceguesa de la neu i encegats per l'absència de paisatge, en la llisor sense referències del torb. Està essent un dels pitjors viatges del món. Sense més èpica que la feixuguesa diària. Aquest és el viatge dels que no sobreviuen per explicar-ho. Fins i tot els gossos estan tan fatigats i desnerits que només Ginger ajuda a tibar els trineus. Dia rere dia els animals van caient, i quan això passa, són carregats al trineu, i d'allà van al fogó. El dia 17 es mengen el gos Johnson. L'endemà el sopar es diu Mary. Dies després fan una bona sopa amb els ossos de Pavlova. El 28 de desembre bullen el crani de Ginger, el parteixen en dos i es mengen el cervell per esmorzar.

I amb Ginger s'han acabat els gossos vius. Ara Mawson i Mertz continuen tirant ells sols el trineu.

La fam i el cansament van passant factura. Mawson no es veu a ell mateix, però segurament Mertz li fa de mirall, i el 5 de gener de 1913 apunta al seu diari (aquell gran mèrit d'escriure un diari en unes condicions com aquestes) que Mertz és tot pell. Acaben decidint descansar tot un dia. El passaran a dins dels sacs de dormir. L'endemà proven d'avançar, però pocs quilòmetres després de lluita contra el torb, l'estat de Mertz els obliga a tornar a plantar la tenda i a descansar una altra vegada. Mawson es veu encara amb energies per arribar a la base on els espera l'*Aurora*, el vaixell de l'expedició, però té clar que Mertz no millora, sinó que empitjora.

El 7 de gener, Mertz es lleva delirant i amb tots els símptomes d'una disenteria que ja és incurable. Durant hores, Mawson dedicarà tots els seus esforços a cuidar el seu company, a netejar-lo, assecar-lo i escalfar-lo de nou a dins del sac fins que, finalment, Mertz aconsegueix reposar. I reposa tan bé que, després que pensi que el seu company porta molta estona quiet al seu costat, a dins de la tenda, Mawson mira Mertz i s'adona que ja no es mourà més. Això passa a la matinada del 8 de gener. També Xavier Mertz acaba de finalitzar el seu pitjor viatge del món.

Aturat pel vent i pel cansament, arrambat durant hores al cos del seu company en la incomoditat de la tenda, Mawson haurà d'esperar fins al vespre següent per treure Mertz a l'exterior i enterrar-lo en la neu, sota uns blocs de gel tallats per ell mateix. Ara Mawson està sol. Sap que és a quasi dos-cents quilòmetres de la persona que té més a prop. El seu estat físic és molt crític. (Heu estat mai sols en un pis? En un edifici? En una illa de cases? En una ciutat? En un país sencer?). A més, Mawson no pot reprendre la marxa fins l'11 de gener a causa del mal temps. Després, quan finalment pot tornar a avançar, comença a notar un dolor cada cop més intens als peus que l'obliga a descalçar-se. Se'ls mira. Aleshores, s'adona que és impossible que pugui avançar sense gens de pell a les plantes. S'han convertit en una massa sangonosa de llagues i butllofes rebentades.

D'alguna manera es farà unes cures d'emergència, però no podrà reprendre la marxa fins al dia 13. I després, durant quatre dies més, continuarà arrossegant-se només amb el martiri que és provar de sobreviure una mica més. Així fins el 17 de gener, quan cau a dins d'una esquerda al gel. El buit. Dolorosa estrebada de la corda a la cintura. Negre. Fer pèndol sobre la foscor. Mirar amunt. L'altre cap de corda lligat encara al trineu, travat per miracle. Ascendir a pols cinc metres fins al caire del precipici. Mirar d'aferrar els dits embalbits al gel. Relliscar i caure de nou, intent rere intent, un cop rere l'altre. I el trineu a punt de caure amb ell cap al fons.

Finalment, a punt de morir com el seu company Belgrave Ninnis, Mawson acabarà sortint sol de l'escletxa després de moltes provatures. Aquest 17 de gener ningú no deu brindar enlloc pel primer aniversari de l'arribada dels anglesos al pol sud.

Avui no hi ha brindis macabre.

Només l'Antàrtida sembla voler brindar amb vides humanes en aquests primers aniversaris de la conquesta polar. Però aquesta vegada no s'empassa Mawson. Ja es va endur els anglesos que van profanar el pol fa un any. Avui donarà encara una altra oportunitat a aquest explorador solitari. Així, els dies següents Mawson podrà continuar avançant. Miraculosament. A un ritme d'uns sis o set quilòmetres diaris. Avenç feixuc. De vegades ajudat pel vent. Altres moments obligat a aturar-se, amb l'embat bufant-li de cara a cinquanta quilòmetres per hora i obligant-lo a plantar el campament. Llarguíssims esforços que ara ha de fer tot sol.

I d'aquesta manera avança penosament, sense cap més sorpresa fins que el 29 de gener veu en la distància una fita de neu, un senyal humà fet pels seus companys Archie McLean, Arthur Hodgeman i Frank Hurley (fotògraf que retrobarem més endavant). Ningú més no ha estat mai aquí. Es desvia per arribar-hi i hi troba unes provisions que li permetran allargar l'agonia, potser també salvar la vida, i una nota dins d'una llauna que indica que el vaixell *Aurora* encara continua esperant els exploradors, i que trenta-set quilòmetres més endavant hi ha un refugi de gel amb menjar al lloc que anomenen Aladdin's Cave. De passada, els companys no es poden estar d'informar que fa un any Amundsen va arribar al pol sud i que

Scott està passant el seu segon hivern al continent. No se sap res encara aquí de la seva mort: són les notícies que hi ha.

Consol i desesper. Mawson troba aquesta nota a les dues de la tarda, i els seus companys l'han signada a les vuit del mateix matí. Impossible atrapar-los. Impensable esperar que tornin. Cal seguir. I cal superar un nou obstacle en forma de glacera, sense grampons, perduts ja en algun moment de l'aventura, relliscant en el gel i envestit pels vents, però amb noves racions de menjar i començant a intuir el final del suplici.

Mawson arriba a la seva miraculosa cova d'Aladí l'1 de febrer. Els últims dies ha anat prou de pressa, però el mal temps li impedeix sortir-ne durant una setmana més. I així, havent superat penalitat rere penalitat, finalment podrà reprendre la marxa i, ara sí, el dia 8 albira la costa, allà lluny, i pot identificar l'*Aurora*. L'*Aurora*, que l'ha estat esperant fins ara, però que tot just acaba de salpar rumb cap a Austràlia.

Res no pot ser pitjor.

Durant els darrers tres mesos ha estat més sol i més lluny del món que ningú, ha enterrat els seus amics, ha matat els seus gossos per menjar-se'ls, ha suportat les tempestes més terribles amb temperatures de vint sota zero i vents huracanats de més de cent quilòmetres per hora, ha perdut carn, pell, cabells, ungles, ha patit congelacions i accidents, ha avançat exhaust i afamat quan era millor morir. I tot plegat per veure marxar l'expedició sense ell. Segona salvació que se li escapa per poques hores. Ara ho sap: per al món, ja fa temps que ell és tan mort com els seus companys Ninnis i Mertz.

Només li queda acabar d'arribar fins a la costa. Només perquè porta setmanes anant cap allà. Una passa. Una altra. Una més. I per fi, al fons del paisatge, unes roques negres despullades de neu, la primera cosa no blanca que li ofereix el paisatge en molt de temps, la badia on hi ha hagut l'*Aurora* esperant-lo. I com un miratge misteriós, unes figures humanes allà lluny. Algú que el veu. I Mawson torna a ser viu.

Sis homes s'han quedat a la base. No servirà de res avisar per ràdio a l'*Aurora* que Mawson ha tornat viu. El gel ja no deixa tornar el vaixell enrere, i amb aquests pocs companys Mawson rebrà les primeres atencions, començarà a recuperar-se i només hauran d'esperar un altre rigorós hivern antàrtic per tornar al món després de dos anys sencers al continent.

Vet aquí un altre pitjor viatge del món.

Perquè aquesta història de Mawson és la història de molts dels que no tornen. Els exploradors engolits per l'oblit absolut no desapareixen sense més ni més. Alguns, com Ninnis, són succionats per la terra com si res. Altres, com Mertz, agonitzen i deliren durant dies de dolor i febre fins a la mort. I encara també n'hi ha que viuen viatges pitjors que els pitjors de tots i que finalment serien herois només que ens n'arribés alguna mena de testimoni. Mawson gairebé és un d'aquests últims, gairebé és un dels engolits per l'oblit més despietat. Però ell torna de l'oblit. Amb paraules. I dona veu als seus amics Belgrave Ninnis i Xavier Mertz.

I mai més no sabrem com és el pitjor viatge del món.

Les naus de l'oblit

Arreu del món hi ha naus exposades en museus o en espais públics, monuments i llibres dedicats a naus històriques, a naus desaparegudes, a naus llegendàries carregades d'èpica... I si hi ha, doncs, espai per a la memòria de les naus, ¿no deuen tenir també aquestes naus els seus herois oblidats? Per molt que tinguin una ànima de fusta, també les naus són protagonistes de la història i per tant de l'oblit. Què són si no els objectes dels museus?

Una d'aquestes naus exposades a la memòria pública es troba avui al Dulwich College de Londres. Allà, per a qui vulgui veure'l, hi sol reposar un vell bot salvavides de set metres d'eslora i una tona de pes anomenat *James Caird*. Poques vegades un d'aquests bots salvavides es guanya el mèrit de passar a la història; la majoria ni tan sols no arriben a tocar mai l'aigua, però aquest, el *James Caird*, ha fet molts de mèrits per no ser un oblidat.

És molt probable que en un primer moment el seu nom no ens digui gran cosa, però si en canvi diem, per exemple, *Endurance*, potser en el nostre imaginari comencin a aparèixer les imatges d'una nau redescoberta al fons del mar de Weddell el 2022; i potser també les imatges del seu naufragi en el gel antàrtic l'any 1915, immortalitzades per Frank Hurley, el fotògraf de la famosa expedició transantàrtica de Shackleton.

Entre les naus marítimes de l'Antàrtida, l'*Endurance* necessita tan poca presentació com entre els exploradors Ernest Shackleton, un dels alumnes il·lustres d'aquest Dulwich College de Londres. Per la seva banda, en canvi, a l'ombra d'aquests noms, el *James Caird* podria ser, en forma de bot salvavides, un il·lustre oblidat de les naus polars: tothom coneix la seva història, però pocs el recorden. Mentre l'*Endurance*, amb el seu nom propi, ha passat a l'imaginari popular gràcies a les fotografies i filmacions de Hurley i a la recent troballa d'aquesta nau, el *James Caird* s'ha convertit en poc més que «la barca amb què es van salvar». Però també és cert que el que queda de l'*Endurance* és allà al fons, sotmès a la lenta digestió marina, mentre que el *James Caird,* en canvi, reposa tranquil·lament en la calma de les sales de museus on de tant en tant és exposat.

No cal, doncs, afegir-hi gaire explicació perquè aquesta és la història més arxiconeguda de l'Antàrtida: quan l'*Endurance* és destruït pel gel l'octubre de 1915, deixa vint-i-vuit homes sols arrossegant tres bots salvavides per l'Antàrtida. Durant mesos, aquests homes s'arrossegaran pel gel fins arribar a l'illa Elefant, on finalment tots aconseguiran ser rescatats amb vida.

Ja comencem a estar avesats a veure homes arrossegant bots salvavides per les regions polars. Durant setmanes i setmanes, durant mesos incerts i extenuants, sentim el soroll dolorós de la quilla dels tres bots rascant i rebotant contra la duresa del gel fins que, finalment, el *James Caird*, l'*Stancomb Wills* i el *Dudley Docker*, tots tres batejats amb noms de patrocinadors de l'expedició, reposen en una platja de l'illa Elefant. Des d'aquí, l'aposta de Shackleton és embarcar-se amb el millor bot cap a l'illa de Geòrgia del Sud, a mil cinc-cents quilòmetres de distància, i demanar un rescat a la colònia balenera que hi ha.

Durant dies, el fuster Henry McNish es dedicarà a preparar el millor bot per a aquest viatge, i el 24 d'abril de 1916 el *James Caird* deixa l'illa Elefant amb sis tripulants a dins: Ernest Shackleton, Frank Worsley, Tom Crean, Henry McNish, Tim McCarthy i John Vincent.

Probablement, gràcies a la fotografia feta per Frank Hurley, aquest és un dels moments més emotius i memorables de tota l'era daurada de l'exploració polar: la imatge d'un grup d'homes acomiadant el *James Caird* a la recerca d'un rescat impossible. En un primer moment, aquesta imatge es va utilitzar per explicar el rescat, com si aquests homes saludessin eufòrics l'arribada d'un vaixell, però en realitat és el comiat del *James*

Caird. A la fotografia, d'esquena i davant la riba, veiem tot de siluetes fosques aixecant els braços en senyal de comiat. És difícil no emocionar-se davant d'aquesta escena en què tots semblen compartir una mena d'optimisme encomanat. Però tant volem veure-hi l'optimisme i la fe cega que quasi ni es nota que, al mig de la imatge, potser enxampat per casualitat en repòs en aquell instant, hi ha un home amb els braços caiguts. Si es vol se li poden veure les espatlles abatudes. I mirant tot seguit els gestos de tots els homes un a un, provant de posar-nos en els pensaments de cadascun d'ells, potser descobrim que aquella mena de convenciment que volíem veure en els braços aixecats se'ns comença a convertir en un últim acte desesperat de voler confiar en el rescat. No de confiar, sinó de *voler* confiar-hi. És gairebé una resignació angoixant. De sobte, un cop ben mirats, ens adonem que tots i cadascun dels gestos de la imatge són gestos cansats i abatuts. I ens adonem aleshores de les seves cares. Poques vegades unes siluetes d'esquena poden mostrar uns rostres tan ben dibuixats. Una mirada al buit, uns ulls llagrimosos, un esbufec d'esgotament anímic...

Aquesta fotografia és avui la imatge de la fe cega perquè tot va acabar bé. Però quina lectura en faríem, en canvi, si s'hagués trobat la càmera i els negatius de Frank Hurley envoltats de cadàvers anys després? Ben mirat, aquest 24 d'abril de 1916, aquests homes saben que estan acomiadant la seva última possibilitat de salvació, una possibilitat protagonitzada per uns altres homes que pot ben ser que vagin cap a la mort.

I aleshores, vista així, la fotografia esgarrifa.

Hem acomiadat ja el *James Caird*. El bot ha acomiadat ja per sempre l'illa Elefant; a poc a poc esquiva els blocs de gel que cruixen al seu voltant, mentre li barren el pas. Des de terra no ho poden veure, però finalment aconsegueix sortir a mar obert. El cruixir fantasmal del gel, la recerca d'una escletxa, l'arribada a mar obert, el vaivé agitat d'ones que s'apoderen de l'interior del bot... Així és aquest anguniós primer dia, potser un dels més plàcids —o dels menys terribles— del viatge que els espera.

Ja des del primer moment, i durant les setmanes vinents de lluita infernal contra els elements, els tripulants es troben xops fins al moll de l'os, dormint escassament per torns damunt l'aigua acumulada al fons del bot, avançant amb constants esforços i orientats només gràcies a la perícia i els càlculs incansables de Worsley, que els permetran mig ubicar-se en aquest oceà gèlid, tempestuós i huracanat, gairebé sempre sense cap referència directa del sol.

No som mai prou conscients del que representa navegar de nit per aigües solitàries i desconegudes. Ni un far, ni una llum, sempre desitjant veure terra de dia abans d'estavellar-se en la negror absoluta contra uns esculls inadvertits. Negror i tempesta contra allò desconegut. Vertigen d'un univers cec i voraç. Sotmesos a un repòs impossible i a una incertesa absoluta, el més difícil d'entendre és que aquest bot no naufragui. Però, finalment, el 10 de maig, després de dues setmanes de martiri resistint totes les inclemències i l'agitació de l'oceà, el *James Caird* és escopit contra la costa deshabitada de l'illa de Geòrgia del Sud. Per poc no es desballesta contra les roques de l'escull enmig de les ones gegants i del vent implacable que els ha assotat durant tot el periple. Finalment, però, ha portat els seus tripulants a terra.

Acaben de sobreviure a una tempesta que no és pas poca cosa. Tres dies abans, un vapor de 500 tones amb vint tripulants, l'*Argos*, ha salpat de Buenos Aires cap a Geòrgia del Sud.

Engolit per la mateixa tempesta, de l'*Argos* tot just es trobaran algunes restes surant no gaire lluny del punt d'arribada del *James Caird*. Poc deu haver faltat perquè en aquesta negra immensitat no s'estavellin uns contra els altres o perquè es demanin mútuament un auxili impossible a la desolada costa sud de l'illa.

Mesos més tard, quan a la costa nord reobri l'estació balenera de Prince Olav Harbour a Possession Bay, els primers baleners que hi arribin hi trobaran set llits improvisats i un cos en descomposició a pocs quilòmetres. Probablement aquests supervivents de l'*Argos* van aventurar-se illa endins amb la mateixa idea que els anglesos del *James Caird* i van arribar al refugi d'aquesta estació abandonada, però no se n'ha sabut res més. Ni tampoc dels cossos. Més oblit, aferrat només a la memòria per l'atzar d'haver estat a prop de topar amb Shackleton enmig de tanta desolació. I qui sap quin hauria estat el destí dels dos grups de nàufrags en cas que s'haguessin trobat. Hi hauria més èpica? O bé més oblit?

Encara més, oblit de l'oblit, entre els senyals de presència humana dels set supervivents de l'*Argos* hi havia també una nota en castellà, incomprensible per al balener que la va trobar i perduda poc després sense que es pugui saber què deia. Un descuit terrible. Hi pot haver la buidor de les paraules no escrites ni dites, com les de tants nàufrags oblidats. I hi pot haver la buidor de les paraules escrites sense saber si seran mai trobades, com les de Scott al pol sud i les de tants altres no trobats mai més. Però l'anècdota d'aquesta nota és encara més desconcertant: una nota que escrius desesperadament, sabent que algú la trobarà, però ignorant que acaba essent llençada abans de ser llegida.

Així, oblidats aquells argonautes, o ignorats encara, tornem als nostres sis homes del *James Caird*. Des d'on són ara, a la banda deshabitada de l'illa, si volen arribar a l'estació balenera de Stromness, els queden més de cinquanta quilòmetres de camí a través de muntanyes de més de mil metres d'altitud i de glaceres que no ha trepitjat mai ningú. McNish i Vincent, totalment defallits, no poden fer aquest camí i es quedaran on són, atesos per McCarthy, protegits sota el bot, ara de nou convertit en una cabana. Mentrestant Shackleton, Worsley i Crean s'aventuraran a peu cap a Stromness. Des d'aquí els esperen trenta-sis hores de camí difícil per terres inexplorades i l'esforç de convèncer les autoritats locals que realment venen de l'Antàrtida (com diu?) i que en plena Gran Guerra (com diu?) cal fer un rescat d'aquesta envergadura.

El rescat de McNish, Vincent i McCarthy serà ràpid i senzill, però encara caldran grans esforços per salvar la resta del grup fins que, finalment, el 30 d'agost de 1916, després de quatre mesos i quatre intents, Shackleton aconsegueix arribar a l'illa Elefant amb el remolcador xilè *Yelcho* i pot rescatar els vint-i-dos homes que estaven esperant. Per fi, després de dos anys d'expedició, tots aquests afortunats podran tornar a casa... abans de canviar l'infern del gel polar per l'infern de foc del front.

A qui li importen doncs les naus? De totes les naus de l'expedició de Shackleton, només el *James Caird* tornarà a Anglaterra. Després de la seva memorable aventura, un cop acabada la Gran Guerra, el bot és recuperat a Geòrgia del Sud per arribar a Liverpool el 5 desembre 1919 a bord del balener *S.S. Woodville*. Finalment, després de ser exposat en diferents llocs, avui reposa al Dulwich College de Londres on Shackleton es va formar.

Mentrestant, l'*Endurance*, la nau mare de l'expedició, tindrà un dels naufragis més memorables de la història. També serà un dels derelictes més buscats. Durant més d'un segle el seu buc reposarà amagat sota la seva freda tomba marina, però l'atzar farà encara que torni un dia a la memòria col·lectiva. El 5 de gener de 1922, Shackleton es troba iniciant la seva última expedició polar quan li arriba la mort en una escala a Geòrgia del Sud, el mateix lloc on un dia havia tornat a la vida. Durant dos mesos el seu cos començarà un periple cap a Londres, però no passarà de Montevideo, i des d'allà serà retornat a Geòrgia del Sud per ser enterrat el 5 de març de 1922. Exactament el mateix dia, cent anys després, el 5 de març de 2022, l'*Endurance* serà localitzat de nou a 3.000 metres de profunditat al mar de Weddell, dret damunt del seu llit i en un sorprenent bon estat de conservació.

Finalment, per la seva banda, de l'*Stancomb Wills* i el *Dudley Docker* només sabem que són abandonats a correcuita a l'illa Elefant quan els bots del *Yelcho* rescaten la resta d'exploradors. Després de mesos arrossegats pel gel, després de ser un bon aixopluc per als supervivents, aquests dos bots queden allà a la platja, de cap per avall, exposats a la brutal erosió que els farà desaparèixer amb els anys. Durant dècades ningú més no trepitjarà aquesta illa (així de difícil era ser rescatats). Quan algú hi torna ja no trobarà cap resta que recordi res del que hi ha passat. L'*Stancomb Wills* i el *Dudley Docker*, ells sí, s'han ben dissolt en l'oblit.

El pol sud 3. Coses de l'aire i el vent

Després de la descoberta de les seves costes i de l'arribada al seu cor, l'Antàrtida sembla impregnada d'aquell ritme de les coses grosses i lentes, que semblen immòbils fins que de sobte, un dia, reben el delicat resultat d'un vol d'una papallona remota i es desplomen, exploten, es precipiten, arrenquen a córrer...

Després de rebre la primera visita llampec dels humans, el solitari pol sud torna a descansar. La presència humana ha sigut només un flaix, una bufetada, una mena d'il·lusió d'aquelles que després només semblen somiades. Finalment, a poc a poc, la tenda i les banderes deixades per aquells fugaços exploradors comencen a ser emportades pel vent, colgades per la neu, invisibles, arrossegades lentament gel avall. I de nou la calma polar, la quietud tempestuosa torna a regnar.

Ningú més no tornarà a arribar al pol sud fins al 1929, quan aparegui al cel un ésser anomenat *Floyd Bennett*, el petit avió de Richard Byrd, el pilot nord-americà que el 1926 ja ha pretès haver arribat al pol nord amb aquell company que ara dona nom a l'aparell. Aquest cop, sens dubte, *Floyd Bennett* sobrevola el pol sud. A bord hi ha també Bernt Balchen, Harold June i Ashley McKinley. Només hi falta l'antic company d'aventures de Byrd, l'autèntic Floyd Bennett, que ja només pot donar nom a l'avió. L'any anterior, Bennett ha mort de pneumònia en ple vol durant una operació de rescat al Canadà. La seva mort va obligar el seu company de cabina, Bernt Balchen, a tornar cap al Quebec amb el cos de Bennett sense vida. Aquests exploradors —els pioners de l'aviació també— potser cauen en errors, però n'hi ha uns quants d'ells que no neguen mai cap ajut. Mai. Bennett, fins i tot malalt de pneumònia i a les portes de la mort, lluitarà fins l'últim alè per ajudar a salvar la vida d'altres pilots accidentats a l'Àrtic.

Així, mort en ple vol a l'altra banda del món, l'aviador ara dona nom a aquest *Floyd Bennett* de metall que continua sobrevolant terres noves i desconegudes, extensions que abans de ser trepitjades per ningú, des de l'aire, que és com van ser batejades, ja rebran també el nom de Terra de Marie Byrd, l'esposa de Richard. Ella l'està esperant pacientment a casa seva. Vet aquí, al cel antàrtic, un home posant noms de la gent que estima a les coses importants... Perquè els que estimen, enyoren, i, si poden, posen noms que els lliguin a aquells que els queden lluny.

Hi ha gent que té monuments en forma d'estàtua o d'avió o de noms de carrers o fins i tot de ciutats, però poques persones corrents (a banda de reis i emperadors, casualitats de poc mèrit) arriben a donar noms a territoris tan extensos. *Terra de Marie Byrd*. Com a monument no està gens malament. I un cop batejat un territori, cal esperar a veure què en farà la història d'aquest nom. En aquest cas, si Byrd pensa que no hi ha res com la llibertat per eixamplar un cor, potser podria estar content. Els exploradors saben prou bé que sempre hi haurà racons del món on no hi ha presència humana, racons que no reclama cap país. L'atzar voldrà que anys més tard, el nom de Marie Byrd sigui precisament el de la *Terra nullius* més gran del món.

Però sobretot caldria que es recordés el més important: Marie Byrd no és el nom d'un territori de ningú a l'Antàrtida; abans és el nom d'una persona que es devia fer estimar.

I aquí els tenim, aquests aviadors, sobrevolant el pol sud. Però els homes que són l'ànima del *Floyd Bennett* no el trepitjaran. El pol sud no tornarà a tenir petjades humanes fins al 1956, quan un equip nord-americà dirigit per Richard Bowers (un cognom molt polar) hi aterri per construir en aquell mateix punt la base científica Amundsen-Scott, permanentment habitada des d'aleshores. Igual com passa al pol nord, l'aviació ha obert el camí i les portes als últims racons del planeta. Lluny quedaran des d'ara les epopeies terrestres per arribar-hi.

Definitivament el camí del pol és al cel, i després que els britànics se'n vagin el 1912, el pol podrà descansar. Fins al 4 de gener de 1958, quan un grup de neozelandesos s'hi planti amb tractors adaptats, no hi arribarà cap altre grup d'homes. Aquests neozelandesos són Murray Ellis, Jim Bates, Peter Mulgrew, Derek Wright i Edmund Hillary, precisament l'home que amb Tenzing Norgay fa pocs anys ha estat el primer a fer el cim de l'Everest.

En aquell moment, Hillary i els seus companys estan participant a la *Commonwealth Trans-Antarctic Expedition*, una expedició dirigida pel britànic Vivian Fuchs, que pretén travessar l'Antàrtida passant pel pol sud. La missió dels neozelandesos és posar uns dipòsits de provisions per a Fuchs durant la segona part del seu trajecte. Però al més pur estil d'Amundsen, de manera improvisada i desobeint ordres de Fuchs, Hillary i companyia aprofitaran que són tan a prop del pol per acostar-s'hi a fer-hi una visita. Hi arribaran dues setmanes abans que Fuchs.

De fet, un cop acomplerta la missió d'aprovisionament, res no impedeix als neozelandesos perseguir un repte personal com el d'arribar al pol sud. També això els permet indicar millor a Fuchs el camí més segur. Edmund Hillary ho explica així, sembla fàcil, però les condicions són les que són. Això és l'Antàrtida i arribar al pol mig improvisadament té els seus perills. Els vehicles es poden espatllar, pot haver-hi un temps inclement, hi ha les esquerdes amagades al gel, jornades extenuants, descansos massa breus... Conduir un vehicle en aquestes condicions pot voler dir, per exemple, passar hores marcant un camí a cops de pala damunt la neu durant gairebé tres mesos. Però no hi ha res que els aturi. Finalment, quan reben ordres de tornar enrere, ja només tenen a l'abast la seguretat de la base Amundsen-Scott. Com ha canviat el pol sud! Gairebé com una broma de mal gust, sembla que per als britànics la història es repeteixi. Cada cop que s'acosten al pol sud, algú altre se'ls avança inesperadament i espera que arribin. Aquest cop, però, quan el 20 de gener Fuchs i Hillary es trobin al pol sud, Fuchs agrairà a Hillary el seu esforç, recollirà totes les indicacions que li pot explicar del camí que l'espera i, despres, Fuchs continuarà el seu periple fins a completar la primera travessa antàrtica de la història.

Gairebé mig segle després de la seva mal anomenada conquesta, Fuchs serà el segon a tornar a peu del pol sud. Mentrestant, Hillary i companyia marxaran del pol en avió. Molt més còmodament. Finalment, el pol sud ha sigut domesticat. Cadascú pot pensar el que vulgui.

La frontera interior. Entre la il·lusió i l'obsessió

Nous camins, nous mars, noves terres, els pols, els cims més alts. Descobrir els límits de la Terra. I també els propis. La lluita contra les adversitats a què els exploradors se sotmeten no és contra les adversitats; la lluita contra les adversitats és una lluita interna contra elles. Darrere d'aquesta lluita hi ha una força interior que s'escapa d'un mateix. Potser per això també els grans exploradors sovint són gent amb un caràcter humà que s'escapa del comú, però en positiu i en negatiu, com tota la gent. Perquè al cap i a la fi no són més que persones normals posades en situacions límit. No és estrany tampoc que de vegades els puguem trobar alguns gestos d'arrogància. Acostuma a passar quan algú aspira a tenir el màxim reconeixement en relació al seu company, aquell que la posteritat deixarà si no oblidat, com a mínim en un segon terme. Vet aquí el xoc de personalitats.

Amundsen, a causa de les tensions que es generen en la llarga expedició antàrtica que arribarà al pol sud el 1911, deixa tres homes fora de la lluita pel pol, Hjalmar Johansen, Kristian Prestrud i Jørgen Stubberud. Els envia a explorar la Península d'Eduard VII mentre ell i quatre companys més es dirigeixen al pol.

L'expert Johansen, que arriba a l'expedició recomanat per Nansen, amb qui va sobreviure aquells quinze mesos perduts a l'Àrtic, és l'únic que pot fer ombra a Amundsen. Johansen ja ha salvat la vida a Nansen a l'Àrtic, i en un primer atac al pol sud dels vuit expedicionaris (només el cuiner Lindstrøm es queda a la base anomenada *Franheim*), també salvarà la vida al seu company Prestrud.

Aquell setembre de 1911, Johansen es converteix en un dels primers a haver intentat els dos pols. Però hi van massa d'hora i es veuen obligats a tornar al campament per provar-ho més endavant. I mentre, l'equip va tornant a tota pressa cap a la base sense esperar-se mútuament. Fins i tot Amundsen incompleix les ordres que ell mateix ha donat. Johansen s'adona que Prestrud ha quedat endarrerit. Després d'una llarga espera a 50 graus sota zero el veu arribar esgotat i amb congelacions als peus, sense haver menjat res en dotze hores. Està esquiant per tal de mantenir l'escalfor en comptes de ser en el trineu de gossos. Des d'aquest moment, Johansen i Prestrud hauran de recórrer junts els trenta quilòmetres que els separen de la salvació. No tenen cap mena de visibilitat. Caminen sota la boira, cada cop més de nit, guiats només pels lladrucs dels gossos de la base. Mentre els primers trineus han arribat a les quatre de la tarda, Johansen i Prestrud hauran de lluitar fins a les dues de la matinada per tornar al *Franheim*, on només el cuiner Lindstrøm els espera despert per oferir-los cafè calent.

L'endemà al matí, davant les recriminacions d'Amundsen pel seu retard, l'expert Johansen acusarà el cap de l'expedició d'haver-los abandonat. Vet aquí la qüestió. Què és un líder? És això un líder? Qüestionar. Però salvar una vida. Però qüestionar. Vet aquí el que no pot tolerar un líder? Johansen prefereix això, qüestionar quan ho veu necessari. Quan cal salvar una vida la prioritat és inqüestionable. I en realitat, sense saber-ho, salvant la vida a Prestrud, Johansen ha arruïnat la seva.

Però Johansen té clars els límits de la seva frontera interior.

Des d'aleshores, un Amundsen cada cop més irritable començarà a buscar la manera d'apartar Johansen del seu camí. Un líder ferm no pot acceptar algú que li faci ombra, que el qüestioni. Amundsen no hauria apostat mai per Johansen. Després de la gesta d'haver sobreviscut al Pol Nord amb Nansen, Johansen s'ha abandonat a l'alcohol, vici que només deixarà quan Amundsen l'hi demani després d'haver-lo enrolat al *Fram* per anar cap al pol sud. Encara que a Amundsen li dolgui, enrolar Johansen és el preu que ha pagat després de la generositat de Nansen, que li ha deixat el *Fram* i l'Antàrtida sencera per a ell sol.

Però també al Pol Sud, Johansen serà relegat una altra vegada. La cursa entre Amundsen i Scott per arribar-hi és, de fet, una lluita d'egos. No hi ha lloc per a ningú més. Només aquests dos contrincants. Amundsen no pot apartar Scott, però sí que pot apartar-ne Johansen. Quan Johansen salva la vida a Prestrud, a Amundsen li sembla que el seu lideratge està amenaçat. Enviarà Johansen, amb Prestrud i Stubberud, a una missió improvisada a la península d'Eduard VII perquè vol treure-se'l de sobre. Mentrestant, els altres cinc companys atacaran el pol. Un cop més, víctima de la mala sort, Johansen serà un oblidat —pitjor encara, un oblidat entre els oblidats: ni tan sols serà «un dels desconeguts que van acompanyar Amundsen al pol sud»—. De retorn a Noruega tornarà a caure en la beguda i la depressió. Pocs mesos després se suïcida. Durant dècades, no serà recordat pràcticament per ningú. Ni tan sols al seu país.

Però Johansen lluita contra el seu jo. La seva lluita és a dins d'ell mateix. En canvi, entre Scott i Amundsen la lluita que hi ha és una lluita d'egos que de vegades se'ls fa incontrolable. En aquest aspecte, són ben diferents de Shackleton i Nansen. Abans de tancar el capítol, doncs, tornarem a fixar-nos en aquests dos exploradors que bé haurien pogut ser els primers d'arribar al pol sud.

En la delicada frontera entre la il·lusió i l'obsessió, per a Shackleton l'obsessió també serà sobreviure: a la seva segona aventura antàrtica (el gener de 1909) arriba als 88° 23' S, es queda a menys de dos-cents quilòmetres del pol sud. Però, malgrat que estigui tan a prop de l'èxit, no dubta a recular davant del risc de posar en perill la tornada. I en la seva següent aventura antàrtica (1914-1916), la més coneguda, aconsegueix que el grup mantingui sempre la confiança en ell mateix. De manera, que aconsegueix també que tothom sobrevisqui. Canviar de plans, sempre amb un ull posat a casa. Tal com diria ell mateix: «El pol no val una vida». Shackleton també sap, doncs, fer els difícils equilibris a la frontera entre la il·lusió i l'obsessió, no arriba a travessar-la mai del tot.

També Nansen és dels pocs que saben navegar per aquesta frontera sense perdre's. Quan Amundsen torna del pol sud convertit en heroi, carregat d'aires de grandesa, s'oblida de les seves promeses i dels seus compromisos, es mostra i fins i tot irrespectuós amb aquells que l'han ajudat. Serà Nansen qui li haurà d'estirar les orelles per posar-lo de nou de peus a terra. En una carta li recordarà: «*He fet un sacrifici més gran per vostè que qualsevol altra persona, en tant que vaig abandonar la meva expedició al pol sud, la culminació de la meva tasca com a explorador polar, i vaig renunciar al* Fram *per tal que vostè pogués anar a l'Àrtic*». I no escriu això perquè vulgui fer-li cap retret gratuït, sinó perquè vol respondre a una arrogància que li sembla excessiva. Nansen no viu obsessionat, viu il·lusionat. Això el fa més feliç que patidor.

No és cap novetat, tanmateix. Nansen sempre sembla tenir més presents els altres que ell mateix. Ho demostrarà també anys després, quan sigui diplomàtic. Són els altres els que ens mantenen a lloc, els que ens donen la mida de la nostra realitat.

Quan Nansen lluita per arribar al pol nord, té una il·lusió i una obsessió, però afortunadament per a ell i per a la resta de la humanitat, la seva il·lusió i la seva obsessió són diferents. La il·lusió de Nansen és arribar al pol. Portarà aquesta seva il·lusió fins al límit, però tindrà el difícil encert de no traspassar la frontera imperceptible que la converteix en una obsessió malaltissa. Molt poca gent és capaç d'arribar a aquesta frontera i veure-la o fins i tot intuir-la. Però com Shackleton, Nansen ho té clar. El pol només és una il·lusió, un punt invisible en una superfície buida i desconeguda. En canvi, la seva obsessió és tornar amb la seva estimada Eva. La seva obsessió és viure. Aquest és el difícil encert de Nansen i el que l'honora més en la seva carrera polar. La il·lusió és al nord, l'obsessió al sud. I quan Nansen és tan a prop de la frontera que gairebé s'escapa dels seus límits, aquest home és capaç de tornar enrere. Per molt que sembli impossible. A la vida. A la seva Eva.

La solitud eterna del pol

Avançar damunt d'un gruix de gel immesurable, molt per sobre de valls i muntanyes colgades sota centenars de metres de gel. Si aquest gel fos transparent, aquests homes solitaris semblaria que volessin molt per damunt dels cims arrossegant uns trineus feixucs en l'aire, com si enfonsessin els peus a dins de núvols de sorra.

Avançar cap al sud amb el vent de cara. Vent del sud. Fins que el vent només pugui venir del nord.

La quietud infinita del pol sud.

La quasi quietud.

Anys més tard que hi arribessin els primers exploradors, una altra gent va aixecar al pol sud la base científica Amundsen-Scott. Això va passar el 1956. Fins avui, no ha deixat d'estar mai en funcionament. Però algun misteri passa encara en aquell precisíssim punt polar, perquè avui, en aquell punt exacte, torna a no haver-hi res. És cert que la base continua viva, però també és veritat que no és precisament damunt del pol.

Com si fos una cosa viva que es mou, el gel s'ha mogut, ha mogut la base i, per tant, avui la base ja no és exactament al pol sud.

I és que sembla que el pol sud acabi rebutjant-ho tot. Com si fos una cosa viva, malgrat la seva lentitud, el gel va apartant-se del pol sud i va avançant cap al nord, cap al mar, fent un viatge de milers d'anys de durada. El gel es mou uns deu metres cada any. Quasi un metre al mes. Dos o tres centímetres al dia. Un mil·límetre cada hora. Un vertiginós «quasi res» que no hi ha força humana que sigui capaç de frenar. Lent, tossut, impertèrrit, quasi immòbil, el gel del nostre temps arrossega amb ell la base Amundsen-Scott. Potser fins i tot arribarà un dia, potser quan ja torni a no haver-hi cap testimoni humà per aquelles latituds, que n'abocarà les últimes restes al mar.

Cèlebes
Jakarta
Roti
Golf d'Exmouth
Gran De
Sorrer
Illa de Dark Hartog
Deser
Gibs
Illes Houtman Abrolhos

Nova Guinea
Illes Salomó
d'Amhem
Estret de Torres
Cap de York
Vanuatu
Cap Keerweer
irrkurra
Desert de
Simpson
Sydney
Tasmània

6. Austràlia

El temps dels somnis

(Al principi tot és en la foscor perpètua. No hi ha temps, ni vida, ni mort. Només una terra plana sense res. En aquesta foscor, els ancestres es desperten i surten de dins la terra amb formes diferents: animals, plantes, persones. Aleshores aquests éssers comencen a canviar el paisatge, creen els rius i les muntanyes, les lleis i els costums...)

Massa sovint encara s'indica l'arribada de James Cook a la badia de Sydney el 1770 com el començament de la història d'Austràlia. I sobretot, encara, s'inicia aquest començament, el dia que es va crear la primera colònia penitenciària en aquell mateix punt el 1788, pocs anys després. Poc més a dir. És cert que va ser en aquesta època quan va començar la recent història de l'Austràlia anglòfona, però no encetarem cap polèmica si recordem que Cook està molt lluny de poder ser el descobridor d'aquest immens territori.

Una altra cosa és que molts dels descobridors de costes llunyanes sabessin fins a quin punt aquella nova costa que havien posat al mapa formava part d'aquesta illa-continent...

Però no avançarem esdeveniments, anirem enrere i començarem pel principi. Perquè potser James Cook només és a la cua dels descobridors del continent australià. Sol ser així, quan parlem de descobridors: només parlem de l'últim, rarament parlem del primer.

(Tota la terra és buida i plana, tot dorm i la Serp de l'arc de Sant Martí dorm dins la terra. Quan la serp es desperta, surt a la superfície i comença a caminar pel món. Mentre avança, va

movent la terra i crea valls i muntanyes. També fa aparèixer l'aigua i neixen la pluja, els llacs i els rius. Després la Serp fa fèrtil la terra i hi fa créixer plantes i arbres. Quan tot està creat, la Serp de l'arc de Sant Martí treu de la terra els altres animals, i després en treu els humans...)

Alguna cosa estranya passa amb aquest continent. Ningú no diria que es tracta de l'illa més gran del món, amb aquesta facilitat que té per amagar-se. Tan difícil és trobar-la per als navegants que, sembla com si fos una illa impossible, sense costes. De fet, aquestes costes no les van trobar ni tan sols els primers que van arribar-hi. Per estrany que sembli, els primers humans que van arribar a aquesta illa van venir a peu.

Devia ser en el temps de la creació, en aquell temps dels ancestres que ara en diem dels somnis, quan la humanitat tot just començava a despertar en aquest planeta verge i desconegut, i quan es movia a les palpentes, com qui tempteja amb les mans endavant per si topa amb algun mur o per si troba un camí en la buidor que els dits van obrint.

En aquell temps fora del temps, en aquell temps dels somnis en què la humanitat comença a palpar el planeta fora d'Àfrica, alguns d'aquests primers pobles exploradors d'allò remot començaran a establir-se a les costes més meridionals d'Àsia.

Establerts en aquelles costes, fent de pescadors, quan encara navegar grans distàncies és un somni quasi impensat, alguns valents s'aventuren de tant en tant amb les seves modestes embarcacions fins a alguna illa que intueixen potser a l'horitzó.

Amb tota certesa, alguns d'aquells valents no tornaran. Sempre ha passat això mateix en el mar. Però alguns altres aprendran el camí d'anada i de tornada. A poc a poc, aquest poble remot i desconegut anirà saltant d'illa en illa, de segle en segle, d'oblit en oblit, fins que arribi a una gran costa darrere de la qual ja no hi ha mar sinó més terra: un continent sencer. Ells que ja fa tant de temps que són gent de mar i d'illes perdudes que havien oblidat fins i tot que hi pot haver terres sense costa.

(Al principi la terra és un lloc fosc, silenciós i tranquil. Un lloc mort, sense valls, ni muntanyes, ni rius, sense arbres ni ocells que cantin. No hi ha res que tingui forma. Enmig d'aquesta foscor, hi ha Mudungkala, una dona cega sorgida de la terra. Mudungkala fa sorgir tres criatures de la terra: les nenes Wuriupranala i Muriangkala i el nen Purukupali. Arrossegant-se de genolls amb els seus fills, Mudungkala crea les muntanyes, les costes, les illes, i després les plantes i els animals... Ningú no sap d'on ve ni on va Mudungkala quan desapareix després d'haver creat les coses...)

És tan remot aquest temps dels somnis que fins i tot la superfície de la Terra és diferent del que coneixem els lectors del futur. En aquella era glacial en què el mar es troba a un nivell més baix, allò que avui anomenem Nova Guinea i Austràlia es troben unides en una gran illa de dimensions immenses.

Ningú més no arribarà a les costes de Papua en aquells temps.

I mentrestant, aquest poble fins ara pescador començarà a avançar a peu per aquest continent.

I a poc a poc, molt lluny, a l'altra banda del món, el gel dels pols es començarà a fondre.

I el mar pujarà.

I Austràlia, ocupada ja, esdevindrà una illa potser abans que algú n'hagi descobert la costa des del mar. Perquè els primers habitants d'Austràlia hi van arribar a peu des de Nova Guinea.

Durant desenes de milers d'anys, si algú descobreix les costes australianes, ho farà des de terra, de dins cap a enfora, a peu. Toparà, doncs, amb l'inici d'un mar infinit i amb un horitzó buit al fons.

A Austràlia no arribarà mai cap barca fins d'aquí a potser seixanta mil anys.

Quina tranquil·litat seria avui això.

No deu ser fàcil, per a una illa tan gran, amagar-se d'aquesta manera.

Aquells primers habitants potser siguin els primers grans exploradors del món. Ningú més no els seguirà durant milers d'anys. En aquell temps dels somnis neix la llavor de la cultura més antiga i duradora de la humanitat. Un món nou, estrany, gairebé fora del planeta.

(Djanggawul i les seves dues germanes Bitjiwurrurru i Madalatj, venen de Baralku, l'illa dels morts, en una canoa. Durant molt de temps remen de nit, sense més llum que l'estrella del dia, Barnumbirr. Quan arriben a la terra de Yalangbarra es fa de dia, s'hi queden a viure, donen a llum els ancestres i viatgen per aquesta terra creant i donant nom als animals, a les plantes...)

Des de la nostra brevíssima experiència, no sabem adonar-nos de la distància del temps. Busquem els descobridors a uns pocs segles de nosaltres, busquem els nostres orígens a dos mil anys enrere, tres mil a tot estirar. No ens aturem a mesurar aquesta distància, a posar-nos a nosaltres mateixos en aquest fil de temps immesurable. Rarament mirem cap a allò que en diem antiguitat per fascinar-nos. Sovint no sabem que fins i tot Cleòpatra és temporalment més a prop de nosaltres que no ho són d'ella les piràmides de Kheops i Micerí, uns monuments que Cleòpatra ja veia com una antiguitat. Passa sovint això: les llargues distàncies dels segles perden el seu sentit quan es poden mesurar. En canvi, quan els mil·lennis es perden en l'horitzó i des del fons de tot ens n'arriba només una veu apagada, tot s'omple de misteri. El temps dels somnis és inabastable per a nosaltres. Fins i tot ens desborda pensar que els egipcis van mantenir-se durant alguns milers d'anys. Però la seva existència llarguíssima empetiteix tot d'una davant d'uns pobles australians que van viure durant desenes de milers d'anys.

No cal dir que han evolucionat, que han canviat, que han aparegut pobles i que n'han desaparegut... Però els europeus encara hem pogut trobar a Austràlia centenars de cultures i de llengües diferents. Fins i tot hi hem trobat algunes pintures rupestres de vint mil anys d'història, al costat de les quals la vida ha continuat fins als nostres dies. Hauríem pogut escriure cinc vegades la història des dels egipcis fins a l'arribada a la Lluna, mentre els somnis de la creació es continuaven explicant a les mateixes parets de la terra d'Arnhem, al nord del continent australià. Enlloc més del món podríem parlar avui amb descendents dels que són les mostres artístiques més antigues de la humanitat. Les seves pintures, fins i tot les corporals, són potser també els missatges més antics, l'escriptura i l'alfabet més remots que ens han pervingut. I les seves línies de cançons són els mapes més antics.

En algun moment de la seva història, cada descobriment era una nova línia de cançó que ens arriba fins avui, a nosaltres que no sabem llegir aquests milers de mapes memoritzats des dels inicis. Saber les cançons de cada lloc és moure-s'hi sense morir en el desert: la cançó et diu on trobaràs aigua, gent, ombra, caça, et parla dels déus i dels somnis de cada lloc... El temps dels somnis és el naixement, és el final, és el temps en què som en un altre temps...

Res que puguem entendre nosaltres. Res que les nostres llengües puguin explicar del tot.

(El món és fosc i no hi ha vida ni mort. Tots els éssers dormen sota la terra. Els ancestres s'aixequen i comencen a caminar per aquesta terra, tots amb diferents formes d'animals i plantes. De fora d'aquesta terra arriben dos Ungambikula que troben animals i plantes mig convertides en humans. Aleshores, amb els seus ganivets de pedra els Ungambikula els acaben de donar forma humana...)

Segle XVI

Després d'aquell llunyà temps dels somnis, quina importància pot tenir ara saber si els primers visitants vindran d'aquí a seixanta mil anys o d'aquí a cinquanta-cinc mil? El despertar que ens espera serà igualment sobtat i confús en aquest món de fora del món; de tan llunyà com és.

Entre l'inici del temps dels somnis i aquells pocs dies que nosaltres anomenem «el segle XVII», no sembla que arribi ningú més a Austràlia. Per als seus habitants no hi ha ningú més al planeta. I qualsevol altra terra que hi hagi més enllà de l'horitzó només forma part del món dels somnis.

Només, com un lapse entre somni i somni, han d'haver arribat fins aquí alguns pescadors de les illes properes, de Cèlebes potser. Sens dubte aquesta costa havia de ser coneguda pels habitants d'aquests arxipèlags propers, també dels habitants de Roti i de Timor. Sigui com sigui, sembla que fa uns cinc mil anys ja hi havia certs contactes entre alguns pobles d'aquestes diferents costes. No tenim cap altra manera d'explicar la misteriosa arribada del dingo fa quatre mil anys. És raonable pensar, doncs, que els pescadors del sud-est asiàtic, disseminats per totes les illes de la regió, van conèixer també aquesta costa. Però no s'hi van establir, o en tot cas no ens hi ha deixat cap més testimoni que el dingo, aquest parent salvatge del gos. I malgrat tot, el dingo ens parla, només amb la seva presència ja ens explica que algú, quatre mil·lennis enrere, havia de tenir un bon motiu per navegar fins aquestes costes, però que en van marxar, ens diu el dingo australià, i van deixar enrere els seus avantpassats amb tot l'espai del món per retornar aquest parent del gos al seu estat salvatge.

I ara, més enllà d'aquesta misteriosa visita, nosaltres, els de fora, només, com a molt, podem fer algunes hipòtesis que situarien els portuguesos en terres australianes al segle XVI. Només hipòtesis. Un misteriós mapa de l'escola holandesa de Dieppe del segle XVI, que segons alguns historiadors mostraria part de la costa australiana i segons uns altres no, és una de les principals portes a tota mena de possibilitats: una suposada arribada a Austràlia de Cristovao de Mendonça el 1522 i que ningú no sap documentar; uns canons portuguesos trobats a la badia de Broome, que en principi es creien construïts al voltant del 1500 però que semblen ser molt posteriors; una suposada intenció dels portuguesos de mantenir en secret certes exploracions per evitar conflictes amb Castella a causa del tractat de Tordesillas... Tot sempre buscant el suport a una hipotètica desaparició de documents arran del terratrèmol de

Lisboa de 1755. Com sempre, qualsevol cosa és factible, raonable... però de tot plegat l'únic que podem conèixer del cert és el terratrèmol de Lisboa.

Res més.

I Austràlia és allà, esperant. Sense pressa. Com més tard millor. Els seus habitants encara no ho saben, però després de milers i milers d'anys, de sobte el món sembla despertar-se, de sobte tenim pressa i també alguns historiadors situarien, al mateix segle XVI, pescadors de Macassar (ciutat de la propera illa Cèlebes) recollint cogombres de mar a la costa australiana per vendre'ls a la Xina. Aquests cogombres eren un producte molt apreciat a la Xina de l'època, sobretot com a afrodisíac, i d'aquell temps semblen identificar-se alguns casos de mestissatge entre indonesis i australians. Però tampoc no en tenim res que estigui documentat.

(Tanmateix el món exterior s'acosta).

(Alguna cosa s'apropa a Austràlia).

Podem descartar-ho ben poc, però probablement, com passa tantes vegades, el que menys podríem descartar és que potser sigui un nàufrag... o uns quants. Com a molt, si algú ha arribat a aquestes costes australianes és un d'aquells dissortats desconeguts que no ens expliquen res perquè no en tornen mai més. Amb un nàufrag només els amfitrions aprenen alguna cosa d'altres llocs. Potser de moment només els australians han descobert que hi ha un món nou horitzó enllà. Però quin món és el nou? Si algun nàufrag ha arribat mai a les costes australianes, si mai ha pogut entendre's amb els seus habitants, potser els haurà parlat del seu món. I els haurà dit que s'està estenent des de fa pocs segles... Tanmateix, l'espai de temps que fa que dura aquesta expansió és curtíssim comparat amb els segles d'història que els australians porten en la seva memòria. Ho sàpiguen o no. En tot cas, els australians acaben de descobrir el món, igual com descobriríem nosaltres l'univers si arribés un nàufrag extraterrestre i ens haguéssim de sentir descoberts. Què li preguntaríem? Quantes coses aprendríem del cosmos? Què gosaríem explicar-li i què miraríem de callar del nostre món? Com que potser ens espantaríem més que no pas ens sentiríem encuriosits, miraríem que aquest nàufrag còsmic no digués res sobre nosaltres a les galàxies també habitades i més avançades, a aquells mons que no tenen res a veure amb el nostre i que, ben segur, com que són molt més avançats que nosaltres, aviat vindrien a saber què els podem oferir, ves a saber a canvi de què.

De moment, en aquesta Austràlia ancestral els terrícoles més antics estan a punt de rebre els seus veïns per primer cop. I no tenen cap motiu per saltar d'emoció.

Al segle XVI, doncs, no podem dir que hagi passat res. Potser sí que va passar, però no ho podem dir. Només sabem que el despertador està a punt de sonar.

Austràlia és realment el món del revés. I sobre Austràlia, en el segle XVI tot és confús. Mentre els europeus van omplint els mapes de noms escrits, sembla que van posant les costes australianes als mapes sense poder dir qui ha descobert aquesta terra anònima, de dimensions tan colossals. La costa australiana apareix dibuixada a diferents mapes holandesos de Dieppe. No hi ha ningú que sàpiga dir-nos qui l'ha descobert. Però no es pot pas dir que hi hagi cap misteri: només hi ha dubtes i desacords, respostes contradictòries sobre l'autoria dels mapes, sobre qui va ser el primer a indicar-ho, sobre qui va ser el primer que ho va dir en l'originalitat, fins i tot no es posen d'acord en les dates.

Hi ha qui diu que ho van descobrir navegants portuguesos, o castellans o holandesos; i que Portugal guarda amb zel tots els descobriments fins que el terratrèmol de Lisboa destrueix les fonts que ens permetrien aclarir els dubtes. També n'hi ha que posen en dubte les dates dels mapes de Dieppe, que diuen que podrien ser posteriors. I fins i tot hi ha els que opinen que no en sabem fer la lectura correcta. Amb tot plegat, l'únic que queda clar és que de moment no hi ha acord sobre l'autoria ni sobre l'antiguitat d'aquests descobriments. I mentre no se sap si una terra existeix, no es pot considerar descoberta. No és fàcil dir «hem descobert una cosa que no sabem dir si existeix».

De moment, per als australians, tant és d'on provenen els forasters. També a nosaltres com a terrícoles ens seria igual que els extraterrestres que ens descobrissin vinguin de la nostra mateixa galàxia o d'una altra de més llunyana. El que seria important per a nosaltres seria el descobriment de vida exterior.

En qualsevol cas, és evident que la clau de la porta australiana és a Malàisia. Primer en mans dels pescadors locals; després, en mans dels forasters. I és a mig camí entre aquests dos on trobem un malaioportuguès que ens obrirà la pista: Manuel Godinho de Erédia. Probablement, si volem trobar un nom, aquest és el que és més a prop de descobrir-nos el continent australià.

Nascut el 1563 a Malacca, fill d'un missioner portuguès i d'una princesa malaia, la vida de Godinho de Erédia passa entre l'Índia i les illes del Pacífic. Considerat portuguès, però sempre lluny d'Europa, com a malai ha sentit parlar de la llegenda de les Illes d'Or. Trobar-les serà durant molts anys un dels seus desitjos més grans. Ubicades aparentment cap al sud (l'única direcció inexplorada), Godinho de Erédia pensa a aventurar-s'hi ja des de ben jove, però per moltes portes que la paraula *or* obrís en aquells temps, de Erédia no aconseguirà mai emprendre la seva desitjada expedició.

Si s'hagués sortit amb el seu propòsit, sense cap mena de dubte hauria topat no amb or, però sí amb Austràlia, on el preuat metall, per cert, va continuar encara massa amagat durant uns segles més.

La idea que possiblement Godinho de Erédia descobrís Austràlia prové d'un mapa que sembla que va fer ell el 1613. En aquest mapa apareix una costa al sud de Java amb la inscripció: «*Nuca Antara foi descoberta no ano de 1601, por Manuel Godinho de Erédia, por mandado do Vice-Rei Ayres de Saldanha*». Novament els dubtes de sempre. I hi ha raons per a això. Què és Nuca Antara? Avui hi ha qui diu que això és terra australiana i altres, que es tracta d'unes costes malaies. Probablement el nom vingui de «Nusantara», arxipèlag en malai. De manera que «descobridor de Nusantara» voldria dir literalment: «descobridor d'illes». I de fet, la inscripció al mapa continua així: «*Terra descuberta pelos Holandeses a que chamaraõ Endracht au Concordia*».

Així doncs, sigui què sigui el que veiem en aquell mapa, el mateix Godinho de Erédia ens assegura que si el 1613 algú ha arribat fins a aquestes costes són els holandesos.

Uns homes blancs

Un dia els homes blancs van venir pel mar amb una casa. Un grup de gent ho va veure i van anar a parlar amb ells, però cap dels homes blancs coneixia la llengua i només es podien comunicar amb signes. Els homes blancs van dir que volien construir cabanes allà on eren i els van oferir algunes coses. Primer tot va anar bé, però després els homes blancs van disparar contra els homes i van agafar les dones...

Vet aquí la que potser sigui la trobada més extraordinària de la humanitat. Dues branques separades per desenes de milers d'anys es descobreixen mútuament. ¿No hauria de ser el retrobament més prolongat que hagi pogut haver-hi mai, un dels moments més emocionants de la humanitat?

Per sort tenim molt ben testimoniat aquest dia tan emotiu amb còpies de documents escrits pels seus protagonistes europeus. Còpies de documents. Res més que còpies, però escrites en paper i fiables, doncs, des del punt de vista occidental. Tan fiables, per descomptat, com la tradició oral australiana que també ens regala els mateixos fets en cançons orals transmeses de generació en generació. Abans que els desmemoriats i desconfiats estrangers copiessin aquella tradició oral en paper, en llocs diferents i persones diferents han anat transmetent més o menys el mateix. Si fa o no fa que *un dia els homes blancs van venir pel mar...* que *van matar els homes...* que *van agafar les dones...*

Tenim aquí uns fets que cadascú explicarà a la seva manera. Comunicació impossible entre mons totalment diferents. I malgrat tot, per què no ha de ser, com dèiem, extraordinària aquesta trobada? Tenim el privilegi de conservar la veu dels protagonistes des de les dues bandes: des de la deplorable carta europea, però també des de la tants de cops silenciada veu dels derrotats. Després de seixanta mil anys de separació això és extraordinari.

D'altra banda, convé que tinguem sempre present la tradició oral. I que la venerem si és que s'ha conservat. Un cop hem perdut els textos originals, els europeus sovint ens desesperem, ens sentim buits, perduts, incapaços de transmetre res amb seguretat. Ja ho deien en temps dels antics egipcis, que l'escriptura estovaria la memòria. Els primers australians desconeixien l'escriptura. Ens toca refiar-nos de la seva tradició oral. Poden faltar-hi dades precises, dades d'aquelles que sembla que els europeus necessitem per entendre les coses, el dia que va passar un fet, el nombre exacte de víctimes, els seus noms i cognoms... Però els fets narrats per diferents versions orals venen a ser sempre els mateixos. I encaixen perfectament amb allò que coneixem per vies secundàries, en aquest cas, a través de fonts holandeses.

És veritat que poden haver-hi algunes divergències en les diferents versions orals, però totes expliquen el mateix. Els fets únics són narrats per veus diferents, fins que aquestes veus es reuneixen de nou en el camí uniforme de l'escriptura dels europeus.

1606. Willem Janszoon

Com que potser poc més que alguns nàufrags han arribat fins a Austràlia, com que no coneixem ningú que n'hagi sortit per explicar Austràlia al món, se sol estar bastant d'acord a reconèixer que el primer desembarcament conegut en aquesta gran illa és el de l'holandès Willem Janszoon a bord del *Duyfken,* el març de 1606. Navegant pel sud de Nova Guinea, el *Duyfken* va arribar a la costa nord australiana, al cap de York. Janszoon pensava que era una part de Nova Guinea. No es pot pas dir, doncs, que el seu descobriment fos gaire lluït. I menys encara quan la seva exploració d'aquestes terres es va tancar en una batalla que va costar algunes vides pels dos costats.

Tot el que sabem d'aquest moment històric és que per algun motiu el desembarcament a cap Keerweer (pròpiament Thewena) es converteix en una batalla en la qual moren nou dels potser vint holandesos. També van morir alguns australians que aquell dia s'havien llevat tan tranquils, més o menys com havien fet ells i els seus avantpassat durant els últims milers d'anys. Després de l'èxit d'aquest primer contacte, els visitants van decidir fer mitja volta i no tornar mai més. Al seu darrere, van deixar segurament els primers europeus que van tenir el dubtós honor de morir a Austràlia. I també els primers australians que van morir a mans d'europeus.

Fins allà on podem saber, abans dels tripulants del *Duyfken* o dels pescadors malais, l'última persona que havia arribat a Austràlia des del nord ho havia fet a peu, uns seixanta mil anys enrere. Des d'aleshores, el mar ha separat aquestes terres de la resta del món, s'ha extingit l'home de Neandertal, aquell món encara ignorat per la humanitat ha desaparegut en una llunyania impossible en la qual altres humans han anat descobrint Àsia, Europa, Amèrica, han navegat per tots els oceans, han descobert les illes més petites d'Oceania... I així, durant desenes de milers d'anys. La branca extraviada de la humanitat que no va arribar a Austràlia ha estat vagant pel planeta, ocupant continent rere continent fins que, finalment, algú més ha tornat a repetir el primer gran descobriment de l'exploració humana. I vet aquí el primer vaixell que arriba a aquestes costes. És rebut amb hostilitats. No està gens malament la carta de presentació d'aquests australians. Però potser la història els donarà la raó i ja fan bé de desconfiar d'algú que ve de fora del seu món.

De moment només podem saber el nom de Janszoon. I per si algú dubta que aquest sigui el primer estranger que va arribar a Austràlia, ben poc després, serà també el segon. L'any 1618. I de nou sense saber-ho. Aquest cop, Janszoon és al capdavant d'una nova expedició holandesa que va cap a Java a bord del *Mauritius*. El 8 de juny d'aquell 1618, el *Mauritius* travessarà el cap de Bona Esperança, i abans d'arribar a Bantam, el 31 de juliol, Janszoon descriurà el descobriment d'una illa al Pacífic. Per la informació que ell mateix dona, no ha descobert només una petita illa, sinó la península de Point Cloates, al golf d'Exmouth. Per tant, ha descobert una petita part de l'illa més gran del món, una illa que ell mateix ja havia trepitjat dotze anys abans, ben lluny d'aquí. Els dos llocs són tan lluny que ni a Janszoon se li acudirà pensar que es tracta de la mateixa illa, la més gran del món; un continent. Mai, ni en el temps dels somnis, ningú no havia arribat dues vegades a Austràlia. Aquest segon cop, per sort, el contacte humà serà més tranquil que la primera vegada. Els tripulants del *Mauritius* no trobaran res més que algunes petjades humanes. Potser per sort, doncs, ningú que espatlli a Janszoon el seu quasi segon descobriment d'Austràlia.

Però tot continua essent ben estrany. En el mateix any 1606 en què Janszoon arribava a Austràlia sense saber-ho per primer cop, un navegant portuguès (aviat coneixerem Quirós) descobria una petita illa i hi veia tot un continent. Dotze anys després, quan Janszoon hi torna, trobarà un continent, però ell només hi veurà una petita illa. Un aplaudiment més per a Austràlia l'enigmàtica.

Però no traiem mèrits a qui se'ls mereix. A nosaltres-observadors-des-del-futur, ens sembla molt fàcil posar les coses al mapa i dir: «Oh! Això és nou! Quin descobriment!». Però, quan un es troba enmig d'un mar desconegut durant mesos, com ha de saber la grandiositat de la terra que s'amaga darrere una costa tot just visitada durant molt poc temps?

Naturalment, un dels objectius de l'expedició del *Duyfken* és trobar or, i quan Janszoon arriba a la península de York, l'or ja hi és, hi és des de molt abans que ningú al món s'interessi per aquest metall tan absurd, però caldrà esperar encara tres-cents anys perquè una dona anomenada Kitty Pluto en trobi al mateix riu Wenlock, on el 1606 uns avantpassats seus van ser els primers australians a contactar amb uns estrangers que buscaven aquest metall preuat. Si l'haguessin trobat, hauria canviat el curs de la història. Qui sap si potser aquells desorientats europeus van passar per sobre del filó que somiaven. I qui sap com hauria canviat tot si haguessin trobat aquest filó d'or de Plutoville. Segur que els del *Duyfken* no són els únics que han estat tan a prop de... Però això és entrar en el terreny de la història-ficció. De fet, no ens ha de servir per res més que per recordar com tot depèn d'algunes casualitats ben petites.

És inevitable pensar quants Janszoons oblidats s'hauran ajagut sobre la seva mina d'or sense saber-ho. O pitjor encara, quants hauran trobat el seu tresor i hauran mort amb ell sense poder tornar mai al món a canviar-ne alguna part per alguna cosa tan útil com un got d'aigua.

1606. Torres, Quirós i el Quixot

Janszoon, el primer nom estranger que coneixem d'una persona que arriba a Austràlia, passa discretament pels llibres d'història. La ignorància sobre el seu descobriment ha acabat portant el record d'aquest home més cap a un record difús, discret, que no pas cap al record d'un fet ridícul. Tot això li confereix encara una certa dignitat. A diferència de molts altres, que, en contrapartida, s'exposen massa feliçment que la posteritat en tingui un record ridícul.

Dèiem que alguna cosa estranya passa a Austràlia. Milers i milers d'anys i, de sobte, en el mateix any, el 1606, dos vaixells passen per aquestes aigües seguint rutes oposades.

Pocs mesos després que Janszoon desembarqui a Austràlia sense adonar-se que ha deixat enrere Nova Guinea, Luis Váez de Torres, travessarà a bord del *San Pedrico* l'estret que separa aquestes dues grans illes sense adonar-se potser que hi ha Austràlia al sud. Si Váez de Torres ha vist aquesta illa, no se n'ha adonat, o no ens ha arribat cap notícia prou clara que se n'adonés. Bàsicament, doncs, més que l'estret al qual va donar nom, el que sabem és que Torres va descobrir la costa sud de Nova Guinea. Ell és el primer que pot explicar al món que Nova Guinea és una illa, que no és aquella *Terra Australis Incognita* que des de Ptolomeu tothom s'entesta que ha d'existir. Els europeus tenen tanta fretura de trobar riqueses que necessiten que hi hagi terres allà on sigui.

Però que Torres pugui explicar-ho no vol dir que ho expliqués. Haurà de passar encara molt de temps abans no transcendeixi el seu descobriment.

Si Váez de Torres i Janszoon es trobessin i parlessin dels seus viatges potser lligarien caps. Vet aquí dos descobridors que no saben que han descobert en el mateix any dues coses diferents al mateix lloc. On Janszoon situa terra navegant de nord a sud, Torres troba mar navegant d'oest a est. Austràlia i l'estret de Torres han sigut descoberts i ningú s'ha adonat de cap de les dues coses. Ja és ben bé que aquest continent sap amagar-se. Quan ja fa quasi un segle que s'han començat a fer les primeres voltes al món, encara ningú no ha topat amb la descomunal Austràlia.

Si fóssiu grans com Austràlia i us volguéssiu amagar, mai no ho faríeu millor que ella.

Però què hi fa Torres navegant per aquelles aigües? D'on surt? Qui és? Doncs precisament algú que acaba de separar-se de l'expedició de Pedro Fernández de Quirós a causa d'una tempesta. I Quirós és l'home que en aquests moments està tornant cap a Amèrica, a Mèxic, tot satisfet, convençut d'haver batejat un nou continent amb el nom d'Austràlia.

No està gens malament aquest 1606 a l'hora de crear confusió.

I vet aquí per què Austràlia es diu exactament així:

El desembre de 1605, el portuguès Pedro Fernández de Quirós salpa del port peruà del Callao al comandament d'una expedició castellana, amb tres naus i tres-cents homes. Està disposat a trobar el continent austral. Durant cinc mesos navegaran pel Pacífic passant per diferents illes deshabitades. Aquells homes van de decepció en decepció. A Pedro Fernández de Quirós cada cop li serà més difícil mantenir els ànims de la tripulació. Els seus homes comencen a patir per la manca de provisions i comença a neguitejar-los l'obsessió quimèrica del somiador Quirós.

Perquè la febre per descobrir i per cobrir-se de glòria és el que mou de debò aquest navegant portuguès. I en aquells temps, es dona tant per fet que hi ha una *Terra Australis Incognita*, que quan finalment el 30 d'abril l'expedició troba una illa prou gran que no ha estat mai trepitjada per cap europeu, Quirós no dubta a pensar que ha descobert aquell gran continent. Mirat amb els ulls d'avui, tant podria ser Austràlia com l'Antàrtida. O tot junt, si fos el cas.

Així doncs, davant l'escepticisme de bona part de la seva tripulació i amb tota la pompositat que pot, el 14 de maig de 1606 Quirós pren possessió formal i solemníssima d'aquesta terra i de la resta de territoris fins al pol. No és poca cosa. I aquest mateix dia, amb la combinació de les paraules *Àustria* (per la corona dels Àustria, que és la corona que regna aleshores a Castella) i *austral* (per la latitud del lloc), bateja el seu descobriment amb el nom de *Terra Austrialia del Espíritu Santo*. I tant de ressò tindrà el seu descobriment que encara avui hi ha qui creu que aquell 14 de maig Austràlia va ser descoberta. Només hi ha un petit inconvenient, i és que aquell dia Quirós es troba a uns dos mil quilòmetres d'allò que pensava haver descobert. Només el nom que dona al seu descobriment i el convenciment de la grandiositat d'aquest ens conviden a la confusió. Però els fets són els fets, i allò que Quirós ha descobert no és sinó l'illa més gran de Vanuatu, avui, senzillament coneguda com a Espíritu Santo. Té unes dimensions semblants a les del descomunal continent de Mallorca.

Però Quirós no sabrà això mai. Viurà encara prou per arribar a Castella i començar a buscar la manera de tornar al seu diminut continent abans que no es dissolgui en l'oceà. Un parell d'anys més tard, mentre intenta convèncer Felip III que li financi una nova expedició, Quirós aconsegueix descriure el seu descobriment amb paraules com: «*La grandesa d'aquestes terres novament descobertes és comparable a la de tota Europa, Àsia menor, fins al Caspi i Pèrsia, amb totes les illes del Mediterrani i l'oceà que hi ha al seu voltant. I hi entren encara les illes d'Anglaterra i d'Irlanda. Aquella part oculta és la quarta part de tot el globus...*». Sens dubte és aquesta la més grandiosa descripció que es deu haver fet mai de Vanuatu. Enhorabona per a Vanuatu. Però finalment Quirós morirà el 1615, mentre està fent els preparatius de l'expedició que ben probablement més vergonya li hauria fet dirigir. Potser morir feliç és una sort.

Però naveguem amunt i avall i correm el risc de perdre'ns...

És cert que després del descobriment de les Índies a Amèrica ja no ens hauria de venir res de nou, però el cas australià tampoc no està gens malament. Així, el 1606, mentre un navegant holandès troba Austràlia sense saber-ho, un portuguès li posa nom sense arribar-hi. Però com a mínim, per a glòria de Quirós, el nom d'Austràlia triomfarà. És veritat que aquest nom encara haurà de recórrer dos mil quilòmetres i que haurà de deixar passar dos segles per tal de ser acceptat per tothom. I també és veritat que mentrestant el nom amb què de moment es començarà a conèixer l'illa més gran i desconeguda del món és el de Nova Holanda. Però Quirós podrà tenir la glòria d'haver-se empescat el nom només dos-cents anyets de res abans, dos segles que en l'escala australiana és com dir demà a la tarda.

Però ja que ens hem trobat amb Quirós, i ja que no ens pot explicar res d'Austràlia a banda del seu nom, potser que aprofitem per descobrir amb ell alguna cosa interessant d'aquelles expedicions europees... Perquè potser aquest portuguès no ens deixarà tan indiferents.

Si una cosa ha de caracteritzar aquells navegants que capitanejaven grans expedicions a la recerca de riqueses, sens dubte ha de ser el desig de grandesa: no són terres el que realment busquen aquests exploradors, sinó honor i glòria. I com que segurament els deliris de grandesa de Quirós tampoc no són poca cosa, ¿què millor que inventar-se un nou orde de cavalleria per celebrar el més grandiosíssim descobriment de tots els temps? Tan gran és la set de títols i descobriments d'aquella època que encara hi ha qui s'inventa ordes cavallerescos. Així, amb motiu d'aquest descobriment tan colossal el navegant portuguès decideix fundar el que anomenarà *Orden del Espíritu Santo*, i tot seguit concedeix el títol de cavaller a tots els tripulants sense excepció, inclosos dos esclaus peruans i un intèrpret de les illes Salomó que no deuen entendre gaire res de tot plegat.

Des d'aquest moment, doncs, tot de cavallers mariners, cavallers grumets i cavallers esclaus es passegen per coberta lluint la seva creu blava al pit, insígnia del nou orde cavalleresc. Segurament, se saluden més fent-ne burla que cap altra cosa. Entretant, continuen fent la mateixa feina feixuga de sempre, a les ordres de cavallers capitans, cavallers almiralls i cavallers sergents.

I Cervantes tan lluny d'aquí!

Però no prou satisfet amb la institució del nou orde i de la solemníssima presa de possessió del nou territori, Quirós nomena les autoritats que calen per donar per fundada també una idíl·lica ciutat de marbre anomenada Nova Jerusalem. Ciutat de marbre que sortirà de les riques pedreres d'aquest nou continent. Els murs i les portes de la ciutat, la catedral, fins i tot les cases seran totes de marbre... una ciutat bellíssima on fins i tot Quirós projecta una societat utòpica i, això sí, per descomptat, cristiana, perquè no es pot entendre res de tot plegat sense l'obsessió per evangelitzar, és clar.

Si Sancho Panza sabés que lluny li queda la seva *ínsula*...

No està gens malament. Segur que havia de ser una experiència ben interessant això d'embarcar-se uns mesos en aquesta mena d'expedicions.

I tot això passa en aquell mateix 1606, durant el qual, precisament als antípodes castellans, s'està publicant el *Don Quixot*.

Quixot i Quirós. Tot és tan confús que fins i tot els noms... Però qui fa cas al cavaller Quixot? I qui fa cas al cavaller Quirós? Naturalment les seves aventures no porten a la glòria i a l'honor. Com ja podem imaginar, quan es constati el poc interès que desperta aquest escampall d'*ínsules* que només servirien a

Sancho Panza, aquestes aigües començaran a ser abandonades per les expedicions castellanes. Estan molt més centrades a anar entre Amèrica i les Filipines, molt més al nord.

El seu intent és meritori, senyor cavaller Quirós, però l'aventura australiana de Castella s'atura amb vostè. Amb Quirós, el nom ha arribat abans que la cosa. Ja tenim, doncs, batejat el territori que encara no hem descobert, un territori que començaran a buscar aviat altres països europeus. Primer de tot, els holandesos.

Perquè ara que ja tenim un nom, ens caldrà trobar l'illa més gran del Pacífic, l'illa a la qual escaigui dir-se Austràlia.

Pel que fa a Cervantes, li caldrà esperar encara fins al 1844 per tenir el seu petit racó a Austràlia. L'hi tindrà quan el balener *Cervantes*, batejat així en honor seu, naufragarà a la costa occidental d'aquesta illa-continent. Encara les restes d'aquest balener reposen a pocs metres de profunditat sota el Pacífic. Ben a prop d'un poble australià que es diu Cervantes, ben lluny, però d'allà on va arribar el quixotesc Quirós. Potser, qui ho sap, si en comptes de Vanuatu, la terra on va arribar Quirós hagués sigut realment l'Austràlia continental, la capital d'aquesta illa avui s'anomenaria el Toboso en comptes de Canberra. Perquè, sigui com sigui, té molt de quixotesc el fet de batejar Austràlia quan l'illa no ha estat encara descoberta.

I d'aquí venia Torres.

L'expedició de Quirós s'estarà a l'illa de Vanuatu durant tot un mes. Durant aquest mes, no para d'haver-hi enfrontaments amb els habitants locals. També les tensions entre Quirós i la tripulació augmenten. Els mariners acaben amotinant-se contra el seu capità. Els sembla cada cop més llunàtic. Costa poc imaginar un motí si don Quixot, per molt bon home que fos, capitanegés una expedició per mars desconegudes durant mesos... Finalment, el 8 de juny, en un ambient encara molt tens, arriba el dia que Quirós, la nau i els seus tripulants marxen del lloc on són i van mar enllà, a explicar al món la grandiosa notícia del descobriment del que ells pensen que és Austràlia.

Però tal com passa sovint al Quixot, les coses sempre acaben torçant-se per un atzar o per un altre. Tres dies després que hagin salpat arriba un temporal que obliga Quirós a ordenar el retorn a terra ferma. Luis Váez de Torres, que capitaneja el *San Pedrico*, obeeix, i passarà allà encara dues setmanes més esperant la resta de l'expedició, que mai més no tornarà a aquest racó de món.

Passades dues setmanes sense tenir notícies de Quirós, Torres ordena reprendre el camí de tornada, però, en comptes d'apostar pel difícil camí cap a Amèrica, s'estima més emproar cap a les Filipines, seguint un rumb de navegació aleshores molt més factible.

I ja tenim Luis Váez de Torres a bord del *San Pedrico*, a punt de posar el seu nom als mapes del món del futur sense saber-ho.

Naturalment, en començar a solcar aigües cap a l'oest i trobar un mar obert en comptes d'un continent, Torres i els seus constataran el que molts ja podien suposar: que allò que ha descobert Quirós no és res més que una illa com tantes altres del Pacífic. I sabent això, el *San Pedrico* avança cap a l'oest fins que uns esculls de corall l'obliguen a desviar-se cap al nord.

A desviar-se molt cap al nord.

Encara més cap al nord...

I vet aquí l'amagatall d'Austràlia.

Una Austràlia amagada darrere un amagatall invisible: la famosa barrera de corall.

No ha de fer gens de gràcia trobar-se amb aquesta barrera sota el buc del vaixell. I menys encara, navegar de nits per aquestes aigües desconegudes.

I la resta ja la sabem: en la seva ruta cap al nord Torres topa amb Nova Guinea, aquella terra que els portuguesos ja han posat al mapa fa un temps. En ressegueix la costa sud, alesho-res encara desconeguda per als europeus. Probablement, en el seu camí intentant esquivar Austràlia, els homes de Torres ve-uen el cap de York, l'extrem nord de la gran illa, però se'n sap poc. Senzillament el periple de Torres passarà desapercebut durant molt de temps. Ni tan sols no es coneix la cartografia del seu viatge. I també qui sap si amb Quirós ja n'ha tingut prou de quixotismes i per si un cas s'estima més dissimular. Perquè en aquests moments Torres ja no està buscant tant d'honor i tanta glòria, sinó potser un lloc on sentir-se com a casa i reposar.

El cas és que finalment, el maig de 1607, acaba arribant a Manila. Hi podrà descansar una mica tranquil i, de passada, si ho vol, podrà explicar que la seva expedició no ha descobert gaire res de l'altre món. I així és com ningú no es recordarà gaire d'ell fins ben bé l'època de James Cook.

Dirk Hartog. Una costa immensa

Nova Holanda. Vet aquí el primer nom estranger per a aquest continent. Al llarg del segle XVII, després que Janszoon trepitgi sense saber-ho Austràlia per primer cop, tot just co-mençarem a trobar un discret escampall de vaixells holandesos traient el nas per aquestes costes inhòspites. Algunes vegades hi arriben arran d'un accident; altres, en puntuals operacions de rescat; i encara, algunes poques vegades, per explorar sense cap més resultat que el d'anar cartografiant a poc a poc una costa que acabaran deixant oblidada després de no trobar-hi gaire res interessant...

Però per fi haurem arribat a un descobriment amb cara i ulls segons els estàndards europeus. Perquè el de Janszoon de 1606 és ignorat per ell mateix; i quan Janszoon hi torni el 1618, en realitat hi arribarà dos anys després que Dirk Hartog s'hagi convertit, per fi, en l'home que diu al món que hi ha una costa de dimensions continentals per aquestes latituds.

Aquests són els temps que els holandesos es passegen per l'illa de Java a la recerca d'espècies i minerals valuosos. Per arribar-hi, el 1611 Hendrik Brouwer ha descobert la ruta dels *rugents quaranta*, menys segura però molt més ràpida. Aquesta ruta consisteix a aprofitar els forts vents de la latitud quaranta, més al sud del cap de Bona Esperança, i deixar-se dur cap a l'est. En aquelles latituds els vents no són frenats per cap terra i t'empenyen amb tota la seva fúria, cosa que permet reduir el trajecte fins a Java en uns quants mesos. L'únic inconvenient és la pèrdua de referents per establir la longitud, de manera que després d'avançar intuïtivament cap a l'est per l'Índic, cal desviar-se al nord quan consideren que es deuen trobar a la longitud de Java. En aquest avenç poc precís a causa de la immensitat desconeguda de l'oceà, no és estrany que algú viri cap al nord massa aviat o massa tard. El que ho fa massa aviat pot perdre un temps preciós, i el que ho fa massa tard es pot trobar amb dues coses: que naufragui davant de les costes australianes o que sobrevisqui a les costes australianes. I això és el que fa el nostre proper convidat, Dirk Hartog.

Pot molt ben ser que els primers europeus que es van integrar en societats australianes siguin nàufrags holandesos avui oblidats. Però l'holandès Dirk Hartog és l'home que el 1616 topa amb la costa occidental australiana i que, en comptes de naufragar-hi, es dedica a recórrer-la durant un temps abans de tornar a aquell altre món que molts anomenen civilitzat. Hartog deu sospitar ben poc que és en el mateix territori trobat per Janszoon deu anys abans. Tot i que la seva experiència és menys tràgica que la de Janszoon, també ell abandona aquestes terres sense trobar-hi gaire res interessant. Bàsicament una costa inhòspita i resseca.

Però aquest és el primer reconeixement forà de la costa australiana. I com que Hartog sí que sap que ha descobert alguna cosa nova, el 25 d'octubre d'aquell any, en passar per la badia de Shark, desembarcarà a l'illa avui coneguda com a illa de Dirk Hartog, plana i erma com qualsevol altre racó d'aquesta extensa costa. Allà, aquell dia, deixarà, en un suport de fusta, el primer objecte i el primer escrit europeu que coneixem a Austràlia: una placa amb una inscripció que testimonia el seu pas per aquest racó de món en aquella data.

I se'n va.

Per primer cop arriba un vaixell de l'altra banda del món, un home deixa un plat en un pal i se'n va.

Un plat amb una inscripció en una platja solitària.

I Hartog que no torna mai més a l'illa a la qual dona nom.

Però la història no s'acaba mai allà on sembla. Aquesta placa absurda en una platja oblidada té encara un bon camí per recórrer. Tan llarg que encara avui està conservada al Rijksmuseum d'Amsterdam.

O l'illa és molt petita o la placa és molt vistosa. O la informació que dona Hartog és molt precisa. O potser també el febrer de 1697 Willem de Vlamingh té una sort extraordinària. El cas és que vuitanta anys després, un altre holandès anomenat Willem de Vlamingh, mentre dirigeix una expedició de rescat, ensopegarà de nou amb aquella illa i amb aquella placa deixada temps enrere per Hartog. I per celebrar-ho, de Vlamingh la recollirà, la portarà cap a Holanda i en el seu lloc hi deixarà una altra placa on, a més de reproduir les paraules de Hartog afegeix les que testimonien també el seu pas per aquest mateix lloc.

I és així com la placa de Hartog se'n torna cap a Europa.

Però de vegades la història es repeteix, com un somni del temps dels somnis. I encara un altre segle més tard, el 1801, quan una expedició francesa (l'*Uranie*) es trobi per aquestes aigües i el seu capità, Jacques Hamelin, faci baixar un grup de mariners a fer un reconeixement de l'illa, un d'aquests mariners, Louis de Freycinet, trobarà la placa de de Vlamingh. Com no podia ser de cap altra manera, Freycinet també la recuperarà i la portarà al capità Hamelin. Aquest capità n'encarregarà una còpia acurada allà mateix. Deixarà l'original al lloc on era i s'endurà la còpia cap a Europa. Però per no ser menys que els altres, a l'illa de Hartog Hamelin també deixarà la seva placa.

I allà tenim de nou un plat amb lletres, fent-se amb paciència un amagatall sota la sorra d'una platja solitària.

Fins que el 1818 el destí torni a portar Freycinet a aquesta mateixa illa durant una llarga circumnavegació del planeta. Aquell dia el francès no se'n sabrà estar. Trobarà la placa de de Vlamingh i se l'emportarà cap a França, on, després d'un naufragi, arribaran ell i el trofeu.

Des d'aleshores, en comptes de consumir-se entre la sorra i el sol d'una platja deserta, la placa deixada per de Vlamingh en aquesta remota illa es conservarà perfectament amagada en els magatzems de l'Acadèmia francesa durant més d'un segle.

L'any 1940 algú la desenterrarà del fons d'un calaix i, en acabar la Segona Guerra Mundial, el govern francès decideix tornar-la a Austràlia. Avui es pot trobar al Maritime Museum de Fremantle, a les proximitats de Perth.

I fins aquí arriben les peripècies del primer objecte euroaustralià que coneixem avui: amb el plat de Hartog a Amsterdam i la còpia de de Vlamingh a Fremantle.

Un plat solemnement abandonat en una platja deserta.

La història d'Austràlia és així d'estranya. Com que els europeus no hi troben res que els sembli gaire llaminer, fa l'efecte que, de moment, estan més interessats a deixar-hi coses que no pas a recollir-ne. I així, mentre la placa de Hartog comença el seu joc de fet i amagar sota la sorra, altres holandesos vindran també a deixar coses importants a la costa occidental australiana. Esquelets, sang, vergonya, i alguns també la dignitat, que tampoc no és poca cosa.

El naufragi del *Batavia*

No gaire lluny de l'illa de Hartog, molt a prop de la badia de Shark, avui encara es poden veure els estromatòlits, la forma de vida més antiga que es coneix. Sense cap mena de dubte es tracta d'una vida plàcida i tranquil·la, pacífica. Els estromatòlits són de fet l'origen de la vida al planeta Terra. Per estrany que ens pugui semblar, aquelles protuberàncies arrapades a les roques llepades per un mar beatífic i lluminós són els nostres avantpassats més antics, els nostres cosins més llunyans. O sigui que estem més emparentats amb aquests estromatòlits que amb la majoria de coses que ens envolten i amb què ens identifiquem tan sovint. Cap objecte, cap casa, cap moble, cap moneda o bitllet, cap peça de roba o cap vehicle, gairebé res de tot el que ens envolta i ens defineix, està més emparentat amb nosaltres que aquests pacifiquíssims estromatòlits.

Però és tan difícil parlar-ne que ens resignarem a fer-los una visita respectuosa i a fer després una passejada pel seu jardí a veure què hi trobem que ens sigui més familiar. A prop, hi ha una placa amb lletres gravades deixada un dia per un navegant antic, i, poc més de tres-cents quilòmetres cap al sud, que en termes australians vol dir a la cantonada, hi ha una història una mica més propera, més nostra, la dels primers europeus australians.

Primer de tot, ens hem de situar a les proximitats de les illes Houtman Abrolhos, un petit arxipèlag a uns seixanta quilòmetres de la costa oest australiana, separat del continent des de fa uns vuit mil o deu mil anys i on de moment no trobarem cap rastre de presència humana. Dels cent vint-i-dos illots que conformen l'arxipèlag, buscarem ara el grup de més al nord, conegut amb el nom de Ualabi. Ens plantarem en aquests illots plans i erms, coberts d'una poc generosa vegetació i envoltats d'uns esculls de corall ben amenaçadors, els més meridionals del món, a una latitud on ningú no espera que n'hi hagi.

Un cop siguem en aquest paisatge desolat, ens caldrà viatjar fins a una matinada de principis de juny de 1629.

I per arribar-hi, caldrà que ho fem amb el *Batavia*, un vaixell holandès capitanejat per Ariaen Jacobsz sota l'autoritat del sobrecàrrec Francisco Pelsaert. Entre mariners, soldats i passatgers, a bord hi ha 341 persones. Fa uns mesos van sortir d'Holanda per anar cap a la ciutat que duu el mateix nom que el vaixell, Batàvia (més endavant Jakarta), a l'illa de Java.

Ja se sap que aquests viatges no són fàcils. I menys encara, quan a les complicacions habituals s'han afegit les inclemències de l'oceà Índic, cosa que els ha dut a navegar més al sud i més a l'est del que haurien volgut. A més a més, les condicions ja habitualment incòmodes d'aquests llargs desplaçaments a vela es veuen accentuades per la manca d'espai per a tanta gent, per la indisciplina i per les tensions entre la tripulació, per la insalubritat cada dia més preocupant, per la manca d'aigua neta per beure o per rentar-se, per la mala conservació d'aliments, molts dels quals es podreixen i s'omplen de cucs, pudor, rates i milers i milers d'escarabats... En aquesta mena de condicions es transportaven els preuats béns de les colònies. Res a veure amb el creuer de plaer que ens agradaria imaginar avui. I lluny també de ser el lloc ideal on portar tot de lingots d'or, cofres plens de diners i altres riqueses per comerciar a Java.

En aquestes condicions, i sabent que Pelsaert i Jacobsz ja es porten malament des d'abans d'embarcar, no és estrany que al *Batavia* comencin a respirar-se aires de motí. Jacobsz ja comença a moure fils i a tenir els seus aliats, entre ells l'apotecari Jeronimus Cornelisz, un polèmic i corrupte comerciant que, si s'ha embarcat en una nova empresa a les Índies, és sobretot per fugir d'Holanda.

No és estrany, doncs, que amb aquests aires irrespirables, Pelsaert no s'acabi de trobar bé. Sobretot també des que, a l'escala de Ciutat del Cap, va agafar una malaltia de la qual no s'acaba de curar. I és així com a la nit del 4 de juny, Pelsaert se'n va a dormir perquè no es troba gaire bé. Però segurament, quan es desperti, oblidarà el malestar que li ha espatllat la nit perquè hi haurà una altra cosa que l'amoïnarà.

Però millor que sortim ara d'aquest vaixell. Avancem-nos al *Batavia* i girem-nos enmig de la nit per sentir-lo com s'apropa. Sentim l'embat de les veles exposades al vent, l'esquitx de l'aigua tallada per la proa del vaixell...

Navega, de nit, una nau enmig de l'oceà, mig adormida potser en la confiança d'unes aigües sense fronteres i inacabables... I un sotrac. Un estrèpit. Una sacsejada del vaixell que es desperta mentre està morint. Aigua, crits, cops, trencadissa, empentes, morts. Tot passa en poc temps fins que, quan el dia clareja, hi ha un grup de nàufrags en una illa sorrenca.

Però reculem. Primer cal que es despertin. Cal que surtin de l'impacte inesperat. Cal que sàpiguen que el vaixell ha encallat amb uns esculls. Cal que valorin fins a quin punt estan en perill.

A sota no tenen més de cinc o sis metres d'aigua. Cal, doncs, que alleugereixin el vaixell de càrrega per veure si el poden fer navegar i poden evitar-ne l'enfonsament. Què és el que més pesa? Les riqueses ni pensar-ho. A la desesperada, els supervivents comencen llençant els canons per la borda. Tot seguit, proven de desfer-se del pal major, però la caiguda d'aquest pal fa encara més destrosses. Ni tan sols no el podran llançar al mar. Per tant, aviat sabran que els caldrà abandonar el *Batavia* i que hauran de mirar d'arribar fins a les illes que veuen a unes poques milles de distància. És així com, després d'uns quants viatges en bot durant el matí, cent vuitanta persones, amb les seves provisions i la seva aigua, aconsegueixen trobar un lloc segur a terra ferma.

Mentrestant, el vaixell es va acabant d'enfonsar a poc a poc. Hi ha encara uns setanta supervivents més. S'emborratxen amb el que queda a les bodegues que acaben de saquejar mentre esperen que els arribi la mort. Només una vintena d'aquests supervivents aniran arribant a terra ferma durant els dies següents, agafats a les restes del naufragi. Entre els últims d'aquests homes, trobarem Jeronimus Cornelisz. Aviat tindrà un paper important en aquest episodi.

Així, un grup de dos-cents nàufrags, homes, dones i criatures comença una de les primeres històries europees que coneixem d'Austràlia.

A les illes Houtman Abrolhos.

Si mirem al nostre voltant, bàsicament tenim rocs, sorra i matolls, un escampall de restes del naufragi i una multitud de cares desolades i desesperades. Crits d'alegria histèrica en retrobar algun parent viu; angoixa per trobar-ne a faltar algun altre.

Com sol passar sovint, els càrrecs més alts, en aquest cas Pelsaert i Jacobsz, tenen la sort de ser entre els molts supervivents. Però no els trobarem en aquests illots durant gaires dies. Conscient de la situació, Pelsaert de seguida decidirà embarcar-se en un bot a rem cap a Java per anar-hi a buscar un rescat. És obvi que es tracta d'un viatge quasi impossible, però és l'única opció. I així, Pelsaert, Jacobsz i un petit grup d'homes emprenen aquest periple que més aviat sembla, senzillament, un viatge cap a una mort diferent.

Sens dubte seran uns mesos llarguíssims per a Pelsaert. Patirà per ell mateix i pels tripulants i passatgers del *Batavia*, però finalment se'n sortirà. Tres mesos després del naufragi, Pelsaert tornarà a les proximitats de les Abrolhos a bord del *Sardam*. Aquest cop, per evitar un altre naufragi, el 17 de setembre Pelsaert s'aproparà a les illes en un bot, disposat a restablir contacte amb els seus i a culminar amb èxit el rescat dels que hagin pogut sobreviure tot aquest temps. Segur que deu estar emocionat quan, ja a prop de la primera de les illes, veu que hi ha supervivents. Encara no ha tocat terra quan se li apropa un bot, en el qual hi ha Wiebbe Haijes, un supervivent que li explica que té a càrrec seu quaranta-set persones que s'han refugiat en aquesta illa per salvar la vida. Li explica que un grup dirigit per Cornelisz ha assassinat més de cent vint-i-cinc homes, dones i criatures. Haijes també li diu que fa dues setmanes que ell mateix ha capturat Cornelisz i que alguns dels seus seguidors han estat executats.

Naturalment la delirant guerra civil que Pelsaert troba a les Abrolhos s'acabarà de seguida que arriba amb el *Sardam*. Immediatament els homes armats seran detinguts. Pelsaert provarà de saber què ha passat. Segur que, abans que torni a aquell lloc tan llunyà anomenat civilització, podia esperar qualsevol cosa abans que el que sentirà explicar durant els dos mesos que dura el judici.

I així, si tornem al juny, veurem començar la primera història australiana purament europea. La primera història dels primers estrangers coneguts que viuran a Austràlia.

Aquell dia de primers de juny, per evitar que hi hagués massa gent que volgués unir-se al petit grup de remers privilegiats, Pelsaert i Jacobsz van marxar cap a Java gairebé d'amagat. Buscaven l'única opció seriosa que tenien per sobreviure, però van deixar darrere seu una colònia improvisada, sense cap autoritat. Gràcies a la seva facilitat per parlar i gràcies també al fet que és una de les persones més instruïdes de totes, Jeronimus Cornelisz assumirà l'autoritat de la colònia en pocs dies. El que encara no s'imagina ningú és, però que, a banda de ser instruït, Cornelisz és també o sobretot un autèntic psicòpata. I no hi ha res més perillós que un psicòpata al poder d'una societat aïllada del món sense opcions de sobreviure, un dement cruel i sanguinari que sap que ningú no vindrà mai fins allà a passar comptes amb ell.

Ningú. Ni Déu.

Més aviat al contrari. Un dels seus motius per deixar Holanda és que se'l persegueix per les seves idees herètiques: per a ell no hi ha més déu que el Diable. Si algú li ha de venir a passar comptes serà el Diable en persona.

Així, ¿per què no sotmet aquest racó oblidat del món a les seves lleis —deu pensar Cornelisz—, si sap que mai ningú no vindrà a buscar-los de nou? I si vingués algú miraculosament, per què no es podria apoderar del vaixell de rescat que arribés? Al cap i a la fi, el motí ja s'estava gestant i Cornelisz ja té els seus sequaços fidels. Estan disposats a tot.

La colònia sanguinària

Agradi o no, els europeus no sempre necessiten trobar habitants nadius per començar la seva presència a nous territoris fent matances sensacionals. En el cas del *Batavia*, durant els primers dies, mentre encara van arribant alguns supervivents del vaixell, comencen a haver-hi també les primeres morts. La colònia pot sobreviure amb les provisions que han rescatat del naufragi. Són administrades per Cornelisz, que ha pres el control de totes les armes, aliments, bots i tota mena d'equipatges.

Per sort, les illes Abrolhos ofereixen encara alguns recursos. Tot i que escassos, la pesca, els ous d'ocells, alguna foca o algun ualabi permeten que tothom s'alimenti un xic. Però poder beure és més difícil. La poca aigua que ha quedat de les poques pluges a dins dels clots d'algunes roques és massa escassa. I sovint, ja és salada. La set serà un dels principals problemes d'aquesta colònia. La set d'aigua d'uns i la set de sang de Cornelisz i dels seus seguidors.

Perquè Cornelisz tindrà seguidors i detractors. I és així com començarà el seu bany de sang. Es desfarà sense cap escrúpol de qui no vulgui acceptar la seva delirant llei del terror. Crearà un sistema organitzat de constant violència, violacions, prostitució forçada, tortura i assassinats sistemàtics. Degollarà, decapitarà i ofegarà dia rere dia.

Matar els rivals i els seus fills, i violar-ne sistemàticament les filles es converteix en la norma de Cornelisz i dels que l'obeeixen. Alguns el segueixen per por; d'altres per fam de poder (sigui el que sigui això del poder i de la por per a gent d'aquesta mena). Però quant de temps pot durar un poder com aquest en un lloc tan desolat? Tard o d'hora caldrà posar-hi un límit. Caldrà entendre's amb tota la societat, una societat amb tan poca gent com aquesta. Potser deu ser per això que un cop Cornelisz convida cordialment a sopar el predicador Gijsbert Bastiaensz i la seva filla gran, Judith. Aquell vespre del 21 de juliol, els Bastiaensz van a la tenda de Cornelisz amb l'esperança d'establir un diàleg amb el tirà, pensant que el podran convèncer, que trobaran un petit cor en aquella carcassa funesta i que fins i tot descobriran que potser és capaç de ser un xic amable. Però s'equivoquen. Mentre són a la tenda sopant, els sequaços de Cornelisz entren a la tenda del predicador i maten els seus altres sis fills a cops d'aixada.

Aquesta és la llei, entén, senyor predicador?

No es pot pensar diferent de qui té el poder.

Potser com a tot arreu. Com sempre. Només que amb resultats més expeditius.

Des d'aquell dia, Gijsbert Bastiaensz sobreviurà sense fills. Només li queda la seva filla gran, Judith, que aquell vespre era al sopar amb Cornelisz. El preu per salvar la vida és ser violada sistemàticament, ser esclavitzada com a concubina d'un dels homes de Cornelisz.

Ah, sí, per això els havien convidat a sopar.

Així són les coses a l'imperi de Cornelisz.

Aprofites tot el que pots i et desfàs de tot el que et fa nosa.

És per això, per treure's alguns rivals del damunt, que un altre cop Cornelisz envia un grup de soldats a explorar un illot veí a buscar-hi aigua. Aquest grup, liderat per Wiebbe Haijes i altres possibles rivals de Cornelisz, són abandonat en aquest illot sense provisions. Els prometen que els aniran a buscar més endavant, però Cornelisz els deixa allà fins que moren. Però de vegades fins i tot el regne més petit és ple de sorpreses inesperades. És així com aquests homes abandonats es convertiran potser en els més afortunats de la colònia: un dia, aprofitant un moment de marea baixa i de bones condicions, aconsegueixen saltar fins a una illa més gran on finalment, vint dies després de ser abandonats, acabaran trobant aigua. Haijes i els seus no dubten a enviar senyals de fum per indicar la seva troballa. D'ençà d'aquest moment, les coses es començaran a tensar encara més en l'assedegat grup de Cornelisz. Per primer cop en molts mesos aquesta gent sap que tenen aigua fresca a prop. De sobte tothom qui pot mira de fugir cap a l'illa de Haijes en balses improvisades. Per no perdre el seu poder, Cornelisz s'acarnissa contra els que volen fugir del seu diminut imperi del terror.

I ja tenim la guerra servida. La set d'aigua contra la set de sang.

Aleshores, en veure el seu poder més amenaçat que mai, el deliri del rei de set-de-sang esdevé encara més diabòlic. Fa matar tothom que vulgui fugir cap a la república de set-d'aigua. Un cop liquidats tots els fugitius que ha pogut, el sanguinari rei Cornelisz de set-de-sang exigirà un jurament de fidelitat a tots els súbdits que li queden. Les opcions per als que queden a prop són molt clares: jurar-li fidelitat o morir a l'instant. Liquidada tota la gent que no li jura fidelitat, potser per no malgastar els escassos recursos que li queden, finalment fa matar fins i tot els malalts. Cornelisz, vessarà tota la sang que pugui vessar.

I és així com ens trobem immersos en una minúscula i absurda guerra, que és també la guerra més gran i més cruel que coneixem en un radi de milers de quilòmetres. I sembla que només s'acabarà quan tothom sigui mort, potser quan Cornelisz es quedi tot sol envoltat de cadàvers. Però el regne de set-de-sang ja no és només cosa de Cornelisz; el deliri s'encomana i els seus seguidors fidels han entrat en una espiral de violència de la qual ja no podran sortir. És així com a finals d'agost, quan ja no queden ni un centenar de persones, Cornelisz i alguns dels seus homes són capturats, alguns són executats i ell és empresonat pels homes de la república de set-d'aigua.

Morta la bèstia, morta la ràbia.

O no.

La tirania de Cornelisz està establerta, la set de sang s'encomana i un cop detingut el líder entra en escena Wouter Loos, un jove de vint-i-quatre anys que assumeix el lideratge dels sanguinaris. Però el seu domini no durarà gaire temps. El 17 de setembre arriba el *Sardam* i el desenllaç es precipita amb la detenció dels amotinats, judicis i execucions que duraran fins quasi dos mesos.

En el judici, el valentíssim i sanguinari Cornelisz no dubta a acusar els seus companys. Queda clar que no és ell qui ha fet un jurament de fidelitat a ningú, però finalment el 2 d'octubre s'executa la sentència: després d'un intent de suïcidi amb un verí que només el torturarà durant la seva última nit al nostre món, a Cornelisz li amputen les mans en viu i el pengen de la forca. Hi arribarà clamant venjança contra qui sap qui o qui sap què. «Venjança», aquest serà el seu últim crit abans de balancejar-se sense haver mostrat en cap moment cap penediment. Més aviat al contrari.

I així és com la diabòlica ment de Cornelisz desapareix del món.

Darrere seu només deixa un grapat de forques a l'illa de les Foques.

Vet aquí: una forca a les solitàries illes Houtman Abrolhos. Probablement això sigui la construcció europea més alta de la història d'Austràlia fins aleshores i durant els cent seixanta anys següents. Ben mirat, no deixa de ser significatiu que entre les primeres coses que van construir els europeus a Austràlia hi hagués una forca per a ells mateixos...

Però Cornelisz no és l'únic condemnat a la forca allà mateix. Altres corren una sort semblant. De tots els condemnats a mort allà mateix, Pelsaert només s'apiadarà d'un jovenet de divuit anys que plora de tal manera i fa tanta pena que Pelsaert decideix revisar el seu cas. És Jan Pelgrom, un jove que durant el juliol ja ploriquejava a Cornelisz perquè li deixessin degollar algú a ell també.

Així, mentre es van esclarint tots els fets, el 27 d'octubre Wouter Loos i el ploramiques Jan Pelgrom són condemnats a l'abandó allà on el *Sardam* localitzi prou aigua dolça. I per fi, el 13 de novembre el *Sardam* salpa amb només setanta supervivents cap a Jakarta, planeta Terra. D'aquests setanta supervivents, catorze viatgen detinguts per ser convenientment jutjats, torturats i cinc d'ells penjats quan arribin a Jakarta. Altres dos, Loos i Pelgrom, són abandonats el dia 16, probablement a la desembocadura del riu Murchison, l'únic regal habitable que la gegantesca costa australiana sembla oferir a l'expedició.

En aquest racó de món hi haurà, segles després, l'actual població de Kalbarri, un petit paradís per a surfistes i turistes, ideal per oblidar-se durant uns dies del tràfec de la civilització moderna. Però en aquell 1629, quan Loos i Pelgrom veuen allunyar-se el poc que els quedava d'aquella seva civilització coneguda, es troben envoltats d'un paisatge més aviat ressec i aspre, amb tot just alguns matolls i arbres que, sense cap mena de dubte, els deuran semblar una autèntica selva després de tants mesos sembrant cadàvers estèrils en uns illots erms. En aquest lloc, això sí, hi ha prou aigua dolça. Aquesta costa inhòspita, probablement és també, doncs, un bon lloc perquè Loos i Pelgrom puguin contactar amb els habitants d'aquestes regions ignotes i perquè hi trobin la manera de sobreviure. Per tal que en puguin tenir alguna opció, Pelsaert els deixa una petita barca, algunes provisions i quatre andròmines per si volen comerciar amb els habitants que trobin. Alguns d'aquests habitants Pelsaert ja els ha vist anteriorment, en el seu doble periple per aquesta costa.

El 16 de novembre de 1629, doncs, és l'últim dia que sabem alguna cosa de Pelgrom i Loos. Alguns diuen que potser van integrar-se als Nhanda; altres, que potser els Nhanda van matar-los. Qui ho pot saber? L'única cosa que se sap del cert és que aquests són els dos primers migrants que coneixem a Austràlia. No està gens malament la carta de presentació.

Mentrestant, qui sap amb quines preguntes al cap deuen tornar a casa els rescatadors del *Sardam*. Si durant el juny Cornelisz hagués continuat emborratxant-se al *Batavia* fins a morir ofegat, quantes vides s'haurien salvat? Quin panorama haurien trobat si haguessin arribat un temps més tard? Qui els hauria explicat els fets? Quin motiu seriós caldria imaginar per a una guerra tan absurda?

Pel que fa a les illes Houtman Abrolhos, avui hi ha les restes més antigues de la presència europea a Austràlia: un escampall d'esquelets enterrats i un petit mur de protecció construït per Haijes, la construcció europea més antiga del continent. Per protegir-se d'altres europeus.

La costa oblidada

Ja veiem que els holandesos del segle XVII fan poc més que naufragar i buscar què troben en aquestes terres. I així serà durant tot el segle. Perquè els holandesos del XVII no hi acaben de trobar gaire res interessant en aquesta costa tan remota. El 1619 Frederik de Houtman recorre la costa oest australiana, el 1623 Jan Carstensz en recorre part de la costa nord, el 1627 s'hi passeja François Thijsen... Tots són descobridors que van ajudant a conformar les costes australianes als mapes, però poca cosa més. Els holandesos del segle XVII no hi troben gaire res que els interessi, cap riquesa, gens d'or. És per això que aquestes terres no tenen cap interès especial per a ningú que no sigui els seus habitants. I així serà fins que els anglesos necessitin fer una de les colònies penitenciàries més cruels i macabres de la història. I finalment, s'hi trobarà or en el segle XIX.

Però de moment, res. L'Austràlia del segle XVII és encara poc més que retalls d'una costa llunyana dibuixada als mapes. Fins i tot així, és un continent misteriós que sap amagar-se millor que ningú. Mirem si no com, el 1642, Abel Tasman volta aquest continent pràcticament sense veure'l i arriba al sud de Tasmània abans de trobar Nova Zelanda. Des d'allà continuarà cap al nord per diferents illes del Pacífic fins a tornar cap al cap de Bona Esperança passant per la costa nord de Nova Guinea. Així, Tasman serà el primer a circumnavegar Austràlia, molt abans que Matthew Flinders es pengi aquesta medalla el 1802, i també molt abans que Cook faci el mateix amb l'Antàrtida. Cook, com a mínim, tindrà la possibilitat d'intuir el continent antàrtic gràcies al gel que se'n desprèn, però el cas australià és molt més digne d'admiració. Realment aquesta terra sap amagar-se.

Dos anys més tard, el 1644, en el seu nou viatge Tasman ja recorrerà bona part de la costa nord australiana, però no es pot negar que de moment tot és molt dispers. Com si el temps dels somnis envoltés encara el continent que es nega a acabar-se de despertar del tot.

I així, al llarg del segle XVII, a poc a poc per a la joveníssima Europa, d'una batzegada per a la somniosa Austràlia, sobretot els holandesos van posant aquest territori als mapes. Però les dificultats per arribar-hi i l'escassetat de beneficis que ofereix el lloc fan que molta gent en perdi l'interès. Senzillament, allò no és res més que una costa llunyana. Res més...

Una costa que es va dibuixant a poc a poc...

1788. L'arribada dels salvatges

Aquesta badia és ampla però ben tancada, protegida dels embats del mar, de clima amable i envoltada d'unes terres generosament productives. Un d'aquells llocs del món que conviden a tenir pocs maldecaps i a viure tranquil; a deixar que la vida flueixi d'una generació a l'altra des del temps de la creació.

En aquesta confortable costa, un dia com qualsevol altre dels últims cinc mil anys, un grup d'australians us trobeu pescant feliçment quan algú veu una cosa inusual a l'horitzó. Sense cap més avís, aquell punt estrany es va fent gran, s'apropa.

Mai ningú no ha vist res semblant. Sembla que és una barca, una barca immensa.

Però si vols menjar cal continuar pescant.

La gran barca s'apropa cada cop més. A alguns us crida l'atenció i us la mireu intrigats. De la barca surt una altra barca més petita, unes persones d'aspecte estrany s'apropen a la costa. No coneixen la llengua i tot el que fan és ensenyar-vos uns objectes estranys i absurds.

Però vosaltres heu de pescar.

'D'acord, d'acord', dieu a aquests estrafolaris visitants. I senzillament esperareu que acabin marxant i que us deixin en pau.

Vosaltres encara no ho sabeu, però per a aquells estrangers els anys es compten en xifres. Aquest és el seu número 1770; el dia, 29 d'abril. L'home que va al capdavant es diu James Cook. I malgrat que se'n tornen cap al lloc d'on venien, no trigaran gaire a tornar. Només divuit anys.

De moment, marxen i continueu pescant, tal com heu fet cada dia d'ençà que els vostres avantpassats van arribar aquí.

I així ho continuareu fent sense cap més sorpresa que les habituals i corrents durant encara un temps.

Fins que un dia d'estiu...

Una gran barca, que és com la que alguns diuen que ja va venir fa anys. Per als visitants, aquest és l'any 1788. Mes de gener. Dia 18.

Aquesta vegada, però, en pocs dies arriba tota una flota amb molta més gent. Gent que —vosaltres encara no ho sabeu— han posat un nom estrany a aquest lloc, Botany Bay, des de l'altra banda del món, i li han donat un destí. Són gent que arriben bruts i malalts, moribunds, molts d'ells encadenats amb grillons que no s'han pogut treure des de fa mesos, grillons rovellats que laceren les llagues podrides dels seus turmells i que els priven de caminar amb normalitat. Entre els visitants també n'hi ha que no van encadenats: són els que donen ordres. El que en dona més es diu Arthur Phillip. Seguint les seves ordres, es descarreguen dels vaixells tot de coses estranyes i comencen a aixecar allò que un dia serà una ciutat de nom també estranger, Sydney.

En pocs dies arribaran encara deu vaixells més, més de mil persones. Totes estan igual de demacrades després de molts mesos de viatge pel mar. I per a qui no obeeix les ordres de Phillip, el seu repòs a terra són fuetades a la carn viva. Tota la ràbia acumulada es descarrega sobre esquenes nues amb assots de diferents puntes. De vegades alguns surten vius d'aquest tracte. Llavors, aquesta massa de carn viva ha de continuar complint les ordres. Definitivament han arribat els salvatges.

Allò que un dia serà Sydney, allò que ha sigut un recés de pesca generosa des del temps dels avantpassats, és de moment una colònia penitenciària on hi ha una crueltat extrema. Aquesta colònia serà una font d'inspiració per als camps de concentració i per als gulags que es perfeccionaran d'aquí a un segle i mig en el continent d'aquests visitants salvatges.

De la Pérouse. La breu presència francesa

Posar un ordre concret a un caos per entendre la història, per explicar-la: agafar uns caps de corda entortolligats en un manyoc de nusos i seguir-ne els fils fins a adonar-se que és impossible de desenredar, fins a entendre que un tros de corda sol no té sentit si no forma part d'un entramat més gros. Explicar la història, doncs, és entendre'n els nusos, és agafar aquests caps de corda i establir la forma de lligar-los, d'aconseguir que el manyoc sigui un teixit amb el qual es pot treballar fàcilment.

Agafem, per exemple, d'aquesta història australiana, uns quants nusos solts i mirem quin teixit en pot sortir. Aquesta vegada, posarem noms francesos a aquests caps de corda, noms com: Jean-François de Galaup de La Pérouse, Napoleó Bonaparte o Dumont d'Urville. I per no perdre el fil d'aquests caps, als nusos també els posarem alguns noms que ens orientin en aquest laberint. Podem anomenar aquests nusos, per exemple: pingüins, Terra d'Adèlia, ferrocarril o Venus de Milo.

I ja tenim els ingredients d'un manyoc per desentrellar.

Perquè en aquest manyoc complex que és la història, tot està lligat.

En el primer cap de corda que estirem trobem, a l'any 1785, un jove de setze anys que prova d'enrolar-se a una expedició al voltant del món. Aquesta expedició està dirigida per Jean-François de La Pérouse, és especialment ambiciosa i necessita fins a quatre-cents tripulants. Però no és fàcil ser-hi acceptat. Calen mèrits, cal passar uns exàmens, i a aquest aspirant no li ha anat prou bé el de matemàtiques. Així doncs, aquest joveníssim noi, de nom Napoleó Bonaparte, es veurà obligat a continuar a terra i a veure com el seu país fa una revolució per tombar la monarquia abans ell no es pugui autoproclamar emperador algun dia.

Tan fàcil com hauria estat aprovar un examen de matemàtiques.

I mentrestant, l'1 d'agost d'aquell 1785 Jean-François de La Pérouse s'embarca feliçment amb la seva expedició científica de quatre-cents tripulants amb el *Boussole* i l'*Astrolabe* en direcció al cap d'Hornos per passar els anys vinents passejant pel Pacífic, Xile, Hawaii, Alaska, Califòrnia, Taiwan, Corea, el Japó, Kamtxatka...

Per prudència o per zel científic, sempre que pugui, La Pérouse es preocuparà de trametre informació a França. Per això el primer a tornar a França serà l'intèrpret de rus, Barthelémy de Lesseps, que el 1787 serà enviat a casa des de Kamtxatka. Trigarà un any a fer el seu viatge. N'informarà Lluís XVI i veurà una revolució, Però no una revolució qualsevol: una revolució de les grosses. Ningú més d'aquesta expedició de La Pérouse tornarà a França. Mentre a París les coses es comencen a complicar per al cap del rei, el *Boussole* i l'*Astrolabe* continuen el seu periple pels mars del sud. A finals de 1787 es planten a Samoa. Allà, sense saber com estan canviant les coses a França, es troben que és el seu propi cap el que corre perill. Atacats pels habitants locals, fugen cap al primer lloc que els sembla que els mapes indiquen que pot ser un bon refugi. Potser la desconeguda i inexplorada Nova Holanda?

L'expedició de La Pérouse arriba a Botany Bay, Austràlia, el 26 de gener de 1788. Justament, hi arriba la mateixa setmana que hi han arribat els primers vaixells de la Primera Flota anglesa, els *HMS Sirius* i *Supply*. De vegades no estan gens malament els capricis de la història; d'ençà que el món és món aquí només hi havia arribat un vaixell fa disset anys i ara, de sobte, n'hi ha una bona dotzena amb quasi dues mil persones de França i d'Anglaterra. Cap dels dos no sabia res dels altres.

Tot i que la precarietat dels anglesos no els permet ajudar gaire els francesos, la trobada és cordial i els homes de La Pérouse s'estaran en aquesta badia fins al 10 de març. En salpar cap al nord, deixaran encara prou informació i cartes als anglesos perquè les enviïn a París. La Pérouse deixa clar que espera ser de retorn a França el juny de 1789. Cap altre europeu els tornarà a veure mai més.

El *Boussole* i l'*Astrolabe* remunten cap al nord, arriben fins a Tonga, continuen cap a l'oest, i a l'illa de Vanikoro els atrapa una tempesta que els estavella contra uns esculls. Durant mesos, els supervivents conviuran amb els habitants de Vanikoro mentre construeixen una embarcació que els permeti tornar a allò que ells en diuen 'la civilització': el país on estan perfeccionant invents tan exquisidament civilitzats com la guillotina. Quan finalment aquesta embarcació estigui a punt, només dos dels francesos decidiran quedar-se a terra ferma. La resta, novament desapareixen sense deixar cap més rastre.

Però de moment, tot això no ho sap cap europeu.

Per molt inquietant que sigui el silenci en què se submergeix l'expedició francesa d'ençà que abandona Botany Bay, a l'estiu de 1789 a París ningú no té el cap per pensar en expedicions als antípodes. Caldrà esperar encara dos anys abans no es comencin a enviar les primeres expedicions de rescat. Tornaran sempre amb les mans buides. Una d'aquestes expedicions serà la del nostre ja conegut Louis de Freycinet, entre 1817 i 1820. Una altra tindrà entre els seus alts càrrecs Dumont d'Urville i es farà entre 1823 i 1825. Però de moment res. Ni aquests ni els primers no troben cap pista de La Pérouse. Finalment, el 1826 el navegant irlandès Peter Dillon navega per l'arxipèlag de Santa Cruz, a les Salomó. En arribar a l'illa de Tikopia descobreix que els habitants locals tenen objectes que pertanyen a aquella expedició francesa desapareguda. Quan els pregunta d'on els han tret, Dillon aclareix que han arribat a Tikopia provinents del comerç amb l'illa de Vanikoro, que és a pocs dies de navegació. S'obre així la pista per saber el destí de La Pérouse, però Dillon trigarà encara un any a trepitjar Vanikoro.

Quan hi arriba, el 1827, un nadiu li explica que anys enrere una expedició havia naufragat en aquella costa. Li parla de la tempesta, dels esculls de corall, dels morts, de la construcció d'un bot i dels supervivents que van marxar per sempre. Segons el testimoni, dels quatre-cents tripulants, només dos supervivents es van quedar en aquella illa durant anys. Malgrat que aleshores aquells supervivents ja són morts, l'irlandès troba proves prou evidents perquè sàpiga que li estan parlant d'aquella expedició francesa.

Per si encara pogués haver-hi cap dubte, mentre Dillon era a Java provant de trobar la pista de La Pérouse, la notícia ha arribat a França. De seguida, s'organitza també una expedició per resoldre el misteri. L'escollit per a aquesta missió al Pacífic torna a ser el reputat i prestigiós Dumont d'Urville.

Encara que tard, d'Urville arriba a Vanikoro el 1828. Troba les restes del *Boussole* a pocs metres de profunditat sota l'aigua, al mateix punt on aquell dia de tempesta el vaixell va ser queixalat pels esculls de corall que ara són el seu llit. Res que no hagués aclarit Dillon recentment, però la troballa de d'Urville és molt més irrefutable.

Amb tot plegat, queda aclarida la desaparició del *Boussole* i de l'*Astrolabe.* I més encara quan alguns dels objectes que tornaran a França seran identificats per Barthelémy de Lesseps, l'home que el 1787 va deixar l'expedició a Kamtxatka i que va ser a temps de veure la Revolució Francesa, l'únic tripulant de la malaurada expedició que va tornar a casa. Només perquè sabia rus.

Com són les voltes del cabdell de la història... Potser si aquell Napoleó de setze anys hagués tingut més sort en un examen de matemàtiques tot hauria anat diferent. El jove Napoleó difícilment hauria evitat el naufragi i sense ell qui sap com hauria sigut el món... Però en fi, la realitat és la que és. Els fets són irreversibles.

D'Urville. Els viatges dels noms

Els fets són irreversibles, però, en canvi, podem entreteixir els nusos de la història de mil maneres diferents. Tot es lliga a tot. Només cal trobar el camí en aquest laberint. Potser és cert que qui entra en un laberint no busca la sortida, sinó la seva Ariadna.

Ara que en aquest laberint hem entrat als passadissos de d'Urville, mirem de continuar fins al final. Tot porta a algun lloc. Darrere de cada cantonada hi ha una resposta, una nova pregunta. I amb d'Urville podem seguir, per exemple, el laberint dels noms. Quantes voltes ha fet la vida abans de deixar un nom a lloc? Quantes voltes han d'haver fet els noms abans d'arribar al seu objecte?

Què tal si fem un petit canvi de rumb?

Potser, cap a la mare de tots els laberints, cap a l'antiga Grècia...

Si obrim un moment aquesta porta, descobrirem que sense la Venus de Milo, probablement d'Urville no hauria trobat les restes del *Boussole* a Vanikoro, ni la terra d'Adèlia a l'Antàrtida, ni tampoc els pingüins d'Adèlia tindrien aquest nom.

Un dia de 1820, a l'illa de Milo, el pagès Giorgos Kentrotas està traient pedres d'unes ruïnes que hi ha al seu terreny per construir un mur. Per fer aquest mur li han servit unes pedres antigues, de molts de segles. Algunes li van molt bé, però algunes altres tenen formes d'allò més empipadores i inútils. Aquell dia, Kentrotas en treu una d'aquestes. Es tracta d'una Afrodita de dos metres d'alçada tallada en marbre. És veritat que no li servirà per al que volia, però de seguida té clar que la troballa és sensacional i que en traurà un bon profit si la sap vendre bé.

Guarda l'estàtua durant uns dies en un seu estable. Finalment, Kentrotas troba el millor postor. Ven la seva Afrodita i el comprador l'embarca cap a Turquia. Però, a l'últim moment, l'oficial de marina francès Jules Sebastien-Cesar Dumont d'Urville aconsegueix que l'ambaixador del seu país pagui més car per aquesta estàtua que el comprador turc. De manera que a l'últim minut la Venus de Milo és enviada cap a França. És així com arriba al Louvre, molt més lluny del lloc on va ser trobada que si hagués anat a Turquia, però potser també més a l'abast de molta gent.

Si cada petit gest ens canvia la vida, què no hem de dir de tenir el mèrit de «trobar» una Venus de Milo i fer-la arribar al teu país? Sobretot en aquell temps en què l'espoli patrimonial era més un mèrit que un robatori.

No és impensable, doncs, que aquest primer episodi memorable catapultés la carrera de Dumont d'Urville. Començarà una important carrera navegant per mars inexplorats, sobretot per l'hemisferi sud, on anirà donant noms als nous llocs que posarà als mapes. Batejar una terra deu ser un compromís delicat. De vegades cal triar: el teu nom, el d'un mecenes, el d'un rei, el d'un tripulant, el d'una persona estimada... la família sobretot.

D'Urville és un home amb fama de malcarat i arrogant. Potser és per això que en triar noms no té por de pensar en la seva gent més propera abans que en reis i mecenes. D'alguna manera sembla dir-nos que les seves persones estimades són per sobre de tot. I així, deixant noms de parents per la geografia del Pacífic sud, l'any 1841 arriba fins i tot a desembarcar a l'Antàrtida, d'on tornarà també feliçment després de donar el nom de la seva esposa Adèle a una terra i a uns pingüins. I és que, malgrat el seu caràcter sever, d'Urville no oblida que es deu a qui l'espera a casa amb ansietat i patiment, i si té la possibilitat de deixar un nom a la posteritat, quin millor que el de la seva estimada Adèle? I vet aquí, doncs, que potser la terra d'Adèlia i els pingüins d'Adèlia deuen el nom a un escultor grec de dos mil anys enrere, i al mur que volia construir Giorgos Kentrotas, i també, és clar, als motius que tenien els sogres de Dumont d'Urville per donar el nom d'Adèle a la seva filla, i...

Qui sap quantes voltes ha de fer el món perquè un nom aterri en un lloc. De les mans d'un escultor grec fins a l'Antàrtida.

Però Dumont d'Urville encara haurà de viure un altre viatge molt més senzill i curt. Serà un viatge recordat tristament. L'afectarà a ell i la seva família. L'any després del seu viatge a l'Antàrtida, el 8 de maig de 1842, els d'Urville van a unes celebracions multitudinàries a Versalles. En acabar els actes, com gran part dels assistents, agafen un tren cap a París. Hi ha coses que no avisen: descarrilament, incendi, tragèdia en el primer accident de tren de França. Entre les desenes de morts, també Dumont d'Urville, la seva esposa i el seu fill.

No heu seguit mai els camins d'una vida? Es trien uns episodis com si fossin cruïlles i sembla que... Un antic escultor grec. Un pagès fent un mur al seu terreny. Un pingüí. Un nom a l'Antàrtida. Un accident de tren...

Mary Bryant

Tancat el parèntesi dels noms, tornem enrere en el nostre laberint i anem de nou cap a aquella Austràlia on de moment tenim encara molta costa per descobrir. Més al nord de la cruelíssima colònia penitenciària de Botany Bay, no es coneix res de la costa australiana. Probablement aquelles latituds només hagin sigut navegades per La Pérouse, i per tant encara ningú no ha sortit d'allà per explicar res d'aquell racó al món.

Aquest cop, qui primer ens en pot dir alguna cosa és una dona anomenada Mary Bryant.

Nascuda en una família de pescadors el 1765 a Fowey, Cornualla, Mary Broad ingressa a la presó el 1786 per haver robat una capa de seda i unes quantes monedes. En un primer moment, el desbordat sistema judicial britànic la condemna a mort, però més endavant li commuten la pena a canvi de set anys de desterrament penitenciari a Austràlia, cosa que en alguns casos serà pitjor que la rapidesa de la forca. En el cas de la jove Mary Broad, però, suposarà tot un seguit de peripècies de les quals es parlarà molt de temps a l'Anglaterra de l'època.

En els seus primers temps de presidi, encara a Anglaterra, Mary Broad coincideix amb el seu futur marit, William Bryant, que també formarà part de la *Primera Flota* de convictes australians. Austràlia en aquell moment no és més que el nom vaporós d'un lloc remot i desconegut, visitat un dia de 1770 per James Cook. Res més. Amb això, ser-hi desterrat vol dir, a la pràctica, no tornar mai més. Ja hem vist, a més, com va ser aquell primer viatge. Durant setmanes, els onze vaixells que formaran la flota esperen al Tàmesi, mentre s'emplenen de presos i preses. Hi sobreviuen en condicions infrahumanes. A la manca d'espai, s'hi suma la insalubritat del lloc, la immobilitat i ferides que provoquen els grillons, la desnutrició, el fred, la humitat, la foscor... Res que no sigui habitual a totes les presons angleses de l'època, és veritat, però en aquest cas s'afegeix també la tortura psicològica pel viatge imprecís sense retorn, que ha de començar ningú no sap quan.

I per fi, després d'aquesta agònica espera, la flota salpa el 13 de maig de 1787 i arriba a Port Jackson, Botany Bay, el 20 de gener de 1788. Per a Mary Broad i William Bryant han sigut vuit mesos més de confinament al *Charlotte*, un buc mercant de 345 tones amb un centenar llarg de persones, cosa que correspon a unes tres tones de vaixell per cadascú. Quasi res. L'atapeïment és total. Durant el viatge, a més, Mary ha tingut una filla. Es dirà Charlotte Bryant, l'han batejada triant el nom del vaixell on ha passat el periple. Portarà el cognom del que és oficialment el seu pare, tot i que —tenint en compte les condicions en què estaven confinats abans de deixar Londres— difícilment William sigui el pare biològic de la criatura.

Després d'un viatge no gaire diferent del dels esclaus africans enviats a Amèrica, els components de la flota troben a Austràlia un món absolutament desconegut i hostil, on cal començar de zero en el sentit més absolut de la paraula. Quan els reus baixen dels vaixells i toquen terra per primer cop en molts mesos, amb prou feines si poden aguantar-se drets, però no hi ha ni un minut de descans. Tal com arriben han de començar la feina de convertir aquest lloc perdut i desconegut en un espai habitable.

Evidentment no troben ningú que els esperi. No tenen més roba que la que porten posada des de qui sap quan, no tenen més aliments que el que van aprovisionar a Ciutat del Cap i el bestiar que arriba viu. Amb prou feines tenen les eines ni els coneixements mínims per sobreviure. A més a més, entre els integrants d'aquesta Primera Flota pràcticament no hi ha pagesos, ni pescadors (William Bryant és l'únic que podem afirmar que ho era), ni fusters, ni constructors... Aquí els únics que semblen experts en alguna cosa són els vigilants que imposen unes condicions de vida draconianes a base de fuetades.

Després d'uns dies de feina per construir les primeres cabanes i per plantar tendes de la nova colònia, el 6 de febrer es desembarquen les dones, i el dia 10, tot just quatre dies després d'haver tocat terra, Mary es casa amb William celebrant el que probablement sigui el primer casament australià de la història. D'aquest matrimoni naixerà encara un altre nen l'abril de 1790, al cap doncs, d'un parell d'anys. Es dirà Emanuel. Però malgrat formar una família, no hi ha res més lluny del que es podria dir que és una vida feliç. Des del moment que arriben a Port Jackson comencen uns anys encara més penosos per a la majoria de deportats.

Gràcies al seu ofici de pescador, William és destinat de seguida a responsabilitzar-se dels bots que estiren les xarxes de pesca que instal·len al moll. Però aquí la vida no és fàcil. Al cap d'un temps és castigat amb cent fuetades per robar peix i vendre'l al mercat negre de la colònia. A partir d'aquest moment, té pressa a portar a cap el seu pla de fuga. El pla passa per aprofitar el seu accés als bots.

Naturalment, ningú no tem que algú s'escapi en bot en un lloc tan remot com aquest. És tan desconeguda la geografia que els envolta, que de moment els únics intents que hi ha hagut han sigut per terra. Potser els que han fugit ho han fet amb l'esperança que sigui certa la llegenda segons la qual caminant cap al nord s'arriba a la Xina en poc temps. I malgrat tot, de moment qualsevol intent de fuga acaba sempre amb la mort, la desaparició o el retorn de cossos esquelètics menjats per la fam i la set.

Però el desconeixement geogràfic dels convictes potser no és tan considerable com voldrà fer creure la llegenda difosa sobretot per les autoritats. En aquesta petita comunitat aïllada hi ha gent de mar. A poc a poc van circulant idees més exactes sobre el lloc on es troben. S'aprofita sobretot qualsevol oportunitat per recollir qualsevol dada útil sobre l'entorn. Quan l'octubre de 1790 el mercant holandès *Waaksamheyd* atraca a la colònia, William aconsegueix que el seu capità Detmer Smit li doni una brúixola, un quadrant, armes i una carta marítima que els dona la pista cap a la colònia holandesa de Timor. Amaga aquests tresors sota els taulons del terra de la seva barraca i comença a preparar a consciència el seu pla. La costa australiana és encara un entorn desconegut i inexplorat, però el contorn del continent i les rutes per vorejar-lo comencen a estar dibuixats.

Durant mesos, William es dedica a reclutar una petita tripulació que prepara a consciència tots els detalls Aconsegueixen amagar eines, armes, municions, roba, estris de pesca i provisions. Sabent la facilitat amb què els oficials fan anar el fuet, és evident que corren un risc enorme, però saben què estan fent. De cap altra manera no haurien pogut planificar tot aquest muntatge i dur-lo a terme sense que ningú no sospités.

Un cop tot és a punt, només cal esperar pacientment el moment adequat. Arriba el 28 de març de 1791. Aquest dia, l'únic vaixell que hi havia a Port Jackson, el *Supply*, ha marxat a avituallar la molt més infernal colònia de l'illa de Norfolk. No hi ha, doncs, cap vaixell que pugui sortir a perseguir cap fugitiu. Aquesta nit, doncs, la família Bryant i set presidiaris més s'esquitllen cap al port i agafen la xalupa de sis rems del governador.

Són onze persones: nou adults i dues criatures. Emanuel només té onze mesos. Hi ha el risc que es posi a plorar o que deixi anar qualsevol so que els delati, però finalment, en el silenci més absolut, aconsegueixen allunyar-se prou de la costa sense que el vigilant nocturn senti ni tan sols una palada de rems.

Amb els quatre membres de la família Bryant, hi ha William Morton, Samuel Bird (àlies John Simms), James Cox (àlies Rolt), William Allen, Nathaniel Lillie, Samuel Broom (àlies John Butcher) i James Martin. Aquest és el grup de fugitius que ara mateix està embarcant i està començant una aventura de dimensions imprevisibles.

Segons la versió que ens deixarà James Martin d'aquest viatge, dos dies després d'haver iniciat la fugida, resseguint sempre la costa cap al nord, els fugitius tenen un primer contacte amb habitants de la zona en un punt indeterminat on s'aturen i on, entre altres coses, es proveeixen d'aliments i de carbó. Aquí —uns dos graus al nord de Port Jackson— passaran dues nits i un dia sencer, temps durant el qual reben la visita d'un grup de nadius. Aquesta primera trobada és pacífica i el grup de curiosos acaba marxant tranquil·lament amb alguns objectes que els visitants els donen com a mostra de bones intencions. A més a més, de passada, es converteixen en els primers a descobrir carbó a Austràlia, notícia que, escampada per aquests fugitius, arribarà abans a Europa que a la mateixa colònia acabada de fundar.

Després d'aquest primer descans en aquest lloc desconegut que anomenen Fortunate Creek, els fugitius continuen el seu camí cap al nord. Però no tot el viatge serà així de plàcid. Les properes trobades amb habitants locals ja no seran sempre tan pacífiques. D'aquí cap endavant, allà on trepitgin terra els esperen tot un seguit de contactes imprevisibles. A vegades, són pacífics, altres violents, i per descomptat, els fugitius passen per un periple de constant cansament, fam, set i fred. Sovint durant llargues setmanes no poden abandonar la barca, remen dia i nit, amb bonança sota sols abrusadors i amb tempesta sobre la negror d'ones enfurismades, sense ni un sol foc, ni un sostre, ni un tros de roba eixuta, sempre a força de braços i al límit del naufragi, traient l'aigua i, quan cal, llençant tot el que es pugui per alleugerir el llast. I no poden fer res de tot això sense que de tant en tant hi hagi les tensions inevitables d'un grup que porta al límit el patiment i la incertesa.

Encara que alguns primers europeus han començat tot just a vorejar aquestes costes en grans naus, és segur que aquests fugitius són els primers estrangers a posar-hi els peus. També són els primers a descriure-la i a posar-ne alguns detalls als mapes. Però la seva exploració no és una exploració apassionada, sinó que és una anguniosa fugida cap a la mort, remant contra uns corrents que sovint s'entesten a enviar-los mar endins. En aquestes condicions, només de vegades el repòs pot arribar a ser serè en un redós deshabitat, però amb aigua dolça i aliment. Altres vegades l'aturada sembla un allargament més de l'agonia: alguns cops és per adobar el bot. S'aturen en un illot erm i sorrenc durant dies... De moment, són lluny de cap llibertat, només han fugit d'una crueltat infernal, però els queda massa camí per fer.

Només amb grans esforços i sense saber massa bé on són, aconsegueixen finalment arribar al llunyà extrem nord del continent, superen el cap de York, travessen l'estret de Torres i entren al golf de Carpentària encarant rumb a l'oest cap a Timor. Però encara no veuen la salvació a prop seu. També en aquest nou mar tornen a ser perseguits per canoes de nadius. Els llancen fletxes. Ells disparen amb mosquets mentre hissen les precàries veles i fugen tan de pressa com poden.

Perseguits aquí i allà, avancen encara centenars de milles més sense repòs fins que es troben al mar de Timor. Semblava impossible, però ja gairebé ho hauran aconseguit. I així, una nit, fugint d'un onatge que amenaça trencar les seves aspiracions de llibertat a l'últim moment, posen rumb cap al nord i per primera vegada en molt de temps comencen a allunyar-se d'aquest continent interminable. Un dia i mig després de deixar-lo enrere, finalment arriben a l'assentament holandès de Kupang. Aquell 5 de juny de 1791 deixen enrere cinc mil quilòmetres i seixanta-sis dies de fugida. De seguida està dit.

Fins i tot a hores d'ara, el seu periple és impressionant. Després d'haver salpat d'Anglaterra, la Primera Flota havia fet escala al Brasil i a l'Àfrica del Sud; Austràlia havia sigut el quart continent que rebia aquests fugitius. Àsia és el cinquè. Però haver arribat fins aquí no és encara cap garantia de llibertat. Com que no deixen de ser uns fugitius, de moment a Kupang es fan passar per supervivents d'un naufragi. Les autoritats holandeses de l'illa els proporcionen aliments i roba i els allotgen mentre esperen un vaixell que els podrà tornar a Anglaterra. Molt probablement aquests siguin els millors dos mesos de la seva vida. Però un dia, després d'una discussió familiar, possiblement sota els efectes de l'alcohol, William es denuncia a ell mateix i denuncia la resta de fugitius al governador. Els empresonen de seguida.

En aquests moments encara és recent el famós cas del motí del *Bounty*, que va acabar amb un grup d'homes abandonats a alta mar fent un viatge semblant per les mateixes latituds entre Tahiti i el mateix Timor. L'amotinat *Bounty* ha estat perseguit durant mesos pel *Pandora*, capitanejat per Edward Edwards. I precisament en aquestes dates, després d'empresonar els amotinats, el mateix *Pandora* acaba naufragant als esculls de corall, de manera que de sobte arriben a Kupang cent vint dels seus homes en condicions semblants a les dels Bryant.

No podria ser més inoportú. El mateix Edwards, que ara es troba a Kupang, es fa càrrec dels fugitius i se'ls emporta encadenats cap a Batàvia, on William Bryant i el petit Emanuel d'un any i mig moren arran d'unes febres fortíssimes a finals d'aquest mateix any. D'allà són portats cap a Ciutat del Cap, En aquest trajecte moren Morton, Bird i Cox. En arribar a aquesta ciutat, sense saber-ho ni voler-ho —els supervivents— Mary, Charlotte, Martin, Allen, Lillie i Broom, tanquen un viatge circular al voltant d'Austràlia un segle i mig després que ja ho fes Abel Tasman —també sense saber-ho—, i deu anys abans que Flinders completi aquesta circumnavegació com si fos el primer. I ignorant aquest estrany honor des d'aquí el grup és embarcat ja cap a Anglaterra. Però durant la travessia, a principis de maig de 1792, encara perd la vida Charlotte després de quatre duríssims anys de vida; nascuda en el viatge d'anada i morta en el de tornada en condicions semblants.

Així retorna Mary a Anglaterra. Ha vist morir en poc temps tota la família que ha format durant aquests anys de tortura. Es veu un altre cop condemnada a un presidi que s'augura tan terrorífic com l'anterior. Però aquesta vegada tindrà la sort al seu costat: Mary Bryant no serà una oblidada més. La història del seu periple ha estat publicada a tots els diaris, tothom parla d'ella, el clamor popular pressiona perquè el govern l'alliberi. Finalment, és alliberada el març de 1793. En el novembre d'aquest mateix any són igualment alliberats Martin, Allen i Broom.

D'aquesta manera, el març de 1793, Mary Bryant es converteix en la primera persona deportada que s'escapa de la llunyana Austràlia i que recupera la llibertat. I amb aquesta nova llibertat acabada d'estrenar, se'n torna a la seva Cornualla natal i desapareix de la vida pública per sempre més.

Tot per una capa de seda i un grapat de monedes que en l'Anglaterra d'aquells anys ningú no devia robar per gust.

Segle XIX. Dibuixa i pinta el teu continent

En el nostre viatge a través del temps australià, arribem a allò que els forasters en diem el segle XIX. Durant els primers segles, aquests blancs que venen de l'altra banda del món han fet poc més que trobar aquesta terra, fer-hi un cop d'ull per constatar que aquí no hi ha res que els sembla que valgui la pena i marxar-ne. Només molt recentment alguns, molt pocs, a poc a poc, han començat a quedar-s'hi. Però aquí tot és lent com els mil·lennis al costat dels segles, i no serà fins aquest segle XIX que aquells estranys començaran a conèixer la forma i el cor d'aquest antiquíssim món que, ara sí, voldran que sigui seu.

De moment, els mapes dels europeus estan posant noms a cadascun dels retalls que van descobrint en aquestes costes. Són tan lluny uns dels altres que es fa difícil creure que són en una mateixa illa. Comença a ser imprescindible, doncs, que algú dibuixi el contorn complet d'Austràlia per tal de saber de què estem parlant. Això és el que farà Matthew Flinders entre el desembre de 1801 i el juny de 1803, quan dirigeix la suposada primera circumnavegació d'Austràlia. Amb permís, és clar, d'Abel Tasman i de Mary Bryant, o de la seva petita Charlotte Bryant, que hi va dedicar tota la seva curta vida.

A bord de l'*Investigator*, durant un any i mig, Flinders en descobreix la forma i en dibuixa els contorns. Acaba demostrant que les costes de Nova Holanda i Nova Gal·les del Sud no són dues grans illes, sinó un sol continent, cosa que fins ara els blancs no sabien clarament. Així, és Flinders qui, l'any 1814, posarà definitivament als mapes per a tot aquest vast territori el nom d'Austràlia, un nom que Quirós ja havia inventat dos segles abans, quan encara era molt lluny d'aquesta illa.

Ja tenim un nou continent dibuixat als mapes. Finalment, en sabem els contorns. Matthew Flinders ha donat forma i nom a Austràlia, ara ja només ens queda poder-lo pintar d'algun color. Ha arribat el moment d'aventurar-se a anar illa endins. La grandiositat dels contorns d'aquest nou continent inexplorat fa suposar que a l'interior d'aquesta illa poden haver-hi terres riques en recursos. Només cal saber a on i quins recursos hi haurà en aquest descomunal tros de món. Així es podrà decidir si es pinta el mapa amb el color verd de les selves i els prats per a pastures, amb el blanc de les neus de grans serralades o amb el blau de mars interiors rics en pesca... Sí, el blau sembla un color prometedor per a aquests estrangers vinguts de mar enllà. Potser la immensa sequedat rogenca del continent continua essent inconcebible per a aquests europeus acabats d'arribar embafats de blau. Encara durant molts anys continuaran explorant els rius i s'endinsaran fins més enllà de les seves capçaleres convençuts que hi ha d'haver un gran mar interior que alimenti els rius en algun lloc d'aquesta vastitud rogenca.

Explorar mars interiors és un repte complicat, sobretot si només són suposats i la idea és arribar-hi i posar-s'hi a navegar el mateix dia que es descobreixen. Potser seria més fàcil trobar-ne primer les costes i després saber cap a on s'ha d'enviar una flota per començar-hi a navegar. Però de sobte aquests europeus tenen pressa. Ara ho volen tot de cop.

Deu ser per això que el 1835 l'explorador Thomas Mitchell s'emporta dos petits baleners cap a l'interior del continent. Aquesta cop, els membres de l'expedició de Mitchell tindran la idea de batejar les seves discretes embarcacions amb els noms de *Discovery* i *Resolution*, en honor a James Cook. Però aquests modestos *Discovery* i *Resolution* estan molt lluny de poder navegar com els vaixells de Cook. A més, faran el seu recorregut en carro i tornaran després d'haver fet milers de quilòmetres damunt la sorra. Han tocat l'aigua molt pocs cops. Segur que els nadius que van trobar al desert van quedar astorats de veure homes blancs, i encara més, de veure els animals que els acompanyaven i les armes de foc que tenien. Però potser el que van trobar més estrany va ser veure aquelles absurdes canoes que arrossegaven pel desert.

Tanmateix, Mitchell no va ser el primer a tenir aquesta idea. Abans d'ell, el 1828, Charles Sturt també es va emportar una embarcació de vela cap al desert inconegut. Com ja podem suposar, com més s'endinsava en el territori, més sec el trobava i, consegüentment, més absurd se li feia portar aquella càrrega. Però estava tan convençut que acabaria trobant aigua que Sturt ho va continuar provant encara durant molts anys. Després de diferents intents fallits, l'any 1844, Sturt va tornar a buscar els suposats mars interiors sortint d'Adelaide i anant cap al nord. Aquest cop, la seva expedició va arribar a endinsar-se uns quants centenars de quilòmetres. Tanmateix no van aconseguir arribar fins al que avui és el desert de Simpson, punt on Sturt esperava trobar el seu anhelat mar interior. En el mes de gener de 1846, l'expedició va tornar amb Sturt pràcticament cec i malalt d'escorbut. Va haver de reconèixer que, a banda d'un sistema de llacs que cada pocs anys s'omplen d'aigua, l'únic mar interior que hi ha a Austràlia és de sorra.

Un cop assumit que aquest continent és un gran oceà de sorra i que, per tant calia pintar en els mapes l'interior d'Austràlia amb els colors groc, taronja o vermell, els europeus comencen a anar-hi havent descartat la il·lusió que hi podrien navegar. No obstant i això, a vegades també hi fracassaran sense deixar cap rastre. D'entre tots els fracassos que s'emportarà el desert australià, n'hi haurà de més o menys memorables i misteriosos. Un d'aquests fracassos és el cas de l'expedició de l'alemany Ludwig Leichhardt, quan el 1848 prova de travessar el continent d'est a oest. Aquell any, Leichhardt i sis homes més, acompanyats d'un gran ramat i ben proveïts de provisions, s'internen cap a l'oest. Però desapareixen en els mateixos dies que Anglaterra sencera està pendent del que passa a l'Àrtic, on Franklin ha desaparegut. L'expedició de Leichhardt també es fon al cor d'Austràlia sense deixar pràcticament cap rastre. Només molts anys més tard es trobaran indicis de llocs per on van poder haver passat aquests blancs, però el misteri de Leichhardt quedarà sempre molt menys resolt que el de Franklin. I això és més sorprenent encara si es té present que la terra ferma no engoleix com fa el mar. Però potser sigui que buscar una expedició alemanya al desert australià no és tan espectacular com buscar-ne una d'anglesa a l'Àrtic. I menys si no hi ha una llegenda que parli de canibalisme i una Lady Jane que vulgui salvar l'honor del seu marit.

Si el desert australià fos d'aigua o de gel, o si Leichhardt tingués l'aparell mediàtic de Franklin, potser encara se n'hauria parlat més. Però aquesta terra té alguna cosa que convida a l'oblit. Pocs recorden que el matrimoni Franklin ha estat també entre els pioners de l'exploració australiana. El 1801, amb només quinze anys, Franklin ja s'havia enrolat com a guàrdia marina a les ordres del seu oncle Matthew Flinders en la circumnavegació del continent. I anys més tard, el 1837, esdevindrà tinent governador de la Terra de Van Diemen, l'actual Tasmània (o la Lutruwita de sempre per als seus habitants). Durant aquests anys, el matrimoni Franklin participa en algunes de les exploracions a Tasmània i al sud del continent, però la seva aventura australiana s'acabarà el 1843 per tornar a Anglaterra, on es posarà al capdavant del seu definitiu i fatídic projecte àrtic. Qui sap si hauria acabat com Leichhardt si s'hagués quedat navegant per aquests deserts australs...

Sigui com sigui, la qüestió és que a poc a poc l'interior del continent comença a deixar de ser un secret. Aviat aquella lentitud mil·lenària s'accelera. John McDouall Stuart es planta al centre geogràfic australià sense trobar res més que desert i més desert: definitivament, no hi ha cap mar interior. I tot just l'any següent, Robert O'Hara Burke, William Wills, Charles Gray i John King aconsegueixen ser els primers forasters que travessen el continent de sud a nord, però només King sobreviurà al viatge de retorn... Sí, tot s'accelera en aquest trepidant món dels blancs, que s'atropellen amb les seves presses, que no pregunten res i que es perden sense acabar d'entendre on s'estan posant... Com tants altres europeus... Potser si escoltessin i aprenguessin dels aborígens que s'hi mouen des de fa milers d'anys, potser si aquests blancs coneguessin les línies de cançons, no se n'hi perdrien tants.

Però les línies de cançons no surten als llibres d'aquests forasters; i no han vingut aquí a escoltar.

Al final del camí més llarg

Yuwali

Als disset anys, la jove Yuwali es troba vivint al desert, com sempre ha fet la seva gent, els Martu. Caminar a la recerca d'aigua i aliment: així és la vida al desert per a aquesta vintena de dones i criatures a qui la mala sort ha deixat sense homes al grup. I així es troben, més soles que mai en aquests temps difícils en què ja gairebé no queda ningú al desert.

Un dia, tornant de caçar, Yuwali veu que al campament hi ha el que li sembla una roca que es mou: són uns homes estranys, amb plats al cap i de pell blanca, com si els haguessin pelat com un dingo quan el cuines. Sense cap mena de dubte són diables caníbals, la seva presència terrorífica ho fa pensar. Mortes de por les noies decideixen esperar amagades fins que aquests visitants del més enllà se'n vagin. No serà fins a la nit, que el gran monstre marxarà, rugint i ensenyant els seus grans ulls lluminosos. Aleshores Yuwali i la seva gent entenen que cal fugir.

Durant els dies vinents, fugiran sense cap altra idea que la de no ser menjades pels diables blancs. No pararan de preguntar-se angoixades per què aquests blancs han vingut al seu país. Però això només ho saben ells, aquests diables blancs que del seu temps en diuen 1964, i d'aquesta terra, *Great Sandy Desert* (el Gran Desert Sorrenc). Només ells saben que aquesta zona és la que han escollit perquè hi caigui el *Blue Streak*, un potent míssil en proves. Per això aquests diables blancs persegueixen aquesta gent, per treure'ls d'allà i salvar-los... de la destrucció que hi portaran. Que ho entengui qui pugui.

Però aquest grup de dones i criatures Martu no saben res de tot això. Fugen amb raó d'un món que de sobte ha deixat de ser el seu. Durant tres dies fugen, i durant tres dies són perseguides pel monstre, fins que el grup és finalment localitzat, atrapat... «salvat» caldria dir?

Quantes històries deuen ser semblants? Els diables blancs et troben, et posen als seus vehicles, et donen roba (sempre el primer que et donen és roba, els blancs no suporten la pell nua). Després, et porten a les seves missions i et diuen que t'oblidis de tornar al desert, que allà ja no hi ha ningú, que tots són aquí.

És així com a poc a poc, als ulls d'aquest nou món de pell emblanquinada, van apareixent els últims nòmades australians, aquells que tanquen la porta de la història més llarga de la humanitat i que ara es veuen obligats a llençar la clau darrere seu, sense que ningú no la pugui tornar a trobar mai més.

El grup de Yuwali és un d'aquests grups que amb la seva desaparició tanquen mil·lennis d'història.

Gairebé podríem dir que els últims del desert, com els primers del temps dels somnis, són els únics que tenen nom. Els extrems d'una llarga corda són els únics punts identificables per ells mateixos. Per als punts del mig, en canvi, la corda és un continu etern amb unes puntes impensables.

Yatungka i Warri

Continuant el nostre viatge a través d'aquest final de viatge aborigen, haurem de fer una inevitable visita al desert de Gibson, considerat una de les zones més àrides i inhòspites del planeta. És aquí on trobarem una parella del poble Mandildjara que veurà immortalitzada la seva història en el llibre *The last of the nomads* (W. J. Peasley, 1983). Gràcies a aquest llibre,

Yatungka (ella) i Warri (ell) són considerats els últims aborígens que fan una vida tradicional. Però la seva història, a banda de ser un final de moltes coses, per ella sola és també digna de ser escoltada.

Nascuts en allò que en diem principis del segle xx, Yatungka i Warri es van enamorar des de ben joves, però des del primer dia sabien que el seu amor no seria recórrer un camí fàcil. Privats de casar-se segons les seves lleis, cap a finals dels anys 1930 decideixen fugir dels seus grups i anar a viure junts al desert, on estaran lluny de cap contacte humà durant més de quaranta anys.

Viuen lluny de tot, espantats, fugint de les lleis que vulneren el seu amor. Fugen, doncs, per amor i mantenen el seu estil de vida tradicional en aquesta seva terra cada cop més deshabitada. Viuran quaranta anys al desert totalment sols, temps durant el qual tindran tres fills. Dos els sobreviuran i tard o d'hora acabaran marxant cap a Wiluna —on hi ha la gent que ha abandonat el nomadisme—, decidits a fer una família, però Warri i Yatungka continuaran la seva eterna fugida al desert.

I allà haurien seguit fins al final dels seus dies si no fos per una continuada sequera que els deixa pràcticament sense opcions de sobreviure. Són aleshores, l'any 1977, una parella d'ancians que està sobrevivint a tres anys de sequera en el desert més cru del planeta. Alguna cosa deuen saber.

Però no sembla que aquesta sequera tingui aturador. Finalment, aquell 1977, la gent gran del grup establert a Wiluna pateix tant pels nòmades que organitza una expedició per anar-los a buscar. Quaranta anys no és prou temps per oblidar ningú o per dubtar que continuïn vius. Així doncs, durant molts dies, els seus vells amics i parents busquen senyals de vida en el desert. No és fàcil trobar rastres de dues úniques persones en una immensitat com aquesta, però de bassa en bassa els seus vells parents encara saben prou bé quines rutes poden haver seguit. La recerca és cada cop més desesperada, tots els punts d'aigua són secs. Aviat sembla impossible que hagin pogut resistir en aquest entorn.

Gairebé se'ls dona per morts quan, finalment, en l'últim dels llocs possibles, potser a l'últim dia, algú descobreix un rastre de fum a la llunyania. No pot ser ningú més en aquesta immensitat inhòspita. Troben Yatungka i Warri sense menjar, desnodrits i en un estat de salut que els dificulta caçar.

Aleshores, sense altra opció i per primer cop en quaranta anys, accepten tornar amb la seva gent i retrobar-se també amb els seus fills. Malgrat tot, continuen tenint la mateixa por que el primer dia, el seu esperit és encara el mateix i encara pensen que seran castigats a causa del seu amor prohibit. Els vells amics, però, els han perdonat. Finalment, ells estan d'acord a ser portats amb els seus a Wiluna.

En aquest assentament s'establiran, per primer vegada junts, Yatungka i Warri. Aquí viuran els gairebé dos anys que els queden de vida. Moriran el 1979, en poques setmanes de diferència. Warri morirà el 28 d'abril. A partir d'aquell dia, Yatungka s'abandona fins que mor també el 23 de maig. Són enterrats de costat, tal com potser haurien volgut, però apartats de la terra on van viure i on van ser ells mateixos.

Com tants altres enamorats del món, Warri i Yatungka han sigut comparats a Romeu i Julieta. Però l'amor d'aquests dos vells australians va més enllà que el d'aquells enamorats venecians. Perdonats, després d'haver desobeït les lleis ancestrals i després d'haver compartit quaranta anys de fugida al desert, Yatungka i Warri moren gairebé a la vegada per acabar sent enterrats ben a la vora un de l'altre. Gairebé fan el mateix que Filemó i Baucis, aquells vellets a qui Zeus premiava la seva humilitat concedint-los el desig de viure, patir i morir junts per amor. Només que aquest Romeu-Filemó que és Warri i aquesta Julieta-Baucis que és Yatungka són reals.

Si fossin europeus de l'antiguitat, els llibres encara n'anirien plens.

Els Pintupi Nou

El món ha canviat per no tornar enrere. La vida tradicional s'acaba i el desert ha deixat de ser una llar on viure. Ja només podem trobar les últimes petges que algú hi deixarà, com les de Warri i Yatungka, que, malgrat tot i gràcies a la lletra escrita d'un blanc, s'emporten la llegenda de ser els últims nòmades del món. Però no són tampoc encara els darrers del tot.

Quan Warri i Yatungka ja portaven anys al desert, i després de segles de persecució i extermini, als anys 50 del segle XX el govern australià intensifica la sedentarització dels últims aborígens que encara mantenen una vida tradicional. En els anys següents, igual com passa en molts altres grups, molts dels Pintupi deixen definitivament la vida nòmada per establir-se en missions properes a Alice Springs, al ressec cor del continent.

Entre aquests Pintupi, però, hi ha una família que en comptes de seguir el camí de la majoria, romandrà desapareguda en el desert i no tornarà a ser localitzada altra vegada fins molts anys més tard. Així, quan els nou membres d'aquesta família, els «Pintupi Nou», siguin trobats el 1984, es convertiran en uns dels últims grups que contacten amb la resta del món; els últims a tenir el món per a ells sols.

Aquell any, el grup està format per dues germanes (Papalya Nangala i Nanu Nangala) de menys de quaranta anys i els seus set fills, tots del mateix pare, entre els dotze i vint-i-sis anys (les noies Takariya Napaltjarri, Yalti i Yukultji Napangati, i els nois Piyiti, Tamayinya, Walala i Warlimpirrnga Tjapaltjarri). En aquelles dates, Yukultji, que té dotze anys i que és la més jove de la família, és potser l'última persona del continent nascuda en el nomadisme. Per a ella, la vida consisteix a moure's d'una bassa a l'altra, sovint caminant desenes de quilòmetres cada dia; a desplaçar-se sempre a la recerca d'aigua, i si no en troben, a caçar goannes, una mena de llangardaix, del qual beuen la sang. I la vida també és caminar a la recerca d'altra gent, sobretot de la resta de la família, en un temps en què tothom sembla haver-se evaporat del desert misteriosament.

De vegades, en aquests mons gairebé aturats, els grans canvis acostumen a venir molt de sobte i sense avisar. Després d'anys estranyant-se de no trobar altra gent al desert, un dia senten l'olor d'unes persones. Veuen fum a uns dos quilòmetres d'on són. S'hi acosten i troben un campament amb altres Pintupi. Són Pinta Pinta i el seu fill Matthew, que han arribat fins aquí amb cotxe des de l'assentament de Kiwirrkurra, on els altres Pintupi de la família estan establerts, a uns cinquanta quilòmetres de distància. Warlimpirrnga, un dels fills grans del grup nòmada, s'acosta a aquests desconeguts per demanar-los aigua, però la situació és confusa i un tret a l'aire disparat per Matthew els espanta. Fugen tots corrent. Uns van de nou cap al desert; els altres, cap a Kiwirrkurra amb el cotxe.

Així que arriben a Kiwirrkurra, Pinta Pinta i Matthew expliquen la trobada als altres. De seguida els més grans tenen clar que es tracta d'alguns dels seus parents, que són gent de la família Tjapaltjarri que continuen fent vida al desert. L'endemà mateix comencen a seguir-los les petjades per retrobar-los. Encara hi ha parents que els recorden, i encara hi ha gent que sap seguir les petjades en el desert. És així com, pocs dies després, els trobaran per poder-los donar —és clar— roba moderna i dur-los a la comoditat (cosa que no vol dir a la felicitat) de la vida sedentària. I així els duen també, és cert, a la seguretat de tenir aigua, a la sort de crear famílies i, en definitiva, a l'única opció que tenien de sobreviure com a grup, ja que el desert, ara abandonat per tothom, ha deixat de ser un lloc per a la vida humana.

Costa d'entendre l'impacte d'un descobriment d'aquesta magnitud. Fins aquell dia, el món de la joveníssima Yalti és un món de silenciosa lentitud entre aigua i aigua. De sobte es veu perseguida, capturada i posada a dins d'un cotxe. No pot fer res més que espantar-se quan es veu tancada en un lloc com aquest i quan s'adona que tota la terra del seu voltant es mou. De sobte, sense saber-ho encara, a dins d'aquest cotxe, Yalti fa un vertiginós salt de desenes de milers d'anys cap al futur. ¿Amb quina angoixa no viuria qualsevol de nosaltres un impacte semblant? Per molt que el seu primer contacte amb el futur sigui amb gent que parla la seva llengua i que té el seu color de pell, es fa difícil que els que ja vam néixer en aquest món que anomenem el present puguem copsar la violència de l'impacte que rep Yalti.

Fet el primer contacte, arriben a Kiwirrkurra on es retroben amb la família. Malgrat que Kiwirrkurra sigui l'assentament més isolat d'Austràlia, el món de Yalti i de la seva família és ben diferent del que ara troben. Estan a cavall de dues realitats, una de les quals haurà de ser rebutjada per sempre. Només l'encanteri d'un verí màgic els podria fer decidir a quedar-se en aquest nou món que acaben de descobrir. I aquest verí és el sucre. N'hi ha prou que els en regalin una mica perquè quedin totalment seduïts per la seva dolçor. Ja no voldran tornar mai més a la vida del desert. Tal com si fos una droga temptadora i destructiva, el sucre els treu definitivament d'aquell desert moribund i els condemna a la vida sedentària per sempre més. Fins avui.

A Kiwirrkurra, els Pintupi Nou descobreixen el millor i el pitjor de la vida moderna. Es meravellaran de descobrir la comoditat amb què l'aigua pot fluir d'un tub o d'una aixeta, però també hi descobriran que a les colònies sedentàries, sovint la situació és bastant depressiva. Aquí no s'hi pot mantenir la vida tradicional. A més a més, la barreja de grups tan diferents intensifica els conflictes que afloren dia rere dia. El plàcid costum de la vida en una comunitat reduïda es veu en aquesta colònia en l'exigència de posar-se d'acord, de dialogar, de cedir, d'escoltar... Tot el que hi havia s'esfondra en nom de la comoditat i de la seguretat. Tot queda enterrat sota aquest sedentarisme que també convida a la desídia, a l'alimentació insana, a l'abús del sucre i de l'alcohol i als problemes de salut que tot plegat implica.

Tot és massa diferent, tant per als nouvinguts com per als que ja fa vint anys que hi són. El salt cap al futur que han fet tots els Pintupi és massa abismal. El vertigen de fer el salt enrere també és un repte excessiu i impossible.

Descobrir el món i el futur, tot a la vegada. ¿No és aquest el descobriment més gran de la història de la humanitat? Només passa que, com tots els viatges cap al futur, aquest és sense retorn. Ja no hi ha opció de tornar al passat a explicar la descoberta als ancestres i quedar-s'hi a viure com si no hagués passat res. Ara, establerts a Kiwirrkurra, han d'aprendre a salvar la dificultat de trobar sentit a la vida. Després de tants mil·lennis al desert, han de trobar la manera de fer créixer alguna cosa aquí, arrelar en un lloc erm que sempre t'havia obligat a moure't, fer que les coses vinguin a tu en comptes d'anar-les a buscar.

Malgrat totes aquestes dificultats, la majoria de membres d'aquesta última família nòmada s'adaptaran al nou món. Com que cada vegada hi ha un reconeixement més important de l'art aborigen, alguns fins i tot es convertiran en artistes de fama internacional. El més destacat, Warlimpirrnga, exposarà en galeries i museus de tot el món. Vendrà quadres a preus desorbitats. Només Piyiti, el fill més gran, d'uns vint-i-sis anys, un bon dia decideix desaparèixer novament desert enllà, I no torna mai més.

Així, sense dir res a ningú, un bon dia Piyiti es lleva i se'n torna de nou cap a l'únic món que considera seu. Esborra les petjades per no ser perseguit un altre cop.

Es fa difícil saber si Piyiti és o no és l'últim nòmada d'aquesta llarga història. La veritat és que en aquest món lent i pausat, al ritme del desert, les notícies poden trigar segles a arribar a tot arreu, i quan Piyiti s'endinsa de nou en el seu territori, potser l'arribada dels blancs encara sigui novetat en algun altre racó desconegut. Dos anys després de l'episodi dels Pintupi Nou, l'octubre de 1986, sembla que un altre grup de set nòmades és vist en el Gran Desert de Victòria. I qui sap si encara en queda algun altre en aquell món ja impossible. Però no. Quan al desert hi havia vida, aquest oferia vida; però ara que són mortes totes les relacions humanes que feien l'entramat de la xarxa de subsistència, sense grups dispersos que s'ajudin uns a altres, sense gent amb qui formar noves famílies que heretin aquests mil·lennis de cultura, la presència humana ja no hi és possible de cap manera. I no, avui ja no hi queda ningú.

Finalment, la vida al desert ja és només un món inexistent i impossible. Després de moure's durant segles d'un punt d'aigua a l'altre, els seus habitants es troben que l'entorn ha canviat, que l'aigua s'asseca i que la caça desapareix. Només Piyiti un dia se'n va anar per ser l'últim a no tornar.

I malgrat tot, el seu germà Warlimpirrnga assegura haver-lo vist una vegada a Alice Springs, casat i amb fills. Es feia dir Yari Yari. Però, tant si això és cert com si no, probablement Piyiti és l'últim que es va endinsar al desert, ben bé a lligar el nus que tanca aquesta llarga corda iniciada en el temps dels somnis.

L'últim nòmada

Avui, després de la connexió d'Austràlia amb la resta del món, hem vist desaparèixer l'últim nòmada d'aquest continent. L'última persona que duia amb ell un bagatge de desenes de milers d'anys. La cultura més antiga de la humanitat. Però potser toca també parlar d'alguna cosa més que de destrucció. Potser toca també parlar de l'admiració que mereix aquesta llarga història de supervivència, de permanència. Mentre naixien i morien gairebé tots els déus que la humanitat ha sabut crear, els australians han continuat allà, transmetent-se els seus mites.

Avui, al nostre món, tenim uns referents culturals (Homer, Sòcrates, Confuci, Buda, Shakespeare, Leonardo...) que ens semblen eterns. Però qui diu que ho siguin? Mirar cap endavant sempre fa un vertigen estrany perquè no hi veiem res. És com mirar al fons d'un precipici en plena nit i no entendre'n la profunditat per molt que sapiguem els metres exactes de caiguda que té. Per entendre el precipici, hem de veure els arbres del bosc que hi ha a baix de tot, les roques contra les quals ens estavellaríem, hem de mirar mil anys cap endavant. A l'any tres mil de la nostra era, al quatre mil, al deu mil, potser arribarà un moment que la quantitat de referents culturals nous que hauran anat apareixent hauran anat entenebrint els referents més antics, hauran anat deixant Homer i Confuci sota un pòsit de pols, un tel transparent al principi però que algun dia, capa a capa, acabarà fent-se completament opac i els amagarà totalment. Ens costa de creure que res del que coneixem avui sobreviurà d'aquí a vint, trenta o quaranta mil·lennis. I això, en canvi, és el que han aconseguit aquests australians triomfadors de la humanitat. Perviure. Són uns triomfadors. L'única cosa que passa és que ens ha tocat veure'n el (o un) final. Perquè res no és etern.

Ara hauríem de lamentar que al nostre món li hagi tocat el paper de botxí i a nosaltres el d'espectadors d'aquest final d'un món tan antic. Però potser, a banda de parlar de mort, sobretot ens caldria primer de tot admirar-los, després envejar-los, i finalment doldre'ns. Potser és moment de gratar ara a les engrunes que queden per recollir-les i salvar-ne tot el possible.

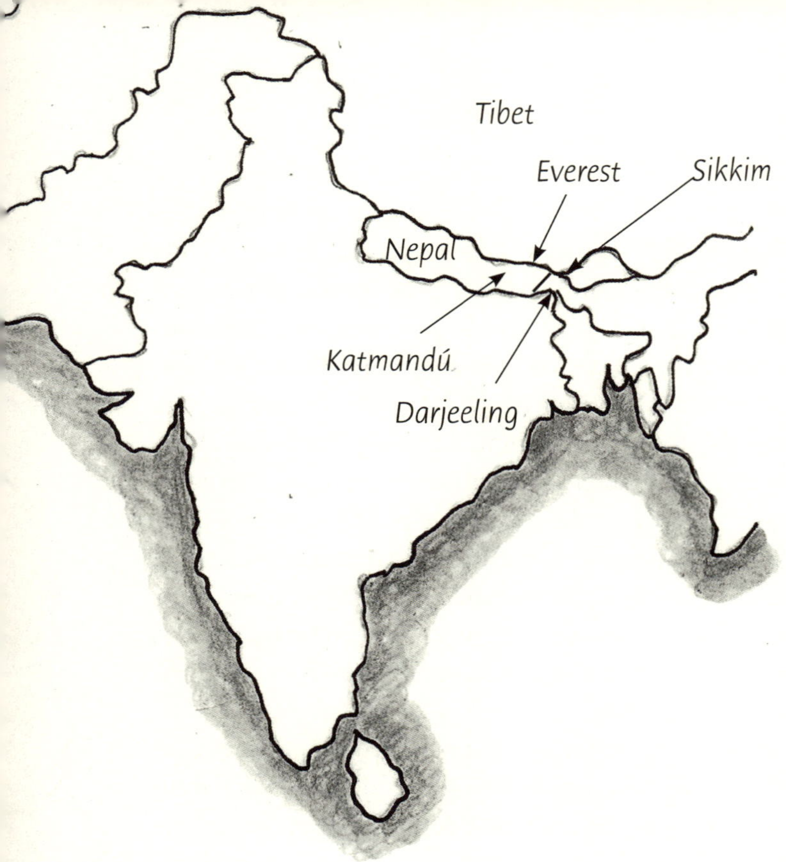
Tibet
Everest
Sikkim
Nepal
Katmandú
Darjeeling

7. El sostre del món

La conquesta individual

Després de dies caminant entre muntanyes imponents i solitàries, el viatger arriba per fi a un modest escampall de cabanes de pastors. És hora de reposar una mica i de tornar a sentir l'escalf d'alguna veu humana. Ben aviat saluda una dona que tira engrunes a les gallines. Ella respon amb educació i timidesa, però no sembla que tingui gaire tirada a dir frases llargues. Aleshores, més per tenir conversa que per saber res, al nou arribat se li acut preguntar el nom de la muntanya que hi ha davant seu. No en té cap dubte, del nom, memoritzats com porta els mapes de la zona, però li sembla una bona manera de trencar el gel. Llavors, sense desocupar les mans que alimenten les gallines, la dona gira els ulls amunt, cap al lloc assenyalat, i, com si s'adonés d'aquell cim per primer cop a la vida, es mira després l'excursionista amb un arronsament d'espatlles per demostrar la indiferència que li inspira aquell inaccessible rocam. El que cal saber és cada quant crien les gallines, com protegir-les del fred, com aconseguir que ponguin més ous...

De què serveix el cim d'una muntanya? Quin sentit té pujar-hi? L'alpinisme és una disciplina més aviat jove dins del món dels exploradors. Allà als cims, on no hi ha res, rarament s'hi ha aventurat mai ningú fins que alguns romàntics del segle XIX van decidir que la seva realització personal demanava descobrir d'una manera esportiva tots els racons del món.

La gent de les muntanyes remotes no solen pujar-hi. En tot cas segueixen els camins que travessen les valls, fan pelegrinatges. És lògic. Quan el ciutadà occidental es passeja enfonsat entre gratacels, només veu edificis, i que algú s'enfili per una d'aquelles façanes li sembla una bogeria. No és gens estrany, doncs, que per als habitants de la muntanya els cims no siguin camins, sinó la llar dels déus, i és incomprensible que algú vulgui pujar-hi. I més encara, que ho faci per plaer, per aventura o per evasió.

Vet aquí l'alpinisme. Un cop descoberta la geografia de tot el món, dibuixats tots els mapes i repartits els territoris entre països i fronteres, sembla que aquesta nova disciplina, amb la seva recerca dels cims, aquests territoris més petits, sovint erms, acabi d'esgarrapar els últims serrells que han deixat els antics exploradors. Els grans viatgers del passat han posat cada racó al mapa. Ja només queda la descoberta vertical, anar fins al final de tot dels últims carrerons sense sortida que hi ha a la geografia per tornar-ne amb les mans buides i l'esperit ple.

Perquè aquesta és, en el fons, l'única conquesta vàlida per a un ésser humà. No la de plantar la bandera en nom d'un rei o d'un país i canviar la vida i la gent dels territoris conquerits, sinó la de canviar un mateix. Perquè malgrat la imposició d'un llenguatge bèl·lic, la muntanya no es *conquereix*, sinó que s'hi arriba amb esforç i se'n marxa de seguida abans no et mati. *Conquereixes* el cim, l'admires, li agraeixes l'esforç que t'ha exigit, i l'abandones havent canviat tu, no pas ell.

Finalment, aquest és l'espai que ens queda a tu i a mi, modestos exploradors moderns que, ara ja, ens podem aventurar als límits del món. Amb el naixement de l'alpinisme, per primer cop fins i tot la gent més discreta sap que hi ha límits a l'abast de la mà. I que pot sortir a explorar i a descobrir què s'amaga darrere la porta de casa, darrere la porta d'un mateix posat al límit dels extrems del món.

Fins ara, darrere l'horitzó sempre hi havia més horitzó. Només s'hi arribava amb grans expedicions, amb temps i amb infraestructures desorbitades. Però ara l'horitzó s'ha enlairat, es retalla en la cresta d'un cim, i si hi arribes amb el teu esforçat pas de formiga, sabràs que a l'altra banda també hi haurà algú mirant cap a tu, a tu que durant uns moments seràs allà dalt, convertit en horitzó de tu mateix i del món.

Perquè tenim limitacions, però no tenim límits. Els límits són una altra cosa que no ens correspon. Són la forma del món, no la nostra.

Txomolungma, Sagarmatha

Tal com el coneixem avui, l'alpinisme és un invent esportiu i romàntic. Al llarg del segle XVIII es comencen a dominar els Alps; el 1760 Horace-Benedict de Saussure (besavi del fundador de la lingüística moderna) inicia la cursa cap al cim del Mont Blanc, cim que Jacques Balmat i Michel Paccard coronaran per primer cop el 1786. Durant el segle XIX, mentre el mapa del món es va completant, l'alpinisme continuarà creixent i buscant nous reptes.

Després dels Alps, allà a on tenen accés els europeus per superar rècords d'altitud és als Andes. El gener de 1897, el suís Matthias Zurbriggen es converteix en el primer alpinista que trepitja el cim de l'Aconcagua, cosa que no per força ha de voler dir que va ser la primera persona. Algunes troballes arqueològiques fan que no es pugui descartar que els inques no haguessin pujat a aquest i a d'altres cims andins uns quants segles abans, evidentment amb finalitats religioses i no esportives. Però, tal com sol passar, tampoc no en podrem tenir la certesa ni sabrem els noms d'aquells que un dia van ser les persones que van arribar als cims més alts del seu tros de món.

Segurament durant segles els Andes han sigut les altituds més transitades per l'ésser humà, força abans que les de l'Himàlaia. Però, tan aviat com pugui, l'alpinisme buscarà cims i noms nous per mirar cap a altres bandes, sempre més amunt encara. Fins que algú identifiqui la muntanya més alta del món i comenci la cursa per ascendir-hi.

Txomolungma des del Tibet, Sagarmatha des del Nepal. Aquests són alguns dels noms de la muntanya més alta del món. Noms que se solen traduir com la *Deessa Mare de les Neus* o la *Mare de l'Univers*, però que per a altres tindrien significats més pràctics com la *Muntanya que cap ocell pot sobrevolar*, o l'encara més prosaic i sorprenent que li donava un pastor local: *Gallina*. Això sí, una gallina ben grossa i estarrufada, no us penséssiu.

Ja sabem que per a molts és més important tenir una bona gallina que una bona muntanya. Però una certa lògica romàntica ens fa quedar amb el significat més estès de tots, la Deessa Mare de les Neus. I de sobte, es fa el miracle: aquesta muntanya és a molts llocs a la vegada. Durant segles, més d'un tibetà o nepalès surt cada matí de casa seva i veu una muntanya que s'alça per sobre de les altres. L'anomena Txomolungma. Però de totes les deesses mares de les neus que hi ha escampades per l'Himàlaia, n'hi ha una que és més alta que les altres.

El 1852, la Royal Geographical Society localitza la que deu ser la muntanya més alta del món. De moment, quan falta molt encara per poder-s'hi acostar des del territori tibetà o nepalès i poder establir un sol nom per a aquesta muntanya que en té uns quants perquè varien segons el lloc, li donaran el senzill nom de cim XV. I així es coneixerà fins que el 1865 Andrew Waugh, topògraf britànic destinat a l'Índia, proposi el nom del seu predecessor al càrrec. Des d'aleshores, aquesta

Deessa Mare de les Neus, el Sagarmatha, el Txomolungma, duu el cognom de George Everest, un home que no ha vist mai aquesta muntanya i que ni tan sols vol que es digui com ell. Però la Royal Geographical Society acceptarà la proposta de Waugh i donarà el nom d'Everest a aquest cim.

Pot semblar molt propi dels europeus això de portar allà on van fins i tot les paraules com a suposada bandera de civilització, però en aquest cas, com en tants altres, senzillament el problema és que cap europeu s'hi pot acostar prou fins molt temps després, quan el nom d'Everest ja ha fet oblidar el de la persona que s'ho deia i s'hagi convertit en el nom del sostre del món.

Waugh, igual com Everest, carregat de bones intencions, és partidari de donar els noms locals als descobriments geogràfics. Aquests homes tenen clar que el món ja estava descobert i ja era conegut abans que ells. Ells no descobreixen res. Però malgrat aquestes bones intencions, només queda recordar que el nom no fa la cosa. Així, segurament, George Everest estaria tranquil i seria feliç si sabés que el seu cognom no farà desaparèixer els noms originals d'aquest cim. Per tant, a la seva salut, que Sagarmatha i Txomolungma, entre tots els altres noms, continuïn essent també per molt temps altres noms d'aquesta muntanya.

Cap al cim

Un cop conegut el cim, a poc a poc la vida de les terres que l'envolten començarà a notar-ne els efectes. Com si hagués crescut de sobte, ara ve gent de fora a dir que aquesta muntanya és la més alta del món sobre el nivell del mar, un mar que aquí ningú no ha vist mai ni ningú no sap exactament on para. Però un cop descoberta aquesta casualitat absurda, per als ex-

pladors europeus ja només queda començar el camí fins al seu cim.

Després dels científics i dels geògrafs arriben, doncs, les primeres expedicions purament alpinistes a l'Himàlaia. William Graham és el primer d'anar-hi empès per aquesta febre. Sembla que el 1883, juntament amb Emil Boss i Ulrich Hauffmann, corona el Kabru, de 7.338 metres d'altitud. Encara que costa de demostrar, si això és cert, serà el cim més alt aconseguit per algú fins i tot encara el dia que Mallory i Irvine moren al Txomolungma. Si no fos així, el cim més alt on s'ha arribat abans d'intentar assolir el sostre del món seria el Trisul, de 7.120 metres. Hi va pujar Tom Longstaff el 1907. Seria igualment el cim més alt assolit durant més de dues dècades.

És així d'absurd, només hi ha ulls per al cim més gran de tots, per a l'última frontera. En tot cas, no serà fins al 1950 quan algú arriba per primera vegada al cim d'una muntanya que fa més de vuit mil metres. La muntanya és l'Annapurna, que en fa 8.091, i els alpinistes que hi arriben són Maurice Herzog i Louis Lachenal. Aquell dia ja fa trenta anys que altres alpinistes proven d'arribar a dalt del Sagarmatha-Txomolungma. Alguns homes ja hi reposen congelats. I alguns d'ells ja havien arribat a una alçada més alta que la de l'Annapurna.

L'Himàlaia té tants reptes oberts, doncs, que sorprèn una mica que hi hagi tan pocs alpinistes que optin per pujar a les altres muntanyes d'aquesta serralada. Des del moment que es planteja la cursa pel sostre del món, però, difícilment hi ha gaire interès per assolir el cim de la segona, de la tercera o de la quarta muntanya més alta del món. El 1885 Alfred Mummery desapareix al Nanga Parbat. Va ser la primera víctima d'uns vuit mil. Gairebé devia semblar una gesta tan absurda com la d'un explorador que volgués anar a les proximitats dels pols, però no pas al pol mateix.

Hi ha tanta gent capficada a ser la primera a pujar al cim del món que quan, a l'any 1921, una expedició britànica provi d'anar-hi, encara no se'n té prou informació. I tampoc no se'n té prou experiència. És una imprudència? És ignorància? És valentia? El fet és que, tot d'una, sembla que tothom vulgui passar dels poc més de set mil metres d'altitud a què ja s'ha arribat als gairebé nou mil que fa el sostre del món deixant de banda totes les altres muntanyes que passen dels vuit mil. Tothom busca superar un rècord, ser el primer a arribar a dalt de tot.

Els anys vint. Primers intents

Cal entendre la muntanya com un territori viu i poderós, però també com un lloc sensible i vulnerable. Es protegirà de seguida que es comenci a veure agredida. Per molt que els alpinistes s'hi apropin amb la humilitat del seu cos en comptes d'anar-hi amb la carcassa protectora dels vaixells de les grans exploracions, la muntanya serà implacable. No perdonarà res. Mentre el gel polar sol esclafar lentament les naus deixant temps per intentar fugides i rescats, la muntanya tracta l'alpinista com qui bufeteja un mosquit que li pica a l'orella.

El 1921 arriba a les faldes tibetanes del Txomolungma la primera expedició britànica de reconeixement. Quasi es pot dir que l'aventura tot just comença, però la decisió està presa. La humanitat ja no s'aturarà fins que algú arribi a aquest cim. De moment encara es tracta de saber quins camins, quines condicions, quin preu exigirà l'ascens. Però un cop fet aquest reconeixement, el 1922 hi ha els primers intents. El 1924 ja hi ha una via per acostar-se al cim. Aquest mateix any, Edward Norton puja sense oxigen fins als 8.570 metres. Serà l'alçada més gran a què ha pujat i ha sobreviscut mai ningú fins al 1952. Però l'optimisme d'aquesta expedició es va estroncar sobtadament quan van desaparèixer George Mallory i Andrew Irvine. No són, ni de bon tros, les primeres víctimes d'aquesta muntanya, però les morts anteriors no han sigut prou europees per omplir els llibres d'història. De poques víctimes del Txomolungma s'ha parlat tant com d'aquests dos escaladors. Són els més recordats i encara avui dels més buscats de la història de l'alpinisme.

Pocs dies després de l'intent de Norton, Irvine i Mallory afronten l'ascens definitiu. Aquell 8 de juny de 1924, un dels seus companys d'expedició, Noel Odell, els veu per última vegada des d'un telescopi, mentre ells pugen per l'aresta nord-est cap al cim. Fa unes hores que han deixat la seva tenda. No hi tornarà ningú fins a l'any 1933. Nou anys després del primer intent, la primera expedició que hi arribarà trobarà, entre altres coses, la llanterna de Mallory. I més amunt, a 8.400 metres, un piolet que només podia haver sigut d'Irvine.

Un piolet no és res que s'oblidi així com així en aquestes alçades. El 1999, uns dos-cents metres més avall de la línia de caiguda on es va trobar el piolet d'Irvine, l'alpinista Conrad Anker troba el cos de Mallory. Després de setanta-cinc anys estirat de bocaterrosa a la neu, si no fos per una cama fracturada, el cos està aparentment intacte per fora, però totalment menjat pels corbs. Duu encara lligada a la cintura la corda trencada que l'unia a Irvine. No porta la màscara d'oxigen i té les ulleres de sol guardades en una butxaca. Que Mallory pogués oblidar la llanterna i no dugués posades les ulleres de sol fa suposar que l'ascensió va començar amb llum de dia i que segurament, en fer-se fosc, encara va tenir temps de treure's les ulleres. Si no és que se les va treure per algun altre motiu com la boira o la necessitat de millorar l'angle de visió. Però res més. No hi ha res que ens ajudi a saber si van fer el cim, si pujaven o baixaven en el moment del fatal accident, si tornaven o reculaven, que no és exactament el mateix. No hi ha res que ens permeti anar més enllà de suposar com van ser les primeres morts humanes per sobre dels vuit mil metres.

Aquesta ha sigut la pregunta eterna sobre Irvine i Mallory: van arribar al cim? I amb tot, malgrat els dubtes, la resposta sempre acaba sent que no, que senzillament era impossible que hi arribessin. El segon esglaó de la cara nord, a 8.650 metres, és un obstacle insuperable per a una cordada de dos homes sols amb una sola corda i un piolet. Fins al 1975 ningú no superarà aquell obstacle. Caldrà una expedició amb un desplegament de recursos molt més complet que amb els que comptaven Mallory i Irvine. Aquell 1975, un grup nombrós de tibetans (oficialment xinesos) obrirà la via instal·lant-hi escales metàl·liques fixes i cordes que permetran superar aquest segon esglaó. Van ser els primers que van fer el cim per la cara nord.

Que l'any 1999 trobessin el cos de Mallory no va ser casualitat. Sempre hi ha una pista per seguir en aquest escampall cada cop més ple de morts que és el camí cap al cim del món. De moment, aquest racó on hem perdut de vista els dissortats britànics va quedar pràcticament oblidat fins al 1960, any en què una expedició xinesa va voler fer el cim per aquesta cara nord. Aquell any, el propagandístic govern xinès va assegurar que, fent una gesta èpica, els seus homes havien superat el segon esglaó després de descalçar-se i de fer una mena de torre humana. Tot seguit havien arribat fins al cim, però, com que era de nit, no havien pogut fer fotografies. El cúmul de mentides inversemblants amb què la Xina va voler demostrar el seu èxit de 1960 va fer que res del que deien els seus alpinistes fos creïble. Tampoc quan un dels membres de l'expedició va assegurar que havia vist el cos d'un dels anglesos perduts trenta-sis anys enrere. Pel que avui sabem, si això fos cert, seria el cos d'Irvine, però també sabem que podria ser una fantasia, perquè, quan no es pot discernir una veritat d'una mentida, la veritat acostuma a no existir. O, com bé diu un proverbi justament xinès: 'Si m'enganyes un cop és culpa teva, si m'enganyes dos cops és culpa meva'.

Però a banda de fantasies i mentides, hi ha qui sí que sap coses de Mallory. El 2013, anys després d'haver trobat el seu cos, es coneix una carta de l'alpinista Frank Smythe a Edward Norton en què assegura que el 1936 havia localitzat el cos d'un dels malaurats alpinistes mentre mirava el sostre del món amb un telescopi. Però per pudor i per respecte, la carta de Smythe va quedar oblidada en un calaix, lluny de la premsa i del públic. És per això que l'única pista que va tenir l'expedició que es va fer el 1999 per trobar els cossos d'Irvine i Mallory va ser la que havia donat l'alpinista japonès Ryoten Hasegawa. Expliquem-ho:

L'any 1979, en una expedició sinojaponesa al Txomolungma, l'alpinista xinès Wang Hongbao explica a Hasegawa que quatre anys enrere (el 1975) havia trobat en el camí cap al cim *el cos d'un anglès antic*, tal com va dir Wang. No hi havia cap dubte que era antic: en una època en què l'alpinisme encara tenia molt camí al davant, precisament quan feia temps que Nansen i Amundsen ja s'abrigaven com els inuits per explorar les regions polars, els escaladors anglesos afrontaven les temperatures polars de l'Himàlaia abrigats amb americanes, gavardines i bufandes de teixits com seda, franel·la, cotó o llana. I així, com ningú no pujaria avui ni un cim de diumenge, era com anava vestit aquell anglès congelat per damunt dels vuit mil metres. Aquesta informació de Wang va cridar l'atenció del japonès Hasegawa. Va voler saber-ne alguna cosa més. I va parlar-ne un moment amb Wang. Però l'endemà d'aquesta conversa breu, Wang va morir en una allau i amb ell van desaparèixer tots els detalls de la misteriosa troballa.

D'aquesta manera, mentre la pista de Smythe queda segellada entre papers personals, la de Wang queda sota la neu. I així sembla evident que tot allò que no és compartit, no forma part de la humanitat, perquè encara que algunes persones han anat trobant el cos de Mallory, el món continua sense saber-ne res.

De moment, amb la pista que Wang va donar a Hasegawa n'hi haurà prou perquè vint anys després s'organitzi una expedició per aclarir si Irvine i Mallory han sigut els primers a coronar el sostre del món. És l'expedició de l'any 1999. Per tercera vegada (que sapiguem) es troba el cos de Mallory, però no s'aconsegueix desentrellar del tot l'enigma que volien resoldre. Més que Mallory, l'expedició de recerca buscava el cos d'Irvine, que era qui duia la càmera fotogràfica i, per tant, qui hauria immortalitzat el cim en cas que hi haguessin arribat. Trobar la càmera i poder-ne revelar les imatges permetria aclarir si van ser ells els primers a trepitjar el cim del Txomolungma. I si s'aclaria això, el 1953 Norgay i Hillary haurien sigut només els segons i no pas els primers.

Però no ens enganyem. Mallory i Irvine no van tenir ni prou temps ni tenien prou recursos per arribar al cim. I ben mirat, fins i tot en l'improbable cas que haguessin reeixit en l'ascens, de què serveix un èxit que no es pot assaborir? De què serveix un descobriment que no es pot compartir? Prou clar que ho deixarà escrit el mateix Mallory: «Al capdavall, el descens forma part de tota l'experiència. Cap alpinista estaria satisfet de pujar un cim i no baixar-ne». I una resposta semblant donaria anys més tard el seu fill John en ser preguntat per la possibilitat que el seu pare hagués arribat al cim: «Per mi l'única manera d'assolir un cim és tornar-ne viu. La feina només està mig feta si no en tornes quan baixes». Res a dir. Tant si havia trepitjat el cim com si no, el seu pare, senzillament, no havia tornat mai més a casa.

Set xerpes oblidats i un segle de morts

John Mallory només té tres anys quan el seu pare és engolit per la muntanya. George, als quasi trenta-vuit anys, deixa una vídua i tres fills, a més de pare i mare. I Irvine, de vint-i-dos anys, massa més jove, mor només com a fill, que és tant o més dramàtic que deixar-ne. Pregunteu-ho si no a qualsevol que tingui fills, pregunteu-ho a Lilian Davies-Colley i a William Ferguson Irvine, pares del plorat i quasi oblidat Andrew, buscat sobretot per si té unes fotos a la càmera. Aquests dos homes senzillament no tornen. Tant se val quina muntanya sigui o en quin punt del camí. No hi ha res més, tornar-ne és l'èxit. I per a qui els espera a casa no té gens d'importància si Mallory i Irvine van arribar al cim o no. Senzillament, han passat a la posteritat com unes de les primeres víctimes del Txomolungma.

Però una vegada més, com en tantes altres aventures, abans d'ells hi ha els oblidats. Els que estan més oblidats encara. La de 1924 ja és la tercera de les expedicions al Txomolungma; Mallory és l'únic que ha participat en totes tres, i ja sap que la Deessa Mare de les Neus pot ser voraç i traïdora.

El 1921, en la primera expedició de reconeixement, Guy Bullock i George Mallory ascendiran fins al Coll Nord, a la cota 7.000, i aquell any la gran muntanya encara serà benèvola. Però el 1922, quan l'ascens al cim comenci a ser una possibilitat seriosa, la Deessa Mare de les Neus començarà a neguitejar-se. Hi haurà ja les seves primeres víctimes. Estranyament algú ens en dirà mai els noms, però el 7 de juny de 1922 una allau al Coll Nord s'emportarà la vida de set portadors xerpes. Set homes absolutament oblidats, amb noms, famílies, amics, vides i futurs esfondrats en un instant. Set noms: Dorje, Lhakpa, Norbu, Pasang, Pema, Sange i Temba. Sis d'ells seran trobats allà mateix entre la runa pedregosa i abandonats en aquest immens mausoleu; un altre quedarà desaparegut per sempre més també allà, empassat per les neus. Mallory, que veu de ben a prop la tragèdia, se'n sentirà responsable la resta de la seva curta vida, però en cap moment abandonarà la seva cursa per assolir el Txomolungma. Malgrat tot, a alguns del seu entorn els interessa més la muntanya que els tibetans, i fins i tot l'alesshores president de la Royal Geographical Society, Francis Younghusband, serà capaç de celebrar que no hagi mort cap europeu. És cert que els xerpes també desperten simpaties entre aquells aventurers britànics i que alguns dels testimonis trobaran injust que no morís cap europeu en l'accident, però és innegable que la mentalitat colonial d'aquelles expedicions aflora més que mai davant la tragèdia.

Dorje, Lhakpa, Norbu, Pasang, Pema, Sange i Temba. Set noms i prou, però amb set vides que podem conèixer a la perfecció. Homes de muntanya, pastors, pagesos, pares de famílies que aprofiten l'arribada d'aquests estrangers com una de les poques oportunitats que la seva terra esquerpa els pot oferir. La vida de cadascun d'ells és, amb tota certesa, la de tantes generacions prèvies i posteriors. Dura i difícil, però també irrepetible i meravellosa.

I no ha canviat res. Encara avui el poble xerpa continua veient aquesta muntanya com l'ha vista sempre. Ells, els grans coneixedors d'aquests territoris, continuen pujant a les altituds com a portadors. Són uns treballadors que s'aferren a una de les poques possibilitats que els ofereix el seu temps i el seu lloc. Continuen escalant i dient que pugen allà dalt perquè no ho hagin de fer els seus fills. En això, les vides de Dorje, Lhakpa, Norbu, Pasang, Pema, Sange i Temba s'assemblen a les dels seus avantpassats i a les dels seus descendents. Treballar amb sacrifici per al bé dels seus fills.

Amb ells, el 1922, comença la llarga llista de víctimes del Sagarmatha-Txomolungma, que s'ampliarà el maig de 1924 quan moren els nepalesos Man Bahadur, a causa d'unes congelacions, i Lance-Naik Shamsherpun, a causa d'una hemorràgia cerebral. I encara uns dies més tard, arribarà la mort d'Irvine i Mallory. Comptant els dos anglesos ja seran onze les vides humanes que s'ha endut aquesta muntanya fins al 1924. Al cap d'un segle, tres centenars de cadàvers s'escamparan per les seves glaceres. Alguns, perduts per sempre en les entranyes del massís, convertits en muntanya; altres, a la vista, fins i tot al mig del pas, convertits en punt de referència i en camí quan cal posar el peu damunt d'un alpinista congelat en la ruta cap al cim, esquinçant-li potser la vella roba amb els grampons.

En plantar-se davant d'aquesta muntanya per primer cop, Mallory la descrivia com un prodigiós ullal que sobresurt de les mandíbules de la terra. Avui, aquest ullal comença a estar corcat. Esforç a esforç, pas a pas, fracàs a fracàs, èxit a èxit, el Sagarmatha es va convertint, a la vegada que en un abocador de deixalles, també en el cementiri més alt del món. A diferència d'altres territoris explorats i domesticats, morir al Sagarmatha no és només cosa dels pioners. Dels tres-cents cadàvers del primer segle d'ascensions, la meitat corresponen al segle xx. L'altra meitat, a les dues primeres dècades del xxi. I de tots aquests, un terç són xerpes que no eren allà per plaer, sinó per necessitat.

Per a qui encara tingui ganes de jugar a ser explorador, doncs, encara avui allà hi ha una porta oberta; així que poca broma en això de perdre el respecte a l'esperit sagrat de les muntanyes. La muntanya és molt voraç i té estómac per a més, però per moltes vides que s'empassi —que ho farà, que ho continuarà fent—, entre els centenars de cossos que van lliscant lentament glacera avall pel seu aparell digestiu hi ha, des d'abans que ningú altre, Dorje, Lhakpa, Norbu, Pasang, Pema, Sange i Temba, enterrats sota el pes de la glacera al Coll Nord. I també sota el pes dels noms d'Irvine i Mallory, que continuen allà, però que en els llibres d'història sempre pesen més.

I mares i fills esperen a tothom amb un patiment idèntic.

Els anys trenta. Shipton i Norgay

La mort d'Irvine i Mallory sembla refredar de sobte les aspiracions britàniques sobre el Txomolungma. Passaran uns quants anys abans no es reprengui l'aventura. Quan es reprèn, l'ant 1933, serà d'una manera diferent, gràcies sobretot a Eric Shipton. Shipton és sense cap mena de dubte l'alpinista més destacat i influent del seu temps. Viatger incansable des de petit fins a la seva mort, tenia una visió molt més oberta i menys colonialista que els seus antecessors. Ell i el seu bon amic Bill Tilman canvien completament la manera de veure l'alpinisme. Lluny de grans expedicions sobredimensionades, Shipton i Tilman aposten per un estil lleuger i proper, miren de portar sempre tan poc equipatge com puguin, volen parlar les llengües locals, integrar-se a les societats que els acullen, consideren sempre els xerpes com uns amics i no pas com uns portadors.

Moguts més per la seva realització personal que per cap altra cosa, a principis dels anys trenta, aquests dos alpinistes es troben recorrent racons inexplorats de l'Himàlaia i escalen nombrosos cims que no ha trepitjat mai ningú. El 1931 Shipton és un dels quatre alpinistes que corona els 7.756 metres del Kemet, a l'Índia, el cim més alt assolit fins aleshores. Per molt que en aquell temps els vuit mil metres d'altitud ja siguin un territori conegut, trepitjat a les parets de l'Everest, encara ningú no havia arribat a un cim d'aquesta alçada. I amb això, el modest Shipton ja sembla donar-se per satisfet. Però als seus vint-i-cinc anys, el seu prestigi li obre les portes per participar a l'expedició de 1933 a l'Everest, la quarta que envien els britànics cap a aquesta fita. De sobte, tot canvia.

Aquest cop, Percy Wyn-Harris i Lawrence Wager seran els que tindran l'oportunitat d'arribar al cim tan desitjat. No tornaran del seu intent amb les mans buides del tot: portaran el piolet de la cordada Mallory-Irvine. A banda d'això, l'expedició de 1933 no dona cap més fruit que la represa del somni més alt de l'alpinisme. De nou els britànics tornen a plantejar-s'ho amb ganes i convicció. Al final de la campanya no queden gaires dubtes que Shipton és el que està més preparat per a afrontar aquest repte amb possibilitats. Rebrà l'encàrrec de dirigir un nou intent ben aviat, el 1935.

D'aquesta manera, ja com a cap de l'expedició, a principis de 1935, Shipton es troba a Darjeeling fent preparatius. Entre altres tasques li toca escollir els quinze xerpes que formaran part de l'equip. En aquell temps, els xerpes ja s'han convertit en els portadors i guies més prestigiosos de l'Himàlaia. En venen de tot arreu. Tots busquen ser contractats a les aventures d'aquests estrafolaris europeus. Aquell any, Shipton pot triar entre un centenar de candidats, però, a banda dels que ja coneix d'altres anys, és difícil saber qui anirà millor. Mira de no contractar inexperts o desconeguts. I tampoc, els que són massa joves. Amb tot plegat, li queden un parell de vacants que haurà d'ocupar d'alguna manera.

Entre el centenar de candidats, hi ha un jove de vint anys nascut a les proximitats tibetanes del Txomolungma, criat en un poblet del Nepal i instal·lat a Darjeeling des de fa dos anys perquè vol aconseguir tenir un lloc en una expedició. El 1933 aquest noi ja havia sigut descartat per manca d'experiència, però, mentre per a altres nepalesos i tibetans la muntanya és una oportunitat de feina, per a ell és també un somni que comença a tenir forma. No renunciarà a provar-ho de nou. Així, aquell dia es repeteix l'escena de dos anys enrere: es planta a la cua de candidats. Quan li arriba el torn, explica als britànics que no té cap experiència, i sense poder-se entendre poc més que amb signes i somriures, li demanen que s'esperi. S'aparta cap a un costat mentre la llista de places es va omplint. Té la certesa que per segona vegada se li escapa l'oportunitat. Ja està pensant com s'ho farà perquè el contractin algun dia per primer cop... A qui no li sona això?

I mentre està així: donant forma a la buidor del seu futur, li diuen que està contractat i tot canvia. Es diu Tenzing Norgay.

Sense tenir cap altra referència, Shipton l'ha triat sobretot pel seu somriure. Un somriure que —el temps no trigarà gaire a donar-li la raó— canviarà el món de l'alpinisme.

A banda d'això, no és cap sorpresa escriure que el 1935 tampoc ningú no arriba al cim de la gran muntanya. Segurament el més memorable d'aquesta expedició sigui l'entrada en escena de Tenzing Norgay. Aquesta serà la primera de les nombroses campanyes en què participarà el xerpa. Ningú com ell perseguirà amb tanta insistència el somni del Txomolungma. Però les expedicions dels anys trenta sota la discreta direcció de Shipton no semblen donar gaire més fruit. És així com acaben les expedicions de 1935, 1938 i 1939. Després, la Segona Guerra Mundial imposa un nou parèntesi en aquesta aventura de l'Everest.

I amb tot plegat, aquells anys trenta ens tenen reservada encara alguna sorpresa més en aquest racó de món. A poc a poc, el somni del cim més alt va deixant de ser només cosa d'empreses nacionals. Mentre Shipton dirigeix les principals expedicions del seu país, altres comencen a posar-hi també la mirada.

Maurice Wilson, *el boig de Yorkshire*

Que amb l'alpinisme ens trobem davant d'un repte nou i diferent ho demostren aventures com la de Maurice Wilson. Fins ara havíem vist grans expedicions que es llançaven a la conquesta de racons remots, èpica culminada amb l'arribada als pols. Les gestes dels Amundsen, Nansen, Scott, Shackleton o Mallory comencen a quedar enrere, l'Everest comença a ser un punt diminut al voltant del qual cada cop és més fàcil accedir sense comptar amb un desplegament de recursos desmesurat. Shipton i Tilman mostren el camí d'aquest canvi quan renoven el món de l'alpinisme impregnant-lo amb un estil més lleuger. Aviat, trobarem altres aventurers capaços de portar aquest minimalisme fins a extrems insospitats. És el cas de Maurice Wilson, que, a causa de la seva aventura d'allò més delirant, va guanyar-se a pols el sobrenom del *boig de Yorkshire.*

Nascut el 1898 a Yorkshire, Wilson és un veterà de la Primera Guerra Mundial que porta una vida desordenada i caòtica d'ençà que va tornar del front. Després d'anys de desordre vital, però, arriba un dia que el seu cervell, alterat per la guerra, acaba trobant un refugi en la religió. És així com un bon dia, quan ja té trenta anys, es lleva convençut que se li ha encomanat la missió divina de demostrar al món el poder de la fe i de les lleis celestials. Per fi sembla que hagi trobat un sentit a la seva vida, i sap que la millor manera d'acomplir el seu deure és aconseguir una gesta quasi impossible.

Està així, pensant quina gesta farà en nom del cel, quan s'assabenta que en algun lloc s'està preparant el primer vol de la història per sobre de l'Everest. De sobte, després d'haver llegit aquesta notícia en un diari, se li encén un enorme ciri mental i una llum encegadora l'enlluerna fins al fons de l'ànima: ell serà el primer a trepitjar el cim de l'Everest. I aquest avió serà el seu trampolí. La gesta sembla ben senzilla: demanarà permís per acompanyar els aviadors i, quan siguin damunt del cim, saltarà en paracaigudes des d'una de les ales fins al mateix vèrtex de la gran muntanya. I així es cobrirà de glòria. Així de fàcil. Gairebé sembla mentida que no ho hagi pensat ningú abans.

Costa d'imaginar la cara d'aquells aviadors en llegir la carta amb la proposta de Wilson. Segurament no cal dir que el vol es va fer sense ell. Envoltats d'una gran expectació mediàtica, al més pur estil del dirigible *Norge* sobre el pol nord, el 3 d'abril de 1933 la *Houston-Mount Everest flight expedition* sobrevola el cim de l'Everest. Els seus pilots (Douglas Douglas-Hamilton i David McIntyre, sense Wilson ni ningú que s'hi assembli) es converteixen en els primers humans que gaudeixen d'unes vistes excepcionals per damunt de l'Everest. Les seves imatges seran un regal magnífic per als alpinistes que vulguin aventurar-se cap a aquell racó de món, però més enllà d'això i dels avenços tècnics que aquest vol representa per al món de l'aviació, a l'Everest ja no s'hi val altra cosa que pujar-hi a peu per deixar-hi la petja.

Amb tot, mentre aquest avió passava per damunt del gran cim, Wilson s'ha quedat a casa fent volar sol el seu cap descontrolat. A hores d'ara, la idea d'arribar al cim de l'Everest amb avió se li ha aferrat amb tanta força que ja no té cap dubte de què ha de fer. Es comprarà una avioneta, volarà fins tan a prop del cim de l'Everest com pugui, aterrarà o l'estavellarà on sigui i farà a peu el trosset que li quedi fins a dalt de tot. Oi que fàcil? De moment només hi ha un problema: Wilson no ha volat mai. I n'hi ha encara un altre, que no ha pujat mai ni una muntanya. I també que... En fi, molts més problemes hi ha, evidentment, però són cosa d'especialistes i a nosaltres no ens toca parlar-ne.

Així, amb aquest pla tan extremadament simple, infantil i forassenyat, el 1933 Wilson es compra un biplà d'ales de tela que batejarà amb el nom d'*Ever-Wrest*. Un cop ha aconseguit l'aparell, s'apunta a unes quantes lliçons de pilotatge que fan posar les mans al cap als seus instructors. De seguida que pot, a l'abril d'aquell mateix any, prova de fer el vol i se'n va cap a l'Everest, després d'haver estavellat i adobat l'avió un cop. El pla li sembla tan senzill i obvi que no li fa l'efecte que necessiti més preparatius. Ni entrenament ni equipament tècnic ni res. Ni tan sols menjar li cal a un asceta il·luminat i obsessionat pel dejuni com ell. L'únic que li cal és marxar de seguida que no fos cas que li deneguin el permís.

Itàlia, Tunísia, Egipte... En poques setmanes de vols miraculosos Wilson esquiva diferents escales internacionals sense permís i, després d'un viatge digne dels millors relats d'aviadors de Saint-Exupéry, durant el mes de maig es planta a l'Índia sense haver-se matat encara. Això sol, ajuntat a la seva imperícia a pilotar l'aparell, hauria de ser prou per considerar que els miracles existeixen. Però per a Wilson no és encara prou. A l'Índia es troba amb l'imprevist sorprenent que li requisen l'avioneta i li deneguen el permís d'entrada al Tibet i al Nepal. Aleshores, aconsegueix vendre l'*Ever-Wrest* i se'n va a peu cap a Darjeeling, on contracta tres xerpes (Tewang, Tsering i Rinzing). S'encamina amb ells Sikkim enllà cap al Tibet en la clandestinitat més absoluta, disfressat de monjo budista, fent-se passar per sordmut per no delatar-se quan algú els pregunta alguna cosa. Sovint viatgen de nit per passar més desapercebuts.

Tot plegat li endarrereix la gesta només un any de no-res. Finalment, a l'abril de 1934, Wilson es troba ja al monestir budista de Rongbuk, punt de partida cap al Txomolungma per la cara nord. I el dia 16 d'aquell mes emprèn el camí tot sol cap al cim sense emportar-se ni tan sols uns grampons. Deu dies després torna a ser al mateix monestir, al límit de les seves forces i sense haver aconseguit el miracle del cim.

Però com que el noi és tossut de mena i no es deixa vèncer així com així, al maig ho torna a provar. Aquesta vegada reprèn l'aventura amb els xerpes Rinzing i Tewang, que l'esperen al camp base, mentre ell torna a enfrontar-se tot sol al fred, al vent, a impossibles parets de gel i a tots els perills que té la Mare Deessa de les Neus. Naturalment, com que per a ell no hi ha res millor que el dejuni, torna a marxar amb ben poques provisions. Potser només el salvarà la sort de trobar els aliments de l'última expedició britànica un any enrere.

Durant aquell mes, un cop rere altre, Wilson va fent intents que el porten a diferents alçades. La muntanya, però, es resisteix. Finalment també se li resisteixen Rinzing i Tewang. Estan tan atònits que deixen de veure clar el seu objectiu. D'ençà de llavors, Wilson es queda sol al Txomolungma amb el seu deliri obsessiu i amb un equipament irrisori. Té, però una confiança en ell mateix tan indestructible com la seva bogeria. Fins al darrer dia continuarà provant d'arribar al Coll Nord i d'escriure al seu diari que ho veu factible. El 31 de maig escriu encara amb optimisme: «Surto de nou, dia esplèndid».

I això és tot. La següent notícia de Maurice Wilson ja ens ve de l'expedició de Shipton de 1935, quan troben el seu cos congelat a gairebé 7.000 metres d'alçada, encaforat en el que queda de la seva tenda. Aquell cop, Tenzing Norgay, en el seu primer contacte amb el Txomolungma, serà un dels alpinistes que trobarà i enterrarà aquest cos al gel de la glacera.

Que Wilson no va assolir al cim és evident. No podem saber a quina altitud va arribar, però mai no deixarà de ser el primer alpinista que va intentar l'ascensió en solitari. I també amb ell queda clar que l'aventura del tercer pol comença a ser una cosa cada cop més a l'abast de somiadors modestos. Abans que la gran muntanya es deixi escalar fins a dalt, començaran a arribar cada cop més candidats particulars que volen fer el cim com qui res.

Earl Denman. Es reprèn l'aventura

A poc a poc, després del parèntesi imposat per la Segona Guerra Mundial, alguns discrets aventurers començaran a tornar a provar d'arribar al cim de l'Everest. El primer de tots, el 1947, serà el jove Earl Denman, el següent —que se sàpiga— a afrontar el cim del món pel seu compte.

Nascut al Canadà i criat a Anglaterra, enginyer de professió, Denman és d'aquell tipus de persones més tocades pel desig d'aventura que per les ganes de dedicar-se a una somnolenta vida professional. De seguida que ha acabat els estudis, fascinat pels relats dels Burton, Livingstone i companyia, Denman decideix anar-se'n un temps a l'Àfrica Oriental. Però aviat descobreix que no és tan fàcil sadollar la seva set d'aventura. Comença a pensar en alguna cosa més èpica, com ara l'ascensió a l'Everest o alguna cosa per l'estil. De moment, mentre va donant forma als somnis, aprofita per preparar-se a les muntanyes Virunga, on s'entrena amb el singular mètode d'anar sempre descalç, fins i tot quan és damunt dels 4.000 metres. Així, sense res més que aquest bagatge excèntric, el 1947 l'inexpert Denman es planta a Darjeeling disposat a contractar un parell de xerpes que l'acompanyin cap al Tibet en una aventura semblant a la de Wilson. Compta entrar il·legalment al país i escalar l'Everest per la cara nord, però sense deliris místics ni avions. Per tant, vol fer-ho d'una manera una mica més sensata. L'empresa semblarà temptadora i fàcil per als dos xerpes que trobarà. Es diuen Tenzing Norgay i Ang Dawa.

En aquella època Tenzing ja és un expert en l'Everest. Ha participat a les expedicions de Shipton dels anys trenta, inclosa la de la troballa de Wilson, i segur que té a la memòria aquell *boig de Yorkshire* quan Denman el contracta. Per descomptat, Tenzing sap que Denman no té possibilitats d'èxit, però, com que no hi ha altres expedicions en marxa des d'abans del conflicte mundial, decideix treure's el cuquet guiant aquest esbojarrat alpinista en l'expedició més petita i discreta feta mai fins aleshores. Ben bé com si aquests que paguen fossin una eina més per arribar algun dia al gran cim, sembla que qualsevol excusa va bé a Tenzing per apropar-se al Txomolungma gairebé com qui juga o s'entrena. I de passada, també podrà aprofitar-ho per tornar al seu poble natal i reprendre els llaços familiars.

Com ja podem imaginar, la història de Denman no tindrà gaire recorregut. Una mica més disposat que Wilson a deixar-se aconsellar, això sí, el canadenc acabarà fent també el seu intent al cim, però, un cop sigui al peu del Coll Nord, haurà de renunciar-hi vençut per la muntanya. Així de senzilla serà l'aventura del primer que torna d'intentar l'Everest en solitari. Mitja volta i cap a casa. Però en qualsevol cas, aquesta aventura deixa petja de simpatia tan forta entre Tenzing i Denman, que aquest se'n va disposat a intentar-ho de nou l'any vinent.

Però l'intent de l'any 1948 no arribarà mai. A vegades somiar és massa fàcil, i quan a l'any següent la realitat s'imposi, Denman demostrarà que no és un boig qualsevol. Renunciarà aviat a aquest absurd impossible i continuarà buscant aventures més a la seva mida. Un senzillíssim final d'aventura. Un premi a l'honestedat.

Però l'Everest en solitari ja s'ha convertit en una llumeta encesa en el cap de molts somiadors del món. La mateixa sort que Denman tindrà encara un altre aventurer semblant, el danès Klavs Becker-Larsen, que prova de pujar a l'Everest l'any 1951. Així, amb petites incursions particulars que no acaben portant gaire enlloc, sembla que a poc a poc ha començat el degoteig definitiu de curiosos assedegats d'aventures. Un degoteig que ja no pararà de créixer fins a esdevenir la canonada d'aigua rebentada dels nostres dies.

Els anys cinquanta. La cara sud

Durant els anys quaranta del segle XX, el món sencer es convulsiona amb la Segona Guerra Mundial, amb l'Holocaust, amb la guerra freda, amb revoltes, amb canvis de sistemes, amb renovacions d'imperis, amb descolonitzacions més o menys efectives... El món canvia molt en poc temps. No hi ha cap racó, per remot que sigui, que no ho noti d'alguna manera. Com no podia ser altrament, això inclou també la frontera més alta del món, a gairebé nou mil metres d'altitud. Així, al voltant de 1950, mentre la Xina tanca les portes del Txomolungma a les expedicions occidentals pel territori ocupat del Tibet, el Nepal comença a obrir-les discretament pel vessant sud del Sagarmatha.

El que no ha canviat és el desig dels britànics de coronar la muntanya més alta del món, i així que poden, tornen a posar fil a l'agulla servint-se de l'experiència d'aquells que ja coneixen el territori. D'aquesta manera, el 1951 es reprendrà el repte de la mà del vell conegut Eric Shipton, mite vivent de l'alpinisme i el màxim coneixedor de l'Everest. O, millor dit, el més reconegut, perquè al seu costat no ha faltat mai Tenzing Norgay, un xerpa que aviat ja tindrà més experiència que ningú al Txomolungma.

Aquell 1951 Shipton dirigeix la primera expedició a l'Everest pel vessant sud, per la banda on el podríem anomenar

Sagarmatha. Aquest cop, la campanya servirà per localitzar la ruta per la glacera de Khumbu i el Cwm Occidental, camí que dos anys després obrirà per fi les portes del cim. A més a més, també en tornarà amb la desconcertant fotografia d'una immensa petjada a la neu que servirà per engrandir la llegenda del ieti. Però sobretot, la campanya servirà per posar en escena un altre dels grans protagonistes d'aquesta aventura.

Shipton ja ha començat la llarga aproximació cap a les faldes de la muntanya, quan rep un missatge del New Zealand Alpine Club que li demana que accepti dos membres seus que en aquell moment es troben a l'Himàlaia. El missatge no li dona ni tan sols els noms d'aquests dos alpinistes. Sense tenir més referències, el més raonable per a Shipton és negar-s'hi. I més encara, després d'haver descartat tanta gent preparada per mantenir l'expedició reduïda i lleugera com a ell li agrada. Només el record dels temps passats a l'Everest el 1935 amb el també neozelandès Dan Bryant fa que accepti a última hora aquests dos desconeguts dels quals no sap ni els noms ni com localitzar-los.

Ningú no entendrà la seva decisió, però Shipton és així. Només el temps li donarà la raó. Fa uns quants anys ja va acceptar un desconegut Tenzing Norgay seduït pel seu somriure, ara convida uns neozelandesos només per nostàlgia. Amb líders així, s'entén que el 1953 la Royal Geographical Society busqués un líder més ferm i organitzat... que, això sí, continuarà comptant amb aquests neozelandesos acabats d'arribar.

Però no marxem encara d'aquell 1951. En aquells moments, els joves neozelandesos Edmund Hillary i Earle Riddiford són uns alpinistes desconeguts que estan fent les seves primeres incursions per l'Himàlaia. Quan s'assabenten que Eric Shipton, l'alpinista més mediàtic del seu temps, es troba en una nova expedició a la zona de l'Everest, aconsegueixen que el New Zealand Alpine Club els obri la porta per fer-los conèixer el seu ídol. Però l'Himàlaia és molt gran i les distàncies inaccessibles semblen fer-lo créixer encara més. Així, quan reben la invitació de Shipton comencen una llarga caminada seguint els seus passos fins que el trobin i es puguin afegir al grup. Atrapar l'expedició britànica no és fàcil. En aquells temps, el Nepal és un territori desconegut i incomunicat. Si volen atrapar-los abans no s'endinsin en les profunditats de les valls més remotes, han de passar per les dreceres més inversemblants. Finalment, però, aconsegueixen localitzar Shipton i els seus. De sobte es troben en una mena de somni: formen part d'una expedició al mític Everest amb el rei de l'alpinisme.

Probablement, una de les primeres sorpreses de Hillary és descobrir que aquest Shipton-rei-de-l'alpinisme és una persona normal i senzilla. Ben mirat, com si no hauria convidat aquests desconeguts? En una de les primeres nits que comparteixen, el neozelandès se sorprèn de veure Shipton com si fos l'home més acomodat del món, arraulit sota una gotera i llegint feliçment dins del sac de dormir amb el paraigua i la pipa. La imatge de la senzillesa és probablement la que millor defineix Shipton i qui sap si és en part el model que seguirà Hillary durant la seva carrera.

De moment, l'expedició de 1951 és una altra expedició de reconeixement. Aquell any encara ningú no arribarà al cim, però tot plegat ha servit per posar en joc tots els elements que culminaran la gesta. Durant aquell any i el vinent, juntament amb Riddiford, Hillary es mou per l'Himàlaia amb l'excitació del jove que es troba de sobte davant dels seus herois. Gairebé com un joc innocent i excitant, com si no tingués més pretensió que jugar a ser el seu ídol, com si les muntanyes més altes del món fossin un pati immens per a un nen de vacances al paradís, Hillary recorre aquestes valls al costat dels seus alpinistes més admirats. En aquells moments, per a ell sembla que pujar algunes d'aquestes muntanyes i admirar l'Everest des d'alguna banda és molt més del que mai no hauria pogut somiar.

I amb això ja es dona per ben pagat. Però en el fons té clar que el seu somni, com el de tots els que es mouen per aquestes regions, és arribar a dalt de tot. I si pot ser abans que ningú, molt millor. Fins i tot ell mateix reconeixerà més tard el seu alleujament quan sap que la competència suïssa no ha trepitjat el cim.

L'expedició suïssa

Fins aquest moment els britànics han tingut la sensació que l'Everest era un territori seu. Han sigut els únics que han enviat autèntiques expedicions al sostre del món. La tranquil·litat de Shipton ja anava bé per anar fent aproximacions al gran cim, però, amb l'obertura de la via del Nepal, les coses són diferents.

El 1951 el govern nepalès autoritza una expedició suïssa per a l'any vinent. És així com, després de l'intent clandestí del danès Klavs Becker-Larsen, aquell 1952 els suissos són els primers que no són britànics que es planten seriosament davant el peu de l'Everest.

L'equip suís, liderat per Edouard Wyss-Dunant, vol aprofitar tot allò que se sap de la muntanya per aconseguir el cim. Per això proposen a Shipton coliderar amb ells l'expedició. A Londres, el Comitè de l'Himàlaia sospesa la invitació, però ara les coses són diferents. De sobte, amb els permisos a altres expedicions, els britànics ja només poden veure aquesta aventura com una nova cursa de l'exploració. No volen compartir el mèrit ni volen ser uns comparses d'un altre equip. De manera que només els quedarà desitjar sort als suïssos i confiar que no els arrabassin el primer lloc.

Ben a punt estaran de fer-ho.

No cal dir que Suïssa és la meca de l'alpinisme. L'expedició estarà formada per autèntics especialistes. Un dels membres de l'expedició, Raymond Lambert, ha sobreviscut ja a tota mena de perills als Alps. Crida l'atenció per les botes tan petites que calça. El 1938, durant una travessa hivernal al Mont Blanc de Tacul, va estar a punt de morir congelat, però finalment només va perdre els dits dels peus. Des d'aleshores es mou per la muntanya amb unes singulars botes fetes a la mida dels seus mitjos peus, però no és res que li impedeixi mantenir-se a l'elit alpinista.

En aquesta expedició, hi haurà també l'incombustible Tenzing Norgay, a qui Wyss-Dunant ha convidat com a alpinista. Per estrany que sembli, després de tants anys a la muntanya, finalment els suïssos són els primers a considerar Tenzing com un alpinista més del grup i no pas com un simple portador o guia.

I sembla que ja ho tenim tot a punt per arribar al cim més cobejat de la història. A la primavera d'aquell 1952, Tenzing i Lambert formaran la cordada que haurà estat mai més a prop de l'èxit. Però en aquells anys, les complicacions més importants ja no semblen venir pròpiament de la muntanya, sinó de l'equipament tècnic, sobretot de les bombones d'oxigen. Un cop més, els eterns problemes amb el sistema de respiració artificial els obligaran a renunciar quan són a tot just tres-cents metres del cim. Amb la mel als llavis, diríem des de baix. Però a aquella altitud, tres-cents metres de desnivell són tot un món o una vida. I aquest és potser el repte més gran de l'alpinisme, saber tornar enrere quan gairebé ja hi ets. Així, Lambert i Tenzing tornen de les portes del cel deixant la cota 8.600 com a fita màxima assolida, una alçada que es mantindrà com a rècord sense oxigen fins al 1978, quan Peter Habeler i Reinhold Messner coronin el cim sense aquest ajut artificial.

Aquesta difícil decisió de renunciar és el que desperta l'interès de gairebé tots els grans relats de l'alpinisme i de l'exploració en general. A partir de quina passa deixem d'avançar cap a la memòria col·lectiva i ho fem cap a l'oblit? Vet aquí el límit, aquella frontera invisible sense retorn que només es descobreix quan ja és massa tard. Quan es té la possibilitat de tornar sense haver arribat al cim, sempre queda la sensació que el primer objectiu era el cim: però el més important era tornar. Després de tant de temps somiant, preparant, patint... a vegades és difícil recordar que assolir el cim és secundari. És així per a la gran majoria, siguin els pioners de l'Everest o turistes que paguen per ser portats fins a dalt de tot, com ha passat més d'un cop en les darreres dècades.

Per descomptat que no cal explicar els avantatges de saber tornar viu. Tampoc no cal dir que un d'aquests avantatges és poder tenir una segona oportunitat. Així, lluny de resignar-se, aquella mateixa tardor de 1952 l'equip suís encara torna a fer un intent desesperat abans no hagin de donar per tancada l'expedició. Novament arriben al coll sud, però l'hivern és massa a prop, l'ascens se'ls fa del tot impossible. Per segon cop tornen enrere en aquesta oportunitat única. Finalment, se'n tornen cap a casa amb poc més que aquella satisfacció amarga d'haver donat una nova mesura a l'èpica.

Amb tot, seria enganyós dir que no hi ha cap més satisfacció que haver provat de pujar aquesta muntanya. Al llarg d'aquests mesos, entre Tenzing i Lambert ha nascut una intensa amistat que es mantindrà viva fins al final dels seus dies. I com a mostra, en acabar la campanya, Lambert regala a Tenzing un mocador amb la confiança que el xerpa pugui portar-lo al cim el 1953.

I mentre Tenzing i Lambert patien per l'oxigen a les alçades, als anglesos també se'ls tallava la respiració patint pel resultat del seu intent. Finalment tornen a respirar tranquils. Els suïssos no han fet el cim i no han pres mal. Les coses apunten bé per a ells.

1953. El cim

Finalment, el 1953 arriba un nou torn per als britànics en el que ara ja és una autèntica cursa contra rellotge. El 1952 ha sigut el torn dels suïssos, aquell mateix any s'especula amb una possible expedició soviètica per la cara nord, i es preveu que el Nepal donarà permís a una expedició francesa el 1954. Amb l'embranzida que ha pres l'aventura, el 1953 els britànics saben que ja no poden fallar en aquest intent. És per això que no escatimaran recursos en el que ha de ser l'intent definitiu.

És evident que primer de tot cal fer l'encàrrec a qui coneix millor el terreny. Sense cap mena de dubte no hi ha ningú més indicat que Eric Shipton, que ha estat cinc cops a l'Everest explorant i reconeixent el terreny. Aquesta vegada, però, el comitè organitzador vol desplegar tots els recursos necessaris per reeixir en l'aventura i Shipton no vol embarcar-se en projectes monumentals i competitius. Amb tot, malgrat que accepta l'encàrrec, finalment hi haurà un canvi d'última hora i es donarà aquesta responsabilitat al coronel de l'exèrcit John Hunt, que té fama de ser més resolutiu i organitzat.

Així, gairebé d'un dia a l'altre, Shipton fa un pas cap a l'oblit i desapareix del mapa himalaienc. Destinarà la resta dels seus dies al seu estil de vida i d'aventura tranquil i feliç, sobretot pels Andes i la Patagònia. A partir d'ara, l'Everest és cosa de Hunt.

Amb l'entrada de Hunt, el canvi de mentalitat sembla molt evident. Comparat amb la quinzena de portadors que contractava Shipton en les seves primeres expedicions, la de Hunt comptarà amb una dotzena d'alpinistes i amb un desplegament desmesurat de 350 portadors i 20 guies. A banda de l'irrisori sou d'una rupia al dia per portador, no s'escatimaran recursos, no es vol deixar res pendent, per descomptat, es recollirà tota la feina feta per Shipton i es buscaran els millors alpinistes disponibles.

Probablement, en aquest canvi de relleu, l'última gran aportació de Shipton deu ser la invitació que el 1952 envia a Nova Zelanda perquè Hillary formi part de l'expedició. Hillary no s'ho pensa dues vegades i, després del sobtat relleu, Hunt tampoc dubta a mantenir el compromís. Més difícil sembla la participació de Tenzing Norgay. No hi ha cap dubte que hauria de ser una peça clau de l'expedició. És per això que, abans d'acabar aquell 1952, ell també rep una invitació. És la persona amb més experiència del món a l'Everest, a més sap tractar amb tothom i serà un enllaç ideal entre els britànics i els portadors.

Però per primer cop a la vida, Tenzing no ho veu tan clar. A la tardor del 1952 l'expertíssim xerpa torna de l'expedició suïssa havent intentat l'ascens per sisena vegada. En baixar del seu quasi èxit, ell i Lambert ja sospesaven la possibilitat que novament s'ofereix al xerpa, però Tenzing ja comença a notar el pas dels anys. Aquesta vegada ha tornat malalt i cansat... Potser si la proposta vingués de Lambert, encara l'acceptaria; els suïssos sempre l'han tractat com un alpinista més de l'equip i s'hi sent unit per una autèntica amistat, però tornar a tenir un rol purament professional ja li dol més. Ja són quasi dues dècades darrere d'aquest objectiu; ja són molts anys, intents, riscos, esforços i patiments per no res. Ha arribat aquell moment en què cal saber-se retirar... Però la temptació és gran. Més encara quan la proposta és contractar-lo com a alpinista. Això sí que és una novetat venint dels britànics. Finalment no sap dir que no a una última oportunitat i accepta la invitació.

Poc va faltar perquè la història donés la raó a la senzillesa de Shipton. És ben sabut que com més complexa és una maquinària, més fàcil és que hi falli alguna cosa. A la primavera de 1953, el camp base del Sagarmatha comença a ser el formiguer d'alpinistes i portadors previst per Hunt. La quantitat de material va arribant lentament a aquest racó de món, i entre aquest material, s'espera tot un carregament de bombones d'oxigen. Ja són en camí entre Katmandú i el camp base, quan arriba l'avís que algunes de les ampolles semblen haver sortit defectuoses. Cal revisar-les totes i assegurar-se que estan en bon estat. Altrament, caldrà avortar tota l'expedició sencera i deixar-ho per qui sap quin any.

Afortunadament, hi ha poques vàlvules defectuoses. Tot continua endavant. Qui sap quantes aventures s'han fos o han estat a punt de fer-ho per culpa de defectes de fàbrica... Perquè no hi ha dubte que l'oxigen, natural o artificial, és un dels grans protagonistes d'aquesta aventura. Les millores en els aparells d'oxigen seran determinants en aquells anys. L'oxigen serà la clau en l'ascensió de 1953. Amb tot, continua essent difícil calcular-ne la mesura exacta. Portar-ne massa és un llast infernal; portar-ne poc és encarar-se a una mort segura.

Finalment, però, tots els engranatges de la maquinària es posen en marxa i encaixen perfectament. Tot sembla anar bé, i després de setmanes de formigueig per la glacera de Khumbu i el Cwm Occidental, tenim un camí de campaments preparats a diferents alçades. El més alt de tots, el camp IX, és a la desorbitada altitud de 8.500 metres.

Tot és a punt i Hunt dona les últimes instruccions per a l'ascens definitiu. Primer ho provaran dos britànics: Charles Evans i Tom Bourdillon. Si no assoleixen el cim, els seguiran Tenzing i Hillary. En saber aquests plans, Tenzing no pot amagar la seva decepció, perquè considera que en el primer intent hi hauria d'haver un xerpa (és a dir, ell), però la decisió ja ha estat presa. El 26 de maig 1953 Evans i Bourdillon afronten finalment la culminació de l'aventura.

Aquell dia, els dos alpinistes repeteixen una situació semblant a la de Tenzing i Lambert l'any anterior. Fins i tot han anat una mica més amunt i han arribat al cim sud, a menys de cent metres de coronar la gran muntanya, però el temps i la manca d'oxigen els obliguen a recular. La decisió no és gens fàcil, són les primeres persones del món que es planten davant d'aquesta esmolada aresta final del Sagarmatha. Sempre més els quedarà el dubte de fins a quin punt haurien pogut posar en risc les seves vides. Vet aquí un cop més l'etern dilema: si tornes viu de l'intent sempre penses que hauries pogut fer una passa més. El límit només es descobreix quan el sobrepasses. I en condicions extremes la frontera és molt fina.

Quan valora la situació, Evans encara té el cap prou clar per tornar enrere, però Bourdillon insisteix que cal provar-ho, que ell es veu capaç de fer-ho encara que hi vagi sol. Finalment, la insistència d'Evans guanya i, en comptes d'arriscar-se a una fatalitat inevitable en voler anar cap al cim, deixen un parell d'ampolles d'oxigen que ja no necessitaran i que podrien ser claus per als alpinistes següents. Un cop alliberats d'aquest llast, tot just tenen forces per arrossegar-se mig caient extenuats pendent avall.

Només els que els veuen tornar al campament saben que no tenien cap opció de sobreviure. La seva tria era entre ser recordats com dues noves víctimes de la muntanya o tornar cap a un confortable oblit a la llar, però la decisió només la podien prendre ells dos, lluny de ningú que els fes tocar de peus a terra.

I així, amb el retorn d'aquests dos alpinistes, el camí és obert per a Tenzing i Hillary.

De vegades la història sembla tenir asos amagats a la màniga. Quan Hunt envia Evans i Bourdillon a la primera cordada cap al cim, Norgay no podia evitar sentir-se molest perquè no hi havia un xerpa. Però finalment acaba passant allò de sempre amb els britànics: que són una gent esplèndida i generosa com pocs a l'hora d'obrir camí. Així, la cordada definitiva —sense cap europeu— ho agrairà infinitament. I vet aquí la temptació de fer-se una inevitable pregunta: qui sap si algun anglès hauria tingut sort en cas d'haver acceptat formar part de l'expedició suïssa l'any anterior?

Fos quina fos la resposta, el cas és que sembla com si el destí o la muntanya s'haguessin repensat alguna cosa i haguessin decidit donar pas al xerpa Tenzing en el seu setè intent. Un per a cada una de les set primeres víctimes d'aquell llunyà 1922. Ningú com ell ho ha intentat amb tanta insistència. I així, amb el consentiment de la Deessa Mare de les Neus, després d'una nit acampats en condicions impossibles a 8.500 metres, el 29 de maig Norgay i Hillary emprenen el tram definitiu.

Ningú no ha arribat mai tan enllà com ells. I arribar a un indret mai trepitjat per ningú sempre genera una mena de vertigen estrany. També Tenzing i Hillary tenen moments d'incertesa. Seguir o tornar? El dubte és inevitable seguramant un més dels difícils elements als quals s'enfronta l'alpinista. Igual com qualsevol que s'hagi jugat la vida en reptes semblants, durant la difícil última nit al camp IX, en el cap de Hillary la pregunta apareix de tant en tant com un fantasma que cal esvair. Quin sentit té tot plegat? Per què plantejar-se bogeries com aquesta?

Però és que ja s'ha fet tanta feina... A poc a poc les coses han anat canviant a l'Everest. Ara ja gairebé tot el trajecte és terreny trepitjat. Durant bona part de l'últim ascens, Tenzing i Hillary van trobant restes de la cordada del xerpa amb Lambert l'any anterior, i de Bourdillon i Evans tres dies enrere. Ja aleshores, a aquelles altituds és evident que allà on abans ha passat algú sempre queden restes: des de menjar congelat fins a providencials bombones d'oxigen que encara poden aprofitar per al descens. Aleshores encara no hi ha consciència del que representen els residus i menys en aquelles condicions. Però fins i tot el primer ascens a l'Everest comença a ser un camí marcat per les deixalles.

Durant hores avancen a un ritme feixuc. Han deixat enrere el cim sud, han començat a progressar per l'aresta final, i ja tenen el cim a tocar quan, amb una necessària barreja de dubtes i convenciment, arriben finalment davant d'un rocam de dotze metres d'alçada que els bloca el pas en el tram final de l'aresta cap al cim. Després de sospesar la situació decideixen provar sort per una esquerda vertical entre la roca i el gel. És l'única opció i l'últim obstacle. Superen aquest obstacle, que a partir d'ara serà conegut com el graó de Hillary, i poc després arriben al cim. La primera cordada a celebrar aquest èxit tan desitjat.

Cim. Ofrenes. Petits rituals. Tenzing porta posat el mocador de Lambert, penyora que més endavant tindrà l'oportunitat de tornar-li. Porta també un barret de l'entranyable Earl Denman i un llapis de la seva filla com a ofrena a la deessa que habita la muntanya.

Per la seva banda, Hillary és més pràctic. Primer de tot, com a demostració del seu èxit, fa una foto a Tenzing aixecant el piolet amb les banderes de l'expedició, després algunes fotos de les vistes i, mentre Tenzing enterra petites ofrenes als déus, Hillary mira si hi ha rastre d'Irvine i Mallory. Res de res. Així venera cadascú els seus ídols. I poc més hi ha per fer aquí. Quinze minuts al cim són més que prou perquè es felicitin, perquè cadascú faci els seus rituals, perquè mengin uns pastissets de menta, perquè deixin les banderes al cim i perquè reprenguin el llarg i difícil camí de baixada.

Que ho sàpiga el món

Per fi s'ha assolit el cim i de sobte comença una estranya cursa a l'inrevés: portar la notícia al món. De vegades la competència periodística pot ser també un món salvatge, més encara quan es tracta d'aquesta muntanya i d'aquestes dates. A cap mitjà britànic se li escapa que seria sensacional donar la notícia del cim de l'Everest el 2 de juny, dia de la coronació de la nova reina, i per això el diari *The Times* ha enviat a l'expedició el periodista James Morris.

Morris es troba al camp IV quan, l'endemà de culminar la gesta, Tenzing i Hillary hi porten la notícia. Aquell mateix vespre, el periodista ja ha baixat fins al camp base, on redacta un missatge xifrat: «*Neu en mal estat STOP camp base avançat abandonat STOP esperant millores*», missatge que a la redacció londinenca voldrà dir: «*Cim de l'Everest aconseguit per Hillary i Tenzing*». Poques hores després, ben de matinada, abans la notícia no s'escampi pel camp base, Morris dona aquest missatge a un xerpa de confiança que, sense notícies del que ha passat a dalt perquè no escampi la primícia a altres mitjans, serà enviat corrent cap a Namche Bazar, l'estació de ràdio més propera, on el missatge arribarà a Katmandú i d'allà a la redacció londinenca.

D'aquesta manera, la notícia ha sortit de les valls del Sagarmatha, però ni el seu portador no sap que la porta. I encara ningú no sap res del que ha passat a dalt de tot, a la llar de la Mare Deessa de les Neus. La llar de la Mare... La mare! La seva llar!

De sobte Tenzing sembla recordar alguna cosa molt important. Perquè a veure si no és cert que de mare només n'hi ha una. Almenys per a ell. Estranys recargolaments del destí, durant aquesta expedició, James Morris ha tingut un fill al Regne Unit, criatura que a partir de 1972 tindrà dues mares, quan Morris culmini un procés de trànsit i es converteixi en l'escriptora Jan Morris. Però de moment, i sobretot per a Tenzing, de mare només n'hi ha una, i mentre uns corren a informar-ne mares pàtries, Tenzing Norgay corre somrient i feliç camp base avall cap al poble de Thamey a donar la notícia a la seva mare. Tot just fa tres dies que es trobava al cim del Txomolungma, i probablement Dokmo Kinzom, la mare de Tenzing, sigui la primera persona del món a rebre la notícia. No cal dir res més.

Gairebé no hi podia haver un final d'aventura més senzill i adequat.

I així, a la salut de les mares, que són sempre les grans oblidades, a veure si no és aquesta una aventura ben acabada.

Encaixada de mans

Per fi s'ha arribat al sostre del món. S'ha obert l'últim gran camí cap a l'impossible. A partir d'ara, la resta serà anar coneixent cada cop més aquesta muntanya. Fins a l'actualitat, quan les multituds s'acumulen fent cua per poder-se fer una foto al cim. I així, amb una imatge de record, gairebé una absurditat a la qual ningú no podria renunciar, tancarem aquest camí d'oblidats al sostre del món.

El 1953 només Tenzing apareix fotografiat al cim del Sagarmatha. En cap moment Hillary demana al seu company de cordada que l'immortalitzi. Per a qualsevol alpinista del món, aquest seria el moment de deixar la càmera al company per tenir també la pròpia foto del cim, però Tenzing no ha tocat mai una càmera i no sembla que aquest sigui el millor moment per iniciar-se amb la tecnologia. Així doncs, no hi ha fotos de Hillary al cim, només la imatge de Tenzing aixecant el piolet enlaire, ben amunt, més amunt que res en el món, com una última extensió de la terra. Amb resignació o sense, lliçó d'humilitat i d'humanitat que ens dona la cordada. Avui milers d'alpinistes es juguen la vida per arribar al mateix cim, i molts d'ells deixarien de dormir tranquils si no en tornessin amb una foto, com si l'experiència per si sola no valgués res. Però per a Hillary deu ser diferent. Posats a immortalitzar, és obvi que només ell ha pogut fotografiar Tenzing allà a dalt. I sigui com sigui, amb aquesta renúncia a ser la cara de l'arribada al cim, Hillary està mantenint el poble xerpa al lloc que li correspon. En paraules seves: «El Nepal és allà per canviar-te a tu, no perquè tu el canviïs a ell». Gestos com aquests gairebé l'honoren més que qualsevol altra suposada conquesta.

Suposada. Perquè conquesta vol dir possessió, i ja sabem que aquesta muntanya no es deixa posseir, en tot cas s'apodera dels pensaments de l'alpinista i el posseeix a ell. Res més. Però malgrat tot, la premsa nacional de l'Índia i del Regne Unit insistiran en aquesta idea de conquesta i es voldran adjudicar el premi de la foto d'arribada. Qui dels dos ha trepitjat uns segons abans el cim, Tenzing o Hillary? Però els dos alpinistes insistiran sempre a dir que és cosa de la cordada, que hi han arribat junts, un com a extensió de l'altre. Aquí s'han unit orient i occident per aconseguir arribar junts a dalt de tot, i cap dels dos es qüestionarà mai qui va ser el primer. Ells són els primers.

I també són ells els que tanquen, des de ben amunt, aquest viatge a la recerca d'exploradors i aventurers que han fet mèrits per ser recordats.

Bibliografia

ALBANOV, VALERIAN: *En el país de la muerte blanca*. RBA, Barcelona, 2001.

ALEXANDER, CAROLINE: *Atrapados en el hielo*. Ed. Planeta, Barcelona, 2008.

ALTADILL, GUILLERMO; ORTEGA, JAVIER: *Aventureros del mar*. Santillana Ediciones Generales, Madrid, 2005.

AMUNDSEN, ROALD: *Al Polo Norte en avión: expedición Amundsen-Ellsworth*. Interfolio, Barcelona, 2008.

ANKER, CONRAD; ROBERTS, DAVID: *La llegenda de l'Everest*. Símbol editors, Sant Cugat del Vallès, 2000.

ARNOLD, MARTIN: *The vikings, a short history*. The history press, Cheltenham, 2008.

BARRADO NAVASCUÉS, DAVID: *De la Tierra a la Esfera Celeste*. INSTITUTO NACIONAL DE TÉCNICA AEROESPACIAL, Madrid, 2014.

BARROS, J. M.: *El descubrimiento de la Antártida. Dirck Gerritsz-Gabriel de Castilla*. Boletín de la Academia Chilena de la Historia (núm. 94), Santiago de Xile, 1983, pp. 217-222.

BERGUÑO, JORGE: *Un enigma de la historia antártica: El descubrimiento de las islats Shetland del Sur*. Biblioteca virtual Miguel de Cervantes, Alacant, 2009.

BERNÁRDEZ, ENRIQUE (trad.): *La Saga de Eirík el Rojo*. Ed. Nórdica Libros, Madrid, 2011.

BEST, ELSDON: *Irihia. The homeland of the Polynesians. Some additional data thereon, culled from traditions preserved by the Takitumu tribes of New Zealand*. The journal of the polynesian Society (vol. 36), Auckland, 1927.

BLACK, LYDIA T.: *Russians in Alaska, 1732-1867*. University of

Alaska Press. Fairbanks, Alaska, 2004.

Bonhomme, Brian: *Russian exploration, from Siberia to Space. A History*. McFarland & Co. Inc., Jefferson, North Carolina, 2012.

Bradley, Peter T. *Navegantes británicos*. Ed. Mapfre, Madrid, 1992.

Bryson, Bill: *In a sunburned Country*. Broadway Books, Nova York, 2000.

Cacho, Javier: *Amundsen-Scott, Duelo en la Antártida*. Ed. Fórcola, Madrid, 2011.

Cacho, Javier: *Héroes de la Antártida*. Ed. Fórcola, Madrid, 2019.

Casariego Córdoba, Pedro (trad.): *Saga de los groenlandeses; Saga de Eirik el Rojo: anónimos islandeses del siglo XIII*. Ed. Siruela, Madrid, 2010.

Causer, Tim: *Memorandoms by James Martin*. The Bentham Project, UCL (University College London), Londres, 2014.

Chadwick, Ian. *The life and voyages of Henry Hudson*. www.ianchadwick.com/hudson, 2007.

Cherry-Garrard, Apsley: *El peor viaje del mundo*. Ediciones B, Barcelona, 2009.

Colón, Cristóbal: *Diario de a bordo. Edición de Christian Duverger*. Ed. Taurus, Barcelona, 2016.

Colón, Cristóbal: *Los cuatro viajes del almirante y su testamento*. Espasa Calpe, Madrid, 2006.

Contente Domingues, Francisco: *O caso Pacheco Pereira*. publico.pt, 14/10/2012.

Cook, James: *A voyage towards the South Pole, and round the world*. W. Strahan and T. Cadell, Londres, 1777.

Cook, James: *Viaje hacia el Polo Sur y alrededor del mundo*.

Espasa Calpe, Madrid, 2004.
Cowie, Winston: *Nueva Zelanda, un puzle histórico*. AECID, Madrid, 2016.
Dash, Mike: *The Most Terrible Polar Exploration Ever: Douglas Mawson's Antarctic Journey*. www.smithsonianmag.com, 27/01/2012.
Day, Alan: *The A to Z of the Discovery and Exploration of Australia*. The Scarecrow Press, Inc., Plymouth, 2009.
Dean, Colin: *The australian aboriginal 'dreamtime'*. Gamahucher press, Geelong, 1996.
Douglas, Ed: *Tenzing Norgay, héroe del Everest*. RBA, Barcelona, 2003.
Ducharme, Steve. *Ship director and Inuk Ranger tell the tale of Terror*. nunatsiaq.com, 23/09/2016.
Elcano, Juan Sebastian; Transilvano, Maximiliano; Albo, Francisco; de Mafra, Ginés; Pigafetta, Antonio: *La primera vuelta al mundo*. Miraguano Ediciones / Ediciones Polifemo, Madrid, 2003.
Fernández-Armesto, Felipe: *Los conquistadores del horizonte*. Ed. Destino, Barcelona, 2006.
Fleming, Fergus: *Barrow y sus hombres*. Ed. National Geographic, RBA, Barcelona, 2005.
Gerritsen, Rupert; et al. *The Duyfken: unveiling the first contact memorial at Mapoon*. Australia on the map & Embassy of the Kingdom of the Netherlands, Canberra, 2013.
Gómez Martín, Jorge Ángel. *Cartografía de los descubrimientos españoles en el Pacífico Sur: La búsqueda de la Terra Australis Incógnita*. Universidad de Valladolid, Valladolid, 2015.
Gozalbes Cravioto, Enrique: *Viajes y viajeros en el mundo antiguo*. Ed. Universidad de Castilla-La Mancha, Cuenca,

2003.

Harwood, Jeremy: *Los confines del mundo. 100 mapas que cambiaron la percepción de la Tierra*. Ed. Blume, Barcelona, 2008.

Hearne, Samuel: *A journey from Prince of Wales's Fort in Hudson's Bay to the Northern Ocean*. The Champlain Society, Toronto, 1911.

Heyerdahl, Thor: *La expedición de la Kon-Tiki*. Ed. Juventud, Barcelona, 1951.

Hillary, Edmund: *Mi camino al Everest*. Desnivel Ediciones, Madrid, 2000.

Hughes, Robert: *La costa fatídica*. Ed. Nueva Galaxia Gutenberg, Barcelona, 2002.

Hughes, Thomas: *The German discovery of America. A review of the controversy over Didrik Pining's voyage of exploration in 1473 in the North Atlantic*. Bulletin of the German Historical Institute (núm. 33), GHI, Washington DC, 2003.

Luque Talaván, Miguel; Mondragón Pérez-Grovas, Carlos. *Et in Arcadia ego. La Terra Australis y la visión utópica de Don Pedro Fernández de Quirós*. Anales del museo de América (núm. 14), Madrid, 2006.

Mallory, George: *Escalada a l'Everest. Escrits complets de George Leigh Mallory*. Cossetània Edicions, Valls, 2020.

Mawson, Douglas, *The home of the blizzard: being the story of the australasian antarctic expedition, 1911-1914*. Lippincott Company, Londres, 1915.

Messner, Reinhold: *La segona mort de Mallory*. Ed. Proa, Barcelona, 2001.

McFarlane, Turi: *Maori Associations with the Antarctic*. Canterbury University, Christchurch, 2008.

Morris, Jan: *La coronación del Everest*. Gallo Nero Ediciones,

Madrid, 2015.

Mutch, T. D.: *The First Discovery of Australia With an account of the Voyage of the "Duyfken" and the Career of Captain Willem Jansz.* Royal Australian Historical Society, Sydney, 1942.

Nansen, Fridtjof: *Hacia el polo. Relato de la expedición del Fram de 1893 a 1896.* Interfolio, Madrid, 2010.

Nansen, Fridtjof: *La travesía de Groenlandia.* Interfolio, Madrid, 2018.

Norgay, Jamling Tenzing: *Más cerca de mi padre.* RBA, Barcelona, 2001.

Palin, Michael: *Erebus, historia de un barco.* Ático de los libros, Barcelona, 2019.

Peláez, Javier: *500 años de frío. La gran aventura del Ártico.* Ed. Crítica, Barcelona, 2019.

Pelsaert, Francisco: *The Batavia Journal of Francisco Pelsaert.* Department of Maritime Archaeology, Western Australian Maritime Museum, Fremantle, 1994.

Pigafetta, Antonio: *El primer viaje alrededor del mundo. Relato de la expedición de Magallanes y Elcano. Edición de Isabel de Riquer.* Ediciones B, Barcelona, 1999.

Powter, Geoff: *Strange and Dangerous Dreams: The Fine Line Between Adventure and Madness.* Mountaineers Books, Seattle, 2006.

Rivera Novo, Belén i Martín-Merás, Luisa: *Cuatro siglos de cartografía en América.* Ed. Mapfre, Madrid, 1992.

Roberts, Dennis: *I'll climb Everest Alone. The story of Maurice Wilson.* Robert Hale Limited, Londres, 1957.

Shipton, Eric: *That untravelled world.* Mountaineers Books, Seattle, 2015.

Sides, Hampton: *1.000 Days in the Ice.* National Geographic

Magazine, ngm.nationalgeographic.com, gener 2009.
THOMAS, HUGH: *La trata de esclavos*. Editorial Planeta, Barcelona, 1998.
THROWER, NORMA J. W.: *Mapas y civilización. Historia de la cartografía en su contexto cultural y social*. Ediciones del Serbal, Barcelona, 2002.
WOODMAN, DAVID C.: *Strangers among us*. McGill-Queen's University Press, Montreal, 1995.

Aquest llibre es va imprimir a la Impremta Pagès, d'Anglès (la Selva), el mes d'agost de 2022. Impressionats per la capacitat de resistència, per la curiositat, pel delit de viure dels éssers humans.